AF559978

A CENTURY OF CHANGE

A CENTURY OF CHANGE

Caste and Irrigated Lands in Tamilnadu 1860s–1970s

HARUKA YANAGISAWA

MANOHAR
2022

First published 1996
Reprinted 2020, 2022

ISBN 978-81-7304-159-4

Published by
Ajay Kumar Jain *for*
Manohar Publishers & Distributors
4753/23 Ansari Road, Daryaganj
New Delhi 110 002

Printed at
Replika Press Pvt. Ltd.

Contents

List of Tables and Figures

Tables

Figures

Preface

This study attempts to clarify the socio-economic changes that occurred in South Indian agrarian society in the period between the 1860s and the 1970s, focussing on the irrigated areas of Tiruchirapalli and other Tamil districts.

The work is based on archival documents, in particular computer-processed data from the village settlement registers for 26 villages in Tiruchirapalli district, and data collected during my field survey of villages in this district. The settlement registers were collected and computer-processed jointly with Professor Tsukasa Mizushima. I have benefited greatly through his suggestions and co-operation and gratefully thank him for permitting me to use the data from the settlement registers. My field survey was undertaken as part of a research project organized by the late Professor Tadahiko Hara, to whom I am deeply grateful. Both the data processing work and the fieldwork were funded by the Ministry of Education, Science and Culture, Japan. Mitsubishi Foundation also supported my study of settlement registers. I am grateful to these organisations.

I was very fortunate to have many excellent teachers, colleagues and friends who supported and encouraged my study of South Indian economic history. In particularly, I received not only intellectual guidance but also emotional and practical support from Professor Mikio Sumiya, who was my supervisor during my years as an economics student at the University of Tokyo. I have benefited enormously from the fertile climate of debate that exists in the Institute of Oriental Culture of the University of Tokyo, where I have been working since 1983. A special debt is due to Professor Toru Matsui and Professor Toshio Yamazaki, who constantly supported the work's development.

A number of teachers, colleagues and friends have provided comments and suggestions on various draft sections, or assisted me with information. Without their helpful criticisms this work would never have been finished. Notable among them are Professor Noboru Karashima, Professor Mitsuru Takahashi, Professor H. Kano, Dr. Peter

Robb, Dr. K. Sugihara, Professor B.B. Chaudhuri, Dr. M.S.S. Pandian, Dr. P.B. Mayer, Professor Y. Kiyokawa, Professor M. Koga, Professor N. Nakazato and Professor S. Taniguchi. Professor Y. Subbarayalu took the time to read the entire manuscript very carefully and gave detailed comments. I cannot adequately thank Professor Dharma Kumar, who has been a great source of inspiration, providing guidance and countless invaluable comments. But for her encouragement, I could not have brought this book to publication.

Librarians and staff of various institutions met voracious demands for source material. I am particularly grateful to the staff of the Tamil Nadu State Archives, Madras, which is a gold mine of information on the history of the Madras Presidency. Thanks are also due to the librarian and staff of the India Office Library and Records, London.

I received help of different kinds from many people during my field surveys. I am particularly indebted to Mr. P. Asai Thambi and Mr. V.S. Kumar Rajah for assisting me in collecting data. My sincere thanks are due to the people of Appadurai village, who warmly accepted me and took the trouble to be interviewed for many hours.

This book is based on my study (in Japanese), *Minami Indo Shakai Keizaishi Kenkyu* (Studies in the Socio-Economic History of South India) (Tokyo, 1991) published by the Institute of Oriental Culture, the University of Tokyo and the University of Tokyo Press. The translation of the book was aided by a Grant-in-Aid for Publication of Scientific Research Results (Ministry of Education, Science and Culture, Japan) and assisted greatly by Ms. Malini Subramanian and Ms. S. Okuda. Ms. Gaynor Sekimori edited with great patience my English text. I am very grateful to the above-mentioned institutions and to Ms. Subramanian, Ms. Okuda and Ms. Sekimori. Needless to say, none of those mentioned bear any responsibility for any remaining errors and misjudgments.

Tokyo Haruka Yanagisawa

Acknowledgments

Portions of Chapters 3 and 5 of the present work have previously appeared in 'Mixed Trends in Landholding in Lalgudi Taluk: 1895–1925', *Indian Economic and Social History Review* 26, 4 (1989). Some sections of Chapters 3, 4 and 5 were presented at the SOAS Workshop held in 1992 and are included in 'Chapter 4.1: Elements of Upward Mobility for Agricultural Labourers in Tamil Districts, 1865–1925' and 'Chapter 4.2: A Comparison with Japanese Experience', in Peter Robb et al. (eds.), *Local Agrarian Societies in Colonial India* (London: Curzon Press, 1996). I would like to thank the editors and publishers of those publications in which the above cited articles appeared, for permission to include them in this book in revised form.

Abbreviations

EPW	*Economic and Political Weekly*
G.O.	Government Order
IESHR	*Indian Economic and Social History Review*
MBEC	*The Madras Provincial Banking Enquiry Committee*
P.B.R.	Proceedings of the Board of Revenue, Government of Madras.
RCLI	*Royal Commission on Labour in India, Evidence,* Vol. VII, Part 1, *Madras Presidency and Coorg, Written Evidence*
TNA	Tamil Nadu State Archives, Madras

1
Introduction

The Debate over Agrarian Change in Colonial India

The present study aims at clarifying more than a century of agrarian change in Tiruchirapalli and other irrigated districts in Tamilnadu since the 1860s. In particular it attempts first to offer a new interpretation of the socio-economic transformation of agrarian society under British rule by identifying two different trends at work during the period and second to interpret the agrarian changes of the post-Independence period in the context of the longer historical perspective.

While a large amount of research has been conducted on the agrarian history of British India, scholars do not concur on one vital aspect of the topic, that is, how the agrarian structure, particularly the class structure in agrarian society, changed during the British period.

Surendra J. Patel's work on agricultural labourers in the Indian Subcontinent pioneered research into agrarian change under colonialism.[1] Pointing out that more than one-third of the agricultural population of India consisted of hired agricultural labourers in 1931, as disclosed by the census, he discusses the process by which the number of agricultural labourers increased rapidly. Agrarian society in pre-nineteenth century India, he argues, consisted of largely self-sufficient and self-perpetuating village communities with no room for the existence of an independent and distinct class of agricultural labourers. During the course of the six decades between 1871 and 1931, the proportion of agricultural labourers to the agricultural population in India increased from one-seventh to more than one-third. Patel attributes the rapid increase in the proportion of agricultural labourers to the disintegration of the peasantry under colonial rule. He argues that such factors as fixed cash revenue demands by the government and the expanding export market for commercial crops were reflected in a vast increase in agrarian indebtedness, which resulted in a massive transfer of landownership

[1] Surendra J. Patel, *Agricultural Labourers in Modern India and Pakistan* (Bombay, 1952).

from cultivators to moneylenders, with the dispossessed peasant being degraded to the status of agricultural labourer or sharecropper. Patel claims that the decline of domestic industry caused by the import of British manufactures also contributed to this process. This view coincides with the argument of the nationalists in the sense that the poverty of the Indian people was attributed to British colonial rule.[2]

While Patel's argument highlights the increase in the number of agricultural labourers and tenants, some historians have emphasised another aspect in the trend towards rural social stratification, that is, the emergence of rich farmers. The emergence of rich farmers in dry districts in South India caught the attention of Washbrook, who argued that rich peasants extended their control over their fellow peasants in the nineteenth and twentieth centuries and, because of their extended influence in rural areas, they played a leading role in the political sphere during this period. He asserts that rises in grain prices and the development of cash-cropping led to the increasing stratification of rural society in the dry zone: large landholders were able to take advantage of the new market situation, whereas their poorer neighbours found it increasingly difficult to continue farming without depending on loans from neighbouring rich farmers. He presents two sources of statistical evidence to support his findings. Between the 1860s and the 1920s, the tiny fraction of *pattas* paying more than Rs. 250 per annum increased their share of revenue from 4.3 to 6.7 percent of the total. Census data of some districts, he says, also indicate the same trend.[3] The emergence of rich farmers in Western India was already remarked in the 1960s by Ravinder Kumar. He attributes the creation of rich peasants in Western India to the introduction of the *raiyatwari* system and other factors that emerged under British rule and argues that the wealth of this social

[2] Ramakrishna Mukherjee holds that the self-sufficient peasantry in Bengal society disintegrated during the British period. Bengal rural society under British rule consisted of three classes: Class 1, landowners and rich farmers; Class 2, self-sufficient peasants; and Class 3, sharecroppers and agricultural labourers. This three-tier class structure was, he argues, created as a result of the disintegration of the traditional village community, which had been formed of a single class of self-sufficient peasants. Ramakrishna Mukherjee, *The Dynamics of a Rural Society: A Study of the Economic Structure in Bengal Village* (Berlin, 1957). See also Utsa Patnaik, 'Development of Capitalism in Agriculture', *Social Scientist* 1, 2 (Sept. 1972).

[3] David Washbrook, 'Economic Development and Social Stratification in Rural Madras: The "Dry Region" 1878–1929', in Clive Dewey and A.G. Hopkins (eds.), *The Imperial Impact: Studies in the Economic History of Africa and India* (London, 1978).

group stood in striking contrast to the poverty of the mass of cultivators, whose position became increasingly desperate with the passage of time.[4]

However, those interpretations which stress the increasing stratification of rural society in the British period have been challenged by later works. A pioneer of this view was Dharma Kumar,[5] who threw doubts upon Patel's notion that the number of landless labourers was insignificant before the British period. She asserts that, in South India, there were many holdings which required several families of labourers, that many Brahman landowners were forbidden most types of manual labour and that, therefore, there was a need for agricultural labourers even before the British period. On the other hand, there were many landless agricultural labourers belonging to agricultural labour castes who were employed by landowners to cultivate their land. Thus agricultural labourers were a sizeable proportion of the agricultural workforce early in the nineteenth century. The class of landless agricultural labourers was not entirely created during the British period through the impoverishment of the peasant proprietor and the village craftsman, and so, she concludes, it is wrong to stress the fact of the rapid increase in landless agricultural labourers in the nineteenth century. Supported by ample evidence, her conclusions make it difficult to argue, as Patel did, that agricultural labourers as a group were largely created in the nineteenth century, at least as far as South India is concerned.

Regarding the period after 1871, J. Krishnamurty has questioned Patel's interpretation of the proportion of agricultural labourers and criticises him for not seriously considering the changes that occurred from census to census in the concept, criteria of classification and area covered. Krishnamurty concludes that the simple model of the decline of employment in the manufacturing sector and the mass conversion of cultivators and artisans into agricultural labourers cannot be sustained for the period after 1870, on the basis of the available census evidence.[6]

In addition to the above arguments regarding the proportion of

[4] Ravinder Kumar, 'The Rise of the Rich Peasants in Western India', in D.A. Low (ed.), *Soundings in Modern Asian History* (Berkeley and Los Angeles, 1968), pp. 25–58; Ravinder Kumar, *Western India in the Nineteenth Century* (Oxford, 1968), p. 229.

[5] Dharma Kumar, *Land and Caste in South India: Agricultural Labour in the Madras Presidency during the Nineteenth Century* (Cambridge, 1965; repr., New Delhi, 1992). A suggestive review of related works appearing in the last 15 years is available in her 'Introduction to reprint'.

[6] J. Krishnamurty, 'The Growth of Agricultural Labour in India—A Note', *IESHR* 9, 3 (1972).

agricultural labourers, Dharma Kumar's research into changes in inequality of landownership among groups of various sizes in South India gave a further blow to the conventional view of increasing concentration of landownership in the hands of moneylenders and large farmers.[7] Analysing the land revenue statistics for the Madras Presidency, she concludes that there is little evidence in them for the view that 'the rich grew richer' during the hundred years between 1853 and 1946, at least in terms of land in the Madras Presidency. Though she admits that the majority of the *raiyats* were in debt and that the volume of debt increased over the period, the indebtedness, she argues, did not lead to an increasing concentration of landholdings. Her conclusion was later supported by C.J. Baker, who comprehensively clarified the structure of the Tamil economy and the changes therein in the British period.[8] Bruce Robert's research into change in Bellary district also denied any concentration of land distribution and further asserted that the modest economic growth the region experienced after the turn of the century was not as detrimental to small and middle-level farmers as indicated by Washbrook, but on the contrary, it provided increased economic opportunities from which many benefited.[9]

Thus, at the present level of the historiography, it is naive to hold to the simple model of dispossessed cultivators and an increasing concentration of landownership in the hands of moneylenders and large farmers, at least as far as South India is concerned.

This view is not confined to studies of South India. Attwood attempted to test whether the process of class-polarisation as envisaged by Marxist theory actually occurred. His examination of changes in landownership in a Maharashtra village between 1920 and 1970 does not support any trend of land concentration in fewer hands, but rather

[7] Dharma Kumar, 'Landownership and Inequality in Madras Presidency: 1853–54 to 1946–47', *IESHR* 12, 3 (1975).

[8] Christopher John Baker, *An Indian Rural Economy 1880–1955: The Tamilnad Countryside* (Oxford, 1984), pp. 320–22.

[9] Bruce Robert, 'Economic Change and Agrarian Organization in "Dry" South India 1890–1940: A Reinterpretation', *Modern Asian Studies* 17, 1 (1983). For changes in colonial Andhra, see also G.N. Rao and D. Rajasekhar, 'Commodity Production and the Changing Agrarian Scenario in Andhra: A Study in Interregional Variations, c.1910–c.1947', and A. Satyanarayana, 'Commercialization, Money Capital and the Peasantry in Colonial Andhra, 1900–1940', in Sabyasachi Bhattacharya et al. (eds.), *The South Indian Economy: Agrarian Change, Industrial Structure and State Policy, c. 1914–1947* (Delhi, 1991).

indicates a tendency for some of the poor to get richer.[10] H. Fukazawa also suggests that the number of agricultural labourers in Western India did not grow rapidly or steadily, and states further that the distribution pattern of Gujarat scarcely showed any change between 1916 and 1942.[11] Rajat and Ratna Ray's research on some districts of Bengal indicates that the available statistics hardly provide evidence to support the notion of a concentration of landholdings and increase in landless labourers, though their view has engendered some debate.[12]

Thus the conventional view regarding the disintegration of peasant society and the rapid increase of agricultural labourers and tenants under British rule has been challenged by many studies and, as Neeladri Bhattacharya has stated, 'Most scholars on the subject now tend to doubt whether there was at all any significant transformation of peasants into agricultural labourers.'[13] The general trend now in the subject is to stress that the small peasants did not disintegrate or were dispossessed but maintained their status quo intact during the British period, though their economic situation did change. Charlesworth admits stratification among Maharashtra peasantry in the nineteenth century but asserts that the economic expansion of the first quarter of the twentieth century may have brought widely distributed benefits within Bombay agrarian society and that the depression of the 1930s hit the employers of labourers most seriously.[14] Sumit Guha's argument goes further. In general he

[10] D.W. Attwood, 'Why Some of the Poor Get Richer: Economic Change and Mobility in Rural Western India', *Current Anthropology* 20, 3 (1979). For a criticism of Attwood's argument, see 'Comment by John Harriss', p. 510 in the same volume.

[11] 'Agrarian Relations: Western India', in Dharma Kumar (ed.), *Cambridge Economic History of India*, Vol. 2 (Cambridge, 1982). See also Jan Breman, *Patronage and Exploitation: Changing Agrarian Relations in South Gujarat, India* (Berkeley, Los Angeles and London, 1974), p. 71.

[12] 'The Dynamics of Continuity in Rural Bengal under the British Imperium: A Study of Quasi-Stable Equilibrium in Underdeveloped Societies in a Changing World', *IESHR* 10, 2 (1973); Ratnalekha Ray, *Change in Bengal Agrarian Society* (New Delhi, 1979). For the debate on Bengali agrarian change, see Nariaki Nakazato, *Agrarian System in Eastern Bengal, c.1870–1910* (Calcutta, 1994).

[13] Neeladri Bhattacharya, 'Agricultural Labour in Punjab', in K.N. Raj et al. (eds.), *Essays on the Commercialization of Indian Agriculture* (Delhi, 1985), p. 123.

[14] Neil Charlesworth, 'Rich Peasants and Poor Peasants in Late Nineteenth-century Maharashtra', in Dewey and Hopkins (eds.), *Imperial Impact*; idem, *Peasants and Imperial Rule: Agriculture and Agrarian Society in the Bombay Presidency, 1850–1935* (Cambridge, 1985), pp. 224–25, 293.

denies both the emergence of rich farmers and the disintegration of peasantry in Western India and concludes that the available data do not show any clear trend of a concentration of landownership. 'On the whole, rural society does not seem to have changed qualitatively during the period of this study [1818–1941].'[15]

Two Different Trends in the British Period: A Hypothesis

Nevertheless, recent arguments that tend to deny any structural change in rural society, particularly in terms of landholdings, should be reconsidered. Dharma Kumar's discussion about the concentration of landownership in South India, and that of Krishnamurty about changes in the structure of occupations, base their arguments mainly on statistics which do not generally indicate any caste breakdown or the social background of such economic categories as agricultural labourer, tenant and landholder. For example, landholders from Brahman communities and those from merchant communities are both included in the same category, namely landholder and, therefore, changes in the composition of the landholders are obscured when analysing these statistics. Similarly, such statistics may not even indicate any significant change, even if, for example, there is a sharp increase in the area held by large landholders from the merchant community and a reduction in acreage held by large Brahman landowners within a period, as these two reverse changes may statistically offset each other. Even radical changes in the socio-economic features of groups comprising 'agricultural labourers' may not explicitly appear in the occupational census data.

[15] Sumit Guha, 'Some Aspects of Rural Economy in the Deccan: 1820–1940', in K.N. Raj et al. (eds.), *Commercialization of Indian Agriculture*, pp. 232–40; idem, *The Agrarian Economy of the Bombay Deccan: 1818–1941* (Delhi, 1985), p. 196. See also B.R. Tomlinson, *The Economy of Modern India, 1860–1970*, The New Cambridge History of India, III, 3 (Cambridge, 1993), pp. 66, 77.

Jairus Banaji tries to specify changes in labour relations in colonial India by characterising them as a process of the formal subsumption of labour. Agrarian capital could form by dominating family-based peasant farms through formal subsumptions. Jairus Banaji, 'Capitalist Domination and the Small Peasantry: Deccan Districts in the Late Nineteenth Century', *EPW*, Special Number, August 1977. For a discussion of this topic, see Gyan Prakash (ed.), *The World of the Rural Labourer in Colonial India* (Delhi, 1992). See also Shahid Amin, *Sugarcane and Sugar in Gorakhpur: An Inquiry into Peasant Production for Capitalist Enterprise in Colonial India* (Delhi, 1984).

In this connection, therefore, B.B. Chaudhuri's argument concerning Eastern India is suggestive. While recognising aspects of continuity between the pre-British and the British period, he points out important changes in the rural structure of Bengal society. He argues that 'though the available data relating to the numerically significant groups of sharecroppers and agricultural labourers could create an impression that their size did not appreciably increase during British rule, at least in certain districts, their origins, composition and functions were considerably different from those in pre-British India.' The role of the loss of land, of the gradual diminution of per capita holdings, and of the impoverishment of a section of small peasants in the development of agricultural labour under British rule is generally admitted, he says, and a consequence of the process was the broadening of the social base of the agricultural labourers.[16] Whether Chaudhuri's argument has been fully backed by evidence is still a matter for debate,[17] but I agree with him in his emphasis on the changes in social composition of those included in each of the economic categories adopted for statistical data. I will attempt, in the following chapters, to advance a hypothesis for interpreting the changes which occurred in rural society in Tamilnadu, particularly in the irrigated area, by means of an analysis of the social composition and origins of the various economic classes.

The hypothesis is as follows. As Dharma Kumar says, the pre-British South Indian rural village was not an egalitarian society composed just of small landowning peasants, but a polarised one consisting of landowning and landless classes. In the middle of the nineteenth century, a large amount of the land in Tamilnadu, particularly in the irrigated districts, was owned by Brahman and other higher-caste landholders (*mirasidars*). This land was cultivated either by the landholders themselves using landless agricultural labourers of the Depressed castes,[18] or by lower-caste landless tenants.[19]

[16] B. Chaudhuri, 'Eastern India', in Kumar (ed.), *Cambridge Economic History*, pp. 86–177, 176.

[17] Binay Bhushan Chaudhuri, 'The Process of Depeasantization in Bengal and Bihar, 1885–1947', *Indian Historical Review* 2, 1 (1975); Sugata Bose, *Agrarian Bengal: Economy, Social Structure and Politics, 1919–1947* (Cambridge, 1986), p. 147.

[18] In this book, I use 'Depressed castes' as a term denoting the so-called 'Untouchable' castes or 'Outcastes'.

[19] This implies that the 'family labour farm', the central characteristic of Chayanov's model, was not the norm in South Indian agriculture and, therefore, Chayanov's interpretation of agrarian change makes little sense regarding an

During the British period, this society witnessed a structural change, a change that involved two different processes at work simultaneously. The first process was the gradual deterioration of the pattern of dominance of landownership by members of higher castes, as seen in the mid-nineteenth century. The landholdings of the Brahman community decreased and this decrease was more pronounced in larger size groups. Some former landless agricultural labourers, however, raised their status to tenant cultivators, and some belonging to lower and Depressed castes came to own small pieces of land.

This process seems to have been promoted by several factors observable in the period: the emigration of upper-caste members to urban jobs; changes in agriculture which favoured intensive cultivation; and the emigration of Depressed-caste members and the gradual development of a sense of independence and self-reliance among them. These changes in South India seem to have their parallels in the agrarian changes which occurred in seventeenth- to nineteenth-century Japan. The common features include the intensification of agricultural production, the acquisition of land by erstwhile agricultural labourer classes and the consequent increase of small farmers, and the decrease in the number of permanent bonded labourers. Moreover, both areas indicate that the general trend in agricultural progress in both Japan and Tamilnadu was towards a smaller rather than a larger family farm. This type of change seems to represent an intensification of internal forces towards change that are inherent in the agriculture of Asian paddy cultivating areas.

The second process that I shall discuss is the concentration of land in the hands of the rich Non-Brahman non-agriculturists who accumulated wealth by exploiting the new economic opportunities that British rule had stimulated. On the other hand, as South Indian agriculture became more commercialised, peasant debts increased and some small cultivator-landholders may have lost their land and sunk to the status of tenants and agricultural labourers. In other words, this process implies increased stratification among Non-Brahmans, an aspect of change that has been stressed by the conventional, or nationalist, view of rural change under British rule.

While there was a growth of large-scale landownership by Non-Brahman communities under colonial conditions in this process, the

---

understanding of agrarian society in this region of India. For a suggestive consideration of Chayanov's model, see Neil Charlesworth, 'The Russian Stratification Debate and India', *Modern Asian Studies* 13, 1 (1979).

growth is shadowed by the sharp decrease in large landholdings by the traditional Brahman landholding community in the first process. The statistics, however, may not indicate any growth of large-scale landownership if a caste-wise breakdown is not given in the statistics. The same holds good for agricultural labourers. While, in the first process, some erstwhile agricultural labourers may have become tenants and some small-scale landholders and cultivators, the second process may have led to the dispossession of landholding peasants and the creation of a new stream of agricultural labourers to supply the labour market. This change may not be noticed if the social composition of the agricultural labourer class is not carefully examined.

While the latter type of change was one of the aspects stressed by the conventional view and, therefore, its process and implications have been well described by many scholars, the former process, the gradual deterioration of the dominance of landownership by higher castes and the emergence of small landholders from members of the lower castes, has not yet been systematically analysed though some scholars have made sporadic references to some of the changes inherent in the process. The present work therefore attempts to interpret the Tamilnadu rural economy by identifying two different kinds of process at work and understanding the changes in rural society as emanating from a combination of both.

This research depends on the descriptions of castes appearing in various records, particularly the caste titles listed in village Settlement Registers, for identifying the social character of each of the economic categories. This does not mean, however, that the study aims mainly at clarifying changes in caste relationships. Neither does it assume the caste system to be the one and only basic formation regulating South Indian society. I depend on descriptions of castes and caste titles chiefly because they provide a key for identifying the social origins of those grouped in an economic class and thus enable us to infer previous economic activities and economic status.

This research also attempts to discuss the implication of the 'subdivision of landholdings'. The increase in the number of landholders, especially of smaller landholders, during the colonial period has been reported by many scholars. The popular explanation for subdivision is population increase and the Hindu law of inheritance.[20] Dhairyabala

[20] W.J. Macpherson, 'Economic Development in India', in A. Youngson (ed.), *Economic Development in the Long-run* (London, 1971), p. 163.

Pandit and more recently Neil Charlesworth[21] have criticised this popular view to some extent. I have outlined above two trends in rural society under British rule; the first highlights the gradual deterioration of the pattern of landholding characterised by the dominance of higher castes and the emergence of new landholders from among low-caste Non-Brahmans and Depressed-caste members who had hitherto been excluded from holding land. The emergence of new small landholders from the Depressed and other lower castes may elucidate an important aspect of the rapid increase in smaller landholdings from the latter half of the nineteenth century. This would partly account for the so-called 'sub-division of landholdings'.

Source Materials: Village Settlement Registers for 26 Villages in Lalgudi Taluk, Trichinopoly District

The main sources used in this study are government records such as the Proceedings of the Board of Revenue and various departments of the Madras Government, together with various government reports and other publications. The data collected during fieldwork in villages in Lalgudi *taluk*, Tiruchirapalli (Trichinopoly)[22] district, are also an important source of information.

Of the archival sources, the most important ones used in this study are the Settlement Registers for each of the 26 villages in Lalgudi *taluk*, Trichinopoly district. A few words may be appended here about the source and the district. In the first half of the nineteenth century, British rule in the Madras Presidency evolved a system to collect land tax which is known as the *raiyatwari* system. It is generally understood that in this system, the government collected the land tax (revenue) directly from the cultivating *raiyats*, though in fact the *raiyats* often did not work the land themselves, as we shall see later. Therefore, the government had to confirm the person or persons responsible for the payment

[21] Dhairyabala Pandit, 'The Myths Around Subdivision and Fragmentation of Holdings: A Few Case Histories', *IESHR* 6, 2 (1969); Neil Charlesworth, 'Trends in the Agricultural Performance of an Indian Province', in K.N. Chaudhuri and Clive J. Dewey (eds.), *Economy and Society: Essays in Indian Economic and Social History* (Delhi, 1979), pp. 130–31.

[22] In the British period, English transliteration was commonly used in administrative documents for denoting place names. I use such Anglo-Indian terms when they denote the district names under British rule; otherwise, I spell place names as they are most widely recognised today.

of land revenue (tax) for each plot of land. Every thirty years, land settlement surveys were conducted to determine or revise the amount of land revenue levied and to identify the person or persons liable for land tax, to whom an official certificate of land rights called *patta* was issued. Each *patta* holder was called a *pattadar*. *Pattas* were of two types, single *patta* (*patta* owned by only one person) and joint *patta* (that owned jointly by more than one person). For example, a person holding the single *patta* No. 26 over 5.5 acres of land could link his name with other *pattadar*(*s*) holding *patta* No. 105 over 12 acres and so could claim a share in those 12 acres.

In the district of Tiruchirapalli, the focus of the present research, land settlement surveys were conducted around the years 1865, 1895, and 1925 under British rule. At the time of each of the settlement surveys, a record called a Settlement Register was compiled for each village. The register meticulously recorded every detail about each plot of land: the name of the *pattadar*, area, amount of land revenue, irrigated or non-irrigated land, source of irrigation, number of crops, government land or land exempted from land revenue, and the nature of the soil. Though the Registers have been recently updated to around 1985, no new Settlement Register has yet been published, making three registers available at present for each village in the Tiruchirapalli district.[23]

The Settlement Registers furnish us with invaluable information that enables us to overcome the limitations of the historical records previously used in studying the history of South India. The most comprehensive statistical research on land distribution in the Madras Presidency, that done by Dharma Kumar, was not based on the Settlement Registers themselves but on the *patta* statistics compiled from the Settlement Registers. As stated above, a landholder could have both a single *patta* and a joint *patta*, and, sometimes, may have registered his name in several *pattas*. Therefore, an accurate understanding of the area held by a landholder must take into account both the areas registered as

[23] For the nature of the Settlement Registers and how their data have been processed, see Haruka Yanagisawa and Tsukasa Mizushima, *Nijisseiki Hajime Minami Indo niokeru Kasuto to Tochihoyu Kozo no Hendo* [Caste and Landholdings in South India at the Beginning of the Twentieth Century] (Tokyo: Institute for the Study of Languages and Cultures of Asia and Africa, Tokyo University of Foreign Studies [hereafter, ILCAA], 1988); Tsukasa Mizushima, 'Village Records on Land Holding in South India and Ways for Processing Them', in *Studies on Agrarian Societies in South Asia* (ILCAA) 5 (1980). Tsukasa Mizushima and I have photocopied the Settlement Registers of about 100 villages in Lalgudi *taluk* kept in the Tamil Nadu State Archives (TNA).

single *patta(s)* and those included in the person's share in the joint *patta(s)*. The Settlement Registers record the names of all the *pattadars*, single and joint as mentioned above. This enables us to compile an accurate list of each *pattadar* and the area held by each. Second, the village Settlement Registers contain the names of all the *pattadars* of each village.[24] The names of these *pattadars*, in most instances, indicate their caste, religion and gender. In many cases, caste titles are included as part of the name. For example, the suffix Ayyar would indicate the Brahman caste. In the case of a name like Chokkalingam Pillai, the suffix Pillai indicates the Vellalar caste. The most commonly occurring suffix in a woman's name is Ammal, though this does not indicate her caste. Further, some names belonged specifically to Muslims or Christians. Therefore, by analysing the village Settlement Registers, it is possible to evaluate accurately the changes in the caste/community composition of landholders, enabling us to elucidate trends in caste relationships and the economic structure of these rural societies. Third, since the new Settlement Registers retain the old survey numbers for reference, it is possible to coordinate the three registers of 1865, 1895 and 1925. This enables us to trace changes in landholders for each plot over a span of 60 years, from 1865 to 1925.

At the same time, it is also necessary to take into account the limitations of the data recorded in the Settlement Registers. First, the *pattadars* registered in the Settlement Registers were identified from the standpoint of land revenue administration. Though in this study we treat registered *pattadars* as owners of the land, whether the *pattadars* can be considered to be equivalent to landowners remains to be discussed. Setting aside the basic problem of how landholding should be conceptualised, there are a number of questions to be considered. What criteria did the British use during their colonial administration of South India to authorise a specific class of people from rural society to be *pattadars*? What was the relationship between land registration and the actual landholding in the case of a joint family? What was the actual position of a wife in landholding? It is also possible that land may have remained unregistered even though it might in reality have changed hands through trade or by inheritance. Second, the data in the Settlement Registers does not reveal relationships among the *pattadars*, barring rare instances, like for example, 'Lakshmiammal, wife of Venkata Pillai'. Where a husband and wife held *pattas* independently in their individual

[24] The entries were both in Tamil and English in the 1865 and 1895 Registers, and only in Tamil in that of 1925.

names, we have no choice but to treat them as different landholders even if they were in reality a single unit. Third, distinguishing the names of various *pattadars* poses a practical problem. For example, within the same village, names like P. Subba Reddi and Subba Reddi are found in the registers. Whether these names refer to the same person or to two different people is very difficult to decipher. For the present study, I have taken any difference in initials as indicating different people, despite the similarity of names. Therefore, my calculations may show a greater number of *pattadars* than actually existed. Fourth, the relationship between titles and communities or castes is not without ambiguity. A title could be used sometimes by different castes, and groups of people did not use the same titles continuously for generations but altered them, as we shall later see. To overcome this problem, I collected information by means of fieldwork in the 26 villages of Lalgudi *taluk* about the connection between titles people used and their communities, particularly about those titles which are supposed to have been used by Depressed castes. As well, some indication of alterations in titles is revealed by a comparison of the names of *pattadars* in a village between different years, as in the case of 'Nadan' and 'Nadavan' *pattadars* in some villages, to which I shall refer later. Still, the information we have is not complete and there still remains room for a re-examination of inferences about caste affiliation in this study.

Tiruchirapalli district is an important area in the present State of Tamil Nadu. The River Kaveri flows through it and there is a wide area of rich wet land in the catchment. Entering neighbouring Thanjavur, the river has created a vast spread-out delta with a network of irrigation canals, which is the granary of all South India. From ancient times, this area was highly regarded as the centre of the Chola empire and historically it has merited many similar compliments. In addition, the area boasts many famous temples which are landmarks of Hinduism. The bank of the Kaveri which faces Tiruchirapalli city has two famous Hindu temples, each of which owns a large area of land in the villages researched in this book. Tiruchirapalli district is situated on the western side of the Thanjavur delta.

Lalgudi *taluk*, under study, can be divided into three areas based on the available irrigation facilities: the wet zone, the intermediate zone, and the dry zone. The area along the Kaveri is very fertile because of canal irrigation. The flow of the river water is controlled by two large dams, the Upper Anicut and the Grand Anicut. The River Kaveri feeds channels, such as the Ayyan Channel, which irrigate the main portion of the wet zone of the *taluk*. Much of the wet land yielded two crops of rice even in the nineteenth century. On the northern side of the long belt of canal-irrigated land along the River Kaveri lies a vast area irrigated by reservoir. Even though a portion of this area is irrigated directly by canal, cultivation in the major part depends on water channelled from reservoirs. With such a system of irrigation, both wet land and dry fields exist in the area. In the northern part of the area are fields mostly dependent on rain water. Though there are some reservoirs, also dependent on rain to maintain their water level, the area irrigated by these reservoirs is limited to just one part of the whole area.[25] The 100 villages chosen for the present study are spread over these three areas and as a result offer a wide variety, from wet villages to dry villages. This has enabled me to make a comparative study of changes among villages with different ecological conditions.

The Research Area

Though Tiruchirapalli district, particularly the irrigated area of the district, is the core area of the present study, I have also tried to include irrigated (wet) areas in other districts in Tamilnadu, such as Thanjavur (Tanjore), Tirunelveli (Tinnevelly) and Chingleput districts. This is because, first, in spite of the differences among the districts, those districts with similar ecological conditions seem to have shared the same socio-economic conditions that prevailed in the wet zone of Tiruchirapalli district, and second, changes revealed by the Settlement Registers for Tiruchirapalli may often be better understood if they are considered together with the information available from other wet districts.

Tamilnadu has two monsoon seasons. While the rainfall is very erratic and unreliable during the south-west monsoon season which starts in June and continues through September, the area enjoys a more steady and abundant rainfall during the north-east monsoon season from the end of September. The most fertile agricultural region is the irrigated area of the Kaveri basin spreading over Thanjavur and Tiruchirapalli districts. While the land in some districts, for example that in the Thanjavur delta, is irrigated by a well-developed river-channel system, a

[25] Tadahiko Hara, 'Introduction', in Tadahiko Hara et al., *Socio-Cultural Changes in Villages in Tiruchirapalli District, Tamilnad, India,* Part 2, Modern Period, 1 (Tokyo: ILCAA, 1983).

considerable amount of land is irrigated by tanks and irrigation wells and some by natural rainfall.[26]

The British colonial government introduced the *raiyatwari* system, under which the land was classified as 'irrigated land' or wet land if the land was irrigated by channels and tanks which the government had the responsibility of maintaining. Other cultivated land irrigated by private wells and rainfall was classified as 'unirrigated land' or dry land and was assessed at a lower land revenue rate. The extent of irrigated land was larger than the unirrigated land in two typical irrigated districts, Thanjavur and Chingleput, whereas Salem and Coimbatore were typical districts with unirrigated land, irrigated land being less than 10 percent of the total cultivated land.[27]

Though the unirrigated land in the Tamil districts was four times larger in acreage than the irrigated land,[28] this does not necessarily imply that the unirrigated region played a much more important role in the economic life there than did the irrigated region. There was a large difference both in yield per acre and population density between the irrigated and unirrigated land. The average rate of land revenue assessed for irrigated land was about five rupees per acre in 1888 while that for unirrigated land was one rupee in the Madras Presidency.[29] If this difference in the revenue assessment can be assumed to reflect the actual difference in yield per acre, the irrigated area as a whole was more important in terms of agricultural production, despite its being smaller in extent. The revenue assessment for irrigated land was raised at the time of the next settlement and the gap in assessment between irrigated and unirrigated land widened further. My analysis of the Settlement Registers of villages in Tiruchirapalli district indicates that while the revenue assessment per acre of land roughly doubled for the irrigated villages, it changed little for the unirrigated villages, which suggests the increasing importance of the irrigated zone as a source of government revenue.

Hereafter, the discussion refers to the wet areas of Tamilnadu if not specifically stated except in some parts where the changes in unirrigated

[26] Baker, *Rural Economy*, p. 23; Arun Bandopadhyay, *The Agrarian Economy of Tamilnadu, 1820–1855* (Calcutta, 1992), Chapter 1.

[27] P.B.R., No. 37, 29 Jan. 1904, pp. 66–67.

[28] For example, the area of wet *patta* land in Tamil districts was 2,451,000 acres for 1900–1901, whereas that of dry land exceeded 9,187,000 acres (ibid.).

[29] S. Srinivasa Raghavaiyangar, *Memorandum on the Progress of the Madras Presidency during the Last Forty Years of British Administration* (Madras, 1893), p. 112.

areas are examined in order to place my findings in a comparative perspective.

Figure 1.1
Tamil Districts, 1929

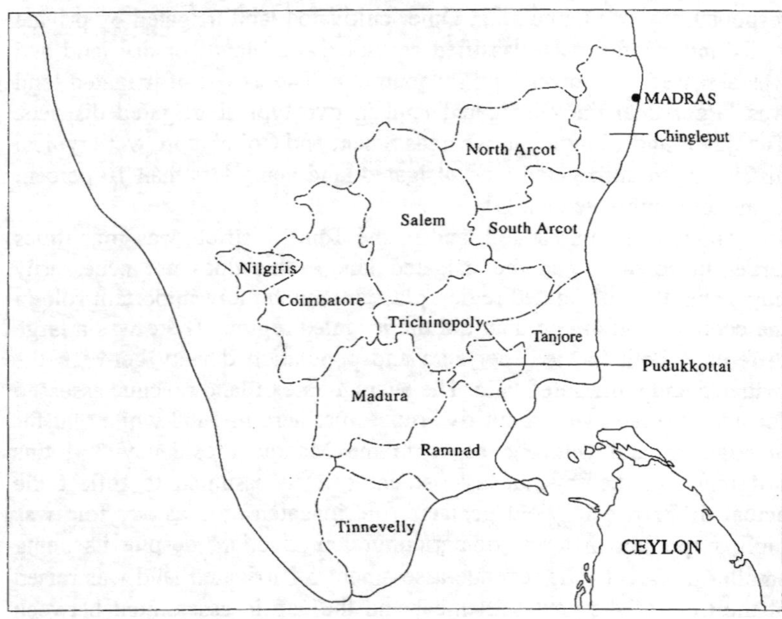

Of the eight chapters which make up this book, Chapter 2 initiates the discussion by reconstructing the agrarian structure of the wet districts in Tamilnadu as being typical of the period between the 1850s and 1870s. This underwent changes after the 1870s. Chapter 3 will concentrate on examining the main factors thought to have stimulated changes in rural society. Of the various factors, only three are considered: intensified agriculture, the emigration of labourers and higher-caste landowners, and the commercialisation of Indian agriculture. The agrarian transformation after the 1870s may be considered in two phases, though the two were closely interconnected: changes in forms of agricultural management and in the pattern of landownership. Chapter 4 deals with the first aspect alone, focussing particularly on the expansion of the tenancy system. Changing patterns of landholding are examined in Chapter 5, and two different trends in landholding are identified. A new interpretation of the sub-division of holdings is presented as well. To examine these observations from a wider perspective, I attempt a comparison with Japanese agrarian change. Chapter 6 is a brief survey of government policy towards members of lower castes.

Chapter 7 presents a summary of my field survey in a wet village named Appadurai in Tiruchirapalli district and attempts to interpret my findings at that time, as well as those reached by other scholars who have recently undertaken similar field surveys in Tamil villages, in the context of the historical changes examined in the previous chapters. Chapter 8 summarises more than a century of agrarian change in the wet area of Tamilnadu.

2

Prologue: Agrarian Structure in the Latter Half of the Nineteenth Century

To clarify changes in agrarian relationships in the period after the 1870s, we need first to reconstruct the agrarian structure in the 1860s and 1870s, and to present it as the prototype against which agrarian society of the later period will be compared. This chapter outlines the agrarian structure as it existed in the 1860s and 70s in this area. The first section of the chapter examines various aspects of landholding mainly through an analysis of the Settlement Registers of Lalgudi *taluk* in Trichinopoly district, the second section looks at patterns of land management and the nature of the labour force, and the last section relates agrarian relationships to agrarian production. This means that neither did the structure I present in this chapter remain unchanged for centuries in the pre-colonial era nor does it serve as an unchanging pattern of rural relationships in South Indian society. Recent studies have shown the occurrence of various important changes in agrarian society in the pre-colonial period and at the earliest stage of colonial rule.[1] Likewise in South Indian rural society, neither the eighteenth century nor the first half of the next century was a period of stagnation with little change in agrarian society.[2] Therefore, the agrarian structure described in this chapter projects a process of historical change from before the eighteenth century, the clarification of which, however, is beyond the main scope of the present study.

[1] C.A. Bayly, *Rulers, Townsmen and Bazaars: North Indian Society in the Age of British Expansion, 1770–1870* (Cambridge, 1983).

[2] D.A. Washbrook, 'Progress and Problems: South Asian Economic and Social History c.1720–1860', *Modern Asian Studies* 22, 1 (1988); David Ludden, *Peasant History in South India* (Princeton, 1985); David Washbrook, 'Land and Labour in Late Eighteenth-Century South India: the Golden Age of the Pariah?' in Peter Robb (ed.), *Dalit Movements and the Meanings of Labour in India* (Delhi, 1993).

Landholdings

Landholdings in the wet zone villages of Lalgudi taluk in 1865

The Settlement Registers, as I mentioned in Chapter 1, provide us with the best information about landholdings in the 1860s. I should add here a few words to explain how the data were compiled from the registers.

Some twenty-six of the one hundred odd villages in Lalgudi *taluk* were chosen and their registers for the years 1865, 1895 and 1925 analysed. The analysis noted every *pattadar* in each of the villages, the area of each *pattadar's* landholding and the amount of land revenue he had to pay. A table was compiled for each village, classifying *pattadars* according to caste (caste title), religion and size of holdings. My priorities in this classification were, in order, (1) caste (caste title), (2) religion (Muslim or Christian), and (3) gender. For example, a Christian of the Muttiriyan (Muttiriyar) caste came under the 'Muttiriyan' division and not under the 'Christian'. In other words, only those names that did not indicate the caste were entered in the 'Muslim' and 'Christian' divisions. The 'female' in the list followed the same criterion—only those female names with no indications of caste or religion were classified as 'female' landholders. The *pattadars* with titles indicating caste were divided into three, based on title: (1) Brahmans, (2) non-Brahman, non-Depressed castes (I shall hereafter use the term 'Non-Brahmans' to denote those who neither belong to the Brahman nor the Depressed castes) and (3) the Depressed castes. In addition there were titles that directly indicated the occupation of the person concerned. For example, *kaval* was the traditional guard of the village, *navitan* the barber, *pusari* the priest of the village Hindu temple, and the like. In my tables, they are included in the larger division, 'Occupational'.

The 26 villages were divided into three zones based on the percentage of irrigated wet land in the total cultivated area, as gleaned from the register of 1895. The 14 villages where irrigated land comprised more than 60 percent of the total cultivated land were classified as wet zone villages, the 7 villages with irrigated land incorporating 10 to 59 percent of the total were grouped as intermediate zone villages, and the 5 villages with dry land as dry zone villages.

Between 1865 and 1895, the administrative borders of these villages changed drastically. The 26 villages, which I have chosen for analysis based on the Settlement Register of 1895, had their origin in one hundred smaller villages that had existed in 1865. On an average, four small villages were combined to form one village. Hereafter, unless

Table 2.1

Distribution of Area by Size of Holding: 14 Wet Villages in Lalgudi *Taluk*, 1865

(acres)

Size Group (Acreage)	1 <0.5	2 <1	3 <2	4 <3	5 <5	6 <10	7 <15	8 <25	9 <50	10 <100	11 =>100	12 Total	(%)
Brahman	17	22	106	105	154	319	201	397	782	1,223	388	3,713	(38.5)
Non-Brahman	19	46	181	153	327	670	373	357	617	344	865	3,957	(41.0)
Chetty	0	1	3	7	3	19	0	15	0	54	0	103	(1.1)
Muttiriyan	1	3	28	9	12	37	40	0	0	0	0	131	(1.4)
Nadan (Nadavan)	8	15	39	54	81	241	83	188	124	200	282	1,317	(13.7)
Pillai	3	8	31	24	93	100	80	40	160	0	460	1,000	(10.4)
Reddi	0	1	0	0	0	0	0	20	0	0	0	20	(0.2)
Udaiyan	4	5	17	10	64	86	85	18	61	0	0	352	(3.7)
Others	3	13	63	49	74	187	85	76	272	90	123	1,034	(10.7)
Depressed castes	0	0	1	3	0	0	0	0	0	0	0	4	(0.0)
Occupational titles	1	9	16	3	24	42	12	0	0	0	0	105	(1.1)
Muslim	0	1	8	12	0	9	0	0	0	0	268	298	(3.1)
Christian	1	1	8	7	5	28	0	0	0	0	0	49	(0.5)
Caste unknown, female	2	1	6	12	3	26	37	0	40	0	0	126	(1.3)
Temple	1	1	15	16	26	59	23	0	74	0	107	322	(3.3)
Others	22	42	63	39	88	117	147	194	96	259	0	1,066	(11.1)
Total	63	123	404	350	627	1,270	793	948	1,609	1,826	1,628	9,640	(100)

Table 2.2

Distribution of Landholders by Size of Holding: 14 Wet Villages in Lalgudi *Taluk,* 1865

Size Group (Acreage)	1 <0.5	2 <1	3 <2	4 <3	5 <5	6 <10	7 <15	8 <25	9 <50	10 <100	11 =>100	12 Total
Brahman	61	29	70	43	41	46	16	22	23	17	2	370
Non-Brahman	80	61	126	61	83	96	31	19	18	5	5	585
Chetty	0	1	2	3	1	3	0	1	0	1	0	12
Muttiriyan	4	4	19	4	3	5	3	0	0	0	0	42
Nadan (Nadavan)	35	22	28	21	21	34	7	10	4	3	2	187
Pillai	9	10	22	10	23	15	7	2	5	0	2	150
Reddi	1	1	0	0	0	0	0	1	0	0	0	3
Udaiyan	18	7	11	4	16	13	7	1	2	0	0	79
Others	13	16	44	19	19	26	7	4	7	1	1	112
Depressed castes	0	0	1	1	0	0	0	0	0	0	0	2
Occupational titles	3	11	11	1	7	6	1	0	0	0	0	40
Muslim	0	2	5	5	0	1	0	0	0	0	1	14
Christian	5	1	5	3	1	3	0	0	0	0	0	18
Caste unknown, female	5	2	4	5	1	3	3	0	1	0	0	24
Temple	4	2	10	6	7	9	2	0	2	0	1	43
Others	74	60	45	17	24	16	12	10	3	3	0	265
Total	233	168	277	142	164	180	65	51	47	25	9	1,361

specified otherwise, the village borders delineated in 1895 will be taken as the standard for counting the number of villages, and by extension, the same standard will be used for analysing the data for 1865—the relevant villages will be combined as one, corresponding to the village of 1895. Table 2.1 shows the caste/title-wise distribution of landholdings of the wet zone villages of the Lalgudi *taluk* in 1865.[3] In the 14 wet zone villages, the cultivated land and public (*purambokku*) land totalled an area of 11,289 acres, of which an area of 1,649 acres was registered as *purambokku* (roads, housing and other public land) and, therefore, has been excluded from the table.

A glance at Table 2.1 reveals that Brahmans clearly stand out as the major holders of large-scale wet land in the irrigated areas. Of the 9,640 acres of cultivated land, 3,713 acres or 38.5 percent were held by Brahmans. In 9 out of the 14 wet zone villages, Brahmans were the biggest landholders. In most of the villages, they held more than half the cultivated land. As the revenue assessment of a plot was fixed based on the condition of the soil and the nature of the irrigation facility, the amount of revenue would be a better index of the assessment of landed properties of different qualities than the mere acreage of land itself. When viewed from the percentage of land revenue paid, the Brahmans' share becomes much larger: of the total amount of land revenue collected from all the 14 villages, the revenue from Brahman-held land accounted for more than 45 percent. Among the Brahmans, the Ayyar group belonging to the Smartha sect held the largest amount of land, outstripping the Ayyangars belonging to the Srivaishnava sect.

The second largest landholding group, after the Brahmans, was the Nadan (Nadar) and Nadavan (Nadavar). They belonged to the Kallar caste. Their large landholdings seem to have been procured by them at a time in the past when they were powerful local leaders, called *nattars*, responsible in part for government administration.[4] However, Nadan (Nadavan) landholdings were mainly limited to only two villages, and therefore were not too significant overall, when all 14 villages of the wet zone are considered. About two-thirds of the total acreage held by

[3] The detailed tables for the three zones in this *taluk* are listed in Haruka Yanagisawa, *Minamiindo Shakai Keizaishi Kenkyu* [Studies in the Socio-Economic History of South India] (Tokyo, 1991).

[4] Personal interview with their descendants in the village. For *nattar*, see Tsukasa Mizushima, *Nattar and the Socio-economic Changes in South India in the 18th–19th Centuries* (Tokyo: ILCAA, 1986).

members of the Nadar and Nadavar communities were concentrated in those two neighbouring villages.

The caste using the title 'Pillai' held 10 percent of the cultivated land, close in percentage to that held by the Nadars, though much less than that of the Brahmans. The caste title 'Pillai' tended to be used by some members of the Vellalar caste, a high ranking agricultural caste occupying a position next to the Brahmans in wet zone villages.[5] Along with the Brahmans, they had a certain amount of power and control in the villages of the area. Though there were also some people belonging to castes other than the Vellalar who used the title,[6] my field studies have shown that most of those using the Pillai title were in fact Vellalars. The Brahmans and Pillais held 55 percent of the total cultivated land in the wet zone villages in terms of the land revenue collected.

However, the Brahmans and Pillais, though owning the majority of land in the wet zone villages, accounted for only a small percentage of the population in this area. The 1871 Village Census reveals the population of the 26 villages surveyed. It is not very clear how the population was divided and grouped in this census. For example, the number of Pariahs (Paraiyars) in the whole area was given as 2,386,[7] about 8 percent of the total population. This, however, is an unnaturally small number if it is taken to indicate the total population of Depressed castes in the area.[8] It is probable that a part of the Depressed-caste population was entered into other categories. Though the numbers do not validate the census as an accurate source of historical data, the census list may be taken as a rough indicator of the population. In the wet zone, Brahmans numbered 1,390 persons or 10 percent of the total population, and Vellalars, to which the Pillais probably belonged, numbered 1,402 (10 percent of the total population), so Brahmans and Vellalars together made up 20 percent of the total. As the Vellalar caste is likely to have included those with the titles of 'Kavundan' and 'Reddi' also, the Brahmans and Pillais together would actually not exceed 15 percent of the total population. Landholdings were thus concentrated in the hands

[5] Ludden, *Peasant History,* p. 87.

[6] Baker, *Rural Economy*, p. 88; *Madras District Gazetteers, Trichinopoly* (hereafter *Gazetteer of Trichinopoly District*), by E.R. Hemingway (Madras, 1907), p. 100.

[7] Calculated from *Census Statement of 1871 in Each Village of the Trichinopoly District Arranged according to Area, Caste and Occupation, Madras* (Madras, 1871), pp. 46–59.

[8] For example, Kumar, *Land and Caste*, pp. 52–63.

of a small section of people, more than half of the land being owned by about 15 percent of the population. The Settlement Registers for the 14 wet villages show that there were 370 Brahman landholders in this zone (Table 2.2). In the Village Census of 1871, the Brahman population was 1,390 and the average family size in the 14 villages was 6.8 people. If we assume that there was no difference in family size across castes, then there would have been 204 Brahman families. An average of 1.8 persons per Brahman family were thus registered landholders.

By contrast, the total number of families of other castes was 2,010, with landholders numbering 991 persons. This means that about half of the non-Brahman families, or about 45 percent of the total families of the villages, did not possess any land at all. Among those people who belonged neither to the Brahmans nor to the Vellalars, two large groups may be identified. The first is the Depressed-caste population: according to the 'castewise division of the population' in Trichinopoly district listed in the 1901 Census, 'Paraiyan', 'Pallan', 'Chakkiliyan' and other Depressed castes occupied 19 percent of the total population. The second group belonging to 'Palli', 'Ambalakaran', 'Muttiriyan' and 'Nattaman' castes formed 25 percent of the total population in 1901. The Pallis were present in large numbers in the dry zone of Tiruchirapalli, and were known by different caste titles like Udaiyan, Vanniyan and Servaikaran, etc. Nattamans also possessed the title of Udaiyan. Ambalakaran[9] and Muttiriyan were in the same caste, and generally held the caste titles of Muttiriyan, Ambalakaran, and Servaikaran.[10] We shall use the term 'low-caste Non-Brahmans' to denote this portion of the Non-Brahman population, who neither belonged to the Depressed castes nor the Vellalars but were members of those castes now classified as 'backward classes'.[11] Low-caste Non-Brahmans and Depressed castes formed more than half the total population of Tiruchirapalli .

In the 14 wet villages in this district too, low-caste Non-Brahmans and Depressed castes accounted for more than half the population. In

[9] *Gazetteer of Trichinopoly District,* pp. 109–10.

[10] Ibid., p. 106.

[11] This does not necessarily mean that all of these communities had been considered 'low', even before the British period and regardless of regional differences. Recent historiography stresses the fluid and adaptable character of Tamil society in the pre-British period and argues that the division among the communities had not been as sharp as that observed in the later period. These important points are, however, beyond the scope of this research. See for example, Nicholas B. Dirks, *The Hollow Crown: Ethnohistory of an Indian Kingdom* (Cambridge, 1987).

the 1871 Census, low-caste Non-Brahmans and Depressed-caste members were likely to have been included in the divisions of 'Vanniyan', 'Sattani' and 'Pariah'. These three divisions included more than 60 percent of the total population of the wet zone.

In sharp contrast to members of higher castes, lower-caste people had only very small landholdings. Land revenue from land held by Muttiriyars was a mere Rs. 455, just 1.2 percent of the total land revenue. The Depressed castes had very little, the paltry land revenue of Rs. 17 indicating that they were almost excluded from landholding. Landholdings were therefore concentrated in the hands of the Brahmans and the Pillais, with little available for the lower castes, though the latter formed a large part of the population. Particularly obvious are the Depressed castes, comprising one-fifth of the population, but virtually totally excluded from holding land. The landless Depressed-caste members and low-caste Non-Brahmans were either employed as agricultural labourers by the Brahmans and farmers, or were small tenants under higher-caste landowners. Later detailed analysis will show that the Brahmans and agricultural castes, like the Vellalars, evolved various methods to prevent or limit people from the lower castes from becoming landholders in order to retain them as labourers or tenants.

The landholdings were concentrated not only in terms of caste but also in terms of size groups. The total land revenue collected from the 14 villages in the wet zone was about Rs. 38,000. Large landholders owning more than 15 acres (size groups 8 to 11), paid land revenue of Rs. 23,205, or 62 percent of the total land revenue. In the wet zone, 132 landholders owned more than 15 acres, representing about 10 percent of the total number of landholders (Table 2.2). Thus, about 10 percent of the landholders owned as much as 60 percent of the land.

It is necessary to add that there were villages where non-residents were the main landholders. Among the 100 villages of 1865 that correspond to the 26 villages of 1895, the main landholders in at least 11 of them were Brahmans or Pillais not living in the village at all. A more careful examination would probably reveal that the area owned by non-residents of the villages formed a greater percentage of village land.

To sum up the landholding patterns in the wet zone of Lalgudi *taluk*, in the mid-nineteenth century, (1) more than half of the arable land was owned by Brahmans and Vellalars, (2) large landholders owning more than 15 acres, a very small 10 percent of the landholders, held 60 percent of the total cultivated land, (3) about 45 percent of the villagers, who belonged to lower castes, did not hold any land at all,

(4) half the number of villagers owning any extent of land are likely to have owned a negligible area of less than two acres, and (5) low-caste Non-Brahmans owned just a small percentage of the land, while the Depressed-caste members particularly were almost completely excluded from landownership.

Landholdings in the intermediate and dry zone villages in Lalgudi taluk

The landholding pattern in the intermediate zone villages, where wet land formed 10 percent to 60 percent of the total area of these villages, was a little different from that of the wet villages. The Pillai (Vellalar) was the major landholding caste accounting for 21 percent of the land revenue collected from the area. [12] The Brahmans followed, contributing 19 percent of the total land revenue. A sizeable 40 percent of the land revenue paid, therefore, came from the Pillais and Brahmans, a situation very similar to that found in the wet zone. A further 11 percent was from low-caste Non-Brahmans such as the Udaiyar, Vanattirayan (assumed to be the caste title of the Kallars), Nadar, Nadavar, Servai, Muttiriyar, and others. Thus in this zone the share owned by low-caste Non-Brahmans was larger than in the wet zone, though not as large as in the dry zone. Out of the 7 villages analysed so far, Pillai landowners predominated in four and Brahmans in two. One village had almost equal strengths of Brahman and Udaiyar landholders. It may be safe to conclude that though it was slightly different from the wet zone villages, the pattern of landholdings in the intermediate zone villages was essentially similar to that of the wet zone villages discussed above.

Unlike the wet zone villages, the dry zone villages in Lalgudi *taluk* can be grouped into two categories of different character. The first type represents villages where most of the village land was owned by people from high castes, like Brahmans, Vellalars or Reddis (Reddiars), while members of lower castes, such as Pallis and Depressed-caste members, were engaged in agriculture either as tenants or agricultural labourers. This feature in 'high-caste dominant villages' is common with villages in the wet zone. The dry zone had a different type of village, where low-caste Non-Brahmans dominated landholding. In such 'lower-caste dominant villages', a group of small landowners owned more than half of the cultivated land and their family farming probably formed the major type of cultivation. In spite of this difference, however, as was the case

[12] See Yanagisawa, *Minamiindo Shakai Keizaishi,* pp. 67–69, Tables 3.8–3.10.

Table 2.3

Distribution of Area by Size of Holding: 7 Intermediate Zone Villages in Lalgudi *Taluk*, 1865

(acres)

Size Group	1	2	3	4	5	6	7	8	9	10	11	12	
(Acreage)	<0.5	<1	<2	<3	<5	<10	<15	<25	<50	<100	=>100	Total	(%)
Brahman	4	7	26	29	45	67	105	321	191	203	132	1,124	(13.9)
Non-Brahman	10	75	144	180	404	800	463	591	218	420	102	3,405	(42.0)
Chetty	1	0	2	0	0	5	0	0	0	0	0	7	(0.1)
Kavundan	0	1	0	0	9	6	0	0	0	0	0	17	(0.2)
Muttiriyan	1	5	12	14	16	7	0	36	0	16	0	107	(1.3)
Nadan (Nadavan)	0	10	11	14	15	19	25	63	29	56	0	242	(3.0)
Pillai	2	11	22	23	85	250	175	201	84	213	102	1,168	(14.4)
Udaiyan	4	21	54	77	157	412	158	104	0	56	0	1,045	(12.9)
Others	2	27	43	52	122	101	105	187	105	79	0	819	(10.1)
Depressed castes	1	2	3	2	3	5	15	0	0	0	0	30	(0.4)
Occupational titles	0	4	19	15	25	32	46	22	26	0	0	187	(2.3)
Muslim	0	1	3	3	4	10	13	23	27	0	0	85	(1.0)
Christian	0	0	3	2	4	13	0	0	0	0	0	22	(0.3)
Caste unknown, female	0	0	0	5	22	11	24	41	46	0	192	341	(4.2)
Temple	2	1	13	9	12	35	41	0	70	0	62	244	(3.0)
No holder's name	1	1	0	0	5	0	12	31	0	99	1,198	1,346	(16.6)
Others	15	29	105	109	150	198	175	138	141	134	112	1,317	(16.3)
Total	33	120	316	354	674	1,171	894	1,167	719	856	1,798	8,101	(100)

Table 2.4

Distribution of Landholders by Size of Holding: 7 Intermediate Zone Villages in Lalgudi *Taluk*, 1865

Size Group (Acreage)	1 <0.5	2 <1	3 <2	4 <3	5 <5	6 <10	7 <15	8 <25	9 <50	10 <100	11 =>100	12 Total
Brahman	11	10	19	12	15	13	12	18	9	4	2	125
Non-Brahman	39	97	100	71	103	114	38	31	8	7	1	609
Chetty	1	0	1	0	0	1	0	0	0	0	0	3
Kavundan	1	1	1	0	2	1	0	0	0	0	0	6
Muttiriyan	2	6	7	5	5	1	0	2	0	1	0	29
Nadan (Nadavan)	3	14	7	6	4	3	2	3	1	1	0	44
Pillai	9	14	16	9	21	36	14	10	3	3	1	136
Udaiyan	10	29	38	31	40	57	13	6	0	1	0	225
Others	13	33	30	20	31	15	9	10	4	1	0	166
Depressed castes	2	2	2	1	1	1	1	0	0	0	0	10
Occupational titles	2	4	12	5	6	5	4	2	1	0	0	41
Muslim	1	2	2	1	1	2	1	1	1	0	0	12
Christian	1	0	2	1	1	2	0	0	0	0	0	7
Caste unknown, female	1	0	0	2	8	3	2	2	1	0	1	20
Temple	5	2	8	4	4	5	3	0	2	0	1	34
No holder's name	3	1	0	0	1	0	1	2	0	1	3	12
Others	35	43	69	43	39	31	15	7	5	2	1	290
Total	100	161	214	140	179	176	77	63	27	14	9	1,160

in wet villages, there were very few Depressed-caste *pattadars* in 1865 in the dry zone, even in 'lower-caste dominant villages', and the majority of the Depressed-caste members were probably agricultural labourers.[13] An important difference was however that agricultural labourers in dry villages were mostly daily coolies; permanent bonded labourers formed only a small section of them, if any.[14]

Dominance by higher castes in landholdings and their command over the labour force in the wet districts

My analysis of the village Settlement Registers in the wet and intermediate zones of Lalgudi *taluk* quantitatively confirms some of the important features depicted in the descriptive sources available for other wet districts. For example, the Manual of Tanjore district indicates that Brahmans dominated landownership. 'There is hardly a family of Tamil Brahmans, which does not possess a competence in landed property; many own valuable estates. . . . Whatever calling they pursue, the one object of every Tamil Brahman, whether he be a Government servant, a trader or a menial, is to reserve his earnings to augment his ancestral estate, large or small, whatever it is.'[15] K. Gough has pointed out that in 900 of the 2,400 villages of Thanjavur, Brahmans were the main landholders.[16] These data point to the conclusion that Brahmans owned large areas of land in Thanjavur district, though we have no data indicating the quantitative share of their land in this district. Vellalar and Brahman landholders were dominant in Tirunelveli: 'By far the largest part of the lands of the district is held either from Government or from the different Zamindars by Vellalars (here popularly known as Pillays), or by the descendants of Telugu settlers, Naiks, and Reddies, by Razus, and by Brahmins.'[17] The best of the arable land with excellent irrigation

[13] The detailed tables showing the landholdings in the dry villages in Lalgudi *taluk* are listed in Yanagisawa, *Minamiindo Shakai Keizaishi*, pp. 262–68. For an excellent account of the landholding pattern of a dry village in Lalgudi *taluk*, see Tsukasa Mizushima, 'Changes, Chances and Choices: The Perspective of Indian Villagers', in Hara et al., *Socio-Cultural Change in Villages in Tiruchirapalli District*, Part 2, 1.

[14] *Manual of Salem District*, by H.Le Fanu (Madras, 1883), Vol. 2, pp. 57–58.

[15] *Manual of the District of Tanjore in the Madras Presidency* (hereafter *Manual of Tanjore District*), by T. Venkasami Row (Madras, 1883), p. 170.

[16] Kathleen Gough, *Rural Society in Southeast India* (Cambridge, 1981), p. 27.

[17] *Manual of Tinnevelly District*, by A.J. Stuart (Madras, 1879), p. 16.

seemed to have belonged particularly to the Brahmans: 'Brahmans are as a rule all the more able to command as the owners in many parts of the district of most of the better irrigated lands.' This is confirmed by Ludden.[18] For Chingleput district, the Tremenheere report of 1891 notes that land in the district was in the hands of the high castes and points out the significance of that fact. The report describes the agrarian population as follows: 'First comes the mirasi body, generally the Brahmans or Vellalas, holding all the lands or at least the best. Then come the non-mirasi pattadars (if any), then the sub-tenants, both perhaps somewhat inferior in caste. Last are the Pariahs, a few of them sub-tenants, but most of them agricultural labourers.'[19] Thus data from Chingleput reveals a situation similar to that of Lalgudi *taluk* in Tiruchirapalli district: *mirasidar* landholders, mainly belonging to the Brahman and Vellalar castes, claimed that they were the founders of the villages and so held most of the land.[20] The concentration of landownership in the hands of a few large landholders was also observable in other districts, as we shall see in the next section.[21]

The Tremenheere report considered the exclusive possession of land by the minority higher-caste groups to be related to the rights asserted by the *mirasidars*. The *mirasidars* claimed that in pre-colonial South India they had held the land jointly and were collectively responsible for the payment of land tax. 'They managed their internal affairs themselves, including the disposal of waste, and were thus able to keep out all strangers except grantees of the Sovereign.'[22] In the Thanjavur

[18] *Gazetteer of Tinnevelly District*, by H.R. Pate (Madras, 1917), p. 106; Ludden, *Peasant History*, pp. 89, 167; idem, 'The Terms of Ryotwari Praxis: Changing Property Relations Among Mirasidars in the Tinnevelly District, 1801 to 1885', in Robert E. Frykenberg and Pauline Kolenda (eds.), *Studies of South India: An Anthology of Recent Research and Scholarship* (Madras and New Delhi, 1985), p. 158.

[19] G.O., Nos. 1010–1010A, Revenue, 30 Sept. 1892, par. 19, p. 617. For *mirasidars* in Chingleput area, see Noboru Karashima, *South Indian History and Society: Studies from Inscriptions, A.D. 850–1800* (Delhi, 1984), pp. 165–80.

[20] Though *mirasi* rights could be held by Paraiyars and a few other castes, the number of such cases was so small as to constitute an exception. *Manual of Chingleput District*, by Charles Stewart Crole (Madras, 1879), p. 50.

[21] See Kumar, 'Landownership and Inequality'.

[22] G.O., Nos. 1010–1010A, Revenue, 30 Sept. 1892, p. 617, par. 11. As early as 1874, the Settlement Report stated that the *mirasidars* were unwilling to see waste land made over to others on *darkhast* and were anxious to keep out these new-comers (P.B.R., No. 2880, 5 Oct. 1874, p. 7804, par. 38; ibid., pp. 7812–13, pars. 57–58). See also *Manual of Chingleput District*, p. 66.

and Chingleput districts, disposal rights over waste land asserted by *mirasidars* were recognised by the British colonial rulers, as we will see in a later chapter. As a result 'a priority of claim to the arable waste is conceded to them, not only as against the traders, the labourers, and other such residents in the village, but *even against other pattadars*, if there should happen to be such, on the ground that the latter are not representatives or assignees of the ancient shareholders, but modern interlopers'. Even in other districts where the *mirasidars*' rights over waste land were not recognised, those *pattadars* already owning land were allowed priority of claim to arable waste land. No land was given to any applicant until the *pattadars* had been given first claim. Thus the government policy of giving *mirasidars* and *pattadars*, who already owned land, priority over waste land had virtually made it impossible for landless lower-caste labourers and tenants to acquire new land. The report goes on: 'If the statement means that a Pariah can in fact obtain waste land as freely as other classes, it is incorrect. He may apply for it, but he has to run the gauntlet of first the mirasidars, and secondly the non-mirasi pattadars, both of which classes abhor the thought of his acquiring land, and one of which cannot get enough land for itself.'[23]

Why were members of low castes like the Paraiyar obstructed from obtaining arable land? According to the report, non-*mirasidar* villagers who were caste-Hindus could obtain a part of the arable land, in the event of trouble among the *mirasidars* in the village, but the Paraiyars [Depressed castes] as a rule were rigidly excluded, because of 'prejudice and fear of a free labour-market. . . . The wretch cut off from the land, bound frequently by iniquitous contracts, and holding his very hut at the mercy of his masters, is obedient as a dog, and works for a rack-rent or for starvation wages. How long would this last if he could get a plot of ground for a home and for a livelihood?'[24] The Collector of Tanjore also indicated that the *mirasidars*, wanting to maintain the labour force, opposed any attempt to improve the condition of the Depressed castes. 'They naturally do not desire to have labour free and their attitude though a selfish one is intelligible.'[25]

As I shall describe in the next section, the Paraiyars and other low

[23] G.O. Nos. 1010–1010A, Revenue, 30 Sept. 1892, pp. 617–18, par. 20. Even later, in 1918, any attempt to improve the condition of Depressed castes by assigning them land met with opposition from the caste-Hindus in North Arcot (P.B.R., No. 60, 18 Mar. 1918, p.19).

[24] G.O. Nos. 1010–1010A, Revenue, 30 Sept. 1892, p. 618, pars. 25, 26.

[25] P.B.R., No. 10, 12 Jan. 1920, p. 106.

castes were used or employed by higher-caste people as the necessary labour force. The higher castes would have lost this advantage and facility if the lower castes became landholders. For this reason they vehemently opposed and banned any changes that might destroy the existing social structure. Arun Bandopadhyay gives an example which illustrates why members of lower castes were prevented from holding land. In 1827, the *mirasidars* in South Arcot district did not oppose the distribution of waste land by the government provided their own under-tenants and slaves did not become owners. As Bandopadhyay correctly points out, the *mirasidars* were well aware that once their slaves and under-tenants were able to cultivate their own land, their hold over them would be weakened. [26]

Agrarian Relations

Patterns of farm management

It was crucial for landowners to keep a firm hold on their under-tenants and agricultural labourers in the wet districts, where the majority of the area was not cultivated by the family of the landowners but was either leased to tenants or cultivated by agricultural labourers.[27]

We have already seen that according to the 1865 Settlement Registers of Lalgudi *taluk* in Trichinopoly district, 70 percent of the *pattadars* in the wet zone were small landholders owning less than 5 acres. Of these, about 40 percent belonged to the Brahman and Vellalar castes and probably did not work the land themselves. The remaining landholders, more than half, belonged to lower castes. As it was technically possible for the landowner and his family to cultivate land of less than 5 acres themselves if they wished to do, it is highly likely that in 1865 more than half of the landowners cultivated their land themselves. On the

[26] Arun Bandopadhyay, 'The Nature of Landownership in Tamilnadu from 1820 to 1855', *Calcutta Historical Journal* 13, 1 (1989) (idem, *Agrarian Economy of Tamilnadu,* p. 214). See also Chitra Sivakumar and S.S. Sivakumar, *Peasants and Nabobs: Agrarian Radicalism in Late Eighteenth Century Tamil Country* (Delhi, 1993), p. 22.

[27] For the period before 1855, see Bandopadhyay, *Agrarian Economy of Tamilnadu,* Chapter 6; Ludden, *Peasant History,* pp. 90–94; Benedicte Hjejle, 'Slavery and Agricultural Bondage in South India in the Nineteenth Century,' *The Scandinavian Economic History Review* 15, 1 & 2 (1967); Kumar, *Land and Caste.*

other hand, as I have shown above, more than half of the cultivated area was owned by large landholders having more than 15 acres each. As it was not possible to cultivate this amount of land by means of the labour of the landholder's family, such land must have been worked by employed labourers or by tenants. Further, since the Brahmans and Vellalars, who did not generally engage in manual work, owned the majority of the wet land, it is safe to conclude that more than half of the arable land in the wet zone in Lalgudi *taluk* was cultivated by non-family, outside labour.

As regards the Tanjore district, the Board of Revenue stated as follows: 'The status of mirassidars in the Tanjore District, who are mostly small holders, more than half of them paying less than Rs. 10 as assessment to Government, differs in no respect from that of ryots in other districts. . . .'[28] It emphasised that the *mirasidars* were a class of cultivator which employed, superintended, and sometimes assisted labourers, comprising everywhere the farmers of the country. The Settlement Report of the Tanjore district in 1892 recorded a table showing the distribution of single *pattas* in the district at the time of the settlement survey.[29] The table confirms the above-quoted statement of the Board of Revenue that more than half of the *pattadars* were small landholders. In the district, whose total arable area including both the irrigated and non-irrigated land was 1,076,646 acres, the average land revenue per acre was Rs. 3.6. According to the table, 58 percent of the total number of *pattadars* were paying less than Rs. 10 and, therefore, are likely to have owned less than three acres, indicating that the largest group in the strata of landholders was the small cultivators. This does not mean, however, that land cultivated with the help of non-family labour existed only to a limited extent in the district. The table demonstrates also that almost half of the total land revenue collected was from large landholders paying more than Rs. 100. In other words, large landholders, owning more than 30 acres but constituting less than 5 percent of the total of landholders, held almost half of the arable land. If we tabulate from a tax level of Rs. 50, or more than 16 acres of landholdings, then 65.6 percent of the total land revenue was collected from this group. In all probability, these landowners managed their land utilizing outside labour and/or by leasing to tenants. The cultivation pattern of Thanjavur in the latter half of nineteenth century is aptly summarised in the following statement: 'Where the Ryot Pattadar is not himself the

[28] G.O., No. 1195, Revenue, 29 Oct. 1885, p. 472.
[29] P.B.R., No. 719, 1 Nov. 1892, par. 58.

laborer (he is generally so in the upland parts of the district), cultivation is carried out by either of two modes, viz., by Panneiyals or hired labor, and by Purakkudis or tenants.'[30]

In the Chingleput district too, as shown above, a large extent of the land was held by Brahmans and Vellalars. According to the Manual, 'Brahmins and Vellalans very seldom themselves work on the farm. . . . The lands of Brahmins and Vellalans are generally cultivated by farm servants, either Pallis or Pariahs. . . . Brahmins and Vellalans very frequently let their lands to Pallis, Pariahs and others, receiving either Melvaram, or share as proprietors, or a Kappattam, money payment.'[31] In this district too, the prevalent system appeared to have been that of utilizing farm servants or leasing to tenants, rather than engaging in family cultivation.[32]

Concerning the district of Tinnevelly, the Settlement Report noted that each of the 136,000 *raiyats* paid an average of Rs. 21.3 as land revenue, which amounted to a total of Rs. 2,900 thousand. Of that number of *raiyats*, 85,000 paid less than Rs. 10, and 31,000 between Rs. 10 and Rs. 30, as land revenue.[33] The majority of the *pattadars* thus belonged to those two divisions of small landholder. In any case, the amount of revenue from *pattadars* belonging to the two smaller divisions could never have exceeded Rs. 1,770 thousand. If we take the middle amount as the average amount of revenue of each division, the total collected from these two divisions comes to Rs. 1,040 thousand. Hence, those paying less than Rs. 30 accounted for less than half of the total land revenue of Rs. 2,900 thousand. In other words, more than half of the land was held by large *pattadars* paying a revenue of more than Rs. 30. As the Manual of this district records: 'Many of the larger ryotwari landholders do not concern themselves personally with the cultivation of their lands. Such is the value of the land in Tinnevelly that sub-tenants are easily found to cultivate for them, . . . there is a wealthy

[30] *Manual of Tanjore District*, p. 379. According to a report submitted by the Deputy Collector to the Collector of Tanjore, 'the ryot-puttadars of Tanjore are not generally the cultivating tenants; that the cultivation is carried on either by panniyals (hired labor) or porakudies (a sort of tenants), and that there are no regular tenants under the Tanjore mirassidars as under the Zemindars' (G.O., No. 1195, Revenue, 29 Oct. 1885, p. 468).

[31] *Manual of Chingleput District*, pp. 50–51.

[32] 'The so-called Mirasidars often cultivate but only a small portion of their puttah lands, leaving the rest to be tilled by Payacarries (under-cultivators) whose tenancy is insecure' (P.B.R., No. 2880, 5 Oct. 1874, p. 7804, par. 38).

[33] G.O., No. 716, Revenue, 4 May 1872, p. 1218, par. 13.

leisure class among the ryots, living on the rent of their lands. This class consists chiefly of Brahmins or Vellalars.'[34] In this district too, it is safe to conclude that landowners holding more than 3 acres owned more than half of the land and that a large number of these large landowners used tenants to cultivate their land. Further, even in the case of Non-Brahman *pattadars*, 'the Sudras largely cultivated their lands themselves, assisted by Pariahs and Pullers as farm servants'.[35] It was thus common to use Depressed-caste members as permanent labourers.

Choosing a village with a population of 929 as a typical example, the Manual of Tinnevelly district tabulates the composition of the village population as follows: Brahmans, 10 families; Vellalar and other 'Sudra' landholders, 61; Chettiar landholders, 4; labourers, 83; others, 137 families. About 75 families of landholders employed 83 families of serfs in agriculture.[36] The number of families of agricultural labourers obviously exceeded that of landowning families in this village. In Srivilliputtur *taluk*, Tirunelveli district, 'more than half of the irrigated land and about a quarter of the unirrigated land is held by Brahmins',[37] though 'the Brahmin never followed the plough'[38] but used an outside labour force.

To summarise, in the latter half of the nineteenth century, the greater part of the wet zone areas of Tamilnadu was cultivated either by tenants or by using permanent labourers like the *pannaiyal*. Though small holdings dominated in terms of the number of *pattadars*, the area cultivated by landowning families themselves was relatively less.

Agricultural labourers

There is no doubt about the importance of agricultural labourers in South Indian agriculture. As mentioned already, Dharma Kumar has argued that agricultural labourers formed a sizeable portion of the total agricultural population at the end of the eighteenth century.[39] Their percentage would be much greater if those who did not actually work in the fields, such as Brahmans and landowning Vellalars, are not counted

[34] *Manual of Tinnevelly District* (Madras, 1879), p. 23.

[35] Ibid., p. 28.

[36] Ibid., pp. 29–30.

[37] G.O, No. 1462, Revenue, 7 Sept. 1878, p. 3098, par. 5. The Gazetteer also stated that the Brahmans were the owners of most of the better irrigated land in many parts of the district. *Gazetteer of Tinnevelly District*, p. 106.

[38] Ibid., p. 28.

[39] Kumar, *Land and Caste*, 'Introduction to Reprint', Chapter XI.

among the agricultural workforce. In this connection, the data from the village survey done by Barnard in Chingleput around 1770 is suggestive. As may be seen in Appendix 1, an analysis of fifty villages reveals that, in the latter half of the eighteenth century, households of agricultural labourers accounted for more than half of the total number of households actually engaged in field labour. Furthermore, it should be taken into account that adult female members of Depressed-caste families in all probability also worked in the fields, whereas women of other communities were less likely to participate in field labour.[40] As the Collector of Trichinopoly reported in 1803, without the Pullers (Pallars) scarcely any land would be cultivated.[41]

In the latter half of the nineteenth century, agricultural labourers still remained the main labour force on which landowners depended. No evidence indicates any decrease in their number in nineteenth century South India. The most important component of the agricultural labourers on whom the landowners relied was permanent labourers such as *pannaiyals* (*padiyals*). The relationship between *pannaiyals* and employers does not need any elaboration.[42] Here I shall merely make a few observations about the *pannaiyals*, many of which have already been examined in previous studies.

First, the yearly income of a *pannaiyal* couple is likely to have been less than that of a cooly couple in some parts of Tamilnadu in the latter half of the nineteenth century, though the evidence we have is too scanty to draw any general conclusion for Tamilnadu. The *pannaiyals* or permanent labourers in the latter half of the nineteenth century were generally remunerated in the following manner in the wet Tamil districts, though there were differences among areas: (1) they were paid mainly in kind (grain, etc.); (2) they were given presents on the occasion of weddings, childbirth and festivals, and also helped on the occasion of deaths in the family; (3) they held the rights to the gleanings after har-

[40] It was said that 'female daily agricultural coolies are almost all Panchamas' (P.B.R., No. 106, 29 May 1918, p. 12). See Hjejle, 'Slavery and Agricultural Bondage', p. 84.

[41] Trichinopoly Collectorate Record, Vol. 3662 (TNA), 29 May 1803, pp. 98–99.

[42] See Kumar, *Land and Caste*; Hjejle, 'Slavery and Agricultural Bondage'; Baker, *Rural Economy,* Chapter 3; S.S. Sivakumar, 'Transformation of the Agrarian Economy in Tondaimandalam: 1760–1900', *Social Scientist* 6, 10 (No. 70) (1978); Ludden, *Peasant History,* pp. 93, 167; D.A. Washbrook, *The Emergence of Provincial Politics: The Madras Presidency 1870–1920* (Cambridge, 1976), pp. 86–87.

vest: (4) they received interest-free loans; (5) they could lease a house with a backyard; and (6) in Thanjavur district, they could lease land from the *mirasidars.*[43] According to a survey done in 1872 in the Valliyur division of the Nanguneri *taluk* in Tirunelveli district, the earnings of a Pallar and his wife during the working season were Rs. 36, and at Shermadevi in the Ambasamudram *taluk* of this district, a couple of same standing was reported to earn the grain equivalent to Rs. 42. On the other hand, 'a cooly or day labourer's wages varied from two annas to three annas four pies per diem and his wife's earnings were taken at from one anna four pies to two annas, . . . a cooly would not work more than two-thirds of a month and the working season could not be put down at more than 8 months; the earnings of a cooly and his wife might accordingly be taken at between Rs. 48 and Rs. 60 a-year. . . .' The source concluded that 'there was, however, no doubt that this class was better off than the hereditary farm servants', suggesting that the income earned by a farm servant and his wife was less than that earned by a couple of day labourers.[44]

Second, the advance given to a *pannaiyal* was one of the traps set by higher-caste landowners to keep him in a condition of servitude. A landowner was eager to pay an advance to labourers, 'as he thereby gets the labourer into the clutches of debt, which prevents his leaving his service . . .'.[45] The purpose of the advance made to *pannaiyals* is more clearly stated in the following observation: 'In almost all cases advances made to padiyals by their masters are, within a certain limit, not intended to be recovered. Indeed in some few villages the mirasidars stated that they would refuse to accept them if they were offered. The object of the advance is to secure a permanent servant at a wage distinctly lower than the market rate, and to make it as difficult as possible for him to change masters, or at least to go to another master in a different village.'[46]

Thirdly, in some districts, *mirasidars* insisted their rights even over

[43] Kumar, *Land and Caste*, p. 151.

[44] Raghavaiyangar, *Memorandum*, p. lxxviii. See also Kumar, *Land and Caste*, p. 151. However, the situation may have differed in Nellore district, where, according to Atchi Reddy, the calculated daily wages of annual farm servants were more than the actual daily wages of day labourers. M. Atchi Reddy, 'The Commercialization of Agriculture in Nellore District 1850–1916: Effects on Wages, Employment and Tenancy', in K.N. Raj et al. (eds.), *Commercialization of Indian Agriculture*, p. 168.

[45] *Manual of Chingleput District*, p. 50.

[46] P.B.R., No. 106, 29 May 1918, p. 19, par. 29.

the house sites of Paraiyar settlements.[47] The threat of eviction was held out to prevent the *padiyal* from leaving his master.[48] Tremenheere reported such cases in Chingleput district. The Sub-Collector wrote: 'This morning I find that most of the paracheri [Depressed castes' settlement] lands are entered in the names of the (*mirasidars*), and they threaten to oust them if they do not work gratis or very cheaply for them.'[49] The information from Thanjavur district and Tirunelveli district points to a common plight of the *pannaiyal*—*mirasidars* asserted their rights over the *pannaiyals*' housing plots or settlements and prevented their freedom of movement with the threat of eviction from those settlements.[50]

Before the abolition of slavery in India in 1843, escaped slaves were caught by the British Collectors and restored to their owners, as observed by Dharma Kumar.[51] The 'abolition of slavery' in 1843 did not really mean a ban on owning slaves or punishment for those who did so. It merely denied slave owners any rights over their slaves and made it unlawful for public authorities to catch and restore an escaped slave to his owner.[52] In fact, a palm-leaf record obtained in a village in Lalgudi *taluk* reveals that Pallar slaves were sold even in 1852.[53] It was not until 1861 when the Criminal Law came into existence that keeping a slave was legally prohibited. Thus though legal action by the government may not have had much actual effect, *pannaiyals* and other bonded labourers acquired a legal basis thereby to leave their masters. The increasing chance of emigration overseas provided them with the opportunity to leave their villages. Payments of advances and threats of eviction aimed

[47] For a case in a village in Lalgudi *taluk*, see Y. Subbarayalu, *Palm-leaf Records of the Tiruchirapalli District* (Thanjavur, 1991), pp. 95–97. The palm-leaf records have been collected by Masao Naito and edited and translated by Y. Subbarayalu.

[48] P.B.R., No. 106, 29 May 1918, p. 21, par. 35; Hjejle, 'Slavery and Agricultural Bondage', p 116. Though later, in 1931, the Gazetteer remarked that the Depressed-caste members in Chingleput district, unlike their castemen in Thanjavur, generally owned a salable interest in the sites on which their houses stood. *Madras District Gazetteers, Statistical Appendix for Trichinopoly District* (Madras, 1931), p. 78.

[49] G. O. Nos. 1010–1010A, Revenue, 30 Sept. 1892, pp. 626–27.

[50] Raghavaiyangar, *Memorandum*, p. lxxxiv.

[51] Kumar, *Land and Caste*, p. 42.

[52] Hjejle, 'Slavery and Agricultural Bondage', p. 98.

[53] Subbarayalu, *Palm-leaf Records*, pp. 32, 90. It was reported in 1856 that many of the Paraiyars and Pallars were privately regarded as slaves to cultivate the land. Board of Revenue, Vol. 2524 (TNA), 18 Apr. 1856.

at limiting the movement of *pannaiyals* and labourers in this new situation.[54]

Day labourers other than *pannaiyals* doubtless also formed an important part of the agricultural labour population, though their numbers in the Depressed castes were probably not as large as those of the *pannaiyals* as we see below.

Varam or tenants

Equally prevalent as the *pannaiyal* system was the *parakudi*, or *varam*, system. While some of those called *parakudis* were practically no different from agricultural labourers except in the method of receiving their remuneration, some were tenants in the sense that they independently managed their farms.

The *parakudi* in Thanjavur was an example of the latter case. Their position was as follows: (1) they provided seed, livestock and cattle; (2) the landowners were responsible for the supply of manure; (3) *parakudis* received $^1/_5$ to $^1/_3$ share of the produce; (4) they had gleaning rights following the harvest; (5) they were offered a housing plot and a backyard; and (6) they were sometimes assigned land as *maniyam*. It is not clear whether the practice of receiving remuneration in the forms of (4), (5) and (6) above was very common in this district. Judging from the fact that *parakudis* provided seed and livestock for ploughing, they may have managed their farms on their own account and therefore can be categorised as tenants, though the lowness of their share in the produce indicates that their economic position was not sharply distinguished from that of agricultural labourers.[55]

[54] Hjejle, 'Slavery and Agricultural Bondage', pp. 100–101.

[55] According to the Manual of Tanjore district, 'in the case of Parakkudi cultivation, the tenant provides the required seed and ploughing stock and, in consideration of it and the labor spent on cultivation, receives a certain share of the out-turn whatever it may be; the share varying in different parts, from 18 to 33 per cent. . . . The tenant's varam does not include Kudimaramat, (the customary farm repairs usually termed "village labor"), or manuring, or the remuneration of village servants, all of which are separately provided for by the Mirasidar or Ryot-proprietor' (*Manual of Tanjore District,* p. 381; G.O., No. 1195, Revenue, 29 Oct. 1885, p. 470). The Sub-Collector of the district reported 'The porakudies are also allowed house-sites and back yards free of rent. But they provide themselves with seeds and ploughing stock and get waram (a share of the produce for cultivating the land)' (G.O., No. 1195, Revenue, 29 October 1885, p. 469). The *tahsildar* of Mayavaram *taluk* of Tanjore district stated, 'The parakudies get a share of the produce as "waram" which varies from $^1/_5$ to $^1/_3$ of

The system of sharecropping in Tiruchirapalli was more complex than that in Thanjavur. Apart from the cultivation by small scale landowners, there were three systems by which the land was cultivated: farm management by owners with the help of day labourers and farm servants; land leased for a rent in grain or money (*kuttagai*); and land leased for a share of the harvest (*varam*). The *varam* system was of two types: the '*al-varam*' ('al' means 'man'), where cultivators were not responsible for the cattle used for cultivation; and the '*mattu-varam*' ('*madu*' means 'oxen' or 'cattle'), where cultivators provided oxen for cultivation. In both cases, the owners were responsible for supplying the manure and seed. *Al-varam* cultivators received $^1/_8$ to $^1/_{10}$ of the farm produce, and *mattu-varam* cultivators received a larger portion of the produce, generally $^3/_{16}$ of the produce and the whole or a part of the straw.[56] The worker cultivating land under the *al-varam* system can be identified as a form of agricultural labourer, since the seeds, manure and ploughing cattle were provided by the landowner, with the worker responsible only for his labour in cultivation. In contrast to this, the *mattu-varam* system was closer to the tenant cultivation system, as the cultivator had to provide the ploughing cattle.

The economic condition of members of lower castes

Another important aspect that must be treated is the connection between caste and occupation among the lower castes in the latter half of the nineteenth century.[57] In wet districts, the majority of Depressed-caste members and low-caste Non-Brahmans were cultivating land owned by others, either as agricultural labourers or tenants.

First, more than half of the Depressed-caste members in wet districts were agricultural labourers. The Tremenheere report on Chingleput stated in 1892 that while a few Pariahs (Paraiyars) were sub-tenants, most of them were agricultural labourers.[58] In Thanjavur in

---

the quantity harvested. They also get some extra remuneration of $1^1/_2$ to 2 measures of paddy as "kalavady". Further an extent of land varying from 75 to 100 gulies are assigned to them for every 15 mahs of land as maniam which will yield about 7 to 10 kalams of paddy' (G.O., No. 1195, Revenue, 29 Oct. 1885, p. 470).

[56] *Gazetteer of Trichinopoly District*, p. 151.

[57] The connection between caste and occupation was previously discussed by Kumar, *Land and Caste*, pp. 60–61. See also Mihar Shah, 'The Kaniatchi Form of Labour', *EPW* 20, 30 (27 July 1985), p. 69.

[58] G.O., Nos. 1010–1010A, Revenue, 30 Sept. 1892, p. 617.

1883, Pareiyas (Paraiyars) were reported to be employed chiefly as agricultural labourers, and the Pallars were 'prædial laborers and are employed exclusively in the cultivation of paddy lands'.[59] In Tiruchirapalli district also Pallar and Paraiyar were stated to be the agricultural labourer castes, who generally tilled the land of others as *pannaiyals*, or permanent farm servants.[60] The situation was same in Tirunelveli district, where the Settlement Report noted in 1872 that the Pullers (Pallars) accounting for about two-thirds of the Depressed-caste population in this district,[61] 'were lately slaves, but are now agricultural labourers',[62] though the Manual of this district stated that about one-third of the male population of Paraiyars was employed as labourers.[63]

Second, a very large portion of these Depressed-caste agricultural labourers were permanent farm servants such as *pannaiyals*. For the Tiruchirapalli district, this is evidenced by the above cited reports from the district. Though the Manual of Tanjore district indicates that the Pallars in this district were praedial labourers, it does not mention what form the employment of Paraiyar labourers took. For the Thanjavur and Chingleput districts, the reports by Tremenheere and Gray are suggestive. The Gray report estimated in 1918 that in the Chingleput district, the number of *padiyals* was probably one-half to two-thirds of the number of male agricultural daily coolies.[64] Since 'the proportion of padiyals to free daily agricultural labourers [in Thanjavur district] is probably higher than in Chingleput',[65] permanent labourers in Thanjavur district are likely to have comprised more than half of the agricultural labourers in 1918. Furthermore, as there was a tendency to replace *pannaiyals* with free labourers, as indicated by the Settlement Report in 1921, the percentage of *pannaiyals* among agricultural labourers as a whole was larger in the nineteenth century than in 1918.[66] Thus it may be safe to conclude that permanent labourers comprised more than half of the total

[59] *Manual of Tanjore District*, pp. 203–4.

[60] *Gazetteer of Trichinopoly District*, pp. 128, 130.

[61] *Madras District Gazetteers, Statistical Appendix for Tinnevelly District* (Madras, 1905), Table VI, p. 6.

[62] G.O., No. 716, Revenue, 3 May 1872, p. 1220 (par. 23). Also, P.B.R., Vol. 2524 (TNA), 18 Apr. 1856.

[63] *Manual of Tinnevelly District*, pp. 15, 28.

[64] P.B.R., No. 106, 29 May 1918, p. 15.

[65] Ibid., p. 21, par. 35.

[66] P.B.R., No. 28, 12 Feb. 1921, p. 49. In 1863, the use of casual labour was reported to be extremely rare in Thanjavur. Kumar, *Land and Caste*, pp. 157–58.

of Depressed-caste agricultural labourers in Thanjavur in the latter half of the nineteenth century. Though no information is available on the percentage of permanent labourers in nineteenth-century Chingleput, the above-quoted 1918 Gray report leads us to presume that they formed nearly half of the total population of agricultural labourers in the latter half of the last century.

Thirdly, many of the low-caste Non-Brahmans in wet districts are likely to have been either tenants or agricultural day labourers, though the data presents a complex picture. The Manual of Trichinopoly published in 1871, referring to the census item of 'cultivator' which comprised 58 percent of the male population, stated 'the bulk of those who engage in cultivation are Vannians in the south, then came the Vellalars and Pariahs in point of numbers. . . .'[67] 'Vannians' in this census included such communities as Kallar, Maravar, Palli and Odars.[68] Since the data from the 1865 Settlement Registers of villages in Lalgudi *taluk* indicate that the percentage of *pattadars* among low-caste Non-Brahmans was very small, it may be inferred that 'Vannian cultivators' should include a large number of landless tenants. The Manual also noted that 'laborers are drawn from all ranks, but chiefly the Vannians and Pariahs'.[69] If we can assume, as indicated by Gray, that the majority of permanent labourers belonged to the Depressed castes, Vanniar labourers were mainly daily coolies. It may be concluded therefore that in Tiruchirapalli district, low-caste Non-Brahmans were engaged in cultivation as tenants and day labourers.

The situation in Thanjavur was no different. According to the Manual of Tanjore district, 'These [Ahamudeiyar, Muppar, Nattamadi or Udeiyar, Padeiyacci, Kallar, Maravar, Palli or Vanniar, Valeiyar, and Kamblattar] are the main divisions of the ordinary peasant population of the district (the Pareiyas or out-castes excepted) known by the general name "Vannia" or "Palli", and, with the exception of the last two, constitute the tenantry of the district cultivating under Ryot proprietors, where the latter do not themselves cultivate their holdings. Considerable numbers of the first five classes are Ryotwary landholders in their own right, some possessing large estates and much wealth.'[70] Among these,

[67] *Manual of Trichinopoly District in the Presidency of Madras,* compiled by Lewis Moore (Madras, 1878), pp. 105, 363.

[68] *Census of India, 1871, Madras* (Madras, 1874), Vol. 1, pp. 156–57.

[69] *Manual of Trichinopoly District*, p. 106; *Census of India, 1891,* Vol. 13, *Madras* (Madras, 1893), p. 246.

[70] *Manual of Tanjore District*, p. 190.

the Kallar seemed to have enjoyed a better economic status: 'The bulk of the Ryotwari proprietors in the richly cultivated part of the Cauvery delta, which constituted the greater portion of the old taluk of Tiruvadi are Kallars, and, as a rule, they are a wealthy and well-to-do class.'[71]

In general an overview of the two districts seems to indicate a predominance of tenants and agricultural labourers among low-caste Non-Brahmans though there was a sizeable number of landholders particularly among the Kallars.

Single Cropping of Paddy and Pannaiyals

In the wet zone districts of Tamilnadu, a large proportion of Depressed castes came under the category of permanent labourers, held in bondage by their employers and fettered in many ways. The status quo was ensured by debts they owed to employers, by the threat of eviction and by other devices to maintain their state of bondage. It goes without saying that the state of agricultural production in South India also hampered their emancipation.

Day labourers had to face a slack season of several months annually, when they had little chance of employment. While the wage per day paid a permanent labourer was probably less than that given to a day labourer (cooly) and, furthermore, his wife and children usually had to serve the master on demand, they had the advantage that they were paid in kind, with food items, etc., for a much longer period of the year than a day cooly was, even though the *pannaiyal* was not automatically entitled to paid employment throughout the year.[72] In some instances, small plots were leased to them for cultivation.

By contrast, the day labourer or cooly had no such benefits, as he was paid daily, and he had no income during the idle months. In the Chingleput district, 'in places work can only be had for twenty days in the month on an average throughout the year; and in other places work is very scarce for about four months during the off season, when there is very little agricultural labour available. . . . During the off season the misery which the coolies and their families have to endure is very great indeed. They have frequently to supplement what they are able to earn by getting herbs and roots from the jungle for food.'[73] In Thanjavur, 'it

[71] Ibid., p. 195.
[72] Hjejle, 'Slavery and Agricultural Bondage', p. 96.
[73] G.O., No. 875, Revenue, 19 April 1916, p. 4.

is sometimes even said that the labourer prefers this dependent position [of *pannaiyals*] to the struggle of finding work under new conditions for himself.'[74] According to the above-quoted Gray report, 'it is true that he [*padiyal* or farm servant] has in most cases the advantage of regular employment and regular wages for the greater part of the year but his total annual income is very low.'[75] This can be regarded as a different angle of the same problem. The existence of idle months and the lack of opportunities to find alternative sources of income in this period made it virtually impossible for them to free themselves from their bonded state.

The seasonal fluctuation of labour demand was very large in the cultivation of paddy. During the entire cycle, the demand for labour was largest at the times of sowing, transplanting and harvesting. On the other hand, for several months a year, during the idle season, there was no demand for agricultural labour. This fluctuation in labour demand was particularly great if the area was single-cropped land wholly cultivated with paddy. On the contrary, if the land was double cropped and sown with a wide variety of crops maturing at different times, the idle season would be shorter and the fluctuation in labour demand less sharp.

In this connection, the contrast seen between the delta area and the upland area in Thanjavur district is suggestive. While the former specialised in a single cropping of rice (to be discussed below), 'the upland ryot has more unfavorable seasons to face, but with transplanted paddy, broad-cast paddy, manavari paddy, and a big assortment of dry crops his risk of total failure is probably less'.[76] The Settlement Report records data about labour demand: 'Owing to the large variety of crops [in the upland], there is little, if any, slack season and labour can always be usefully employed. On the other hand in such of the delta villages as contain no garden or padugai lands, there is long off season and it is not always possible to keep the labourer effectively employed for the whole year.'[77]

It has to be borne in mind that in the Thanjavur and Chingleput districts, single cropping of paddy was in vogue, making the idle season particularly long. The River Kaveri is the source of an intricate network of irrigation channels. The water level of the river rises in mid-June, making cultivation possible. Continuing to supply water, the river

[74] *Gazetteer of Tanjore District*, p. 111.

[75] P.B.R., No. 106, 29 May 1918, p. 15, par. 24.

[76] P.B.R., No. 28, 12 February 1921; G.O., No. 1537, Revenue, 25 Aug. 1922, p. 12.

[77] G.O., No. 1537, Revenue, 25 Aug. 1922, p. 12.

swells again when the south-west monsoon starts in mid-July. Irrigation is further boosted when the north-east monsoon starts around October-November. The land lies dry only for three months, from March, which means this area had an adequate water supply for nine months of the year.[78] Benefiting from the Kaveri channel system, the Thanjavur district had a high percentage of irrigated land. According to the Settlement Report of 1892, 70 percent of the land, or 803,107 acres, was irrigated.[79] Hence, as much as 78 percent of the total area was cropped with paddy.[80]

Surprisingly, however, in spite of good irrigation facilities, Thanjavur district had very few areas with double cropping. In 1902–3, of the 889,000 acres irrigated by the Kaveri, only a little over one-tenth was cultivated with a second crop.[81] What was the reason for this under-utilisation of the irrigated land? According to the above Settlement Report, 'undoubtedly shortage of manure frequently prevents the raising of two crops even when the water-supply is adequate.'[82] The delta areas could not afford to supply the necessary amount of manure to double crop the area. A comment in the 1883 district Manual suggests the reason for this lack of manure. 'It is hardly possible that the required quantity of manure can be found for the whole of the Cauvery delta. There are not sufficient cattle, sheep or goats for it, and owing to the absence of pasture, a sufficiency of these cannot be maintained.'[83]

Chingleput district was no different, in the sense that agriculture in the irrigated area was characterised by the single cropping of paddy. The 1874 Settlement Report states that in the Saidapet, Ponneri and Tiruvallur *taluks,* irrigated land was 118,665 acres and non-irrigated land 85,602 acres. Ninety-five percent of the former area and 20.84 percent of the latter were under rice cultivation, comprising 63.7 percent of the total land area. In 1872, these three *taluks* had a total of 20,899 acres, or a mere 10.2 percent, under double cropping.[84]

The lack of double cropping in this district was partly due to limitations in the irrigation system in the district, and partly related to the development of a closer economic link between Chingleput agriculture

[78] P.B.R., No. 719, 1 Nov. 1892, p. 5

[79] Ibid., pp. 18–19.

[80] Ibid., p. 21.

[81] *Gazetteer of Tanjore District*, p. 99.

[82] P.B.R., No. 28, 12 Feb. 1921; G.O., No. 1537, Revenue, 25 August 1922, p. 20.

[83] *Manual of Tanjore District*, p. 348

[84] P.B.R., No. 2880, 5 Oct. 1874, pp. 7814, 7855.

and Madras city, as revealed by G. Djurfeldt and S. Lindberg.[85] The following statement from the Settlement Report illustrates how straw, important as feed for livestock, and bratties produced in this district were taken away to the Madras market. 'Of course, anything that the Ryots like to produce and bring for sale, finds a ready market at Madras, and this, I cannot help thinking, is one cause of the bad cultivation and the bad condition of the Ryots of these Taluqs. They can, in fact, live from hand to mouth so easily by bringing in straw, bratties, firewood or poultry, which all command a high price, and that they . . . neglect their cultivation. . . .'[86] Since locally produced fodder was taken away to Madras, 'the locally bred cattle are poor and stunted'.[87] It was therefore very difficult for the district to supply enough manure to increase the area under double cropping until it started importing manure and cattle from other districts, as we shall see later.

It may be concluded that (1) single cropping of rice was a typical pattern of cultivation in the wet areas of Thanjavur and Chingleput districts and that (2) the long idle periods created by this pattern of cultivation probably prevented bonded labour from becoming free day labour.

Conclusion

An analysis of the Settlement Registers has revealed a highly concentrated pattern of landholding in Lalgudi *taluk*. More than half of the land was owned by Brahmans and Vellalars, particularly by a few large landowners. The majority of the villagers held no land or owned a negligible area of less than two acres. Members of low Non-Brahman castes owned a small percentage of the land, while those belonging to Depressed castes were virtually excluded from landownership. This type of ownership was prevalent in other wet districts such as Thanjavur and Chingleput. Though small holdings dominated in terms of the number of *pattadars*, the area cultivated by the landowning families themselves was relatively less. The greater part of the wet area was cultivated either through a sharecropping system or by using permanent labourers like the *pannaiyal*.

[85] Göran Djurfeldt and Staffan Lindberg, *Behind Poverty: The Social Formation in a Tamil Village* (Lund, 1975), p. 66; Bandopadhyay, *Agrarian Economy of Tamilnadu*, p. 20.

[86] P.B.R., No. 2880, 5 Oct. 1874, p. 7801.

[87] P.B.R., No. 299, 19 Aug. 1909, p. 39.

The key labour force, on which landowners had to rely for the cultivation of their land, was permanent labourers and under-tenants belonging to the Depressed castes and to low Non-Brahman castes. The higher castes would have lost their advantage and the use of cheap labour if the members of lower castes became landholders. In addition to the exclusion of members of lower castes from landownership, debts owed to employers and the threat of eviction were the main devices used by landowners to keep their labourers in a state of bondage. The nature of the agricultural production in South India also hampered the emancipation of these permanent labourers. The single cropping of rice, a pattern typical of the wet areas of Thanjavur and Chingleput districts which developed as a result of the integration of local agriculture into the wider network developed under colonial rule, created a long idle season, which seems to have prevented bonded labourers from becoming free day labourers.

3
Background to the Change

Agrarian society in Tamilnadu underwent a marked change after the 1870s. Though this transformation represents the cumulative result of various factors, the following three developments seem to have most instrumental: intensification of agricultural production, the emigration of lower- and higher-caste people to estates and urban areas respectively, and the integration of South Indian agriculture into the network of world trade.

Intensification of Agricultural Production

The change in agricultural practices in the Tamil districts that began in the latter half of the nineteenth century was one of the factors that promoted changes in agrarian society. My hypothesis is that agriculture in the period showed a gradual tendency towards intensification, with cultivators giving more care and attention to obtain a better yield. This change in agricultural practice may have been underpinned by an increase in the demand for agricultural products, particularly for paddy, from both the foreign and domestic markets between the late nineteenth century and the 1920s. A trend towards rising prices of such products was noticed during this period.[1]

First, irrigation in the Tamil districts improved from the latter half of the nineteenth century. The increase in the number of wells was particularly remarkable. Between 1852 and 1890, areas irrigated by private wells increased by 138 percent in the Madras Presidency.[2] The three decades after 1891–92 witnessed an increase of 50 percent in the area irrigated by wells in Tamil districts (see Table 3.1).

Records for the districts confirm this. To cite some examples, in the

[1] Baker, *Rural Economy*, pp. 186, 241; Kumar, 'Agrarian Relations: South India', p. 231.

[2] Raghavaiyangar, *Memorandum*, p. 48.

Table 3.1
Irrigated Area in Tamil Districts
(thousand acres)

	1891–92	1902–3	1912–13	1922–23
Government canals	1,349	1,389	1,442	1,436
Private canals	4	7	27	23
Tanks	1,358	1,407	1,970	2,063
Wells	785	796	989	1,206
Other sources	74	93	149	139
Total	3,570	3,690	4,577	4,867

Source: *Season and Crop Reports.*
Note: Tamil districts: Chingleput, North Arcot, South Arcot, Salem, Coimbatore, Trichinopoly, Tanjore, Madura, Ramnad and Tinnevelly.

Salem district, the number of wells increased from 51,000 to 54,000 between 1871 and 1876.[3] The Settlement Report of the district in 1903 stated that a remarkable feature in the agricultural history of the previous thirty years was the increase in the number of wells.[4] For Madurai district, the Gazetteer indicated an enormous increase in the number of wells,[5] and an increase in the number of wells was also reported in the Coimbatore and Tirunelveli (Tinnevelly) districts.[6] According to the Settlement Report of Trichinopoly district, areas irrigated by wells almost doubled, from 51,000 acres in 1905–6 to 100,500 acres in 1919–20.[7] Table 3.2 has been compiled from village census data given in the Settlement Registers for 60 villages in Lalgudi *taluk*, Trichinopoly district. The villages are grouped into three categories, wet, intermediate and dry zones. The average number of wells per village increased from 18 to 33 between 1894 and 1925.

There seems also to have been an improvement in canal irrigation in some areas, though this is not as remarkable as in well irrigation. The village Settlement Register describes how the land of each plot in a village is used. Figure 3.1 shows water channels in Appadurai village in Lalgudi *taluk* as reconstructed from descriptions in the Settlement

[3] *Manual of Salem District*, Vol. 1, p.153.

[4] P.B.R., No. 205, 15 June 1903, p. 17.

[5] *Gazetteer of Madura District*, compiled by W. Francis (Madras, 1906), p. 131.

[6] P.B.R., No. 1760, 26 June 1878, p. 5735; P.B.R., No. 565, 4 Nov. 1910, p. 5; *Manual of Tinnevelly District*, p. 25. See also Ludden, *Peasant History*, pp. 147–48.

[7] P.B.R., No. 86, 26 Nov. 1923, p. 27, par. 22.

Table 3.2
Village Census Data for 60 Villages in Lalgudi *Taluk* :
Average per Village for 1894 and 1925

Zones Number of villages		Wet 18	Intermediate 20	Dry 22	Total 60
Total cultivated area (acres)	1894	594.2	735.6	1428.4	927.7
	1925	591.1	739.3	1585.4	981.4
Wet land (acres)	1894	553.9	518.0	180.2	414.3
	1925	556.8	543.0	205.4	432.6
Area double cropped (acres)*	1894	352.3	273.5	108.1	235.9
	1925	364.7	304.6	153.1	266.4
Area cultivated with paddy (acres)*	1894	877.8	686.9	202.3	566.5
	1925	920.4	795.7	294.4	649.3
Area cultivated with *ragi* (acres)*	1894	24.6	73.1	150.3	86.8
	1925	3.7	30.6	158.3	69.4
Area cultivated with other cereals (acres)*	1894	8.6	82.9	822.3	331.7
	1925	2.2	42.6	697.9	270.8
Area cultivated with sugarcane (acres)*	1894	15.9	34.6	19.0	23.3
	1925	3.8	13.8	9.5	9.2
Area cultivated with cotton (acres)*	1894	0.0	3.7	37.4	14.9
	1925	0.0	0.6	64.9	24.0
Area cultivated with groundnut (acres)*	1894	2.2	6.4	12.2	7.3
	1925	0.2	13.1	109.6	44.6
Number of wells	1894	0.0	2.4	47.7	18.3
	1925	0.0	3.7	88.1	33.5
Number of cattle	1894	516.1	645.2	852.2	689.0
	1925	622.7	735.2	975.7	786.5
Number of carts	1894	25.9	28.3	28.5	27.7
	1925	38.9	43.5	55.2	46.4
Number of ploughs	1894	107.4	113.5	172.0	133.7
	1925	129.8	145.0	256.1	179.9

Source: *Settlement Registers for Villages in Lalgudi Taluk, Trichinopoly District* (c. 1895); *Settlement Registers for Villages in Lalgudi Taluk, Trichinopoly District* (c.1926).

Note: * Area cropped for 1894 is the average for five years ending 1894, whereas that for 1925 is for a single year, 1925.

Register for 1865, and Figure 3.2 shows the situation in 1979.[8] A comparison of two figures reveals an important difference in canal configuration. In 1864, only the main trunks of the canals existed, hardly any of the network of branches then existing (Figure 3.1). I have omitted the 1895 map, since it shows no noteworthy differences from the map of 1979 given in Figure 3.2. The inference is that the ramifying canal branches were constructed during the 30 years between 1864 and 1895.

The case of Appadurai village indicates another change in the village irrigation system. The River Kollidam (Coleroon) flows along the western part of the village, and land along the bank remained largely non-irrigated until 1864. By 1895 however much of the area had become irrigated, resulting in a reduction in area of non-irrigated land from 144 to 78 acres. The river bank had originally functioned as a natural embankment. It had to be high enough to prevent the flooding of low-lying arable land, for river levels fluctuated widely. The renovation and improvement of the Upper Anicut dam towards the end of the nineteenth century reduced the grave uncertainties of the Kollidam water levels. With the stabilisation of the water level, villagers started lowering the land along the bank to irrigate it.[9]

Second, the increase in the number of wells and the improvement of canal irrigation resulted in an increase in the gross area of irrigated land. M. Hodgson noted in 1808 that in 'Tanjore, the dry grain cultivation does not amount to 50 in the 100',[10] though he did not define the bounds of the area referred to as 'Tanjore'. Eighty years later, the Settlement Report of the district made it clear that in 1892, 70.8 percent of the total area reserved for cultivation was irrigated land, indicating a marked increase in the area under irrigation.[11] For the whole Madras Presidency, in addition to the above-mentioned increase by 138 percent in land irrigated by private wells between 1852 and 1890, the increase in the area of cultivation in this period was 25 percent for unirrigated land and 41 percent for land irrigated by sources of irrigation maintained by the government.[12] The irrigated area further expanded after the 1890s. The irrigated area in Trichinopoly district increased from

[8] Haruka Yanagisawa, *Socio-Economic Changes in a Village in the Paddy Cultivating Area in South India* (Tokyo: ILCAA, 1983).

[9] Ibid., pp. 25–28.

[10] W.H. Bayley and W. Hudleston (eds.), *Papers on Mirasi Right* (Madras, 1862), p. 117 n.

[11] P.B.R., No. 719, 1 Nov. 1892, pp. 18–19.

[12] Raghavaiyangar, *Memorandum*, p. 48. For government irrigation, see Ludden, *Peasant History*, pp. 142–46.

Figure 3.1
Land Use in Appadurai Village, 1864

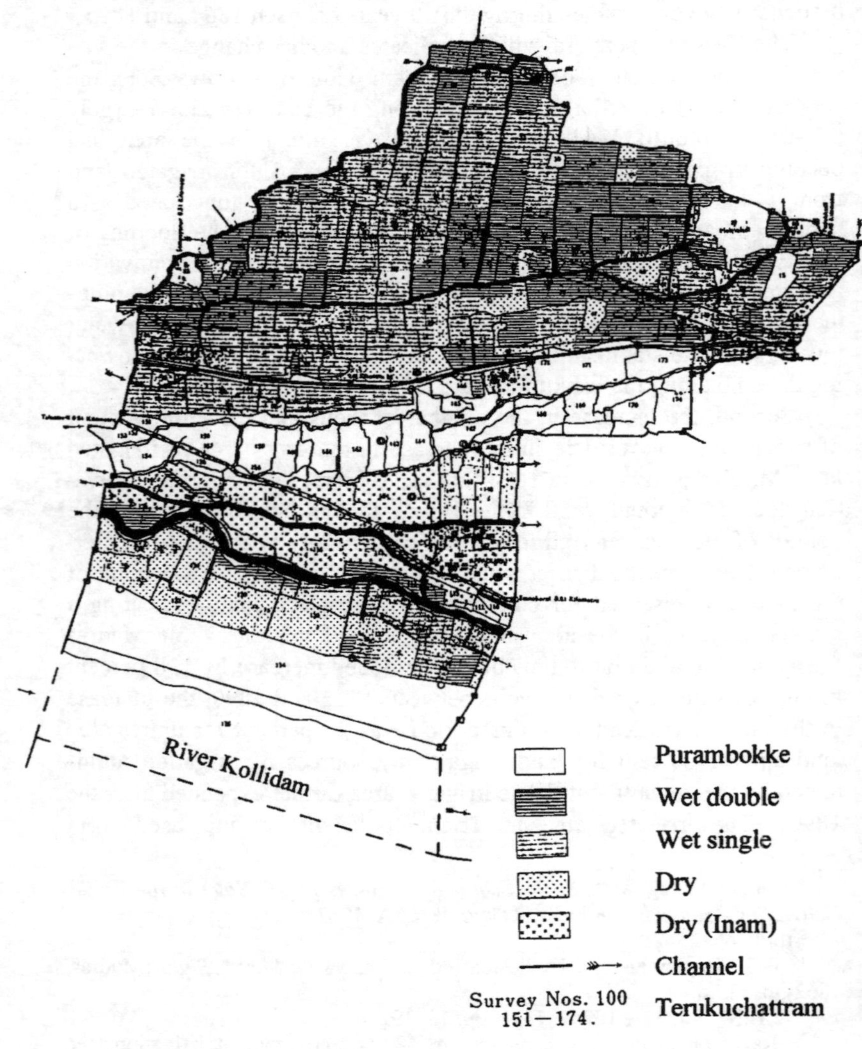

Figure 3.2
Land Use in Appadurai Village, 1979

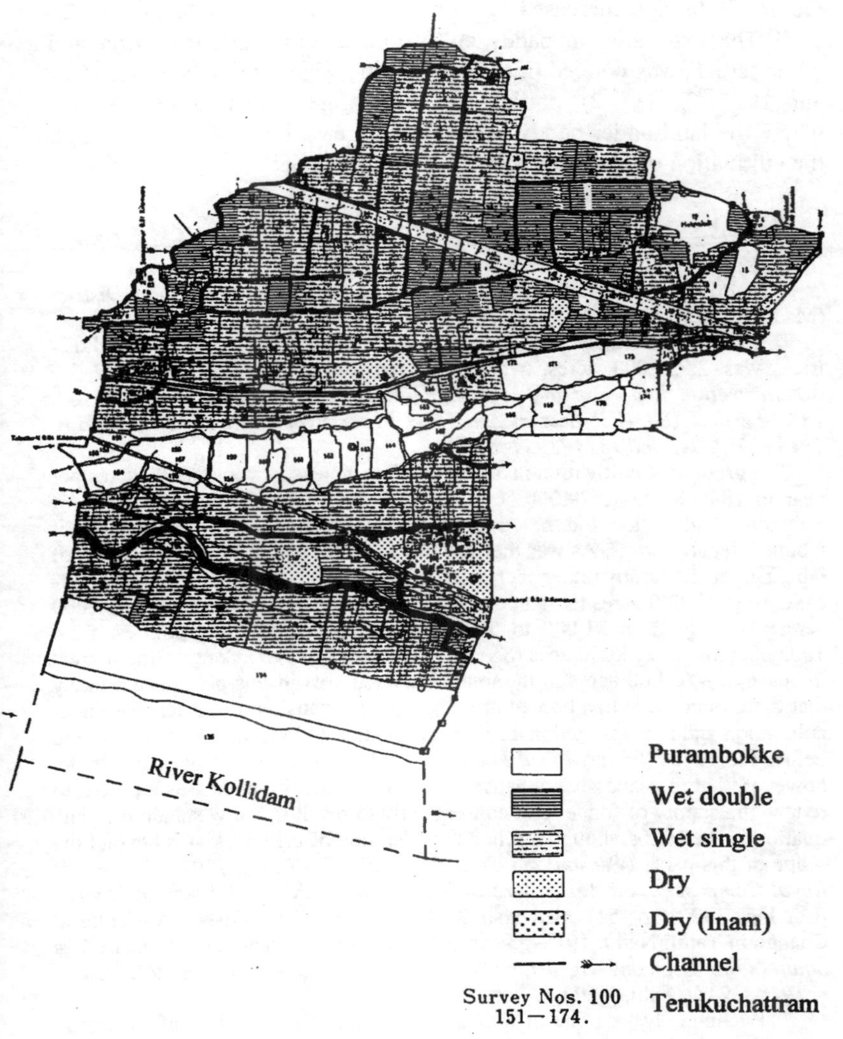

210,000 acres in 1902–3[13] to 280,000 acres in 1930–31,[14] while for the all the Tamil districts, the increase was about 36 percent in the three decades after 1891 (Table 3.1). This increase was accompanied by a rapid expansion of paddy cultivation. The area cropped with paddy in the Tamil districts increased by 68 percent between 1880–82 and 1932–34.[15] The expansion in paddy cultivation at the expense of *ragi* and other cereals was noticed in the villages in Lalgudi *taluk* between 1894 and 1925 (Table 3.2), particularly in the intermediate zone villages, where the land under paddy cultivation increased by 109 acres, though the cultivation of sugarcane decreased by 21 acres.[16]

[13] *Madras District Gazetteers, Statistical Appendix for Trichinopoly District* (Madras, 1905), p. 9, Table VIII.

[14] *Madras District Gazetteers, Statistical Appendix for Trichinopoly District* (Madras, 1933), pp. 14–15, Table IX.

[15] The average area cultivated with paddy per year in 1880–82 in Tamil districts was 2,753,000 acres, whereas it jumped to 4,612,000 in 1932–34. *Administration Report of the Madras Presidency during the years 1880–81, 1881–82 and 1882–83; Season and Crop Reports for Fasli 1342 (1932–33), 1343 (1933–34) and 1344 (1934–35).*

The groundnut cultivation in Tamil districts increased from 66,000 acres per year in 1880–82 to 1,229,000 acres in 1932–34. However, this expansion of groundnut cultivation did not accompany a reduction in the cultivation of labour-intensive crops. As was the case of paddy, the cultivation of a number of labour-intensive crops rather increased between 1880–82 and 1932–34: sugarcane, from 17,000 acres to 45,000 acres; plantains, from 26,000 acres to 68,000 acres; tobacco, from 31,000 to 55,000 acres; spices including chillies, from 100,000 acres to 195,000 aces (*Season and Crop Reports)*. Considering a great increase of 4,654,00 acres in the total cultivated area in this period, it is likely that the groundnut cultivation contributed to the expansion of the acreage under cultivation and thus resulted in a fuller exploitation of land, at least in the period before the 1920s (Baker, *Rural Economy*, p. 149). It is also important to note, however, that the excessive expansion of groundnut cultivation was reported to reduce the supply of fodder and consequently to result in a low standard of cultivation in the 1920s, though a fuller consideration of the problem is beyond the scope of this paper (*Season and Crop Report for Fasli 1334 [1924–25]*, p. 16; *Royal Commission on Agriculture in India,* Vol. 3, *Evidence Taken in Madras* [London, 1927], p. 51). See also K.N. Nair and A.C. Dhas, 'Agricultural Change in Tamil Nadu: 1918–55', in Sabyasachi Bhattacharya et al. (eds.), *The South Indian Economy: Agrarian Change, Industrial Structure and State Policy, c. 1914–1947* (Delhi, 1991).

[16] Trichinopoly was one of four districts where the reduction of sugarcane cultivation was most marked in 1925, due to an insufficient supply of water for irrigation. Therefore, though the figures for 1925 in Table 3.2 suggest a reduction of sugarcane cultivation in the Lalgudi villages, it may be inappropriate to accept the figures for 1925 as indicating any general trend in sugarcane cultiva-

Third, and even more important, double cropping grew remarkably.[17] As Table 3.3 shows, the area under double cropping in the Tamil districts roughly doubled between the 1890s and the 1940s. The data in Table 3.2 confirms the increase in the double-cropped area in Lalgudi *taluk*, Trichinopoly district, even though 1925 was a year when Tanjore and Trichinopoly were among the few districts that suffered from a serious insufficiency in water supply.[18]

Table 3.3
Area Cropped More Than Once

(thousand acres)

	1891	1902	1912	1922	1933	1944	1946
Chingleput	58	153	168	233	213	237	271
South Arcot	175	286	162	267	255	272	242
North Arcot	153	247	203	287	255	287	327
Salem	190	235	202	269	234	269	263
Coimbatore	213	310	276	304	324	348	334
Trichinopoly	85	107	193	171	149	219	183
Tanjore	93	111	98	121	172	341	289
Madura	98	140	171	176	171	231	196
Ramnad	–	–	49	74	56	64	65
Tinnevelly	200	216	232	219	239	214	206
Total	1,265	1,805	1,754	2,121	2,068	2,482	2,376

Source: *Administration Report of the Madras Presidency during the Year 1891–92* (Madras, 1892); *Season and Crop Reports*.

Note: A division of Tinnevelly district and also one of Madura district were amalgamated into a new district, Ramnad, in 1910.

Fourth, the expansion of the double-cropped area was closely connected with important improvements in agricultural practice. The rapid, if uneven, spread of the practice of transplanting paddy around the turn of the century was noted by Baker, though the source of this information was not mentioned.[19] Sources from Thanjavur indicate a spread of the use of manure in the district. As discussed above, the Thanjavur

tion. A clear trend of decline is not discernible in the area under sugarcane cultivation in Trichinopoly district after 1891–92, when it grew from about 2,000 acres in 1880–81 to about 6,000 acres (*Season and Crop Reports*).

[17] Baker, *Rural Economy*, pp. 176, 221–22, 574 n.135.

[18] *Season and Crop Report for Fasli 1335 (1925–1926)*, pp. 3–11. *Madras District Gazetteers, Statistical Appendix for Trichinopoly District* (Madras, 1905), p. 9, Table VIII; *Madras District Gazetteers, Statistical Appendix for Trichinopoly District* (1933), p. 15, Table IX.

[19] Baker, *Rural Economy*, p. 176.

delta witnessed a shortage of manure in the 1880s. According to the Manual of the district published in 1883, 'As a rule, in the case of irrigated nansei [wet land] or rice cultivation, it is only the fields on which two crops are raised that are manured every year, and even these not invariably, for it is not always that the required manure is available. Single crop lands are generally manured once in five years; in some cases not at all. . . .'[20] However, the situation changed during the next twenty years. In 1906, the Gazetteer of the district noted that 'the ryots have found that it is not impossible to secure manure for their fields, and enquiries now reveal that its use has greatly spread. It is now apparently not an exaggeration to say that there are few wet fields which are not manured every year.'[21] As a witness wrote to the Madras Provincial Banking Enquiry Committee, 'It is a fact that a large number of people have begun to use chemical fertilisers.'[22]

The spread of the practice of using manure was reported from other districts. According to the Settlement Report of Chingleput district in 1909, a large amount of manure was brought from Madras, and its continued application greatly improved soils, so that many of the red soils took on the appearance of black loam.[23] Regarding Tiruchirapalli district, Puckle stated in 1860 that manure was very seldom used with river irrigation, as the deposit left by the Kaveri water was considered to be sufficiently fertilising.[24] Thirty-five years later, the 1895 Settlement Report described a change in the situation. After citing Puckle's 1860 statement, the report stated: 'Enquiries now made show that this is still true to a large extent so far as the first crop is concerned, but that for the second crop the practice of using leaf manure is more or less general, and that this practice is more extensively followed now than was formerly the case.'[25] The Gazetteer of the district also reports a large increase in the use of manure during the last quarter of the last century.[26]

[20] *Manual of Tanjore District*, p. 348.

[21] *Gazetteer of Tanjore District,* by F.R. Hemingway (Madras, 1906), pp. 101–2. For the increase in the demand for green manure, see G.O., No. 676, Revenue, 29 June 1904.

[22] *MBEC,* Vol. 2, *Written Evidence*, p. 139. See also *Royal Commission on Agriculture in India,* Vol. 3, p. 164.

[23] G.O., No. 2240, Revenue, 14 Aug. 1909, pp. 104–5, par. 80.

[24] *Papers Relating to the Survey and Settlement of the Trichinopoly District,* Selection from the Records of the Madras Government, No. L (Madras, 1876), p. 9.

[25] P.B.R., No. 2, 4 Jan. 1895, p. 18.

[26] *Gazetteer of Trichinopoly District,* p. 141. Companies trading in fertilisers were reported to be entering villages at the end of the 1920s. *MBEC,* Vol. 2,

A remarkable increase in the application of manure between 1916 and 1957 was reported in Gangaikondan village in Tirunelveli district.[27] In Vadamalaipuram village in Ramnad district, chemical fertilisers, which had not been used in 1916, were reported as being applied in 1936.[28] The use of manure on dry land also increased. In Thanjavur district, dry land was treated a little less generously than wet land, but still received plenty of attention.[29] As the Director of Agriculture noted in 1911, 'in the Southern Districts much more capital is now being put into dry lands. The soils are being improved by carting silt on to them while much greater efforts are being made to adequately manure such lands.'[30]

The increase in the use of manure was facilitated by local cart trade among the neighbouring districts. Green-manuring was especially popular in Tiruchirapalli district. The favourite leaves used in the district were wild indigo, which were carted in great quantities from Coimbatore and Salem districts.[31] Wild indigo was the favourite green manure in Tirunelveli district also, where it was grown on the red soils of the dry *taluks* and often brought 20–30 miles to the river valley.[32] The Settlement Report of Coimbatore district stated in 1910 that a rise in the price of paddy enabled the *raiyats* who cultivated land irrigated by the Kalingarayan channel to increase their expenditure on manure; hence the radius within which employment was provided in the plucking and carting wild indigo expanded.[33] In Thanjavur district the movement of cattle among neighbouring districts enabled *raiyats* to obtain a supply of

Written Evidence, p. 159.

[27] V.B. Athreya, *Gangaikondan 1916–1984: Change and Stability* (Madras: Madras Institute of Development Studies, 1985), p. 74.

[28] V.B. Athreya, *Vadamalaipuram: A Resurvey* (Madras: Madras Institute of Development Studies, 1984), p. 65. It was reported that 'evidence is not wanting to show that much greater efforts than formerly are being employed to manure such lands [wet lands]. . . . Much greater pains are taken than formerly to exploit every source of manure supply' (*Season and Crop Report for Fasli 1321 [1911–1912]*, p. 4). For the increase in the use of artificial manure, see *Royal Commission on Agriculture in India*, Vol. 3, p. 43.

[29] *Gazetteer of Tanjore District*, p. 102.

[30] *Season and Crop Report for Fasli 1321 (1911–1912)*, p. 4. According to Supplement to the South Arcot District Gazetteer, 'Recently green manuring has become common in the district and large areas of dhaincha, kolinji and indigo are grown year after year in wet lands for being ploughed in as manure' ('Supplement to the South Arcot District Gazetteer', *Statistical Appendix for South Arcot District* [Madras, 1932], p. xvi).

[31] *Gazetteer of Trichinopoly District*, p. 141.

[32] P.B.R., No. 94, 1 Apr. 1907, p. 24, par. 34.

[33] G.O., No. 102, Revenue, 10 Jan. 1910, p. 9.

manure. A shortage of cattle, sheep and goat manure owing to the absence of pasture land in Thanjavur district was noted around 1880, as discussed in the previous chapter,[34] but the Gazetteer stated in 1906 that herdsmen from the Marava country brought cattle to the district to fertilise the fields during the cultivation season and that the lack of local grazing land was compensated for by the *raiyats'* driving their cattle across the Kollidam into the forests of South Arcot.[35] Later, in the 1930s, an increase in the cultivation of wild indigo for use as green manure was reported from Thanjavur and Madurai districts.[36]

Noteworthy in this connection was a remarkable increase in the number of bullock carts and ploughs in Tamil districts between 1880 and 1919: plough number more than doubled from 1,001 thousand to 2,175 thousand, while carts more than tripled in number from 134 thousand to 482 thousand. Thus the period witnessed a decrease in area per plough, indicating a trend towards a smaller farming unit.[37]

The impact of these changes was not uniform across the sub-regions. The increase in the number of wells was more remarkable in dry areas than in wet areas. A more frequent use of manure is discernible in a highly irrigated zone such as the wet zone of Lalgudi *taluk*, though the land here was already highly double cropped by 1895, and therefore the expansion of the area under double cropping was not so dynamic. In spite of this diversification across the sub-regions, each change was more or less noticed in each of sub-regions and the evidence reveals a basic similarity in the nature of change within Tamilnadu in this period.

The increase in the number of wells, the expansion of the double-cropped area and the increase in the application of manure indicate that South Indian agriculture was tending towards intensive cultivation, which required more labour input per acre and a greater degree of care and attention. Information from Thanjavur district indicates such an increase in labour input per acre. The Manual of the district published in 1883 states that the area of land which could be cultivated by means of one plough with a pair of bullocks and one farm labourer was assumed

[34] *Manual of Tanjore District*, p. 348.

[35] *Gazetteer of Tanjore District,* p. 102.

[36] K. Ramiah, *Rice in Madras: A Popular Handbook* (Madras, 1937), p. 84.

[37] *Report on the Administration of the Madras Presidency during the Year 1880–81* (Madras, 1881), p. cxliv, table E, (20); *Season and Crop Report of the Madras Presidency for the Agricultural Year 1919–20* (Madras, 1920), p. 28, Appendix G. See also P.B.R., No. 94, 1 Apr. 1907, p. 10, par. 14; P.B.R., No. 565, 4 Nov. 1910, Appendix XV.

to be six-sevenths of a Thanjavur *veli* (1 *veli* = about 6.5 acres), equal to 5.67 acres.[38] Thirty-eight years later, in 1921, 'at least two men are required for the efficient cultivation of one veli of land'.[39] As S.S. Raghavaiyangar remarked in 1893, 'lands also are believed to be much more carefully cultivated now than in the old days'.[40] 'My enquiries tend to show that, under the stress of necessity and the additional incentives to individual exertion promoted by the break up of the joint family system, greater care is now bestowed on cultivation of lands in Tanjore district than in times past; and this is to some extent the case in other districts also.'[41] This trend was also observed in a village survey in South Arcot district in 1916. Here, where it was no longer possible to extend the cultivated area, the *raiyats* resorted to more intensive cultivation, and were vigorously attempting to dig wells.[42] The Gazetteer of Tinnevelly district also noted 'the growing tendency towards intensive methods' in 1918,[43] and the Settlement Report of Coimbatore district stated that the progress of the district since the last settlement had chiefly been in the direction of intensive cultivation.[44] Agriculture in South India had turned towards intensive cultivation, with expanded double cropping through more efficient and careful management of water and manure resources.[45]

[38] *Manual of Tanjore District*, p. 382.

[39] P.B.R., No. 28, 12 Feb. 1921, p. 54.

[40] Raghavaiyangar, *Memorandum*, p. 202 n. 85.

[41] Ibid., p. 56. In the Shiyali *taluk* (Thanjavur district), more efficient cattle power was employed for ploughing, and the cattle were better fed and less vulnerable to epizootics (ibid., p. ccxcix).

[42] Gilbert Slater (ed.), *Some South Indian Villages* (Oxford, 1918), p. 225.

[43] *Gazetteer of Tinnevelly District*, p. 192.

[44] G.O., No. 102, Revenue, 10 Jan. 1910, p. 12.

[45] This does not necessarily imply that South Indian agriculture witnessed an increase in output per acre. A change towards intensive agriculture could occur along with a decline in productivity. In fact, it is probable that the increased application of manure in Thanjavur district, as mentioned above, may have been the farmers' reaction to a decline in the fertility of the Kaveri water and the resultant soil starvation (P.B.R., No. 28, 12 Feb. 1921, p. 12). I shall briefly consider the data pertaining to the change in agricultural productivity in Appendix 2 and indicate that the paddy yield per acre seems to have steadily risen during the period between the 1870s and 1917 in a majority of the districts in Tamilnadu.

Migration and Urban Job Opportunities

Emigration to estates

Another important factor that encouraged changes in rural South India was the increase of emigration. Emigration to the coffee estates of Ceylon (Sri Lanka) began growing in the 1830s, and the expansion of tea and rubber estates in Ceylon caused a rapidly escalating exodus of labour from South India from the middle of the century. By the 1880s, the annual movement was about 40,000, and by 1921, there were around 600,000 Tamils in Ceylon.[46] There was also a steady flow of 4,000–6,000 emigrants to Malaya every year between the 1860s and the 1890s. Most of the Tamil emigrants to Malaya worked on sugarcane and coffee estates and later on rubber estates. In the mid 1920s, there was a boom in rubber production triggering the entry of 160,000 emigrants from South India, and by 1921 Malaya had 390,000 Tamils. Meanwhile, rice cultivation was gathering momentum in Burma and by 1921, the country had 270,000 Tamil and Telugu emigrants from South India.[47] In the period 1923–28, a large number of people emigrated from the Madras Presidency: about 100,000 to Ceylon, 90,000 to the Straits Settlements and 10,000 to Assam each year on an average, besides a large number to Burma and the estates and plantations in and near the Madras Presidency.[48]

Overseas emigrants formed not an insignificant percentage of the population at least in some of the Tamil districts, as seen in the census data (Table 3.4) for the period of 1921–31. In Gangaikondan village of Tirunelveli district, the number of villagers who emigrated between 1921 and 1931 was 1,023 persons or 23 percent of the total population in 1921.[49] The emigrants were of two types: those moving to plantations and those to urban areas. According to the village survey of 1936, the

[46] Baker, *Rural Economy*, p. 101.

[47] Ibid., p. 100. For the emigration from South India, see Kumar, *Land and Caste*, Chapter 8; R. Jayaraman, 'Indian Emigration to Ceylon: Some Aspects of the Historical and Social Background of the Emigrants', *IESHR* 4, 4 (1967); Hugh Tinker, *A System of Slavery: The Export of Indian Labour Overseas, 1830–1920* (London, New York and Bombay, 1974); Barbara Evans, 'From Agricultural Bondage to Plantation Contract: A Continuity of Experience in Southern India, 1860–1947', *South Asia*, n.s., 13, 2 (1990).

[48] *RCLI*, p. 298.

[49] P.J. Thomas and K.C. Ramakrishnan (eds.), *Some South Indian Villages: A Resurvey* (Madras, 1940), p. 58.

Table 3.4
Numbers of Emigrants (1921–31)

District or state	Approximate number of emigrants	Percentage of 1921 population
Tanjore	263,500	11
Trichinopoly	505,500	27
Pudukkottai	88,300	21
Ramnad	276,200	16
Tinnevelly	517,500	27

Source: *Census of India, 1931,* Vol. 14, *Madras*, Part 1, p.92.

migration had started thirty years earlier when the first plantations of the Western Ghats came into being. The emigration 'is of a seasonal nature and is confined to the depressed classes like Pallars and Pariars', the number of emigrants amounting to as many as nearly 200 per year. As a result, the number of Depressed-caste families in the village fell from 215 to 199 families between 1916 and 1936. According to the 1931 Census, of the total number of people who migrated between 1921 and 1931, 41 percent belonged to the Depressed castes.[50] For the district of Tiruchirapalli, as early as 1863 the Settlement Report pointed out a decrease in the number of labourers in the district due to emigration,[51] and still later the Manual of the district observed 'there is a considerable amount of emigration out of it, principally of labourers to Ceylon and the Mauritius. As a rule, however, those who leave the country return again to it before very long.'[52] Overseas emigration by labourers was not confined only to the districts referred to in Table 3.4. Such districts as Chingleput, South Arcot, Salem, Coimbatore and Madurai also experienced it.[53]

Labourers could, in addition to emigration to estates abroad, work on domestic plantations. The tea and coffee estates in Malabar, Nilgiris and Coimbatore offered job opportunities to the rural labour force. In

[50] *Census of India, 1931,* Vol. 14, *Madras,* Part 1 (Madras, 1932) p. 84. In 1926, the Labour Commissioner estimated that about 52 percent of the emigrants were from the depressed classes (*Royal Commission on Agriculture in India,* Vol. 3, p. 334).

[51] Cited in *Manual of Trichinopoly District,* p. 217.

[52] *Manual of Trichinopoly District*, p. 108.

[53] *RCLI,* p. 298. For Madurai district, see P.B.R., No. 86, 1 Mar. 1893, pp. 6–7, and for South Arcot district, see P.B.R., No. 10, 12 Jan. 1920, p. 96.

1931, the Labour Commissioner, G. Paddison, put on record the presence of 50,000 labourers on plantations throughout the Madras Presidency.[54] Most of the labourers were Depressed-caste members coming originally from the districts of Coimbatore, Salem, Tiruchirapalli, Madurai, Mysore and Malabar.[55] They worked on the plantations for ten months of the year, returning to their villages for the remaining two months,[56] though an increasing number tended to remain on the plantations. Of those who did return to their villages for a brief stay, 60 percent to 90 percent tended to go back to the same estates where they had worked before.[57]

On an aggregate, Tamils either employed on plantations in India or emigrating overseas exceeded in total a million and several hundred thousand.

Factory workers

In contrast to the emigration to overseas plantations, the impact of the labour demand from the industrial sector in South India was much more limited. First, those employed in the factories in India were small in number, not exceeding two hundred thousand even in the 1930s. According to the 1921 Census of India, in Madras Presidency, 867 factories regulated by the Indian Factory Act were employing 131,000 workers in 1911, whereas 1921 saw the presence of 1,384 factories of the same standing with 166,000 workers.[58] In the early 1930s, the total number of industrial labourers in factories consisting of not less than ten persons was less than 200,000.[59] In addition, about one-third of the registered factories were only seasonal. Cotton ginning and groundnut decortication factories operated for only about four months a year,[60] and depended to some extent on migrating labourers.[61] Thus, while over 10 million people were engaged in agriculture throughout the Madras

[54] *RCLI*, p. 7.

[55] Ibid., p. 251.

[56] Ibid., pp. 6, 8, 155.

[57] Ibid., p. 155.

[58] *Census of India, 1921,* Vol. 13, *Madras,* Part 1, Report (Madras, 1922), p. 190.

[59] *RCLI*, p. 7. According to the annual report on the working of the Indian Factory Act, in 1928, there were 136,973 persons working in the factories in the various district of the Presidency (ibid., p. 297).

[60] Ibid., p. 8.

[61] Ibid., p. 108.

Presidency in 1930, the number of workers employed in factories was only 0.2 million, a number too small to cause any significant change in the agricultural population.

Second, a considerable number of industrial labourers were settled in towns and therefore the movement of rural labourers to the factories was not large enough to produce a noticeable impact on rural society. The rural connection of industrial workers varied greatly depending on whether the factories were within Madras city or outside. In 1921, 79 percent of the roughly 530,000 persons residing in Madras city were born there. This implies that the majority of labourers employed in the factories in Madras were not new immigrants. Of the total of about 12,000 persons employed in large mills in the city, 81 percent were adult males and only 5 percent were women. This proportion is quite different from factories outside Madras city.[62] For example, at the Buckingham and Carnatic Mills, an old cotton mill in the city already in existence for over fifty years by 1931, 'there has been an increasing tendency for succeeding generations of the same family to work in the same factory. . . . The labour in our Madras mills is now very settled and there is practically no migration.'[63] Eighty to ninety percent of the workforce of this factory were virtually permanently settled.[64] According to the Madras Labour Union, only a small number of textile workers in the city went back to their villages to spend a few days there.[65]

The situation outside Madras city was to some extent different. In Madurai, for example, a large number of textile workers had come from villages and had settled in towns near the mills, taking houses.[66] In Tuticorin, half of the textile workers lived in the town and the rest commuted from villages two or three miles away.[67] Outside Madras city, the percentage of children and women employed in cotton and spinning factories was higher, being 14 percent and 21 percent respectively.[68] Thus, except for the movement of rural labourers to the factories located in mofussil towns, such as Madurai, Coimbatore and Tuticorin, large scale migration of industrial labourers from rural to urban areas was not discernible in this period.[69]

[62] Ibid., p. 103.
[63] Ibid., p. 133.
[64] Ibid., pp. 133, 211.
[65] Ibid., p. 164.
[66] Ibid., p. 90.
[67] Ibid., p. 89.
[68] Ibid., p. 103.
[69] Ibid., p. 204.

Third, in contrast to the plantation workers, who were generally of the Depressed and other low castes, factory labourers were from different communities and classes and this lack of cohesion may have weakened the impact of factory employment. A castewise breakdown of the 45,000 skilled workers who were employed in the factories regulated by the Indian Factory Act gives Vellalars 7,000, Christians 6,000, and Vanniars and Depressed-caste members about 5,000. As for the unskilled labourers in factories of the same standing, their caste breakdown was Depressed-caste members 18,000, Vellalars 14,000, Muslims 9,000, Christians 9,000, and a few Vanniar and Thiya caste members.[70] The factories thus offered job opportunities to a variety of social groups and therefore their employment did not have the concentrated impact that emigration had on the Depressed castes.

It is not necessary to elaborate on why the labour demand from the industrial sector was too small to cause any significant impact. There is no doubt that industrial development was seriously hampered by the suppressive policy of British colonial rule. The economic policy of the Government of India remained geared to preserving the British imperial order.[71]

Apart from factories employing more than ten workers, a number of small-scale cottage industries were present in most districts of South India. They included the handloom industry, *beedi* manufacture, embroidery, tailoring, masonry, leather goods manufacturing, and furniture manufacturing.[72] With a few exceptions, those engaged in such pursuits were generally confined to members of one or a few specific castes and therefore these occupations attracted few from the agricultural population. Thus the direct impact on the agrarian population of employment in these occupations was very limited, though further research needs to be done on how these cottage industries influenced rural change in South India.

[70] *Census of India, 1921*, Vol. 13, *Madras*, Part 2, Table XXII; ibid., Part 4, p. 314; ibid., Part 5, p. 324.

[71] Amiya Kumar Bagchi, *Private Investment in India, 1900–1939* (Cambridge, 1972).

[72] For changes in the handloom industry of South India, Baker, *Rural Economy*, pp. 393–413; Konrad Specker, 'Madras Handlooms in the Nineteenth Century', *IESHR* 26, 2 (1989); Tirthankar Roy, *Artisans and Industrialization: Indian Weaving in the Twentieth Century* (Delhi, 1993); Haruka Yanagisawa, 'The Handloom Industry and Its Market Structure: The Case of the Madras Presidency in the First Half of the Twentieth Century', *IESHR* 30, 1 (1993).

Professionals

Government employees made up a large portion of the urban population, larger than that of factory workers. Baker shows that in the 1951 Census, those employed in health, education, public administration, railways, etc., constituted 11.4 percent of the urban working population, forming the single biggest category.[73] The number of government employees and their dependents formed a fifth of the urban population in 1891, and accounted for a third of the increase in urban population between 1891 and 1951.[74] The 1931 Census of the Madras Presidency recorded 180,000 people in the category of Public Administration, 130,000 in Instruction, and 20,000 in Law.[75]

Most of these occupations were virtually monopolised by Brahmans and other higher castes. As noted in the 1921 Census, Brahmans predominated in the 'Public Administration Services'.[76] The second largest group of people employed in this category were the 'Paraiya' and 'Panchama', who probably held lowly ranked jobs related to the collection of revenue. Vellalars were the third largest. In the field of education also, Brahmans comprised the greatest number of employees, followed by Christians and two communities of high-caste Non-Brahmans, the Vellalars and the Nairs. The Brahmans dominated the legal circles. Apart from the Depressed-caste members who were employed probably in lowly ranked jobs at rural government offices, coveted urban public service jobs such as public administration, education and law were the prerogative of the Brahmans and high-caste Non-Brahmans.[77] A large number of Brahmans and Vellalars migrated from rural to urban areas in order to be employed in these jobs or to train for them. In Gangaikondan village for example, Brahman families dwindled from 100 to 75 over a period of ten years (1926–36), probably due to urban migration.[78] K. Gough also reports that the exodus of Brahmans

[73] Baker, *Rural Economy*, p. 388.

[74] Ibid., p. 389.

[75] *Census of India, 1931,* Vol. 14, *Madras,* Part 2, p. 112.

[76] *Census of India, 1921,* Vol. 13, *Madras,* Part 2, Imperial and Provincial Tables, Table XXI, p. 259.

[77] The Manual of Trichinopoly district (p. 105) describes the breakdown of communities in the Civil Service in this district as follows: Vellalars, 721; Vanniars, 440; Brahmans, 383; Muhammadans, 315; Pariayars, 155. The percentage of Brahmans in the civil servants in this district was lower than the corresponding figure for the whole Presidency in the 1920s, probably because many Brahman civil servants lived in Madras city.

[78] Thomas and Ramakrishnan (eds.), *Some South Indian Villages: A Resur-*

from Kumbapettai village in Thanjavur began about 1870 and that by 1900, a large proportion of Thanjavur Brahmans lived in Madras and other cities.[79]

Export-Oriented Commercialisation of Agriculture and the Development of Internal Trade

Development of the transport system

The patterns of commercialisation of agriculture under British rule also determined the nature of rural change in South India. The development of trade was facilitated by a rapid expansion of the railway system, a well-known fact that requires no further elaboration.[80]

Another prominent feature of the rural transport system which formed the infrastructure for trade was the bullock cart. As early as 1840, a Collector reported a spread in the use of these carts: 'The introduction . . . of pack bullocks and carts reduced the cost of carriage of goods to 50 per cent. of what it was 20 or 30 years before.'[81] The data from the Settlement Registers in the Lalgudi *taluk* of Trichinopoly district also reveal an increase in the number of bullock carts between 1895 and 1925. In this *taluk*, the increase was particularly remarkable in the intermediate and the dry zones, which witnessed 1.5 and 2.0 times increases in the number of bullock carts respectively, as shown by Table 3.2.

The condition of roads also improved. The 1860 Settlement Report stated concerning road conditions in the dry areas of Trichinopoly district: 'The tracts leading from village to village are hardly passable in dry weather for a wheeled conveyance, and a heavy shower or rain will put a stop to all traffic for days together. . . . The greater part of the grain and merchandise is transported on pack bullocks.' In the irrigated

---

vey, p. 58.

[79] Gough, *Rural Society in Southeast India*, p. 201. See also Washbrook, *Emergence of Provincial Politics,* pp. 219–20; B.M. Bhatia, 'Growth and Composition of Middle Class in South India in Nineteenth Century', *IESHR* 2, 4 (1965).

[80] Baker, *Rural Economy*, p. 80.

[81] Raghavaiyangar, *Memorandum,* p. 33. In the early nineteenth century, there were very few carts in Tamil country. See Jean Deloche, *Transport and Communications in India Prior to Steam Locomotion,* Vol. 1, *Land Transport,* trans. James Walker (Delhi, 1993), pp. 258–59.

areas too, 'during the monsoon, when the country is under water, they are sometimes completely isolated and cut off from all communication with the neighbouring villages'.[82] The Gazetteer of the district published in 1907 compared the conditions with those of 1860: 'Much has been done since those days, and at present the district is traversed from north to south by main road, and the other roads in the district are fairly numerous and tolerably good.'[83] Fifteen years later, further improvement was reported in the 1923 Settlement Report: 'There are country cart-tracks everywhere, and it is quite easy to get into interior villages except in the black soil tract and there only in the rainy weather.'[84] Thus improved roads made more villages accessible by cart, altering the situation considerably from the 1860s when goods had to be carried by bullock. As a result, the number of carts continued to increase, and consequently trade expanded.[85]

Export-oriented commercialisation of agriculture

At the beginning of the nineteenth century, Madras was exporting handloom textiles to many parts of Asia and Europe, and importing a variety of luxury goods. However, by the 1850s, the commodities had changed—raw materials were being exported and imports were largely manufactured goods. Ships from Madras began to sail away with a variety of agricultural goods and to bring in Lancashire cotton and metal wares from England.[86]

It is a well-known fact that India's trade developed as a part of a multi-national network of world trade centring around the British economy. India's trade with Asian countries was one important part of this world-wide trade network.[87] The South Indian economy played an important role in the network. The main export items from Madras were rice and handloom textiles to Ceylon and Southeast Asia, raw cotton to Japan, groundnuts and hides to Europe and plantation products, such as

[82] *Papers Relating to the Survey and Settlement of the Trichinopoly District*, pp. 6–7, pars. 34, 37.

[83] *Gazetteer of Trichinopoly District,* p. 180.

[84] P.B.R., No. 86, 26 Nov. 1923, p. 17, par. 15.

[85] For the improvement of the road and transport, see Kumar, 'Agrarian Relations : South India', p. 362.

[86] Baker, *Rural Economy*, p. 98.

[87] Kaoru Sugihara, 'Patterns of Intra-Asian Trade, 1898–1913', *Osaka City University Economic Review* 16 (1980); S.B. Saul, *Studies in British Overseas Trade, 1870–1914* (Liverpool, 1960).

tea and coffee, to Britain. While Asian countries were importing an important part of South Indian products, the products imported into the presidency came mainly from Britain, even though a trend towards diversification in imported items, such as an increase in the import of foodstuffs, is discernible later in the period.

Rice was one of the main commodities exported from Madras to the regions of Asia. Rice from the Kaveri delta and other areas of South India was being exported to Ceylon even from earlier times. The export continued to escalate, keeping pace with expanding emigration from India and reaching the shores of Malaya as well. Handloom textiles from South India were another important export item to Asian countries, due to the demand of the exploding numbers of Indian emigrants.[88]

South Indian agriculture was seriously affected by this marked increase in the export of agricultural products. In the 60 villages of Lalgudi *taluk*, Trichinopoly district (Table 3.2), the cropping pattern changed considerably between 1895 and 1925 towards an export-oriented pattern in response to the market. In the wet zone villages, the area cropped with paddy noticeably increased, while the area under *ragi* was drastically reduced. The change was more remarkable in the intermediate and dry zones. In the intermediate zone, cultivation of *ragi* and other miscellaneous cereals decreased and that of rice increased. In the dry zone villages, miscellaneous cereal crops were considerably reduced and partly taken over by paddy, groundnuts and cotton. The increase in groundnut cultivation in this zone was especially remarkable: an average of 12.2 acres per village growing groundnuts in 1895 grew to a great 109.6 acres in 1925, though it should not be overlooked that much of the dry zone still produced miscellaneous cereals. The entire Tiruchirapalli district witnessed the same type of change.[89] Agriculture in the Tirunelveli and Madurai districts also showed a similar trend. The Settlement Reports reveal that in a span of 30 years paddy and cotton cultivation expanded tremendously and *cambu* and other miscellaneous cereals decreased considerably in those districts.[90]

Some instances reported by village surveys illustrate the process of the integration of South Indian agriculture into the international com-

[88] Baker, *Rural Economy*, pp. 102–6; Yanagisawa, 'Handloom Industry'.

[89] *Manual of Trichinopoly District*, p. 368, Table 7-A; *Madras District Gazetteers, Statistical Appendix for Trichinopoly District* (Madras, 1905), p. 9, Table VIII; *Madras District Gazetteers, Statistical Appendix for Trichinopoly District* (Madras, 1933), p. 15, Table IX.

[90] P.B.R., No. 565, 4 Nov. 1910, p. 5, par. 8; P.B.R., No. 117, 29 Apr. 1915, p. 18, par. 18.

mercial network. Dusi is a village about four miles from Kanchipuram town in Chingleput district,[91] and the following quotation is from the 1916 survey of the village.

> The chief commodities bought for agricultural purposes are: (1) the chemical manure sold by Parry & Co., (2) rock salt, (3) pig manure.
>
> The inhabitants of the village have to purchase all articles necessary for food excepting rice and tamarind. The chief among these are:—salt, chillis, pepper, asafoetida and all kinds of pulse.
>
> The chief produce sold by the villagers is paddy. They do not convey it to the market. Corn dealers from abroad come with bandies and gunny bags and pay for the paddy and then take it to the market to sell at a profit. Each landlord retains as much paddy as is necessary for his own consumption and sells the rest to the corn-dealers for money.[92]

Paddy was cultivated in the 518 acres of irrigated land, and plantain, etc., grown in the 221 acres of dry land in the village. The second survey of the same village done in 1936 says that:

> Since Conjeevaram [Kanchipuram], a big town, is very near, people take the cow-dung cakes to this place and find a good sale there.[93]
>
> Chillies, sugar, gram, dholl, etc., are all bought from Conjeevaram. At times, onions, red gram, black gram and sugar are all brought from Conjeevaram in cartloads and sold in the streets. . . .
>
> Vegetables are brought in headloads from the neighbouring villages and sold in the streets. . . .
>
> About 80 per cent of the groundnut harvested is sold out. About 25 per cent of the paddy produced is sold out and the rest is retained for home consumption. . . .
>
> Paddy is sold in the mandies at Conjeevaram. Groundnut is taken to Conjeevaram but is also sold to the Vania Chettiars who press the oil and sell it. . . . Now the ryots have to take the paddy to the mandies at Conjeevaram at their own cost.
>
> The kist installments do force the ryots to sell their produce at

[91] The village was re-surveyed by M.R. Haswell (*Economics of Development in Village India* [London, 1961]) and a fourth survey has been recently conducted by S. Guhan and K. Bharathan (*Dusi: A Resurvey* [Madras: Madras Institute of Development Studies, 1984]).

[92] Slater (ed.), *Some South Indian Villages*, p. 90.

[93] Thomas and Ramakrishnan (eds.), *Some South Indian Villages: A Resurvey*, p. 195

> whatever price they may get. Generally, the ryots incur some loss because of this.[94]

The case of Gangaikondan village in Tirunelveli district also illustrates this change. The village had a total cropped area of approximately 4,000 acres, of which 1,000–1,200 acres were devoted to paddy. Cotton was grown on 940–1,070 acres and the remaining area produced a variety of cereals like *cambu*, *cholam*, *ragi*, gram and gingelly.[95] The average production of rice per year was about 6,000–7,000 *kottahs*, and the quantity needed to feed the people of the village was about 8,400 *kottahs*. However, in spite of this deficit in domestic requirement, according to the estimate by a landowner, 3000 *kottahs* of rice, 500 *kottahs* of *ragi* and 100 *kottahs* of *cholam* were sent out annually to be sold in the Kythar market.[96]

> The prices at these centres determine the price of paddy or other grains in the village. They are also sold in the neighbouring villages. The grain merchants visit the village on alternate days during the season. There are about 3 local dealers also. They discourage competitors from outside by creating trouble for them in numerous ways. Paddy goes even as far as the Sathankulam market, about 40 miles distant from the village.[97]

The following example further illustrates how deeply the farmers were involved in the commercial network. A farmer in the village operating ten acres of land, cultivated paddy and other crops, which earned him a total income of Rs. 603 on the produce. His expenditures incurred in cultivation were Rs. 404 in cash, added to which were *kist* and cess amounting to Rs. 65. This figure does not include the wages paid in kind to his three permanent labourers (on an average, the equivalent of about Rs. 110), livestock maintenance and seed cost except in the case of *ragi* cultivation.[98] Poor farmers too were similarly involved. A survey of a wet village in Madurai district done in 1918 described a poor *raiyat* who had to sell his paddy on the threshing floor at eight measures of rice the rupee, and later in the year had to buy it back again for family consumption when the price was higher, at six measures the rupee.[99]

[94] Ibid., pp. 199–200.
[95] Ibid., p. 74.
[96] Ibid., pp. 101–2.
[97] Ibid., p. 102.
[98] Ibid., pp. 84–85.
[99] G.O., No. 1779, Revenue, 7 May 1918, p. 3.

What emerges from the above is: (1) In these villages, a considerable portion of the necessities for cultivation had to be bought in cash. Especially important was the fact that manure used in Gangaikondan was purchased from outside the village.[100] (2) The produce sold outside the village was not what was in excess after deduction for domestic consumption, but was taken out of the village to market at the cost of domestic consumption. This is particularly true of Gangaikondan village, where almost half the rice produced was sold outside the village. The share of the village produce thus sold outside would be much larger, if we take into account the cultivation of other commercial crops such as cotton, which was grown on one-third to one-fourth of the total cultivated area, the major portion of which was probably sent to outside markets. (3) Many of daily goods needed by the villagers were bought from outside. (4) While a part of the produce was traded with neighbouring villages, the major part reached urban markets and was even conveyed to distant places by way of the towns.

The growth of an export-oriented pattern of cropping led to a loss of self-sustaining economic independence in some districts. The case of Thanjavur district, a typical paddy producing area, illustrates this. The increase on the irrigated area in this district, as pointed out earlier, was accompanied by an expansion of rice cultivation at the cost of dry crop cultivation. Prior to the establishment of rail transport, rice and paddy produced in the Thanjavur delta were shipped mainly to Ceylon. But with the advent of railways, they began to be traded with northern districts. Calculated in terms of money per year, the paddy and rice transported by railways was worth Rs. 16,000,000; combined with those commodities transported by ship, the amount of rice and paddy exported beyond the district boundary came to Rs. 20,000,000.[101] This means that the value of paddy exported from each acre under paddy cultivation came to Rs. 20. However, this large-scale transport of rice out of the district did not have a long history, but started under British colonial rule. While almost all the rice produced in Thanjavur was consumed within the district up to 1807, the district rapidly expanded paddy production and captured the Madras market from Bengal.[102]

Notwithstanding the huge exports of paddy and rice, many food-

[100] In a village in Madurai district, *ryots* purchased city rubbish and night-soil as manure. See ibid., p. 4.

[101] P.B.R., No. 28, 12 Feb. 1921, pp. 173–91.

[102] A. Sarada Raju, *Economic Conditions in the Madras Presidency, 1800–1850* (Madras, 1941), pp. 63, 67.

stuffs like grain and pulses were imported into Thanjavur from other districts. 'Of the imports the most noticeable are grain and pulses. . . . Pulses are produced to only a comparatively small extent in south India and are consequently largely imported; and the cheaper Burmese rice, in spite of the large production and export of Tanjore, is sometimes imported in great quantities, especially in times of scarcity, for the consumption of the poorer classes throughout the south.'[103] An examination of the import data given in the Settlement Report of Tanjore district reveals that the import of rice, paddy and pulses into this district amounted to about Rs. 7,000,000 in 1911–12.[104] The average area cropped with miscellaneous cereals was 230,000 acres during the five year period of 1913–17. If we assume the maximum yield per acre was Rs. 20, then the total miscellaneous cereals produced in the district were worth Rs. 4,600,000, indicating that the import of grains and pulses was much larger than the production of miscellaneous cereals in the district. Though it is wrong to assume that all grain and pulses imported into Thanjavur were consumed in the district itself, there is no doubt that the district largely relied upon imports from other areas to provide foodstuffs for the poorer classes of people. It may not be incorrect to say that, partly because of the expansion of paddy cultivation geared to the markets in the north and abroad, and partly because of competition from cheap rice imported from Burma,[105] the cultivation of dry crops like miscellaneous cereals was largely abandoned or neglected by farmers in the Thanjavur delta, resulting in a sharp decrease in the output of miscellaneous cereals.

In this way the agrarian economy of South India became deeply involved in the international trading network, losing its self-sustaining economic independence. While a large proportion of agrarian products was exported to remote markets, a similarly large proportion of necessities had to be imported from remote areas.

The local markets held in Thanjavur district projected the export-import-oriented pattern of the economy of the district. The Settlement Report stated: 'They [markets] are not very numerous and their importance is considerably less than in more backward districts. The paddy crop is almost always sold by the ryot in his village either to agents of the big exporting firms or rice mills, or to rural traders acting as

[103] *Gazetteer of Tanjore District*, p. 131.

[104] P.B.R., No. 28, 12 Feb. 1921, pp. 173–91.

[105] W.R.S. Sathyanathan, *Report on Agricultural Indebtedness* (Madras, 1935), p. 29.

middlemen.'[106] As the district specialised in the production of paddy for export to remote markets, trade among local farmers in local market places may have dwindled to marginal significance.

Export-import-oriented commercialisation and the development of internal trade: an analysis of rail-borne trade statistics

We have so far observed the way agriculture under British rule was commercialised, oriented to exports and imports. The reorganisation of South Indian agriculture was, of course, accompanied by the development of trade and transport closely geared to the international network. At the same time, an important growth in internal trade, though not as remarkable as the export-oriented trade, was also discernible in the same period. I will examine in this section rail-borne trade statistics, the *Review and Returns of the Rail Borne Trade of the Madras Presidency*, in order to identify these two different trends in transport and trade.

In 'Statement III showing the trade by rail between the different blocks of the Madras Presidency' listed in the above statistics, the area was divided into eight or ten 'Madras Sea-ports' blocks, and nine 'Madras Presidency, excluding sea-ports' blocks. The amount of goods transported among the blocks was tabulated in the Statement. To elucidate the changes in the movement of goods, I have chosen data for two benchmark years, 1900–1901[107] and 1913–14[108] and selected 40 important items whose individual value in terms of amount transported by rail was more than Rs. 2,000,000 in 1900–1901. I have excluded 'Metals', though their traded value exceeded this amount, since the content of this category seems to have changed between 1900–1901 and 1913–14.

I have separated the transport of goods in the Madras Presidency into two categories: 'inter-inland movement', denoting the movement of goods within and between the non-port blocks, and 'inland–port movement' indicating both transport between non-port blocks and port blocks and among the various port blocks. This gives us a clear picture of the two phases of trade activity, one the movement of goods to and from overseas markets, and the other the transport of goods within South India. Needless to say, this categorisation is not absolute because a

[106] P.B.R., No. 28, 12 Feb. 1921, p. 15.

[107] *Review and Returns of the Rail-Borne Trade of the Madras Presidency for the Official Year 1900–1901* (Madras, 1901), pp. 148–99.

[108] *Review and Returns of the Rail-Borne Trade of the Madras Presidency for the Official Year 1913–14* (Madras, 1914), pp. 178–283.

sizeable amount of goods would have been transported by ships between ports within India and therefore, the 'inland–port trade' would not always have indicated trade abroad. Despite these limitations, data thus attained may be taken as more or less reflecting the export-import-oriented commercialisation of goods transport and the movement of goods within South India.

We first examine the growth rate in relation to the total amount of the item transported by rail.[109] Topping the list are 'Oil seeds–earth nuts', 'Tea–India', and 'Leather–unwrought', indicating the dominance of goods either for export or related to export production. This surely reflects the strengthened link between the South Indian economy and the overseas markets. In the entire Madras Presidency, the total movement of goods registered a 236 percent growth as against 184 percent in the inter-inland movement. This also indicates a shifting emphasis towards export-import-oriented commercialisation.

It is important to note that along with this rapid increase in inland–port trade, rail goods transport within South India also increased markedly. When viewed against the inland–port movement, the 1.8 times increase in the inter-inland movement of goods appears too low, but this increase was of considerable magnitude for the thirteen year period. It is not appropriate to interpret the increase as resulting merely from substituting rail transport for other transport facilities. This thirteen year period did not witness any rapid construction of new railway lines that might have substituted for other means of transport. Furthermore, as was pointed out earlier, bullock carts increased in number. Thus the increase in the inter-inland movement of goods was not achieved at the expense of other modes of transport but reflected a real growth in internal trade.

Next, to study the background of the expansion of inter-inland trade, I have calculated the rate of growth in the total amount of each item unloaded in the non-port blocks either from the port-blocks or from other non-port blocks. The items ranked at the top of the list thus indicate the goods for which demand grew during the period in the non-port blocks. The statistics for 1913–14 did not record the value of the various goods moved. Therefore, assuming no changes in price, the prices of 1900–1901 have been applied to the goods imported into the non-port blocks of the Madras Presidency. Even though this assumption is

[109] The result is listed in a table in Yanagisawa, *Minamiindo Shakai Keizai-shi*, p. 117.

somewhat unrealistic, it serves the purpose of allowing us to study the comparative importance of the various items.

The result reveals that the highest percentage increase is seen in unwrought leather and Indian tea unloaded in non-port blocks. However, the absolute value of these two items unloaded in the inland blocks was much less than that of the other goods. The amount of unwrought leather and Indian tea unloaded in the non-port blocks in 1900–1901 had been so small that the rate of increase between 1901 and 1914 appeared very large. In analysing the background to the increase in amounts unloaded in non-port blocks, it may be better to omit these two items, along with earthnuts, which also had registered a low absolute value in 1900–1901.[110]

Excepting these three, the goods which doubled in the amount unloaded in the non-port blocks can be grouped as follows:

(1) Goods whose local production had suffered an extreme decrease or been suspended due to overwhelmingly strong competition from imports. Coming under this category were 'Grain and pulse–gram and pulse' and 'Cotton–manufactured piece-goods–Indian'. To these should be added 'Cotton–manufactured piece-goods–European', a typical example of an item imported in huge amounts, in terms of the large absolute value, though the rate of increase in this period was not very remarkable. Almost all of these goods were brought through the ports and made their way to non-port areas of the Madras Presidency, thus exemplifying the port-centred development of trade.

(2) The second type of goods was industrial raw materials, the demand for which increased in South India. A typical example was raw cotton. The consumption of cotton expanded as a result of the development of cotton spinning mills in South India, which supplied cotton thread to the handloom industry. This suggests the existence of a kind of industrialisation, a pattern of economic change different from export-import-oriented commercialisation.

(3) The third group of goods included daily necessities, such as 'Fruits and Vegetables–fresh', 'Wood–timber–unwrought', 'Sugar–refined', 'Oil seeds–til or gingili', 'Oils–kerosene', 'Spices–chillis', 'Tobacco–unmanufactured', and 'Oils–others'. Unlike the goods in group (1), the production of most of these items was not destroyed either by the inflow of imported goods or by the shift of production from goods for domestic demand to those for export. Rather, the production of most of these items grew. Eight items can be categorised in

[110] Ibid., p. 120, Table 4.7.

this group and they form a major part of the total of 15 items that doubled in amount their transport into non-port blocks. We shall further examine the background to this growth of trade in the goods categorised in the last group.

It is not absolutely clear which class was the main consumer of the goods categorised in the third group. The case of tobacco however is somewhat clear. The main consumers of tobacco were apparently the lower classes of society. Even though there were various kinds of tobacco, such as *beedis*, cigarettes and cigars, the bulk of unmanufactured tobacco seems to have gone into *beedi* making. While the Manual of Salem district noted that tobacco was used by all castes,[111] 'beedies are mostly consumed locally by poorer classes and also exported to Ceylon and Rangoon',[112] as the *Report on the Survey of the Cottage Industries* stated in 1929. The report went on to note 'the flooding of the country with indigenous beedies and handy cigarettes which have become fashion of the day'.[113] These data indicate the increase in consumption of tobacco by the lower classes.

Table 3.5 compares the food items of higher castes like the Brahmans with those of lower castes like the labourers in a village near Coimbatore at the end of the last century. While the table reveals a sharp difference between the higher and lower castes in the consumption of staple foods and ghee, chillies showed no variation. As the Manual of Tanjore district agrees, dry chillies as well as salt and tamarind were the most indispensable ingredients for all, both rich and poor.[114] Gingili oil too was consumed equally by all sections of the population in the village.[115]

Even though vegetables were eaten by all, the higher castes consumed a much larger quantity and the lower castes a pitifully small amount.[116]

[111] *Manual of Salem District*, Vol. 2, The Taluks, p. 96.

[112] D. Narayana Rao, *Report on the Survey of Cottage Industries in the Madras Presidency* (Madras, 1929), p. 204.

[113] Ibid., p. 202.

[114] *Manual of Tanjore District,* p. 213

[115] Gingili oil was chiefly used for bathing (ibid., p. 128).

[116] The Director of Nutritional Research, Pasteur Institute furnished the Royal Commission on Labour in India with examples of diets actually eaten by various classes of workers. The examples reveal that the amount of vegetables eaten by coolies was less than that by higher grade workers, such as mechanics (*RCLI*, pp. 234–37). 'Vegetables are used occasionally by the labour class', but 'it is the labouring classes that consume vegetables least' (Thomas and Ramakrishnan [eds.], *Some South Indian Villages: A Resurvey*, pp. 143, 404).

Kerosene oil was used by both higher and lower castes, the higher castes registering a higher figure in this table. However, according to the Gazetteer of Tanjore district, kerosene was rarely used to light kitchens by any but poor persons, because of the unpleasant taste imparted to food by a hand which had touched the lamp. The poor were reported to use kerosene extensively because of its cheapness.[117] Thus, a large portion of the kerosene oil was probably used by the lower classes.

Table 3.5
Scale of Diet in Use among the *Raiyat* Population
in a Village near Coimbatore

Higher castes	Rs.a.p.	Lower castes	Rs.a.p.
Rice	2-0-0	Cholam	1-0-0
Salt	0-1-6	Horse gram	0-1-0
Dholl	0-1-6	Salt	0-1-6
Chillies	0-0-6	Chillies	0-0-6
Tamarind	0-1-0	Onions	0-0-6
Black gram (powdered)	0-2-0	Sundries	0-1-0
Butter-milk	0-2-6	Kerosene-oil	0-1-6
Ghee	0-5-0	Gingelly-oil	0-2-0
Kerosene-oil for light	0-2-6	Tamarind	0-0-6
Gingelly-oil	0-2-0	Betel leaves, areca nut & tobacco	0-4-0
Firewood	0-8-0	Total	1-12-6
Vegetables	0-1-0		
Total	3-11-6		

Source: S. Srinivasa Raghavaiyangar, *Memorandum on the Progress of the Madras Presidency during the Last Forty Years of British Administration,* p. ccxxxv.

The market demand for sugar in the 1930s was detailed in the 1942 *Report on the Marketing of Sugar*. According to the report, while a small part of locally produced unrefined sugar or *gur* was consumed in industrial production, refined sugar was rarely used for this purpose. In the Madras Presidency, about 70 percent of the refined sugar was used for drinks. Coffee and tea were the most common beverages, accounting for 76 percent of sugar consumption in drinks. Since per capita consumption of sugar for drinks in the Presidency was 3.0 pounds and that

[117] *Gazetteer of Tanjore District,* p. 128.

of *gur* for drinks was 0.7 pound, refined sugar accounted for almost 80 percent of the total amount of sugar and *gur* used for drinks.[118]

In the latter half of the 1930s, at the time the above report was prepared, South India was the major coffee-consuming area in the whole of India;[119] this however represented a change in consumption habits of the people. In 1906 the Gazetteer of Tanjore published interesting observations about changes in consumption habits of labourers: the Brahmans and other higher castes ate hot food at lunch and dinner, had coffee in the morning and a light snack at 3 P.M., while the lower classes on the other hand had cold rice and water at 7:30 A.M. with meat soup on rare occasions, hot or cold rice for lunch, and hot rice, meat, soup or curry at 7 or 8 P.M. for dinner. 'Of recent years however a tendency has become noticeable among Sudras, even of the poorer classes, towards the use of coffee in the early morning in preference to cold rice. On the other hand, this beverage is said to be losing favour with the higher classes, who regard it as unwholesome.'[120] The same trend was noticed in Tiruṅelveli district in 1917. The Gazetteer of this district pointed this out: 'The old practice of taking *kanji*, or cold rice-water, in the early morning is rapidly giving way to coffee drinking, . . . Even Pallans in some parts insist on having their cup of coffee before they go to work; with the younger members of the richer classes the custom of drinking coffee is almost general.'[121] Tea, on the other hand, was apparently much less popular with the people. Changes in beverage consumption, in the course of the previous twenty years, were noted by a village survey made around 1936: in a village in Ramnad district while coffee consumption shot up,[122] tea was not drunk; in Parakurichi village in Thanjavur district also, while coffee drinking was the general custom among Nayudu families, tea was rarely used.[123] I have already mentioned that refined sugar was mainly used for drinks in South India. As tea was not popularly drunk in South India in this period, the steep increase in the demand for sugar was obviously caused by the spread of coffee consumption. Thus the popularisation of drinking coffee among the lower castes resulted in an increase in coffee consumption in South

[118] *Report on the Marketing of Sugar in India and Burma* (Delhi, 1942), pp. 166, 170, 180.

[119] Ibid., p. 172.

[120] *Gazetteer of Tanjore District*, p. 65

[121] *Gazetteer of Tinnevelly District,* p. 105.

[122] Thomas and Ramakrishnan (eds.), *Some South Indian Villages: A Resurvey*, p. 46.

[123] Ibid., p. 143.

India and thus caused a sharp increase in sugar consumption. It may be safe to conclude that an increase in consumption by the lower classes was one of the main factors in the growing demand for sugar, like tobacco and kerosene, etc.

The increase in the transport of 'Wood–timber–unwrought' into inland blocks may be due principally to the needs of railway companies, though considerable research is necessary into the various uses of raw wood.

Reverting to the earlier grouping, my examination has revealed that most of the items in group (3) were consumed by the lower as well as the higher classes, and some were in demand by the lower classes in particular. Hence the increase of goods reaching the non-port blocks at that time indicates a development of trade based on an expanding internal market for goods consumed by a large lower class group in the villages. In other words, the analysis of railway statistics reveals the existence of a trade pattern different from export-import-oriented commercialisation.

Let us now examine the relationship between the increase in inter-inland trade, referred to earlier, and the growth in consumption of some items by the low classes. For this purpose, I have re-arranged the goods in descending order in terms of their growth rate in inter-inland trade.[124] The share of the inter-inland movement as a percentage of the total amount moved by rail has been also calculated. Among the items that more than doubled in amount transported, the share of inter-inland trade for a few of them, such as tea, raw hides and groundnuts, was conspicuously low. This was mainly because the absolute value of inter-inland trade had been so small in 1900 that it appears to have grown very rapidly. Such goods will therefore be excluded from the present analysis.

Among the goods registering a high growth rate of inter-inland trade as well as occupying a large share of the inter-inland trade in the total trade, were wood, fruits and vegetables, chillies, tobacco and cotton yarn. Most of these, as seen earlier, belonged to group (3), confirming the role of the lower castes in creating market stresses for consumer goods, which in turn spurred inter-inland trade in the Madras Presidency.

It has already been pointed out that the custom of morning coffee, which was a privileged habit of the higher classes, gradually spread to the lower classes. At the same time, staples also underwent a change. As

[124] Yanagisawa, *Minamiindo Shakai Keizaishi*, p. 125, Table 4.8.

shown in the above table, in nineteenth-century South India, members of higher castes generally ate rice as the staple food, whereas people from the lower castes had *cholam* or other cereals,[125] except in some of the paddy producing areas. However, this also changed in the early twentieth century. A report on the life of an average agricultural family stated, 'The poorer classes of ryots and labourers, who once mainly ate the healthy cholam, ragi and cumbu, have now to a noticeable extent gone over to the cheap broken rice from abroad.'[126] The same information was found in a research report of the Madras Presidency.[127] A study of a village in the Godavari district noted, 'the giving up of harder grains like cholam and kambu and the increasing use of milled rice are the most obvious changes in the dietary of the villagers in the last 20 years',[128] indicating that this shift in the staple food was quite a common phenomenon, seen in various parts of South India.

The spread of rice among the poorer classes was partly due to the decline of the production of miscellaneous cereals as the result of the inflow of cheaper Burmese rice. In addition to this economic explanation, it can be understood as reflecting the tendency among the lower castes to imitate the life-style of the higher castes. A report from Madras University made the following observation: 'But by 1936, a large percentage of people had taken to rice as their staple food, partly because of its greater convenience to the housewife and partly because it signified a rise in the social scale.'[129] Adopting the life-style of the higher castes to climb the social ladder has been termed as 'Sanskritization' by M.N. Srinivas,[130] and viewed from this perspective, the spread to other castes of both the morning-coffee habit and the consumption of rice as the staple food could well be a part of it. A record of the customs of the Paraiyar, published in the 1906 Gazetteer, noted that they 'are actually beginning to copy the social ways of the higher castes',[131] corroborating the existence of the Sanskritization process.

[125] For Trichinopoly district, see *Papers Relating to the Survey and Settlement of the Trichinopoly District,* p. 50.

[126] Sathyanathan, *Report on Agricultural Indebtedness*, p. 29.

[127] Thomas and Ramakrishnan (eds.), *Some South Indian Villages: A Resurvey*, p. 46.

[128] Ibid., p. 254.

[129] Thomas and Ramakrishnan (eds.), *Some South Indian Villages: A Resurvey*, p. 403.

[130] M.N. Srinivas, *Social Change in Modern India* (Berkeley and Los Angeles, 1966; repr., Bombay, 1977), Chapter 1.

[131] *Gazetteer of South Arcot District,* by W. Francis (Madras, 1906), p. 105.

However, a consideration of other aspects of the everyday life of the lower castes reveals that not all changes represented Sanskritization. For instance, the habit of smoking tobacco seems to have become commoner: 'Drinking, smoking and chewing betel or tobacco are common among all classes except Brahmans.'[132] While Brahmans and other higher-caste members abstained on religious grounds from drinking alcohol,[133] the Paraiyars were known for their 'love of intoxicating drinks',[134] contributing to an increase in the consumption of alcohol.[135] Meat-eating, taboo for Brahmans, was reported to be increasing among the lower castes.[136] Thus such habits spread among the lower castes, even though they were taboo in the Brahmanical way of life. Therefore, it would be wrong to assume that changes occurring among the lower castes at the time were merely a simple process of Sanskritization.

In the following chapters, we shall examine the process of the emancipation of the lower classes including the Depressed castes from a state of servitude. In the process they tried not only to liberate themselves from socio-economic control by higher-caste landlords but also to pursue freedom in their social life, releasing themselves from social restrictions. As we shall see in later chapters, some Depressed-caste members were in the process raised from the status of mere agricultural labourers to that of tenants and some even to small landowning farmers. The increase in the consumption of various items by the lower classes, as discussed in this chapter, seems to have been underpinned by the increasing liberty of the lower castes, who were gradually acquiring small plots of land. On the other hand, the markedly increased consumption of food items like chillies, sugar and tobacco seems to have supported the small low-caste farmer by providing him with a market for his products, as I shall discuss in Chapter 5.

The fact that the lower castes not merely imitated the eating and social habits of the higher castes but also increased their consumption of certain food prohibited to Brahmans[137] may be easily understood, if put

[132] *Gazetteer of Trichinopoly District,* p. 85.

[133] Ibid.; *Manual of Tanjore District,* p. 215.

[134] Ibid., p. 206.

[135] Raghavaiyangar, *Memorandum*, pp. xc, ccxi. For the increase in the consumption of spirits, see G.O., No. 1937, Revenue, 13 Aug. 1901; G.O., No. 2023, Revenue, 24 July 1909; G.O., No. 460, Revenue, 13 Feb. 1914; *Royal Commission on Agriculture in India,* Vol. 3, p. 414.

[136] Raghavaiyangar, *Memorandum*, p. xc.

[137] The Collector of South Arcot district, identifying the larger consumption by labourers of such items as we have discussed, asserted that he could not

in the context of the long historical process of the emancipation of the lower castes.

The analysis of railway statistics has revealed a growth in internal trade. In this connection, we should also note that local trade by bullock carts also contributed to the development of internal trade within South India. As discussed earlier, local trade in manure by bullock cart facilitated the supply of manure to those districts which formerly had not been able to produce an adequate amount of manure themselves.

To summarise, trade in South India began evolving, on one hand, into an export-import-oriented commerce, and this formed the major structural change at the time. On the other hand, internal trade started to increase at the same time, triggered by the changing needs of the lower class villagers. The latter change reflects the increasing freedom and emancipation of the lower castes.

---

attribute this to the higher wages given to the labourers, because, he said, though the wages of unskilled labour other than agriculture had advanced about 25 percent during the previous twenty years, the price of food had gone up in proportion. He argued that 'it is due mainly, I think, to the steady and ever-increasing demand for labour throughout the year, so that the man or woman who is willing to work need never want. . . . In former days, within my own recollection, it was a very difficult matter for the labouring classes to tide over those months of the year during which agricultural operations were at a standstill' (Raghavaiyangar, *Memorandum*, p. xc). My argument is that the increase in the consumption of these items by the lower classes was a reflection of their emancipation. In this connection, the existence of a long agricultural off-season in the year was an important issue, standing as an obstacle to the emancipation of agricultural labourers from the control of the landlords. The Collector's observation seems to agree with me as to the importance of the steady demand for labour throughout the year, though he does not imply this too clearly.

4

Two Paths to the Tenancy System

The developments delineated in the previous chapter contributed to the transformation of the agrarian structure of the wet districts in Tamilnadu. This transformation took place in two closely linked areas: the pattern of agricultural management and that of landholding. This chapter traces the transformation of patterns of agricultural management, focussing particularly on the expansion of tenant cultivation.

The Growth of the Tenancy System

The tenancy system was prevalent in early twentieth-century South India, particularly in wet areas. An enquiry into subletting in a typical area in North Arcot district revealed in 1912 that out of a total of 13,253 acres of irrigated land, 3,918 acres or 29.5 percent were under tenant cultivation; and of 16,096 acres of dry land, 686 acres or 4.2 percent were sublet. The report indicates that the practice of subletting was far more prevalent in wet than in dry lands. This was because the dry land hardly generated sufficient income to meet taxes, cultivation expenses and the living expenses of the tenants, unless the land had been improved by sinking a well.[1] In Ambasamudram *taluk*, Tirunelveli district, 55 percent of irrigated land was under tenant cultivation, compared to only 22 percent of dry land.[2] Concerning this *taluk*, 'in the Tambraparni valley very few of the pattadars cultivate their own lands; in the river-irrigated tracts at the foot of the hills, it is more common, but even here, it is the general rule that the lands are cultivated by tenants either on a year-to-year lease or on waram.'[3] Similar statistics were reported for government land in Udumalpet *taluk*, Coimbatore district,

[1] G.O., No. 3594, Confidential, Revenue, 9 Dec. 1914, pp. 18–19.

[2] Ibid., p. 112.

[3] 'Notes to G.O. Nos. 3594–95, Revenue, 9 December 1914', p. 75. The Gazetteer of the district also states that in this area, at least two-thirds of the land was leased to tenants (*Gazetteer of Tinnevelly District*, p. 189).

where almost 82 percent of the 5,871 acres of wet land was under tenancy, while a mere 10 percent of the 29,190 acres of the rainfed dry land, and 22 percent of the 6,273 acres of garden land were sublet.[4]

The prevalence of tenant cultivation was noted in many districts of South India. In Thanjavur district, land was cultivated under several systems. Reporting on the district in 1894, Krishnamurthi Iyengar divided cultivation into three categories: (1) the *pannai* system, under which the *mirasidars* themselves cultivated their land with the help of *pannaiyals* or hired labourers, (2) the *varam* system, under which landowners were responsible for supplying manure and for some other expenditures, while the tenants bore the other main expenses relating to cultivation; a fixed percentage of the produce from the land was shared by the landowners and the tenants; and (3) the lease system, where a fixed amount of the produce was taken by the landowners. According to the Gazetteer, the most widely prevalent type in the Thanjavur delta was the *varam* system and the least practiced was the lease system.[5] Though some *varam* cultivators may have been virtually no different from agricultural labourers, there is no doubt that at the end of the last century the tenant system was prevalent in this district. It can be said therefore that at the beginning of the twentieth century, the tenancy system was quite prevalent particularly in irrigated land in South India, despite regional differences.

Scholars, however, do not concur on whether or not the tenant system developed in South India. Dharma Kumar threw doubt on the popular view that tenancy grew up along with commercialisation and with absentee landlordism and inequality in landownership. A decrease in the percentage of non-resident landowners in relation to the total was noted in three of the four districts of Madras Presidency (North Arcot, Coimbatore and Cuddapah), from 1911–13 to 1947. Tirunelveli district alone registered an increase from 7 percent to 31 percent. On the other hand, Dharma Kumar points out that if one compares the figures for the percentage of land let in 1911–13 with the census figures for 1961, the percentage fell in Tirunelveli, though non-resident landowners increased; it rose in North Arcot, where absentee landowners decreased; and was stable in Coimbatore district.[6]

Two points should be considered in relation to this argument. First, since 'it is not by any means only the absentee who sublets his land in

[4] G.O., No. 3594, Confidential, Revenue, 9 Dec. 1914, p. 52.

[5] 'Notes to G.O. Nos. 3594–95, Revenue, 9 December 1914', pp. 66–67.

[6] Kumar, 'Agrarian Relations: South India', p. 236.

some districts at least',[7] the change in the percentage of absentee landlords may not correlate directly with fluctuations in the percentage of land sublet. A decline in the percentage of absentee landlords in relation to the total is not necessarily incompatible with the growth of the tenancy system. Second, by 1961, when the census data were collected, land reform, including the regulation of the tenancy system, had been enforced. It is highly probable that landlords either had already reduced the area under tenant cultivation or tried to conceal a part of the leased-out area when the census data were collected. Therefore, the 1961 Census data for tenancy area cannot be considered a suitable index for judging the changes that occurred before Independence.

There are reasons to believe that the tenancy system spread in Tamilnadu after the 1880s, though there is no statistical evidence available regarding changes in the area let to tenants. One of the most reliable sources for tenancy in the Presidency is a confidential Government Order of 1914, which included full and detailed reports about sub-tenants by special settlement officers in various districts. A note to this Government Order states that 'it seems quite clear that the number of sub-tenants under ryots is much larger now than it was in Chentsal Rao's time [in 1881], and it is also most probable that the number of non-cultivating ryots who sub-let is on the increase.'[8] Accounts in the *Jamabandi* Reports, annual revenue reports submitted by the Collectors for each district of the Presidency, also indicate a growth in the subletting system. An examination of reports for the three years 1903, 1904 and 1905 reveals that subletting had grown even in this short period in such districts as North Arcot, South Arcot, Madurai and Tirunelveli, while it was already prevalent in the districts of Tiruchirapalli and Thanjavur.[9]

[7] 'Notes to G.O. Nos. 3594–95, Revenue, 9 December 1914', p. 91.

[8] Ibid., p. 33.

[9] In North Arcot for Fasli 1313 (1903), 'the growth of subletting in ryotwari tracts will be prominent only in districts where Brahmans form the chief land-holding class'; in South Arcot, for Fasli 1313 (1903), 'the practice of subletting land appears from the various reports received to be gradually increasing'; in Thanjavur for Fasli 1313 (1903), 'the practice of subletting is very prevalent in all the taluks', except Puttukkottai; in Tiruchirapalli, for Fasli 1313 (1903), 'it is true that there is a good deal of subletting, many wet villages being practically owned by mirasdars, often not living on the spot, who sublet their holding under one system or other'; in Madurai, for Fasli 1314 (1904), 'the system of subletting lands in ryotwari tracts has slightly increased in recent years in the Periyar-affected areas of Periyakulam, Madura and Melur taluks, where a large number of non-resident ryots and capitalists have purchased waste lands'; In Tirunelveli

The information we have on the tenancy system for the period after 1914, though very scanty, points to a continuation of the same trend. Referring to a rise in the 1921 Census as compared with the Census of 1911 in the number of cultivating tenants per thousand, the Labour Commissioner stated that the middle classes were taking to other pursuits and that some of these landowners instead of farming themselves were leasing their land out to tenants.[10] A growth in the tenancy system in a few areas of Madras Presidency was noted in the village survey done by the Madras University in 1936. For example, in Gangaikondan village, Tirunelveli district, 'All the ryots whom I consulted are certain that there has been a great increase in the number of tenants in the last 15 or 20 years. The majority of them are of opinion that 50 per cent of the total agriculturists are tenants exclusively and about 10 per cent are both tenants and petty land holders. Many of these tenants are also agricultural labourers in the spare time.'[11] Later, K.G. Sivaswamy, who conducted a survey of the tenancy system in South India in 1941 and in 1946, stated that absentee landlordism had made strides during the twentieth century.[12] The *Jamabandi* Reports for the period of between 1915 and 1926 often noted a growth of subletting in Chingleput district, though, for the Madura district, an expansion of the tenant system in the area under the Periyar and a decrease in Tirumangalam *taluk* are noted.[13]

These scanty references suggest that on balance it is probably appropriate to conclude that in the period between the 1880s and 1940s,

---

for Fasli 1313 (1903), 'subletting is on the whole increasing' (ibid., pp. 20–22).

[10] *Royal Commission on Agriculture in India,* Vol. 3, p. 341. See also *MBEC,* Vol. 4, *Oral Evidence*, p. 397.

[11] Thomas and Ramakrishnan (eds.), *Some South Indian Villages: A Resurvey*, p. 71. For the increase in the cases of lease in Vadamalaipuram village in Ramnad district, see p. 10. For a village in Kistna district, see Slater (ed.), *Some South Indian Villages*, p. 112 and Thomas and Ramakrishnan (eds.), *Some South Indian Villages: A Resurvey*, p. 216. In reply to a question issued by the Madras Provincial Banking Enquiry Committee, a witness in Tirunelveli stated that the landholders had given up the habit of cultivating their own land, indicating a spread of tenant cultivation (*MBEC,* Vol. 2, *Written Evidence*, p. 334).

[12] K.G. Sivaswamy, *The Madras Ryotwari Tenant* (Hereafter, '*Tenant*'), Part 1 (Madras: South Indian Association of Agricultural Workers, 1948), pp. 8, 19–20.

[13] *Report on the Settlement of the Land Revenue of the Districts in the Madras Presidency* (Hereafter, *Jamabandi Report*) *for Fasli 1325 (1915–16)* (Madras, 1917), p. 13; *Jamabandi Report for Fasli 1332*, p. 10; *Jamabandi Report for Fasli 1328*, p. 12.

Tamilnadu, especially its wet zones, witnessed a growth of the tenancy system.

Decrease in the Share of Agricultural Production Paid as Taxes

The spread of the tenancy system was attributable to several factors, of which I shall consider here only the important ones. Essential to the expansion of this system was a decrease in the share of agricultural production paid as taxes. According to Raju, in 1837 the taxes paid accounted for as much as 50 percent of the total agricultural products,[14] and after the subtraction of taxes and production costs from the total agricultural product, the remaining profit was reported to be a bare one-tenth or one-fifth of the produce. However, around the beginning of the twentieth century, the share of taxes slid drastically to as little as 10 percent. For example, in 1916, the share of taxes was only between 3 and 4 percent of the produce in villages in Ramnad district, and 15 percent in a village in Tiruchirapalli district.[15] It is beyond the scope of this study to clarify the implication of this decrease in the share of products paid as the taxes, in spite of its importance. I shall consider only, in a later chapter, the change in the composition of government revenue and the economic effects of this change on the various classes.

The decline of land taxes as a percentage of the total product was a prerequisite to the development of the tenancy system. If land tax collected by the government amounted to nearly 50 percent of the total product, it would be hardly possible for a tenant farmer to have any profit from which he could pay rent to his landlord. The decrease in the relative burden of the government land tax enabled tenants to pay rent to the landlords and thus made possible a parasitic class of people living on income from rents. The Manual of Tinnevelly district states, 'it has

[14] Revenue Consultation, 5 Dec. 1837, cited in Raju, *Economic Conditions in the Madras Presidency*, p. 73. Recent work done by Bandopadhyaya also reveals that the assessment amounted to about 40 to 50 percent of the gross produce in this period (*Agrarian Economy of Tamilnadu*, p. 155). See also, Kumar, *Land and Caste*, p. 83.

[15] Slater (ed.), *Some South Indian Villages*, pp. 51, 225–26. Sivaswamy states that land revenue dwindled from one-half of the gross produce to about one-tenth over the century from the middle of the nineteenth century (Sivaswamy, *Tenants*, Part 1, p. 51). See also, Ludden, *Peasant History*; Sugata Bose, *Peasant Labour and Colonial Bengal since 1770*, The New Cambridge History of India, III, 2 (Cambridge, 1993), pp. 113–14.

everywhere been found possible to obtain from the land besides what is needed to support its actual cultivator and to pay the Government assessment, a rent sufficient to keep up an idle class.'[16]

Commercialisation of Agriculture and Dispossession of Peasants' Land: Towards the Spread of Tenant Cultivation (1)

There seem to have been two ways through which the tenancy system in South India developed. First, the tenancy system spread as a result of the acquisition of land by merchants and moneylenders and the resultant dispossession of farmers from the land.

As I mentioned in Chapter 1, it has been the conventional view to believe that the increasing commercialisation of agriculture and the integration of farmers into international trade networks put farmers more and more at the mercy of merchants and moneylenders, and ultimately led to the loss of their land, reducing them to mere peasants. I have referred to Dharma Kumar's severe criticism of this opinion. To reiterate, she concludes, based on her analysis of land tax statistics for each district of South India, that there is no trend towards the concentration of landownership in the hands of large landholders, and that if there was an increase in indebtedness among farmers, it did not necessarily lead them being deprived of their land.[17]

In spite of Dharma Kumar's criticism, my data seems to indicate not only a growth in the number of rich traders, moneylenders and some *nouveaux riches* who exploited the new economic opportunities developed under British rule, but also a transfer of landownership to these classes of people as well. In Chapter 5 I will analyse changes in the patterns of landownership in detail and attempt to demonstrate that landholding by traders and moneylenders increased, thereby presenting a new interpretation of Dharma Kumar's analysis from a different angle. In this chapter, I delineate how the tenancy system expanded as a result of the commercialisation of agriculture, without presenting the evidence for changes in landownership, as it will be examined in the next chapter.

[16] *Manual of Tinnevelly District*, p. 31.

[17] Kumar, 'Landownership and Inequality', p. 257; G.G. Kotowski, 'Pacht und Pachtverhältnisse in Tamilnad (Südindien) von 1917–1939', in Walton Ruben (ed.), *Die ökonomische und soziale Entwicklung Indiens* (Berlin, 1959), p. 278.

Price fluctuations

The increase in agricultural exports and the integration of agricultural production into global trade networks, discussed in Chapter 3, were accompanied by some important changes in the economic performance of South Indian agriculture. First, differences in price levels among different parts of South India apparently diminished in the nineteenth century. Changes in the price of rice (amount of rice per one rupee) in several places of South India between 1809 and 1887 are shown in Figure 4.1, demonstrating a clear trend towards a decrease in price differences among various parts of South India.[18]

Second, and more important, is that yearly fluctuations in prices of foodgrains became sharper as agriculture was integrated into the wider economic network. A village survey comments, 'The fluctuating area of cultivation of the crop is due to the price factor which is entirely controlled by a foreign market. To the villagers it appears as a gamble.'[19]

Figure 4.1
The Prices of Second-Sort Rice in Terms of Seers of 80 Tolas per Rupee in Various Places in South India

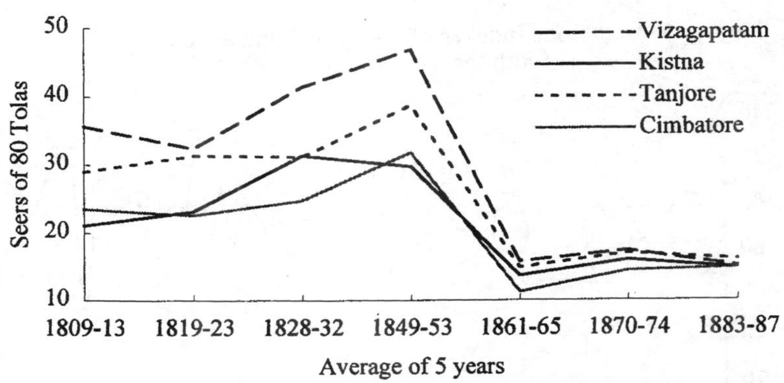

Source: Compiled from Raghavaiyangar, *Memorandum*, p. c, (a) Table showing the prices of second sort rice in terms of seers of 80 tolas per rupee (average for quinquennial periods excluding famine years).

[18] See also G.O., No. 711, Revenue, 11 Aug. 1902, p. 23; John Hurd II, 'Railways and the Expansion of Markets in India, 1861–1921', *Explorations in Economic History* 12, 3 (July 1975).

[19] Thomas and Ramakrishnan (eds.), *Some South Indian Villages: A Resurvey*, p. 79.

Figure 4.2
Price Indexes of Paddy in Comparison with the Year Before: Tanjore

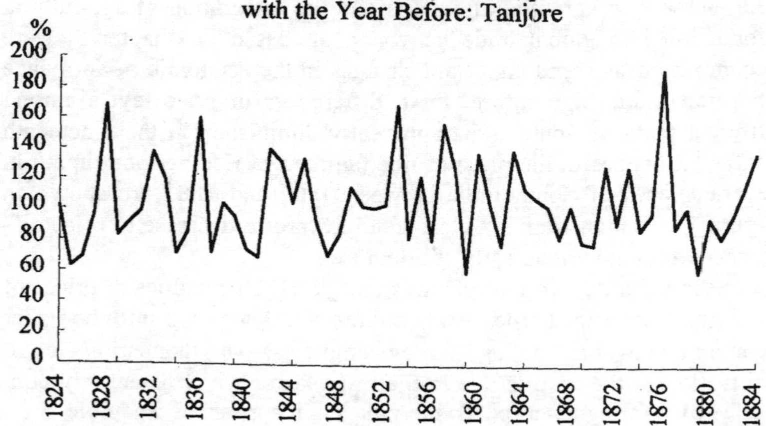

Source: Compiled from Raghavaiyangar, *Memorandum*, p. cvii, Statement showing the mahanum prices of paddy per Tanjore kalam (24 Madras measures) for a series of years in the Tanjore District.

Figure 4.3
Price Indexes of Paddy in Comparison with the Year Before: Palghat

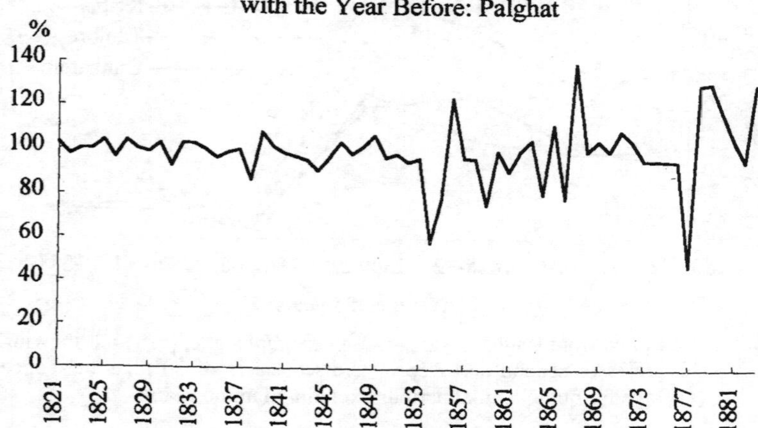

Source: Compiled from Raghavaiyangar, *Memorandum*, p. civ, Statement showing the number of padies of paddy sold for a rupee at Palghat for a number of years compiled from the accounts preserved in the family of a rich landlord in Malabar.

In Figure 4.2, I attempt to show the yearly fluctuation in rice prices in Thanjavur by plotting price indexes in comparison with those of the year before. The resulting figures reveal that the price of rice in this district fluctuated wildly every year from 1825. As detailed in Chapter 3, the rice produced in Thanjavur had been so organised as to reach distant places like the markets of Madras since the beginning of the nineteenth century and this solid integration of Thanjavur agriculture into the wider market network probably explains the sharp fluctuation in rice prices in that district. As we have seen above, agricultural production in various districts in South India other than Thanjavur were also gradually being connected with the wider economic network. As this occurred, the sharp fluctuations seen in Thanjavur became common in other areas of South India as well. Records preserved by a landlord family in Malabar district show the changing prices of paddy over a 62 year period in the Palghat area (Figure 4.3). The graph depicts yearly changes in the amount of paddy sold for a rupee. The figure reveals an apparent tendency towards a sharper fluctuation in paddy price in this area, mirroring the greater integration of the area into the wider trade network.

Increase in farmers' debts

The sharp fluctuation in the price of paddy seems to have seriously affected the economic position of farmers, deeply involved in the commercialised economy, and led to their disintegration.

The process started with an increase in farmer debt. Of course, farmers debt existed even before the 1850s, probably even before British colonial rule. A report from Bellary district stated in 1851: 'About 49 per cent. [of farmers] are obliged to borrow money by mortgaging their crops and stock and 34 per cent. are obliged to sell their crops as soon as reaped and even their stock to pay their kists.'[20] The majority of moneylenders were small traders and most of them made advances to farmers with the sole purpose of usurping the produce.[21] These moneylenders and traders not only earned interest on their loans, but also took forcible hold of the produce from the land, thereby making a double profit.[22]

Many scholars concur that moneylenders increased their activity as agriculture became ever more commercialised. A government report of

[20] Raghavaiyangar, *Memorandum*, p. 30.
[21] *MBEC*, Vol. 1, *Report*, pp. 30, 109.
[22] Sathyanathan, *Report on Agricultural Indebtedness*, p. 19.

1893 stated: 'It [the income of moneylenders] is much larger than was the case formerly in this country, and, being made up of smaller profits than before, denotes increased activity of trade.'[23] A 1902 memorandum on the material condition of the Madras Presidency admitted an enormous growth in debts.[24] The Madras Provincial Banking Enquiry Committee recorded in 1930 that mortgage debts doubled between the years 1895 and 1917,[25] and that almost 60 percent to 70 percent of the farmers were under considerable debt and were required to repay at least a small part of it during the harvest season.[26] It further pointed out that on average, the debt per acre came to Rs. 62 in Tamil districts or Rs. 19 for one rupee land tax assessment for the Presidency.[27]

Farmers' debts had increased further by 1936–37. A village survey conducted at that time by Madras University revealed that the construction of a dam in the Mysore area had restricted the water supply to the irrigated land of Dusi village in the North Arcot district. Partly because agricultural production was badly affected by an insufficient supply of water and partly because the price of paddy fell from Rs. 85 per cartload in 1927 to Rs. 25 in 1937, farmers were forced to incur debt. Fifty percent of the *pattadars*, especially those owning wet land, had to mortgage their land. Only 10 percent of the debtors were reported to be able to repay their loans.[28] In Gangaikondan village of Tirunelveli district, the total debt incurred by peasants almost tripled in the course of 17 years—from Rs. 100,000 in 1916 to Rs. 270,000 in 1934. According to the survey, a period of boom prices enhanced the borrowing power of the *raiyats* but it was followed by a period of depression which reduced their capacity to repay. The Maravar, one of the main farming castes of this village, had an average debt of Rs. 1,500 per family. As a farmer managing a land of 10 acres scarcely earned even Rs. 600 a year, the amount of debt a family had was too large for an average farmer to repay.[29]

[23] Raghavaiyangar, *Memorandum*, p. 160.

[24] G.O., No. 711, Revenue, 11 Aug. 1902, p. 25.

[25] *MBEC,* Vol. 1, p. 80.

[26] Ibid., p. 105.

[27] Ibid., p. 76.

[28] Thomas and Ramakrishnan (eds.), *Some South Indian Villages: A Resurvey*, p. 201. In Tinnevelly district, in a typical tract about one-half of the tenant population were debtors, and the Gazetteer presumes that the same would apply to *raiyats* (*Gazetteer of Tinnevelly District*, p. 194).

[29] Thomas and Ramakrishnan (eds.), *Some South Indian Villages: A Resurvey*, pp. 105–6.

There is evidence that the increase in debt resulted in the spread of the tenancy system. The farmers, unable to repay their debts, lost their land and became tenants. For example, in Iruvelipat village, South Arcot district, 'when the cultivators failed to repay, as was usually the case, there was transfer of land, and the former landowners have sunk to the position of tenants cultivating the same land on Varam or Kuthagai.'[30] In Gangaikondan village, Tirunelveli 'of the total amount of money lent at present, it is expected that only one-third can be recovered in cash, and that too in several installments; one-third will be returned in the form of landed property and the rest can be recovered in part through the civil courts'.[31] The Labour Commissioner also admitted that the increase in the number of tenants was partly due to the fact that a cultivating landowner had to part with his land to clear his debt.[32] In this way, the commercialisation of agriculture brought mounting debts and hardship to farmers. Pressured to give up or sell their land, these farmers were forced to become tenants. Tsukasa Mizushima's analysis of the 1929 Madras Provincial Banking Enquiry Committee Report brought to light some such instances.[33]

Acquisition of land by merchants and moneylenders

As we shall see in the next chapter, the statistical analysis of the village Settlement Registers indicates there was a transfer of land to the newly rich, including merchants and moneylenders. Their acquisition of land also resulted in the expansion of the tenancy system.

In contrast to the growth of farmer debt, merchants and moneylenders accumulated wealth through commercial activities and moneylending. According to a table compiled by S.S. Raghavaiyangar showing the classification of income tax assessees in Madras Presidency for the year 1890–91, no other category of assessees was paying a larger amount of income tax than the group engaged in 'Money lending and changing' (under 'Part–IV(b) Commerce'). Together with other related items, the total income tax assessed in the section labelled 'Commerce' was about Rs. 680,000. As the total amount of income tax, about Rs. 1.58 million, was levied on a total taxable income of Rs. 65.12

[30] Ibid., p. 153.

[31] Ibid., p. 107.

[32] *Royal Commission on Agriculture in India,* Vol. 3, p. 341.

[33] Tsukasa Mizushima, 'Minami Indo Nosonno Ruikeika no Kokoromi [Some Types in Villages in South India]', *Shigaku Zasshi* 87, 7 (1978), pp. 8–9.

million, the taxable income per rupee of income tax came to Rs. 41.16.[34] If we can assume that the same rate of income tax was levied on the income from commerce, the total income from 'Commerce' including money-lending becomes Rs. 28 million, of which money-lending accounted for Rs. 14.78 million.[35]

The income from commerce and money-lending stands comparison with the profit from agriculture in terms of the total amount. For the one year period of 1889–90, the total land revenue was Rs. 50.3 million, of which Rs. 20.6 million derived from irrigated land and Rs. 17.4 million from dry areas.[36] On the other hand, it was estimated in 1892 that the net profit after subtracting both cultivation expenses and land taxes was about half the amount of land tax in the case of irrigated land and almost the same as the tax in the dry areas.[37] Assuming this estimate to be correct, the total amount of the net profit made by farmers from agriculture comes to Rs. 27.7 million. Thus, the total taxable income earned through commercial activities, including money-lending, namely, Rs. 28 million, turns out to have been as large as the total net profit earned in the agricultural sector. Though the definitions of 'taxable income' and 'net profit' are not clear and therefore the estimate made is not completely reliable, it may be safely inferred that a large portion of agricultural income was creamed off by traders and moneylenders.[38]

In Thanjavur and other districts, the latter half of the nineteenth century witnessed land becoming an object of 'safe investment',

[34] Raghavaiyangar, *Memorandum*, pp. cxc–cxciii, Statement showing the classification of the incomes on which the income-tax was collected in the Madras Presidency during the year 1890–91. According to the 1886 Act, income tax was levied on incomes of all kinds except those either derived from agriculture or below Rs. 500. *Report of the Indian Taxation Enquiry Committee 1924–25* (Madras, 1926), Vol. 1, p. 189; V.K.R.V. Rao, *Taxation of Income in India* (Calcutta, 1931), p. 25.

[35] According to S.S. Raghavaiyangar, the total income earned by moneylenders with incomes exceeding Rs. 500 was estimated at Rs. 16 million. Raghavaiyangar, *Memorandum*, p. 160.

[36] Raghavaiyangar, *Memorandum*, p. cxli, Statement showing the growth of the Land Revenue and extension of occupied areas of land fully assessed in the Madras Presidency.

[37] Ibid., p. 198.

[38] At the end of the last century, Frederick A. Nicholson estimated the amount of interest annually paid by borrowers in the Madras Presidency at Rs. 67.5 million. Frederick A. Nicholson, *Report Regarding the Possibility of Introducing Land and Agricultural Banks into the Madras Presidency*, Vol. 1 (Madras, 1895), p. 241.

because of a decrease in the burden of land taxes.[39] In 1881, the Deputy Collector of Salem district reported that the urban Brahmans and traders were procuring land and this land was sublet to tenants:

> The wet lands and the more fertile and improved dry lands are largely held on patta by persons belonging to the non-cultivating classes, who are frequently non-resident in the villages where they hold the lands. The holders are usually Brahmans and Chetties in the towns. The possession of land is sought as an investment of a secure kind and the rate of interest expected on the principal sunk is very low.[40]

The evidence for the acquisition of land by moneylenders and traders is presented and examined in the next chapter, where I will discuss overall changes in landholding by analysing the data compiled from the Settlement Registers. In this chapter, I aim only to establish that land transferral to merchants and moneylenders resulted in the expansion of the tenancy system. A report from the North Arcot district mentions: 'Land purchased as an investment, pure and simple, is almost invariably sub let.' In this district, according to a survey conducted in 1914, about 60 percent of wet land and 55 percent of dry land leased out were owned by non-resident *patta*-holders.[41] Of the total area of land sublet to tenants, 25 percent belonged to government officials and lawyers, 20 percent to traders and moneylenders and the remaining 55 percent to landholders with no other profession or occupation.[42] The moneylenders and traders thus did account for a considerable proportion of the leased land in this district. The spread of the tenancy system was specially intense in the Periyar area of Madurai district. 'The growth of subletting continues especially in the Periyar tracts. As in last year the system is resorted to in the main by Vakils and Nattukottai Chetties (traders).' In Coimbatore district, 'generally, the non-agricultural class of people and public servants who happen to own lands and who do not find time to devote to them, lease their lands to agricultural labourers on favourable rentals, either in cash or in grain'.[43]

People who had become wealthy through trade or money-lending were not confined to professional traders and moneylenders. The Report of the Madras Provincial Banking Enquiry Committee noted in 1930

[39] Raghavaiyangar, *Memorandum*, p. 111.
[40] G.O., No. 3594, Confidential, Revenue, 9 Dec. 1914, p. 8.
[41] Ibid., pp. 19–20.
[42] 'Notes to G.O. Nos. 3594–95, Revenue, 9 December 1914', p. 103.
[43] Ibid., pp. 21–22.

that 'the ryots themselves form the biggest community of lenders'.[44] While moneylenders in wet land areas were mostly professionals, farmers in dry areas borrowed money from rich farmers.[45] Towards the end of the nineteenth century, in not less than 80 percent of cases, moneylenders were reported to be farmers.[46]

Such money-lending farmers also tended to lease out their land. In this context, the following quotation from the 1935 Report on Agricultural Indebtedness is of value:

> Absentee landlordism is steadily on the increase. It is especially increasing among those who lend money to agriculturists, whether professional money-lenders or agriculturist and trader money-lenders. Land was a safe investment till a few years ago, though the return it yielded was meagre. So those, whose professions gave them a surplus for investment, invested in land. Hence, we have absentee landlords among Government servants, lawyers, and retired men. Professional money-lenders, and traders and agriculturists who lend money are gradually turning out to be big absentee landlords. When their loans are not returned, they eventually take the land of their debtors in full or part payment. It being impossible for them to cultivate this growing volume of landed property themselves, the land is let out on lease to tenants. This tendency of land to pass into the hands of those who will not or cannot cultivate in person has been much aggravated by the economic depression.[47]

Appadurai village in Tiruchirapalli district, for which data was collected through village records and interviews with the villagers in the course of my field work, offers ample instances of newly rich traders buying wet land as a safe investment and leasing it to tenants. As an interesting example, a Muslim trader, who appeared as a *pattadar* of 8 acres of village land in the 1925 Settlement Register, had migrated to Burma at an early age and had opened a fuel shop there. Returning to Tiruchirapalli city at the age of 30, he operated a rice shop for ten years, and bought a total of 13 acres of land near the Grand Anicut of the River Kaveri and in and around Appadurai village, because, according to his descendants, the land was very fertile. All his land was leased to tenants and he himself carried on his trading business in the city.

[44] *MBEC,* Vol. 1, p. 30.

[45] Mizushima, 'Minami Indo Nouson no Ruikeika', p. 7. See also, Washbrook, *Emergence of Provincial Politics,* pp. 71–73.

[46] Raghavaiyangar, *Memorandum*, p. 254; P.B.R., No. 28, 12 Feb. 1921, p. 33, par. 33.

[47] Sathyanathan, *Report on Agricultural Indebtedness*, pp. 4–5.

Another Muslim family, whose ancestors lived and owned land in Madurai, provides a second instance. Early in the twentieth century, they started a timber business in Tiruchirapalli city and bought land in Appadurai village to provide rice for home consumption, selling off their land in Madurai. In addition, a textile merchant from the Kaikola Chettiar community living in Srirangam town procured land in Appadurai, which was all leased out to Appadurai villagers.[48]

I suggested at the beginning of this section that there were two ways through which the tenancy system of South India developed. To sum up the first, when colonial India started commercialising its agriculture and structuring trade towards international markets, agrarian management by farmers became unstable, as a result of the instability of the foreign market, and the farmers who depended financially on merchants and moneylenders tended to disintegrate. It is highly probable that some farmers lost a part or the whole of their land and were reduced to the status of tenants of their former land. On the other hand, an increasing amount of land was bought by merchants and moneylenders, who had accumulated wealth as a result of the increasing commercialisation of agriculture. Thus, the commercialisation of agriculture under British rule resulted in an expansion of the tenancy system.

Leasing out of Land Formerly Operated by Large Landholders: Towards the Spread of Tenancy Cultivation (2)

I shall now examine the second way the tenancy system spread in South India, a way that has so far attracted little scholarly attention. Here, an expansion of tenant cultivation resulted from the fact that some higher-caste large landowners leased out a part or the whole of their land, which they themselves had formerly managed with hired permanent labourers.[49]

[48] Yanagisawa, *Socio-Economic Changes*, pp. 61–62. As a witness in Tiruchirapalli stated, 'a debtor cultivator cannot be expected to be enthusiastic in the cultivation of his land' (*MBEC*, Vol. 2, *Written Evidence*, p.145). Gough's research on a wet zone village in Thanjavur gives more instances of a similar turn of events. In the early nineteenth century, most of the land in the village was held by Brahmans. Later, though, increasing numbers of village Brahmans left for the cities in search of better jobs and sold some land to outside merchants and landlords, resulting in an expansion of *kuttagai* tenure with fixed rent. Gough, *Rural Society in Southeast India*, p. 202.

[49] Marshall M. Bouton has already indicated that *pannai* cultivation was gradually transformed to tenant cultivation in Thanjavur district after the mid-

Emancipation of agricultural labourers

The emancipation of agricultural labourers was an important factor in promoting the trend for large landholders to lease out their land. The exodus of a considerable number of Depressed and other lower-caste members from villages to plantations in India and abroad, as discussed in Chapter 3, brought about a noticeable change in their socio-economic status.

The influence the emigration from villages had on the condition of labourers was already being recorded in the 1860s: 'There was a considerable improvement in the condition of non-agricultural labourers also, as, owing to the construction of several railways and other public works, the demand for labour was great and continuous.'[50] According to the 1863 inquiry by the Board of Revenue, 'grain wages also had in some instances risen, though not in the same ratio as the payment in money. In consequence of the greater demand for labour, the condition of the agricultural labourers had not deteriorated, but on the contrary had generally improved; and this was no less the case with other classes of labourers, whose wages had fully kept pace with the enhanced price of food, being in some cases doubled and trebled.'[51] Though the various reports did not concur as to whether labourers' wages rose or not, it seems certain that job opportunities outside the villages did affect the economic position of labourers considerably.

Emigration to overseas estates seems to have supported the efforts of low-caste labourers to emancipate themselves from their state of bondage. In the South Arcot district, 'the only way of escape for the padial from this condition of servitude and poverty is emigration. . . . Needless to say the emigration of padials is discouraged by their creditors. It is impressed upon the padial that it is a point of honour for him never to leave his master; and he is given to understand that he cannot legally do so. In some districts the creditors adopt the device of making the padial sign a fresh document every few years, so that in a court of

---

nineteenth century. Marshall M. Bouton, *Agrarian Radicalism in South India* (Princeton, 1985), pp. 183–84.

[50] Raghavaiyangar, *Memorandum*, p. 39. Bandopadhyay reveals that the influence of the emigration of Pallar labourers was noticed in the 1840s (*Agrarian Economy in Tamilnadu*, p. 131). The Collector of Trichinopoly district reported an interesting case, in which the *raiyats* complained that their cultivation was impeded owing to the frequent emigration of their Pallars and that 65 Pallars had deserted their villages (Board of Revenue, Vol. 2331 [TNA], 14 June 1852, pp. 6893–94).

[51] Raghavaiyangar, *Memorandum*, p. 39.

law it may be made to appear that a fresh debt has been incurred.'[52] Another record says 'sometimes some of them run away to the emigration depot at Nagapatam. Otherwise, as they are not able to discharge their debts, they have to toil for their masters perpetually.'[53]

There were many instances where an employer of labourers could not deter them from emigrating overseas even though he had made advances to them. As the Manual of the Tanjore district noted in 1883: 'These advances, however, are not unfrequently lost by the laborers emigrating to Ceylon or the Straits or otherwise failing to work them out.'[54] The 1921 Settlement Report of Tanjore has the following entry: 'Though "Kalavadi" is theoretically due at harvest time, it is alleged that some mirasidars defer payment till the next cultivation season is approaching in order to minimise the risk of their pannaiyals' desertion.'[55] Instances of *pannaiyals* deserting the *mirasidars* were thus not rare.[56]

Many low-caste emigrants returned to their native villages in India a few years later and some of them could buy livestock, agricultural

[52] Slater (ed.), *Some South Indian Villages*, p. 9.

[53] Ibid., p. 209. B. Hjejle and P.B. Mayer have already indicated the importance of the alternative employment available on the plantations as the real factor in the movement towards emancipation of low-caste agricultural labourers. Hjejle, 'Slavery and Agricultural Bondage'; P.B. Mayer, 'The Penetration of Capitalism in a South Indian District: The First 60 Years of Colonial Rule in Tiruchirapalli', *South Asia*, n.s., 3, 2 (1980). See also Christophe Z. Guilmoto, 'Towards a New Demographic Equilibrium: The Inception of Demographic Transition in South India', *IESHR* 29, 3 (1992), p. 287.

[54] *Manual of Tanjore District*, p. 311.

[55] P.B.R., No. 28, 12 Feb. 1921, p. 27, par. 31.

[56] The Manual of Tanjore district states that 'the general complaint now is, that the Panneiyals desert the Mirasidars, without working out their advances, and that the advances are often lost from want of assets' (*Manual of Tanjore District*, p. 381). 'In the good old times, the panniyals were actual slaves and the porakudies more obedient to the mirasidars. But owing to advancement of civilization and litigation, the mirasidars are now-a-days more annoyed by porakudies and pannials than the latter by the former. The mirassidars are, therefore, now in the habit of taking bonds from panniyals for moneys lent to them, and deeds of rent from them and the porakudies for house-sites, as the latter claim ownership thereto by reason of long enjoyment. The panniyals and porakudies are in these days at full liberty to resort to emigration whenever they like, and do what they please' (G.O., No. 1195, Revenue, 29 Oct. 1885, p. 469). Later in 1918, the Collector of Tanjore district noted that 'within the last 10 or 15 years the pannaiyal has become more independent and has been more inclined to contest the right of the mirasidars to the house-sites' (P.B.R., No. 10, 12 Jan. 1920, p. 104).

implements and even land with the money they had saved and brought back. The Royal Commission on Labour in India commented on this situation in 1931:

> To take the emigrants to Burma, it is largely true to say that many workers live there for more than two years, although everyone of them hopes to come back to his native village sooner or later and to set himself up as an independent landowner, or fairly well-to-do tenant or a small business man. Most of the emigrants go to Burma for a season or two and are therefore only temporary workers on the other side of the Bay. Similarly, but for a few thousands of workers, who have made Ceylon their permanent country, the others always look forward to go back with their savings to their villages in Southern India.[57]

In Madurai, 'agricultural labour classes [such] as "Kallars", "Pallars" and "Valayars" go to Ceylon and Malaya and with their savings buy a pair of cattle etc., and bid for lands as tenants'.[58] Similar data is available for the South Arcot district too: 'Their economic condition in Ceylon is vastly improved, and they have opportunities of saving money, and if they choose, of returning to their native districts and buying land.'[59] In Thanjavur, 'both classes [of tenants and labourers] emigrate, though chiefly the labourers, and all return with considerable savings, by means of which the porakudi becomes a landholder and the labourer sets-up as a tenant.'[60]

Probably more important than this direct economic impact is the fact that emigration had a great influence on the minds of the lower classes of rural society. They developed a sense of independence from the high-caste large landholders. According to the Census Report:

> One social effect of emigration has been indicated above, viz., a growth in independence and self-respect on the part of the depressed classes who go abroad. This is all to the good. A man who, little removed from praedial serfdom [such as *pannaiyal* system] in Tanjore, finds himself treated on his own merits like every one else when he crosses the sea, paid in cash for his labours and left to his own resources, must in the majority of cases benefit from

[57] *RCLI*, p. 322.

[58] Sivaswamy, 'Agricultural Leases in Ryotwari Areas', in *Tenant*, Part 2, p. 50.

[59] Slater (ed.), *Some South Indian Villages*, p. 9; ibid., p. 74.

[60] Raghavaiyangar, *Memorandum*, pp. 145–46. See also, *Royal Commission on Agriculture in India,* Vol. 3, pp. 362, 412, 601.

> the change, and it is probably the existence of the emigration current that has contributed most to the growth of consciousness among the depressed classes in India. . . .[61]

Though the above description of the census is over optimistic about the impact of emigration on labourers in the sense that it did not take into account the miserable conditions and low wages prevailing in the plantations where they worked, it cannot be denied that emigration had great impact on the minds of the labourers.

In this connection, the following record about the situation in Parakurichi village in Thanjavur is suggestive: 'Emigration of padials or poor tenants or peasant proprietors to foreign cities, such as Colombo, Rangoon, Singapore and Penang, is common. As these people do not go there with any capital, they seldom make profits, and as many of them go there through emigration depots they return poorer and emaciated. But their account of their wanderings and experiences in such foreign places (which have a halo of romance about them) usually induces people to try their chance and thus causes a general unrest in the village and its neighbourhood.'[62]

As early as 1879, the Manual of the Tinnevelly district noted that 'the spirit of independence has reached the laborer, who carries his labor into the best market and does not scruple to leave his master if he thinks he can better himself'.[63]

It was unavoidable that the relationship between masters and permanent labourers in South Indian villages was affected both by the appearance of new job opportunities and by the changes in the outlook of labourers. Since permanent labourers had been the nucleus of the agricultural labour force in wet areas hired by landowning higher-caste communities, landowners encountered increasing difficulty in securing the necessary labour force to cultivate their farms. According to the Settlement Report of Trichinopoly district, 'the facility of emigration, and the high wages paid to coolies by the Railway Company, have much

[61] *Census of India, 1931,* Vol. 14, *Madras,* Part 1, p. 93. See also Kumar, *Land and Caste*, p. 142. Weakening of the labourer's traditional dependence on the landlord was asserted by Kumar, 'Agrarian Relations: South India', p. 232.

[62] Slater (ed.), *Some South Indian Villages*, p. 82.

[63] *Manual of Tinnevelly District*, p. 30. Though about the later period, J. Harriss commented that sentiments of equality were reinforced to some extent by the experience of low-caste people outside the village and by the experience of some Depressed-caste members especially in the Army. John Harriss, *Capitalism and Peasant Farming: Agrarian Structure and Ideology in Northern Tamil Nadu* (Delhi, 1982), pp. 248, 269.

reduced the number of agricultural labourers in the neighbourhood of Trichinopoly, and the Merasidars now complain that they have not hands enough to get their wet crops off the ground before they are very ripe and the grain becomes loosened in the ear.'[64] Later, in 1907 in the same district, 'these [wage] rates are said to be much higher than those paid in the past, but they need to be higher yet to check the emigration which is now going on to other countries, and the supply of *pannaiyals* is not at present equal to the demand. . . . Daily wages have also risen everywhere, but the supply of day labour is as unequal to the demand as that of *pannaiyals*. . . . The complaints of landowners of the scarcity of labour are loud.'[65]

Difficulties in securing labourers were common in the Presidency. 'The tendency everywhere appears to be for an increase in grain wages, and the complaints often made are that it is difficult to obtain labourers for the due customary rates of wages or to make them work with zeal or full time as in the old days for these wages. . . . This shows that custom is gradually giving way to competition.'[66] And 'a struggle is going on to adjust the old customary rates of wages to the new conditions under which there is increasing mobility of labour.'[67]

A scarcity of labour was also reported in Thanjavur district, in most parts of which landholders complained bitterly about the defection of their serfs and the scarcity of labour in general. The result was that the remaining labourers could demand much better terms than their fathers. Everywhere working hours were reported to have decreased.[68] The Set-

[64] *Papers Relating to the Survey and Settlement of the Trichinopoly District*, pp. 9–10. The Collector of Madura district was of opinion that great number of labouring classes emigrated to Ceylon and the Straits Settlements and that it was difficult to get labour for ordinary repairs to roads and tanks, etc. (G.O., No. 366, Confidential, Revenue, 27 May 1888, par. 24; P.B.R., 14 Feb. 1893, p. 12).

[65] *Gazetteers of Trichinopoly District*, p. 152. See also Mayer, 'Penetration of Capitalism'.

[66] Raghavaiyangar, *Memorandum*, p. 151 n. 70.

[67] Ibid., p. 290. For the shortage of agricultural labour in Thanjavur, see Evans, 'Agricultural Bondage to Plantation Contract', p. 60.

[68] *Gazetteer of Tanjore District*, p. 111. The Director of Agriculture reported in 1906 that 'in the Tanjore delta, many complaints are heard from landowners of the growing scarcity and independence of the day labourers in consequence of emigration' (*Season and Crop Report for Fasli 1316 [1906–1907]*, p. 4). The shortening of the hours of work put in by agricultural labourers has been already discussed by M. Atchi Reddy, 'Work and Leisure: Daily Working Hours of Agricultural Labourers, Nellore District', *IESHR* 28, 1 (1991). While the shortage of labour caused a rise in the wage paid to daily labourers, the grain wage paid to permanent labourers was reported to be unaltered. However, the *raiyats*

tlement Report of 1921 confirms this: 'Returning to the delta pannaiyal, my inquiries show that increase in grain wages is distinctly exceptional. It is more generally alleged that pay has risen indirectly by shortening of hours of work or by an increase in toddy money.'[69] In Palakkurichi Village in Thanjavur, 'the landlords complain that it has become very difficult nowadays to extract work from pannayals, as they fight for more leisure. At the time of my visit I was told that one Pannayal had run away and the master was trying to get him back by force. There is no unemployment among agricultural labourers or educated persons.'[70] Both an increase in emigration and a scarcity of labour for repairs to roads and tanks and for coffee estates were reported by the Collector of Madura district in 1888.[71] The situation was no different in Tirunelveli district, where the number of homestead labourers was comparatively small and decreasing annually. Emigration to Ceylon was exceptionally easy, and the Tinnevelly Pallar knew that both there and on the tea estates of the high ranges he could command a good wage. 'I do not mean that labour is fully mobile, but that if a landlord does not treat his labourers fairly according to their ideas, the latter are not slow to seek employment elsewhere.'[72]

Later, Sayana noted that in the past labourers on the East Coast had for a generation or more been in the habit of emigrating to Burma, Ceylon or the Straits whenever times were bad or the master troublesome, and that in Thanjavur at any rate the labourers were skilled at threatening emigration to extort better conditions from the master.[73] And, with

---

had to offer various small additions in the shape of occasional free meals, etc., in order to retain the services of the permanent labourers (*Season and Crop Report for Fasli 1317 [1907–1908]*, p. 4; *Season and Crop Report for Fasli 1321 [1911–1912]*, p. 4).

[69] P.B.R., No. 28, 12 Feb. 1921, p. 28, par. 31. See also *Season and Crop Report for Fasli 1316 (1906–1907)*, p. 4. It was also stated that 'emigration and the rice mills are drawing off labour from the land in Tanjore and landlords are being forced to give better terms to retain their labour' ('Notes to G.O., No. 748, Confidential, Revenue, 29 Mar. 1919', p. 8).

[70] Thomas and Ramakrishnan (eds.), *Some South Indian Villages: A Resurvey*, p. 141.

[71] G.O., No. 366, Confidential, Revenue, 27 may 1888, par. 24.

[72] 'Notes to G.O. Nos. 3594–95, Revenue, 9 December 1914', p. 76. For Chingleput district, G.O., No. 2435, Revenue, 26 June 1918, p. 9. See also a report of the Director of Agriculture in *Season and Crop Report for Fasli 1316 (1906–1907)*, p. 4; *Season and Crop Report for Fasli 1317 (1907–1908)*, p. 4.

[73] V.V. Sayana, *The Agrarian Problems of Madras Province* (Madras, 1946), p. 252.

the widening of opportunities for emigration and various kinds of employment, 'the "Pannaiyal" too began to feel the irksomeness of tied service and longed for some amount of freedom'.[74]

The rapid expansion of groundnut cultivation in South India accelerated this trend in some districts. As the Director of Agriculture stated in 1906, 'at Palur [in South Arcot district] so many labourers now cultivate small patches of ground-nut on their own account that it is found very difficult to obtain labour for the picotas [an indigenous water lift] during the season of the irrigated ground-nut'.[75]

Thus, available evidence points to the increased mobility of labourers, the development of a sense of independence among them and the difficulty the large farmers had in securing them as permanent labourers.

Evidence from early twentieth-century Tiruchirapalli indicates that some resistance on the part of labourers took the form of a mass movement. The Collector of Trichinopoly district, in the wet land area of the Kaveri delta, noted instances where attempts were made to cut down the grain wages of labourers but these attempts were not successful since the labourers went on strike.[76] Later, in 1930, the Annual Report of the Labour Department states that *Adi Dravida padiyals* in Chingleput district went on strike on the grounds that their wages were inadequate and thereby won an increase.[77] In the 1940s, the labour force showed even stronger and better organised resistance.

Led by a leader they dictate their wages for doing harvesting or

[74] Sivaswamy, *Tenant*, Part 1, p. 64. The Director of Agriculture also stated in 1926: 'There is much discontent, now that he [landless labourer] has discovered that to be such a slave is neither pre-ordained nor in the eternal fitness of things. The efficiency of the worker has been lowered by such discontent. . . .' The labourers were reported to be wakening up in a most remarkable degree (*Royal Commission on Agriculture in India,* Vol. 3, pp. 59, 336). In some cases, the depressed classes had got, even by the door of election, into such organisations as co-operative societies and village *panchayats* (ibid., p. 341).

[75] *Season and Crop Report for Fasli 1316 (1906–1907)*, p. 4; *Season and Crop Report for Fasli 1317 (1907–1908),* p. 4. See also Baker, *Rural Economy*, p. 152.

[76] P.B.R., No. 243, 3 July 1908, p. 9.

[77] G.O., No. 3218L, Labour Department, 21 Dec. 1931, pp. 3–4. In this connection, a witness in Ellore presented an interesting case before the Indian Industrial Commission. The workers in his factory, who had been recruited from the ordinary agricultural cooly class, tended to go on strike. Indian Industrial Commission, *Minutes of Evidence,* Vol. 3, *Madras and Bangalore* (Calcutta, 1918), pp. 127–28.

groundnut picking as piece-work. In the Tanjore area they have resisted their subjection to Kallars about whom we will shortly refer, and been able to rise in the social scale as share-tenants and farm servants. In the Godavari and Kistna deltas untouchables prefer to be casual workers rather than permanent farm servants. 'The Panchamas' who were once satisfied with being engaged as 'Palerus' are today extremely reluctant to work as such. For instance, they prefer to go to forest work . . . or are more anxious to become cultivators of others' lands. They prefer to be casual workers in almost every deltaic place. Thus there has been a steady and even very marked decrease in the last twenty years in the number of people who are willing to work as Palerus.[78]

Thus, as a result of increased emigration, landlords began to experience not only labour shortages but also difficulties in getting their *pannaiyals* to work as hard as they used to. It is possible to argue that, together with the effect of the intensification of agriculture (to be discussed below) this difficulty induced landlords to lease out a part or whole of their land instead of cultivating them using the hired labour. In South Arcot, for example, 'this practice [of subletting] is reported to be on the increase in the Tirukkoyilur division owing to the difficulty experienced by landowners in procuring labourers who prefer to cultivate lands themselves to getting wages for their work every day.'[79] A similar trend was reported in Chingleput, where subletting was on the increase as the Depressed-caste members who had hitherto worked as farm servants 'now own lands themselves and are becoming more and more independent of the landowning classes'.[80] In 1914, subletting was, on the whole, increasing in Tirunelveli, where 'the spread of education may account for this in part by exciting a repugnance to field labour on the one hand, and on the other, a preference in the actual cultivation for the status of a tenant rather than that of a cooly'.[81]

[78] K.G. Sivaswamy, *Caste and Standard of Living versus Farms Rents and Wages* (Madras: Servants of India Society, 1947), p. 13.

[79] 'Notes to G.O. Nos. 3594–95, Revenue, 9 December 1914', p. 20.

[80] *Jamabandi Report for Fasli 1332 (1922–23)*, p. 10.

[81] Ibid., p. 22. In Vadamalaipuram village in Ramnad district, the 1936 survey revealed not only an increase in the area let to tenants but also the dearth of labour, which made even large landholders work in the fields with their family members (Thomas and Ramakrishnan [eds.], *Some South Indian Villages: A Resurvey*, pp. 10, 40). This case also seems to suggest the possible relationship between the dearth of labour and the expansion of the tenancy system. The acquisition of land by labourers stimulated this trend. In Nellore district also, 'the assignment of land to the members of the depressed classes has to some

As Sivaswamy has shown, the *varam* was an evolution from the older custom of permanent farm service, a custom which fell into disuse with a breakdown in the sense of mutual obligation and its replacement by a wage relationship.[82]

Intensification of agriculture

It is important to note that these labour problems appeared just when agriculture was becoming more labour intensive and more painstaking care and industry from labourers and farm managers were required for a better crop yield, as mentioned in the previous chapter. The intensity of labour input and the hours of labour attained greater importance as a factor determining agricultural productivity.

The advantage enjoyed by a larger farm over a small peasant-run farm tended to lessen in this period. As a general rule, a large farm depending upon non-family labourers required very strict supervision of labourers by the farm manager to make them work as industriously as family labour. Even with such strict control, it may have been difficult to secure from non-family labour the same quality and intensity of work that family members produced, particularly when agriculture was

---

extent induced them to refuse to work as farm servants and tended to increase the growth of sublettings' (*Jamabandi Report for Fasli 1332 [1921–22]*, p. 10). A similar trend was observed in other districts in South India: N.G. Ranga's survey of villages in Guntur district clarified that 'the tendency among Panchamas is to favour independent life . . . and the efficiency of the present generation of annual servants is much lower than that of the past generation. This is one of the reasons why more and more ryots prefer to lease out their lands' (N.G. Ranga, *Economic Organisation of Indian Villages*, Vol. 1, Deltaic Villages [Bezwada, 1926], p. 182). A case observed by M.N. Srinivas, though in later decades, deserves attention: in a Mysore village, 'Harijans had begun to claim all kind of rights' and, since bigger landowners found it difficult to secure enough labour, they generally leased out a part of their land to tenants in order to reduce their management problems (*The Remembered Village* [Berkeley, Los Angeles and London, 1979], pp. 197, 212).

[82] Sivaswamy, 'Agricultural leases in Ryotwari Areas', *Tenant,* Part 2, p. 48. Eric Stokes has also considered the loosening of the hold of rich farmers over predial labour. Eric Stokes, *The Peasant and the Raj: Studies in Agrarian Society and Peasant Rebellion in Colonial India* (Cambridge, 1978), p. 276. See also Ian Stone, *Canal Irrigation in British India: Perspectives on Technological Change in a Peasant Economy* (Cambridge, 1984), p. 122; Tom G. Kessinger, *Vilyatpur, 1848–1968*: *Social and Economic Change in a North Indian Village* (New Delhi, 1979), pp. 139–46, 197.

becoming more intensive, and much more care and attention from labourers was required.

It was observed in 1916 in Eruvelliput village in South Arcot district that 'the customary method in transplanting is to put several plants together into one hole in the levelled mud of the rice field. Experiment has proved that if each seedling is separately planted and all are evenly spaced, there is a considerable saving of seed and a heavier crop. The new method is spreading, but as yet very slowly. . . . The cooly whom they employ will not change their methods unless compelled to do so by strict supervision. They want to do their work in the semi-automatic manner attained by unchanging habit, and not to tax their brains and think about what they are doing.'[83] Again, 'it [the new method] required more personal supervision'. Another interesting observation is that 'those who cultivate the land themselves find it enough if they supply only 12 cartloads, while others who cultivated with the help of labourers have to apply about 24 cartloads of manure, for the land is not so well ploughed as in the other case'.[84]

A source from Thanjavur indicates the difficulty a large farm encountered in securing enough labour at the peak season. 'After the grain has ripened, it is allowed to dry for two to three weeks before it is reaped; but in the case of large estates, the reaping is delayed a few days longer from the amount of labor required not being at once forthcoming.' The same source also suggests that the application of manure in single crop land was often neglected 'where the holdings are very large'.[85] In Tirunelveli, 'the method of cultivation followed by the small holder in this country, especially if he holds dry lands or wet lands under a precarious source, is as a rule better than that adopted by the owner of extensive safe wet lands'.[86] The fragmented state of landhold-

[83] Slater (ed.), *Some South Indian Villages*, p. 5.

[84] Thomas and Ramakrishnan (eds.), *Some South Indian Villages: A Resurvey*, pp. 163, 167.

[85] *Manual of Tanjore District*, pp. 379, 348.

[86] P.B.R., No. 200, 5 June 1909, pp. 7–8.

A. Satyanarayana revealed many important findings in his recent publication on Andhra peasants (*Andhra Peasants under British Rule: Agrarian Relations and the Rural Economy 1900–1940* [Delhi, 1990]), in which he stresses the technical superiority of the large farmers. He remarks: 'The settlement officer of Guntur came across instances where "large ryots" carried on (paddy) cultivation more scientifically. They "imported" manure "in large quantities" from the neighbouring districts' (p. 114). However the report of the settlement officer of Guntur, on which Satyanarayana bases his assertion, seems to indicate a different fact. 'In only two places did I find ryots who had actually purchased manure

ings in South India further offset the possible advantage a large farm might have possessed. The landholdings at this time were formed mostly of small plots of less than one acre. For instance, in Dusi village, North Arcot, a large land area of 11.94 acres was made up of 26 small plots, of which the largest was 1.1 acres.[87]

The importance of care and attention paid by the farmer and his family to cultivation is well illustrated in the following case from Tirunelveli district, where the amount of land still available for cultivation was in all *taluks* negligible and the growing tendency towards intensive methods was reported to be the most satisfactory feature of the economic outlook.

> All these are the places where it is not enough that the landowner shall wait for the season and then give orders to a 'tenant'. The supply for the wet lands is precarious, and, if it does not come or comes out of season, resources and patience are needed; a gingelly crop must be sown in the nick of time in place of the paddy that has failed, or the last drop of water left in the tank must be husbanded

---

last year for their fields. One of them was a very large ryot at Karenchedu where cultivation is carried on more scientifically than in most places in the delta. He told me that he imported *pig* manure in large quantities from the Nellore district and proved to me that he sustained a loss on every acre of paddy he grew. (He explained this away afterwards). But even here in my inspection I came across a few acres of molakolukulu paddy which bore at least twice as good a crop as the neighbouring fields. It was explained to me that it belonged to some Gollas (shepherds) who are able to manure the crops well. Again and again I found a similar patch and was told that the owner had only two or three acres and so could manure all his lands. The custom undoubtedly is for a ryot to take up more lands than he can farm properly. I heard of a well authenticated case of a man who was compelled to sell half his land and obtained a much larger produce from the remaining half than he did for the whole farm before' ('Report of the Settlement Officer of Guntur', P.B.R., No. 463, 17 Dec. 1903, p. 24). The settlement officer clearly asserted, contrary to Satyanarayana's interpretation, that the large farm was less properly managed and that the yield of the smaller farm was higher than that of the larger farm.

Satyanarayana also argues that in Coastal Andhra districts of Guntur and Nellore 'big ryots' increasingly used chemical manure (p. 115). Though the evidence surely indicates the existence of large farmers who used chemical fertilisers in Nellore district, the total amount of sales of chemical fertiliser mentioned in the document shows that the number of such cases was very few, probably only one or two, in the district (*Royal Commission on Agriculture in India,* Vol. 3, p. 762). It may be an exaggeration to conclude from this evidence that large *raiyats* in general increasingly used chemical fertiliser.

[87] Thomas and Ramakrishnan (eds.), *Some South Indian Villages: A Resurvey*, p. 184. See also Slater (ed.), *Some South Indian Villages*, p. 7.

> and led to the field at the critical moment; the land is by the register entitled only to a dry crop, but the united labour of a family will lower it till water is bound to reach it, and fearless of 'penal rates' the peasant owner will turn a dismal waste into a smiling garden. In many places the tank fills only during *pisanam* and to the non-cultivating owner the value of such land is but one crop in the year. The cultivating owner can make double, or even three times, that income; wells are sunk, and, by the steady labour of himself, his family and joint owners, precious crops—chillies, onions, brinjals and cholam, exceeding in value even the paddy of *pisanam*—fill up the interval between the paddy seasons.[88]

The importance of a farmer's personal participation and attention to cultivation is further evidenced by the following statement from the Settlement Report of Tinnevelly district: 'Thus in one village in which at last settlement the Brahmans owned some 2,000 acres and now possess less than 200, a Brahman villager pointed out a Naicker who was going to his field, to plough his land taking his food for the day with him, saying that that man was worth about Rs. 10,000. He added "How can the Brahman compete with the Naick? Suppose a Naick's land yields four pothis of cotton, the Brahman's close by of equal extent will give less than two".'[89]

It is appropriate to conclude that, with the development of intensive cultivation, the direct participation and devotion to cultivation of the farm managers was an important factor in securing a better yield; large farms employing non-family labourers encountered difficulties making hired help work as industriously as family members on their own small farms, thus lessening the advantage large farms had possessed in the past.[90] This conclusion is in accord with the view advanced by Francesca Bray, who has mainly studied East and Southeast Asian countries and concluded that as rice cultivation became more intensive, there was a marked tendency for units of management to become smaller

[88] *Gazetteer of Tinnevelly District*, p. 192.

[89] P.B.R., No. 565, 4 Nov. 1910, p. 15.

[90] In this connection, an observation made by N.G. Ranga in the 1920s deserves attention. His farm-cost enquiry in wet villages in Guntur district revealed that most *raiyats* found it more profitable to lease out their land after such holdings exceeded the limit of ten acres than to cultivate it and it was much more profitable to do so once the holding exceeded twenty acres (Ranga, *Economic Organisation*, pp. 57, 62, 88, 90).

rather than larger, usually taking the form of family farms supplying the bulk of their own labour.[91]

Higher caste migration to the cities

The third factor which stimulated the second path to the expansion of the tenancy system was the emigration of people from higher castes to urban jobs. The higher-caste landowning communities, especially Brahmans, grew interested in urban employment, and a considerable number of people migrated to urban areas to take jobs and obtain a better education for their sons, consequently losing their commitment to agricultural management.

The case of Gangaikondan village in Tirunelveli district illustrates the changes brought about by the increasing interest of the Brahman community in urban work. As revealed by the University of Madras survey of 1936, the number of Brahman families in the village decreased from 100 to 75 between 1916 and 1936.

An aged Brahmin gentleman told me that some fifty years back

[91] Francesca Bray, *The Rice Economies: Technology and Development in Asian Societies* (Oxford, 1986). This implies that intensification of agricultural practice does not necessarily strengthen the economic position of large farmers versus their farm servants or lead to an intensification of labour exploitation by the masters under any circumstances.

The advantage a small family farm possessed over a larger farm has been stressed by Sumit Guha, who stated that in the Deccan economy between 1916 and 1947, the area owned by landholders owning less than 15 acres increased, indicating the tendency towards smaller units of cultivation and that the large farm had no advantage over the small, since the latter could superexploit its own family labour (Sumit Guha, 'Some Aspects of Rural Economy in the Deccan 1820–1940', pp. 238–40). The importance of family labour in raising the yield in paddy cultivation has been suggested by Alan Heston and Dharma Kumar, 'The Persistence of Land Fragmentation in Peasant Agriculture: An Analysis of South Asian Cases', *Explorations in Economic History* 20, 2 (Apr. 1983), p. 207. D.W. Attwood, who studied the changes in landholdings in a village in Maharashtra state between 1920 and 1970, observed a tendency of some of the poor to get richer instead of getting poorer in terms of landholding and found one reason to explain this in the fact that small holders have been shown to invest more labour and supervision per acre, generating higher yields than those obtained on larger farms with nonmechanised technology (Attwood, 'Why Some of the Poor Get Richer'). See also Donald W. Attwood, *Rising Cane: The Political Economy of Sugar in Western India* (Boulder, San Francisco and Oxford, 1992), Chapter 7. See also Robert, 'Economic Change and Agrarian Organization', pp. 75–76.

> they were 120 families strong, possessed 100 ploughs between them, owned 800 acres of nanja [irrigated] land out of the 1000 acres, 3000 out of 3,500 acres of black soil and 3,000 out of 3,500 acres of red soil in the village with a further right to a poramboke area of 3500 acres for purposes of grazing cattle—all between 106 share-holders. But their total possessions in the village today have dwindled to 250 acres of nanja land, 100 acres of black soil land and 1000 acres of red soil land of which only 100 are cultivable. This is because the Brahmins ceased to take personal interest in land. They were content with merely letting the land on lease or varam on terms more or less dictated by the tenant. From active agriculturists they have degenerated into idle rent-receivers. . . . The increasing resort to higher, English education, has been another drain for Brahmin families. They were not only the first to take to it, today they are almost the one community in the village who have sought it wholesale. Although this may not fully account for their decline in numbers in the village, it is certainly the cause of emigration of a considerable number of Brahmin families and their lack of interest in land. It looks as though the Brahmin thrives best in towns and the rural soil is uncongenial to his genius.[92]

What is indicated here is that (1) though the Brahmans had been active agriculturists some decades before, they had ceased to take a personal interest in land, gave up hands-on farm management and (2) began to let their land out to tenants; (3) this change led them to lose some of their land; in addition, (4) their increasing desire for higher education was one of the causes of their emigration to urban areas and their decreased interest in land.

Similar instances can be seen in other districts. In North Arcot district, it was reported in 1904 that subletting was prevalent where Brahman landowners had other commitments, as lawyers, officials or traders. In Thanjavur also, the practice of subletting was widespread, especially in Brahman villages, and also where land was passing out of the hands of the cultivating class into the possession of pleaders, officials and merchants. In Tiruchirapalli, subletting was reported as being resorted to by absentee landlords and by those who followed professions other than agriculture.[93]

[92] Thomas and Ramakrishnan (eds.), *Some South Indian Villages: A Resurvey*, p. 61. The Gazetteer states that the general story was that, 'where fifty years ago there were thirty or forty families [of Brahmans], there are now but five left' (*Gazetteer of Tinnevelly District*, p. 373). See also Ludden, *Peasant History*, p. 158.

[93] 'Notes to G.O. Nos. 3594–95, Revenue, 9 December 1914', pp. 20–21.

Thus the second path leading to the expansion of tenant cultivation may be summarised as follows: (1) Due to the increasing emigration of agricultural labourers to overseas estates and their growing sense of independence, large farmers experienced mounting difficulties in securing labourers and making them work as hard as before. (2) With the general trend in agriculture being towards intensive cultivation, the relative advantage of the large farm disappeared;[94] instead, care and attention paid to cultivation by farmers acquired greater importance. (3) At the same time, the Brahman community, the largest landowning community in the wet villages, became increasingly interested in urban jobs and higher education; some Brahmans migrated to urban areas, losing their interest in cultivating land.

All these changes induced some high-caste landowners who formerly had managed their farms by employing labourers to lease out a part or all of their land to tenants, who would devote themselves to cultivating the leased land with the help of family members. Some landowners even sold part or all of their land. Thus 'cultivation by owners with the aid of farm-servants, which was in vogue in 1916–17, has been slowly giving way to lease of lands on share or fixed rents' and 'the number of tenants are increasing while the number of farm servants are decreasing'.[95]

[94] Charlesworth also indicated the trend among farmers to input more family labour in Western India. Charlesworth, *Peasants and Imperial Rule*, p. 220; idem, 'The Impact of the Interwar Depression on Agriculture in the Bombay Presidency: A Case of Further Arrested Development?' in Clive Dewey (ed.), *Arrested Development in India* (Delhi, 1988), p. 265.

[95] Thomas and Ramakrishnan (eds.), *Some South Indian Villages: A Resurvey*, p. 349; Sivaswamy, 'Agricultural leases in Ryotwari Areas', *Tenant*, Part 2, p. 48. A village in Thanjavur, according to K. Gough, witnessed both a significant decrease in the number of farm servants and a rapid expansion of tenants in the Depressed-caste population. She reports that, by 1951, 38 percent of the Depressed-caste members had become sharecroppers, whereas the percentage of tied labourers had fallen to 22 percent (E. Kathleen Gough, 'The Social Structure of a Tanjore Village', in McKim Marriott [ed.], *Village India: Studies in the Little Community* [Chicago, 1955], p. 43). Sivertsen also observed the same change in a Thanjavur village (Dagfinn Sivertsen, *When Caste Barriers Fall: A Study of Social and Economic Change in a South Indian Village* [Oslo, 1963], p. 16). In Nellore district also a transformation of a large section of farm servants into tenant cultivators was suggested by M. Atchi Reddy ('The Commercialization of Agriculture in Nellore District 1850–1916', p. 180; M. Atchi Reddy, 'Agrarian Structure of Nellore: Tenants and Tenancy 1800–1980', *Social Scientist* 166 [March 1987]).

Satyanarayana asserts that the peasant-bourgeoisie in colonial Andhra

Two Types of Tenants

As may be expected from the above analysis of the two paths to the tenancy system, the tenants in South India at that period were of two types, originating from different social groups: (i) former *pattadars*, who belonged to the cultivators' caste but had been reduced to tenants as a result of the commercialisation of agriculture, and (ii) members of lower castes who had become elevated from permanent or daily labourers to tenants.

In 1912, a report from North Arcot divided tenants into two kinds: (*a*) those who were *pattadars* themselves in a village cultivating others' land on the *varam* system; and (*b*) those who were more or less

---

attempted to increase their occupational holdings by leasing-in the land of others (*Andhra Peasants,* p. 112). One piece of evidence to which he refers is a description from Baliga's study, which stated that the pattadar 'whose lands are *sufficient* for all their requirements' took additional lands on lease to make up an economically viable holding (B.S. Baliga, *Studies in Madras Administration,* Vol. 2 [Madras, 1960], p. 130; emphasis added). Though the name of the government document on which Baliga based his description is not given, he was certainly citing sentences from a 1914 Government Order ('Note to G.O. Nos. 3594–5, Revenue, 9 December 1914'). What the original document said, however, was: 'The pattadar whose patta lands are *insufficient* for all his requirements' took additional land on lease (ibid., p. 102; emphasis added). Baliga made a crucial mistake when he cited the original government report; he wrote 'sufficient' instead of the original 'insufficient'. N.G. Ranga's 1925 survey of Guntur district does not simply point to the trend for big *raiyats* to lease-in land: while noting that, 'in the last four years', big *raiyats* 'have begun to rent others' lands', it also reports, as mentioned already, that in most places, most of the *raiyats* found it more profitable to lease out their lands when such holdings exceeded a limit of ten acres than to cultivate them (N.G. Ranga, *Economic Organisation,* Vol. 1, Deltaic Villages, pp. 62–63). The result of the 1930 Economic Enquiry Committee also reveals that while in villages in dry zones of Kistna district and in upland *taluks* of East Godavari district, most rented land was occupied by bigger *raiyats,* landless people and smaller *raiyats* were the main lessee classes in irrigated villages in delta zones, leasing-in more than half of the rented area there (*Report of the Economic Enquiry Committee*, Vol. 1 [Madras, 1930], pp. 33–35). Sayana's study, to which Satyanarayana referred, also emphasised that the bulk of the tenants were small farmers and landless people and that cases of large landlords' leasing-in were observable only in some villages (V.V. Sayana, *The Agrarian Problems of Madras Province* [Madras, 1949], p. 198). Thus, while, as correctly indicated by Satyanarayana, there were some big *raiyats* who leased-in others' land in some areas of colonial Andhra, it may be misleading to exaggerate the trend in the large landowning class to increase operational holdings, considering that the large landlords were the main lessors of tenancy land. Rather, the general trend was for the smaller peasants and the landless peasants to increase their operational holdings.

labourers living in the village without any *patta*, and who worked not as farm-servants of *pattadars* but as independent lessees of land generally owned by Brahman *pattadars* in the village.[96] Though the criterion adopted for the classification is not exactly the same as mine, the observation roughly accords with my categorisation of tenants.

The existence of tenants who had formerly been labourers is suggested by some documents. A report on Thanjavur tenants stated in 1914 that 'the Tanjore porakkudis, as I know, consist mostly of Pariahs and Pallis, the latter more commonly known by the name of Padayachis. Both are low in their social status'.[97] As we saw in Chapter 2, in nineteenth century Thanjavur, most Paraiyars were agricultural labourers, while the Pallis or Padayachis were mainly agricultural labourers or tenants though some were landholding farmers. Thus it may be inferred that some low-caste agricultural labourers became elevated from the status of labourers to that of tenants. A report from Tiruchirapalli more explicitly indicates that some tenants or sharecroppers evolved out of the agricultural labour class. As discussed in Chapter 2, *mattu-varam* was one type of *varam* sharecropper, one who ploughed the land with his own oxen. 'The position of a *mattu-varam* man may not be quite satisfactory as that of the *varam* tenant but it evidently is an improvement on that of the agricultural labourer from whom he has sprung and to whom he has to revert in case a landlord does not care to entrust him with the cultivation of the land.'[98] The 1948 report of K.G. Sivaswamy states that in the Kulittalai *taluk* of Tiruchirapalli, wet land was leased to Pallars on a sharecropping basis.[99] These reports serve as evidence that some tenants had their origin in the labourer stratum.

Sivaswamy's observation presents a slightly complex picture of the tenants in Madurai. In the Periyar area of this district, while agricultural communities such as the Kallars and Thevars were reported to have large blocks on lease from absentee landlords and to be subletting them to Pallars and others, agricultural labour classes as Kallars [*sic*], Pallars and Valayans went to Ceylon and Malaya, as mentioned already, bought a pair of cattle etc. with their savings and bid for land as tenants. Some of the Perumalai Kallars of Usilampattinadu settled as tenants around Madurai. In the Cumbam and Periyakulam areas, Pillai belonging to the

[96] G.O., No. 3594, Confidential, Revenue, 9 Dec. 1914, p. 32.
[97] 'Notes to G.O. Nos. 3594–95, Revenue, 9 December 1914', p. 69.
[98] Ibid., p. 75.
[99] Sivaswamy, 'Agricultural leases in Ryotwari Areas', in *Tenant*, Part 2, p. 44.

Vellalar caste were the main tenants.[100] In this district also, Sivaswamy reveals, the tenants were of two groups: those from 'agricultural communities' like Kallars; and those from Depressed and other low castes who purchased cattle and tried to elevate themselves to tenants.

In the Coimbatore district, land irrigated by wells (garden land) could be cultivated eight months a year. However, to cultivate garden land, two sets of oxen were needed to raise the water from the wells, and sheep and goats were necessary to fertilise the fields. 'Leases of garden lands necessitate a higher class of tenant than leases of wet lands. . . . He [tenant] must be a man well removed from the field labourer class.'[101] Unlike Thanjavur, tenants cultivating garden land in this district belonged to the type (i) mentioned earlier. In the Salem district also, because well-irrigated garden land demanded high expenditure and outlay for cultivation, the people of Depressed castes were in no position to afford it and resorted to cultivating dry land.[102]

To summarise, (1) there were then two types of tenant, having different origins: one belonging to the Vellalar and other 'agricultural' castes, and the other being Depressed-caste members and low-caste Non-Brahmans who had been formerly working as agricultural labourers, and (2) the former often cultivated the land of absentee landlords, while the latter worked as sharecroppers under village landlords.

Tenant Farms

As we have seen already, tenants may be categorised into two groups, sharecroppers and fixed rent tenants. The Tirunelveli district furnishes us with a detailed account of the tenant system as practiced in 1912.

> *Kinds of lease*—(*A*) *Wet lands*—(*a*) *Fixed rent* (*Ver. 'Kattu-kuttagai'*):—The rent may be either in money or in kind. The usual terms are—(i) The cultivator enters upon the land at the beginning of the agricultural season, that is, in the month of Chitrai (April–May). (ii) It is the cultivator's duty to manure the land according to a customary scale. This process includes the penning of sheep in the land. (iii) The cultivator bears all expenses of cultivation. He

[100] Ibid., p. 40.
[101] G.O., No. 3594, Confidential, Revenue, 9 Dec. 1914, p. 56.
[102] Sivaswamy, 'Agricultural leases in Ryotwari Areas', in *Tenant*, Part 2, p. 46.

may receive an advance from the pattadar; if so, he will repay it at any rate of interest up to 20 per cent. or so. (iv) The straw goes to the tenant; the pattadar may receive a bundle from a field as a sort of gratuity. (v) If the rent is in kind, the produce is handed over to the pattadar at the threshing floor. If the land is cropped twice, three-quarters of the lease amount will be paid at the harvest of the first crop. (vi) The pattadar receives no rent for land required for the purpose of a seed-bed. If the pattadar has no seed-bed land, he pays the lessee four to eight annas for every 8 cents of land so used, the amount being deducted from the rent fixed. (vii) If the crop gives a short outturn and the tenant cannot be blamed, the pattadar will occasionally forego part of his demand. If the crop fails altogether, the pattadar gets nothing and the tenant loses the cost of cultivation. (viii) The pattadar pays the Government assessment.

(*b*) *The Varam tenure.*—By this system, the produce of the land is divided at the threshing floor between pattadar and tenant in a fixed proportion. The tenant's share varies from one-third to one-half of the gross produce. The lease is invariably for one year only. Of the conditions, which I have enumerated as attaching to leases for fixed rent, numbers (i) to (iv), (vii) and (viii) apply to the varam lease also.[103]

The relationship between the ecological condition of a region and the type of tenancy most dominant was so varied according to locality that it seems very difficult to draw any general conclusion. In North Arcot, around the same time, the system in vogue was almost entirely a sharing one: the landlord paying the assessment and taking a certain share of the gross produce, while the tenant bore all the expenses of cultivation and received the rest of produce and the straw. The leases were generally orally contracted and were for one cultivation season only. Out of 4,604 acres only 368 were leased out for a fixed rent in kind or money and the remaining 4,532 acres were let on *varam* (sharecropping).[104] In the Salem district, where wet lands occupied only a small part of the total area, the general practice was sharecropping. Fixed rent tenancy was confined to such wet and garden land as were assured of a water-supply.[105] In the Madathukulam area of Coimbatore district, while wet land in river irrigated areas was leased at a fixed amount of produce, dry land and garden land were leased for a fixed

[103] G.O., No. 3594, Confidential, Revenue, 9 Dec. 1914, p. 112.

[104] Ibid., p. 19. Annual lease was the common form of contract in the wet land in Coimbatore district and in Tirunelveli district (ibid., pp. 53, 118).

[105] G.O., No. 1029, Revenue, 7 Oct. 1903, p. 23.

sum of money. Sharecropping occurred only in areas irrigated by minor rain-fed tanks.[106] In Tirunelveli district, the most common form of rent in wet land was fixed rent in produce; rent in money was demanded only for the best paddy land and land planted with plantains and betel vines. The *varam* tenure prevailed in the case of rain-fed wet land and river-irrigated land where the water-supply was not assured. Dry land when leased was almost invariably let on the *varam* system.[107] It may be gathered from the above that as a whole, (1) leases for a fixed rents payable in produce existed either in the most fertile wet areas with an assured water-supply or in garden land irrigated by wells, (2) leases for fixed monetary rents were common in the case of well-irrigated land cropped with plantains and other fruits, and (3) the dominant form of tenancy in both dry and wet land with an unassured water-supply was sharecropping.

However, this generalisation needs to be qualified for the Kaveri basin. In Thanjavur district, the form of tenancy depended upon whether the land belonged to a resident owner or not. In this area, sharecropping was the more common system, and was particularly preferred by resident landholders, while non-resident landlords chose the fixed rent method for cultivating their land.[108] In Tiruchirapalli district, 'the *varam* system is commonest in the river-side wet land, and the *kuttagai* method in the dry land in the uplands or in properties held by absentee landlords or persons like Brahmans and merchants who do not care to supervise their cultivation personally'.[109] In this area, therefore, the form of tenancy was more closely associated with the type of landholder than with the ecological conditions of the land, but this point needs further examination.

The amount collected by a landholder from his tenant, though not the same across the country, tended to be high. The 1914 Government Order provides us with detailed data on the tenancy system in Thanjavur district. In the sharecropping system, the commonest system of tenant cultivation in this district, the balance left after deducting harvesting expenses from the gross produce was shared between the landholder and his tenant in the proportion of one-fifth or one-fourth or 33 percent to the tenant and the rest to the landholder. The landholder, on his part, was responsible for the payment of land tax and also for the following

[106] G.O., No. 3594, Confidential, Revenue, 9 Dec. 1914, p. 87.
[107] Ibid., pp. 112–13..
[108] 'Notes to G.O. Nos. 3594–95, Revenue, 9 December 1914', p. 67.
[109] Ibid., p. 75.

expenses: cost of manure, labour charges for lowering the level of the field to allow channel water to spread to all the corners of the field, and cleaning the canals. The tenant, on the other hand, had to provide his personal labour in the cultivation of his landlord's land and pay all charges connected therewith. The richest landholder in the district stated that the tenant's share was generally one-third of the gross produce.[110]

In Chingleput district also sharecropping was the common custom. The tenant bore the cultivation expenses and was entitled to all the straw after threshing. The landlord paid the land tax and generally shared the grain produce equally with the tenant. Where irrigation was by baling water, tenants would get three-fifths of the produce. For the better wet land, the tenant's share was often smaller than half and might be two-fifths, or more commonly one-third.[111] In a wet land village near Tiruchirapalli city, where land was let out on *varam* tenure, the tenant got only 18.5 *kalams* as his share out of every 100 *kalams* of gross out-turn. In wet land near Lalgudi town, the landholder collected four-fifths of the produce. In a wet village towards the tail end of irrigation canals there was *varam* only in certain poor land suffering from drainage troubles, and here the share was half.[112]

The garden and dry lands of Coimbatore district when leased out were also managed by sharecropping. The landholder undertook to bear half of the cultivation expenses, and in return collected half the land's produce. The tenant got all the straw after threshing, besides his share in the produce. There were also instances where the landholder did not contribute at all towards the cost of cultivation and collected only one-third of the produce for himself. Only poor tenants who had no capital and in consequence received petty advances from landholders resorted to this system of subletting.[113] As indicated above, most of the wet land sublet in this district was cultivated by tenants whose rents were based on a fixed quantity of the produce. The result of a survey of several wet villages in this district indicates that the rent for wet land was very high, in most cases being more than 11 times the land assessment and amounting to more than 80 percent of the outturn.[114]

[110] Ibid., p. 67.

[111] Ibid., p. 61. According to the Settlement Report of Salem district, when the land was let on *varam*, the tenant generally received a half of the produce. Little change had taken place in the apportionment of the share in the previous thirty years (G.O., No. 1029, Revenue, 7 Oct. 1903, p. 23).

[112] P.B.R., No. 86, 26 Nov. 1923, p. 23, par. 19.

[113] G.O., No. 3594, Confidential, Revenue, 9 Dec. 1914, p. 87.

[114] Ibid., pp. 66–68, Appendixes III, IV, V.

Information from other districts also suggests that tenants had to pay a high rent. In Tirunelveli, wherever sharecropping was adopted, the produce of the land was divided at the threshing floor, the tenants taking a half or one-third of the gross produce, though in the dry land they took three-fourths.[115] In irrigated areas, the generally prevalent system was fixed-rent lease. A survey of 43 villages in Ambasamudram *firka* of Tirunelveli district listed the proportion by which the net yield or the yield minus expenses was divided between the landholder and the tenant, indicating that the proportion of rent to net yield worked out generally at 70 percent in the case of wet land.[116]

On the whole, whatever the regional differences, landlords in South India took a large portion of the produce as rent and the result was that 'the straw and the remaining half share of the grain are considered to be very little more than enough to cover the expenses of cultivation and to support the cultivator and his family'.[117] Thus the income a tenant could earn by cultivating land hardly exceeded the sum of the cost of cultivation and the wage he and his family members might have earned if they had been hired for the cultivation of the same land. 'These expenses whittle away the allowances for cultivation expenses till he is left with, perhaps, half of the total cost of cultivation in hand as remuneration for the time and labour he and his family spend on the holding. This I believe to be practically the bare cooly wages they would get if they did the same work on another man's land.'[118] This reference is a fairly accurate indication of the income level of tenants in South India at the time.[119]

Because of the heavy rent burden, a large number of tenants were in debt. In 27 villages of the Ambasamudram area in Tirunelveli, nearly half the tenants were in debt, and moneylenders were the most important source of money borrowed, followed by landholders.[120] One method

[115] Ibid., pp. 112–13.

[116] Ibid., p. 120, Statement showing the results of enquiry in the subletting of lands in Ambasamudram firka, 43 villages; 'Notes to G.O. Nos. 3594–95, Revenue, 9 December 1914', p. 75; G.O., No. 3594, Confidential, Revenue, 9 Dec. 1914, p. 97.

[117] 'Notes to G.O. Nos. 3594–95, Revenue, 9 December 1914', p. 62.

[118] G.O., No. 3594, Confidential, Revenue, 9 Dec. 1914, p. 55.

[119] The village survey done by Madras University confirms this (Thomas and Ramakrishnan [eds.], *Some South Indian Villages: A Resurvey*, pp. 92–93). Later, Sivaswamy reported that the income of a tenant was 12 to 14 annas a day in Thanjavur district, whereas a day labourer got a wage of Rs.1-4-0 (Sivaswamy, *Tenant*, Part 1, p. 17).

[120] G.O., No. 3594, Confidential, Revenue, 9 Dec. 1914, p. 124, Statement

of money-lending was to advance money on the condition that it was repaid at harvest in paddy rated at a money value far below the current market-price. Money and paddy were advanced also to be repaid with interest in the usual way. These were the methods of the professional moneylender and the interest demanded varied between 12 and 50 percent. The landholder who advanced grain or money was reported to demand a more moderate rate of interest varying from 12.5 to about 18 percent. It was also reported that all tenants who had debts of around Rs. 100 possessed assets in the shape either of *patta* land, farm stock or houses in excess of their liabilities. For example, in the village of Kodarangulam, out of nineteen tenants whose debts exceeded Rs. 100, fifteen owned *patta* land.[121] Tenants in the Coimbatore district could not borrow money from the traders of the region because they had nothing to offer as security on the loans. Hence, many farmers (an estimated 23 percent) resorted to borrowing from landholders. According to a report, 'there can be no doubt that the grant of loans to tenants is a concession made in order to secure a high rate of rent and is one of the concomitants of rack-renting.'[122] In Thanjavur also, landlords advanced cash to tenants to buy oxen, seed, and necessities related to cultivation. 'The mirasdar, as a rule, contrives to keep his porakkudi indebted to him for advances of money or seed and thus has a perpetual hold on him.'[123] Whatever the form of debt, advances granted by landlords enabled them to extract high rents from their tenants.

Under this system of rack-renting, there was little margin for tenants to sublet the land to under-tenants. They had to cultivate it by their own and their family labour. A report from Tirunelveli states, 'Instances of persons holding under the pattadar's tenant are very rare', and it was reported that it was more common for tenants to cultivate the land by their own personal labour than to cultivate it by hired labour.[124]

In the Ambasamudram *taluk* of Tirunelveli district, each tenant cultivated an average area of 1.8 acres of irrigated land and 1 or 2 acres of dry land. Every acre of wet land brought him an average net income of Rs. 28 a year after the deduction of cultivation expenses.[125] A tenant's income from cultivation was hardly sufficient to support a family.

---

showing the status of tenants and the extent of their indebtedness in Ambasamudram firka, 27 villages.

[121] Ibid., p. 117.

[122] Ibid., p. 57.

[123] 'Notes to G.O. Nos. 3594–95, Revenue, 9 December 1914', p. 67.

[124] G.O., No. 3594, Confidential, Revenue, 9 Dec. 1914, p. 111.

[125] Ibid., p. 114.

Unless he owned a bit of *patta* land also, he could hardly afford even daily necessities on his income as a tenant. This is made clear in a report concerning North Arcot district.

> Sub-tenants who are pattadars themselves seldom borrow money for cultivation. . . .
>
> When the pattadar sub-tenant finds that his farm does not keep him and his bullocks fully engaged, or that he does not make a satisfactory living on his own farm, he takes others' lands for cultivation and the earnings on the combined farm would generally permit him to maintain the status of a ryot. He may occasionally find some savings to purchase lands.
>
> The non-pattadar sub-tenant, on the other hand, is always at the mercy of the landholder and will invariably find it difficult to satisfy his demands and clear his debts to him. It is not generally possible for him to purchase lands and become a ryot himself.[126]

It should be also noted that, as revealed by the case of a village in Coimbatore district, tenants owning no *patta* land at all predominated among tenant farmers in terms of both number and the total area of operational holdings.[127] To supplement their income, these *patta*-less tenants had to earn wage income by hiring themselves out as cooly labour. A report concerning the Coimbatore district provides an example.

> Turning now to the number of days in the year on which there are agricultural operations going on in paddy fields, it becomes obvious at once that the cultivation of paddy will not provide the tenant and his family with more than, say, three months' work in the year, and the cultivation expenses do not leave the tenant anything beyond his cooly wage for the days he actually works. Some additional employment must therefore be sought by the tenant and his family, and they of course help to plough, manure, transplant and harvest the crops of other tenants. When the seasons for these operations are over then the men of the family will often take out their bullock cart for hire if they have one and own bullocks.

In fact, it was also reported that the tenant worked as a field labourer on the land of others for cooly wages for the same number of days in the year he worked on his own leased land.[128]

The situation was the same in Tirunelveli district. In 27 villages in

[126] Ibid., p. 32.
[127] Ibid., p. 86.
[128] Ibid., p. 55.

this district, 55 percent of a total number of 3,139 tenants were found to be coolies; 16 percent had some other independent means of livelihood, either in the way of landed property or money-lending; 29 percent followed their hereditary occupations as oil-mongers, palmyra-climbers or artisans; and only 2 percent depended solely on the cultivation of their leased land.[129] The report further states that tenants often regarded cultivation as a tenant as supplementary and even subsidiary to their other occupations. To illustrate this, in 1916, a Pallar tenant owning no land earned a net return of Rs. 40 from the cultivation of three acres of wet land, whereas the wage income he, his wife and his son earned amounted to as much as Rs. 77.[130]

Thus the majority of tenants did not own *patta* land at all and had to work as cooly labourers. The dominance of non-*pattadar* tenants seems to reflect again that the tenant class included many members of low castes who had evolved from the status of mere labourers.

Tenants' side jobs were not limited to hereditary occupations and daily wage agricultural labour. An interesting case was reported from a village called Vikramasingapuram in Tirunelveli. There, hundreds of cooly workers were employed by the Tinnevelly Cotton Mills. Not content with the monotony of life as a mill hand, a large number of workers competed eagerly to obtain the lease of small plots in the village for cultivation. To cultivate them they obtained leave of absence for two weeks a year, and managed to sow and reap 'by working during this time and such time as they can snatch on other days before 6-30 A.M. and after 6 P.M.'.[131]

This does not mean that the tenant had the same socio-economic standing as the labourer. A reference from a report of Coimbatore district illustrates the distinction between them: 'But there is a difference, the tenant more often than not owns cattle of his own which are more frequently she-buffaloes than bullocks, and the tenant has a certain status which enables him to command a small credit'.[132] And, 'if a tenant wants at any moment to borrow money, he has his prospective share of the crop as security and can easily do so'.[133] In addition, he was entitled to the straw—'The straw relieves this pressure, the search for work need

[129] Ibid., p. 115.
[130] Slater (ed.), *Some South Indian Villages*, p. 75.
[131] G.O., No. 3594, Confidential, Revenue, 9 Dec. 1914, p. 115.
[132] Ibid., p. 55.
[133] Ibid., p. 116. The same situation was reported for Tirunelveli (*Gazetteer of Tinnevelly District*, p. 190).

not be made every day of the remaining nine months of the year. The straw therefore helps the tenant supplement his income by cart-hire. . . .' Another not negligible product was the manure from the cattle on the holding.[134]

The advantage a tenant had over a mere labourer was well illustrated by an instance of a Depressed-caste tenant in Tirunelveli. He cultivated 1.08 acres of double-cropped land for two years. After paying rent and deducting cultivation expenses, he was able to get about 1 *kotta* (= 112 Madras measures) of paddy and all the straw. When there was no work to be done on his lease, he worked as a cooly for his landlord, getting two *podis* (maybe *padi*: 1 *padi* is about 2/3 Madras measure) of paddy per day as wages. In addition, he did other cooly work such as mud work, wood cutting, repairs to ridges, etc., to earn extra income. His wife and two of his four sons (aged 18, 14, 8, and 5 years) helped him in the field and did cooly work as well. He owned a pair of oxen and used them to plough for others. When questioned, he replied, 'I stick to tenancy because I do not get cooly work always and I get straw for my oxen'.[135]

The above case confirms that (1) the income a tenant could earn from his farm was so small that his whole family had to work as coolies to supplement the income, (2) the farmer preferred tenancy in spite of its low income because cooly jobs were not available regularly, and (3) the availability of straw to feed his oxen, a great asset to the tenant, was an important incentive and reason for his sticking to tenancy cultivation. Thus the position of a tenant was advantageous over a mere labourer in that he owned a pair of oxen and could obtain straw to feed them. 'Tenants take a pride in maintaining their status as such.'[136]

Furthermore, the status of tenants seems to have stabilised in some districts. In most areas, as mentioned above, tenant cultivation was undertaken on a one-year contract and the landlord had the right to evict the tenant at any time after the end of the one-year term. In Coimbatore district at the end of the last century, landlords were reported to have evinced an inclination to turn out their customary tenants for casual

[134] G.O., No. 3594, Confidential, Revenue, 9 Dec. 1914, p. 55.

[135] Ibid., p. 116. For the importance of straw for tenants, see also *Royal Commission on Agriculture in India,* Vol. 3, p. 444. The importance of a greater security of income from their own farms for the farmers, even if the plots they owned or leased were very small, has been considered by Krishna Bharadwaj, *Production Conditions in Indian Agriculture: A Study Based on Farm Management Surveys* (Cambridge, 1974), p. 23.

[136] G.O., No. 3594, Confidential, Revenue, 9 Dec. 1914, p. 58.

bidders who offered higher rents.[137] However, in the early twentieth century, in the same district, tenants were seldom reported to have lost their tenant's status and 'no case of eviction of tenants' was reported as having occurred.[138] As a report from Tirunelveli district notes, the status of tenant tended to be a permanent one. When 20 villages were surveyed to examine how many people had changed their status from tenant to some other in the previous ten years, a total of 213 persons, or 11 persons per village, were reported to have 'relapsed' from the status of tenant.[139] In Tirunelveli district at that time, the average number of tenants per village in 27 villages surveyed was 116 persons.[140] Therefore, at a rough estimate, a mere 10 percent of the tenant population lost their status as tenants in a span of ten years, suggesting that the majority of tenants had secured their status as tenants for many years. Furthermore, if we take into account the fact that, as the report suggests, many of the above 213 cases of change in status were attributable to the growing demand for labour outside agriculture and that cases of transition from tenant to ordinary labourer was extremely rare in those villages,[141] we can safely conclude that tenant status was quite stable in the district in the first decade of the century, though in the 1940s a survey reported that the position of tenants was deteriorating owing to a keen struggle for livelihood among tenants, and that in many places of Thanjavur, in the Solavandan area in Madurai district and in parts of Tirunelveli district, agitation by tenants led to their eviction and replacement by outsiders.[142]

What is more important is that becoming a tenant was a vital step for members of lower castes in raising their status to small landholders. 'In and around Ambasamudram are a number of small pattadars of the Panchama caste; it is only through the path of tenancy that they have risen to this position. A tenant has very often his poultry and a few sheep; to buy his cattle he may incur a debt, but by the labour of his own hands in his lease holdings he will earn himself a return and pay for them. Cultivation is his stand-by, his one occupation that in four years out of five is certain to give him a return; in addition to this he has many resources in the labour market in cultivation, in road work, house-

[137] *Manual of Coimbatore District*, quoted in 'Notes to G.O. Nos. 3594–95, Revenue, 9 December 1914', p. 64.

[138] 'Notes to G.O. Nos. 3594–95, Revenue, 9 December 1914', pp. 101, 106.

[139] G.O., No. 3594, Confidential, Revenue, 9 Dec. 1914, pp. 118–19.

[140] Ibid., p. 124, Appendix B.

[141] Ibid., pp. 118–19. See also *Royal Commission on Agriculture in India*, Vol. 3, p. 443.

[142] Sivaswamy, *Tenant*, Part 1, pp. 26–27.

building or in his hereditary craft.'[143] It sometimes happened that tenants of *raiyatwari pattadars* purchased the land they had originally cultivated as tenants and became *pattadars* themselves.[144]

The 1874 Settlement Report of Chingleput district records: 'No doubt amongst these small Pattadars are Payacaries who wishing to rise to the dignity of holding land of their own, have managed to commence in a small way, with the hope of adding to their three or four acres, as time and opportunities offer.'[145] This reveals that the tenants were making continued efforts to own land, however small in area. In the Appadurai village of Tiruchirapalli district, chosen for my field survey, every Depressed-caste landholder had spent some years as a tenant cultivator. The villagers said that a mere labourer was not capable of saving the money needed to purchase a plot of land. Essential for the acquisition of land was a number of years of experience as a tenant.[146]

To summarise, the tenancy system developed in two ways: (1) the commercialisation of South Indian agriculture under colonial conditions led to the growth of traders and moneylenders and to the decline of some farmers, and (2) the intensification of agricultural practices and the emigration of labourers and members of higher castes discouraged higher-caste landowners from hiring labourers and induced them to lease their land to tenants. The composition of tenants also confirms my observation: there were two types of tenant, one from the former landowning families and the other from the former landless classes.

Because of the high rent tenants had to pay to the landlords, the income they could earn from their own farms was so meagre that they had to supplement their income by working as hired coolie labourers. However, becoming a tenant was the vital step for people from lower castes in raising their status to that of landholder. In the next chapter, I will present cases exemplifying the acquisition of land by tenant farmers.

[143] G.O., No. 3594, Confidential, Revenue, 9 Dec. 1914, p. 117.
[144] 'Notes to G.O. Nos. 3594–95, Revenue, 9 December 1914', p. 90.
[145] P.B.R., No. 2880, 5 Oct. 1874, pp. 7805–6, par. 42.
[146] Yanagisawa, *Socio-Economic Changes*, p. 164.

5

Mixed Trends in Landholding

The tenancy system, as shown in the previous chapter, developed along two paths. This change in agrarian relationships was accompanied and accelerated by changes in the pattern of landholdings in wet zone villages in Tamilnadu. Certain descriptive evidence for the shift in landholding patterns was noted in the previous chapter. In this chapter, I will analyse statistical data compiled from the Settlement Registers of the villages in Lalgudi *taluk*, Trichinopoly district, as well as sources from other districts, in order to trace changes in landownership after the 1860s.

Decline of Higher-Caste Dominance in Landholding

Increase in landownership by Depressed-caste members and low-caste Non-Brahmans: Lalgudi taluk

The structure of landholding in the 14 wet and 7 intermediate zone villages as seen in 1865 was detailed in Chapter 2. Each of these villages was re-surveyed twice, in 1895 and 1925, and a new Settlement Register for the village was compiled each time. The data in the Settlement Registers for 1895 and 1925 was processed in approximately the same manner as the 1865 Settlement Registers.

The sixty years after 1865 witnessed notable changes in the pattern of landholding in Lalgudi *taluk*, the most conspicuous being the increase in the area owned by members of lower castes.

In 1865, Depressed-caste members like the Pallar and Paraiyar held only 4 acres of land in 14 wet zone villages. Even if the extent owned by the *vettiyans*, village servants who discharged the lowest offices, such as those of scavenger, etc., and are presumed to have belonged to Depressed castes, is added to this, the total amount of land held by this community hardly exceeded 10 acres, indicating that Depressed-caste members were practically excluded from landownership. However, the situation was to change. The data indicates a definite increase in landholding by these lowest castes in subsequent years. In 1895, people of Depressed castes owned 39 acres, and by 1925 that area had more than tripled, to 138 acres (Tables 5.1 & 5.3). In none of the 14 wet zone villages did their landholdings decrease between 1865 and 1895 and in the next three decades every village without exception witnessed an increase in the amount held by Depressed castes. The same trend was discernible in the intermediate zone, where in seven villages the area owned by Depressed castes, which in 1865 had been only 30 acres, had roughly tripled to 96 acres in the next thirty years and further increased to 313 acres by 1925 (Tables 5.5 & 5.7). Every village in this zone witnessed an increase in Depressed-caste landownership.

Furthermore, changes in the area of land owned by Christians should be taken into account. Land held by Christians increased markedly in the thirty years after 1895, especially in the 14 wet zone villages. The 49 and 48 acres in 1865 and 1895 respectively (Table 5.1) more than doubled to 132 acres in 1925 (Table 5.3). The intermediate zone showed a similar trend, from 22 and 30 acres in 1865 and 1895 (Table 5.5) to 84 acres in 1925 (Table 5.7). Since, as the Manual of Trichinopoly district notes, Christianity spread mainly among the lower classes,[1] the actual increase in the land owned by Depressed castes was probably larger than it appeared.

From the beginning of the present century, the Government of Madras adopted a policy of assigning uncultivated arable land to Depressed-caste members, distributing this land either directly to members of that community or through Christian missionaries, as will be described in Chapter 6. Was the acquisition of land by Depressed castes, as indicated by the Settlement Registers of Lalgudi *taluk*, attributable to this government policy?

To clarify the characteristics of land acquisition by Depressed castes, I have examined the cases of land transfer to them between 1895 and 1925 in a village in Lalgudi *taluk*.[2] In this village, Depressed castes owned a total of 20 *pattas* in 1925. For each of plots included in these *pattas*, I have clarified the name(s) of the *patta*-holder(s) who had

[1] *Manual of Trichinopoly District*, p. 101. See Henriette Bugge, *Mission and Tamil Society: Social and Religious Change in South India (1840–1900)* (London, 1994), Chapter 6.

[2] The details of the cases are listed in Yanagisawa, *Minamiindo Shakai Keizaishi*, pp. 193–95, Table 7.13.

Table 5.1

Distribution of Area by Size of Holding : 14 Wet Villages in Lalgudi *Taluk*, 1895

(acres)

Size Group	1	2	3	4	5	6	7	8	9	10	11	12	
(Acreage)	<0.5	<1	<2	<3	<5	<10	<15	<25	<50	<100	=>100	Total	(%)
Brahman	61	71	177	182	269	439	332	669	986	439	172	3,795	(40.0)
Non-Brahman	66	157	315	278	512	702	578	454	177	262	555	4,065	(42.9)
Chetty	1	7	6	8	13	17	12	33	44	0	0	142	(1.5)
Muttiriyan	14	30	63	15	53	111	45	21	0	0	0	356	(3.8)
Nadan (Nadavan)	16	27	55	107	143	158	136	132	60	179	360	1,371	(14.5)
Pillai	10	26	56	14	88	98	160	90	47	83	195	867	(9.1)
Reddi	1	0	2	3	3	11	13	23	0	0	0	56	(0.6)
Udaiyan	5	19	44	37	72	121	82	52	0	0	0	432	(4.6)
Others	19	48	89	94	140	186	130	103	26	0	0	841	(8.9)
Depressed castes	2	10	10	8	10	0	0	0	0	0	0	39	(0.4)
Occupational titles	2	4	15	14	19	54	0	0	0	0	0	107	(1.1)
Muslim	2	3	15	0	24	47	23	0	0	0	227	341	(3.6)
Christian	3	5	16	0	8	5	10	0	0	0	0	48	(0.5)
Caste unknown, female	20	43	52	50	74	121	24	25	30	0	0	439	(4.6)
Temple	10	18	32	26	28	34	71	36	69	0	0	323	(3.4)
Others	29	33	48	51	41	71	39	14	1	1	0	322	(3.4)
Total	195	344	680	609	985	1,473	1,077	1,198	1,263	702	954	9,479	(100)

Table 5.2

Distribution of Landholders by Size of Holding: 14 Wet Villages in Lalgudi *Taluk*, 1895

Size Group (Acreage)	1 <0.5	2 <1	3 <2	4 <3	5 <5	6 <10	7 <15	8 <25	9 <50	10 <100	11 =>100	12 Total
Brahman	347	98	122	75	67	59	28	35	28	6	1	866
Non-Brahman	382	214	223	114	130	105	48	24	5	4	2	1,251
Chetty	5	10	4	3	4	2	1	2	1	0	0	32
Muttiriyan	81	41	44	7	13	15	4	1	0	0	0	206
Nadan (Nadavan)	90	38	39	44	37	24	11	7	2	3	1	296
Pillai	49	35	41	6	23	15	12	5	1	1	1	189
Reddi	5	0	1	1	1	2	1	1	0	0	0	12
Udaiyan	34	24	30	14	17	19	7	3	0	0	0	148
Others	118	66	64	39	35	28	12	5	1	0	0	368
Depressed castes	9	13	8	3	3	0	0	0	0	0	0	36
Occupational titles	12	4	10	5	5	8	0	0	0	0	0	44
Muslim	16	4	9	0	6	6	2	0	0	0	1	44
Christian	15	7	10	0	2	1	1	0	0	0	0	36
Caste unknown, female	93	63	38	20	19	18	2	1	1	0	0	263
Temple	37	24	23	11	7	4	6	2	2	0	0	116
Others	143	49	35	21	11	10	3	1	0	0	0	265
Total	1,054	476	478	249	250	211	90	63	36	10	4	2,921

Table 5.3

Distribution of Area by Size of Holding: 14 Wet Villages in Lalgudi *Taluk*, 1925

(acres)

Size Group	1	2	3	4	5	6	7	8	9	10	11	12	
(Acreage)	<0.5	<1	<2	<3	<5	<10	<15	<25	<50	<100	=>100	Total	(%)
Brahman	50	74	187	161	324	565	375	522	388	237	0	2,884	(30.5)
Non-Brahman	155	285	550	357	506	698	271	227	212	279	789	4,328	(45.8)
Chetty	3	11	44	18	21	55	0	64	36	69	0	322	(3.4)
Muttiriyan	47	80	109	60	94	92	22	18	0	0	0	522	(5.5)
Nadan (Nadavan)	22	35	69	36	82	51	43	15	33	0	101	487	(5.2)
Pillai	17	31	83	45	41	121	73	35	49	79	474	1,047	(11.1)
Reddi	1	6	8	11	22	37	0	0	94	0	214	392	(4.1)
Udaiyan	16	34	77	71	122	210	82	15	0	76	0	703	(7.4)
Others	49	88	160	116	124	132	51	80	0	55	0	855	(9.0)
Depressed castes	26	42	49	13	0	8	0	0	0	0	0	138	(1.5)
Occupational titles	4	8	18	2	13	11	0	0	0	0	0	56	(0.5)
Muslim	10	22	32	8	8	6	11	0	0	0	109	206	(2.2)
Christian	21	28	40	9	12	21	0	0	0	0	0	132	(1.4)
Caste unknown, female	49	113	149	142	126	147	13	16	0	0	0	755	(8.0)
Temple	14	29	44	44	31	62	36	35	144	52	229	720	(7.6)
Others	42	41	69	35	31	16	1	0	1	0	0	231	(2.4)
Total	371	642	1,138	771	1,051	1,534	707	800	745	568	1,127	9,450	(100)

Table 5.4

Distribution of Landholders by Size of Holding: 14 Wet Villages in Lalgudi *Taluk*, 1925

Size Group (Acreage)	1 <0.5	2 <1	3 <2	4 <3	5 <5	6 <10	7 <15	8 <25	9 <50	10 <100	11 =>100	12 Total
Brahman	359	102	136	67	83	77	31	28	11	4	0	898
Non-Brahman	953	385	388	150	132	101	23	12	6	4	5	2,159
Chetty	20	14	30	8	6	8	0	3	1	1	0	91
Muttiriyan	309	109	76	26	24	14	2	1	0	0	0	561
Nadan (Nadavan)	166	46	48	15	22	7	4	1	1	0	1	311
Pillai	94	41	58	19	11	17	6	2	1	1	2	252
Reddi	4	7	6	5	5	6	0	0	3	0	2	38
Udaiyan	82	49	57	29	31	29	7	1	0	1	0	286
Others	278	119	113	48	33	20	4	4	0	1	0	620
Depressed castes	110	56	35	6	0	1	0	0	0	0	0	208
Occupational titles	24	9	13	1	3	2	0	0	0	0	0	52
Muslim	51	31	22	3	2	1	1	0	0	0	0	112
Christian	114	37	30	4	3	3	0	0	0	0	0	191
Caste unknown, female	275	158	113	58	33	20	1	1	0	0	0	659
Temple	59	39	32	18	8	9	3	2	4	1	1	176
Others	275	60	48	14	8	2	0	0	0	0	1	407
Total	2,220	877	817	321	272	216	59	43	21	9	7	4,862

Table 5.5

Distribution of Area by Size of Holding : 7 Intermediate Zone Villages in Lalgudi *Taluk*, 1895

(acres)

Size Group (Acreage)	1 <0.5	2 <1	3 <2	4 <3	5 <5	6 <10	7 <15	8 <25	9 <50	10 <100	11 =>100	12 Total	(%)
Brahman	21	28	28	47	125	159	236	263	212	219	0	1,337	(18.6)
Non-Brahman	57	129	354	306	608	964	641	334	316	203	0	3,907	(54.3)
Chetty	0	1	11	5	4	13	14	0	0	0	0	47	(0.7)
Kavundan	1	7	12	2	8	33	0	18	0	0	0	80	(1.1)
Muttiriyan	6	11	11	19	15	22	26	0	0	72	0	181	(2.5)
Nadan (Nadavan)	4	9	16	17	35	53	86	22	73	0	0	313	(4.4)
Pillai	7	30	81	82	116	184	161	131	182	79	0	1,053	(14.6)
Udaiyan	13	23	77	83	257	390	148	110	0	0	0	1,102	(15.3)
Others	26	48	146	98	173	269	206	53	61	52	0	1,131	(15.7)
Depressed castes	5	7	22	12	10	26	12	0	0	0	0	96	(1.3)
Occupational titles	1	4	13	9	11	35	33	21	38	0	0	166	(2.3)
Muslim	2	2	6	5	4	0	0	0	0	0	0	19	(0.3)
Christian	4	4	8	2	5	7	0	0	0	0	0	30	(0.4)
Caste unknown, female	13	20	53	61	84	85	103	31	0	0	0	450	(6.3)
Temple	5	14	23	27	40	90	73	21	92	0	0	384	(5.3)
No holder's name	0	0	0	0	4	16	0	0	45	51	0	116	(1.6)
Others	17	40	82	100	129	172	66	50	30	0	0	690	(9.6)
Total	125	248	589	569	1,020	1,554	1,164	720	733	473	0	7,195	(100)

Table 5.6

Distribution of Landholders by Size of Holding: 7 Intermediate Zone Villages in Lalgudi *Taluk*, 1895

Size Group (Acreage)	1 <0.5	2 <1	3 <2	4 <3	5 <5	6 <10	7 <15	8 <25	9 <50	10 <100	11 =>100	12 Total
Brahman	80	38	21	18	32	23	17	14	7	3	0	253
Non-Brahman	224	176	246	123	155	140	50	17	9	3	0	1,143
Chetty	1	1	6	2	1	2	1	0	0	0	0	14
Kavundan	3	8	8	1	2	4	0	1	0	0	0	27
Muttiriyan	14	16	8	8	4	3	2	0	0	1	0	56
Nadan (Nadavan)	11	12	11	7	9	7	7	1	2	0	0	67
Pillai	27	43	54	33	30	27	12	6	5	1	0	238
Udaiyan	62	34	55	32	65	56	12	6	0	0	0	322
Others	106	62	104	40	44	41	16	3	2	1	0	419
Depressed castes	16	10	16	5	3	4	1	0	0	0	0	55
Occupational titles	7	5	9	4	3	4	3	1	1	0	0	37
Muslim	9	3	4	2	1	0	0	0	0	0	0	19
Christian	15	5	6	1	1	1	0	0	0	0	0	29
Caste unknown, female	44	27	38	25	22	13	8	2	0	0	0	179
Temple	17	18	15	12	11	13	6	1	3	0	0	96
No holder s name	0	0	0	0	1	2	0	0	1	1	0	5
Others	70	61	60	40	33	25	6	3	1	0	0	299
Total	482	343	415	230	262	225	91	38	22	7	0	2,115

Table 5.7

Distribution of Area by Size of Holding: 7 Intermediate Zone Villages in Lalgudi *Taluk*, 1925

(acres)

Size Group	1	2	3	4	5	6	7	8	9	10	11	12	
(Acreage)	<0.5	<1	<2	<3	<5	<10	<15	<25	<50	<100	=>100	Total	(%)
Brahman	13	26	67	59	97	158	81	34	0	62	0	595	(8.1)
Non-Brahman	164	351	661	485	876	944	340	284	105	62	0	4,275	(58.5)
Chetty	3	18	24	22	36	36	24	0	0	0	0	163	(2.2)
Kavundan	11	27	51	36	90	41	0	44	27	0	0	328	(4.5)
Muttiriyan	20	39	72	50	66	119	0	15	0	62	0	443	(6.1)
Nadan (Nadavan)	4	9	22	10	20	92	40	42	0	0	0	238	(3.3)
Pillai	24	46	80	43	176	148	121	147	78	0	0	862	(11.8)
Udaiyan	47	104	201	192	308	310	90	36	0	0	0	1,289	(17.6)
Others	55	108	211	132	180	198	65	0	0	0	0	952	(13.0)
Depressed castes	30	51	88	50	22	34	34	0	0	0	0	313	(4.3)
Occupational titles	4	11	26	20	16	30	0	0	0	0	0	108	(1.5)
Muslim	2	7	8	16	4	0	0	0	0	0	0	37	(0.5)
Christian	7	12	21	16	24	5	0	0	0	0	0	84	(1.1)
Caste unknown, female	44	87	155	116	93	110	26	0	0	0	0	632	(8.6)
Temple	10	21	28	19	54	148	62	37	30	0	180	590	(8.1)
No holder's name	0	1	3	0	0	0	0	0	0	70	0	73	(1.0)
Others	40	55	117	80	142	107	27	16	26	0	0	603	(8.2)
Total	314	622	1,174	861	1,328	1,536	570	371	161	194	180	7,310	(100)

Table 5.8

Distribution of Landholders by Size of Holding: 7 Intermediate Zone Villages in Lalgudi *Taluk*, 1925

Size Group (Acreage)	1 <0.5	2 <1	3 <2	4 <3	5 <5	6 <10	7 <15	8 <25	9 <50	10 <100	11 =>100	12 Total
Brahman	66	33	46	24	25	22	7	2	0	1	0	226
Non-Brahman	695	480	472	200	228	144	28	15	3	1	0	2,266
Chetty	22	26	16	9	9	5	2	0	0	0	0	89
Kavundan	43	37	34	15	24	6	0	2	1	0	0	162
Muttiriyan	84	55	54	20	15	19	0	1	0	1	0	249
Nadan (Nadavan)	12	3	6	0	2	5	1	0	0	0	0	29
Pillai	119	62	57	18	47	22	10	8	2	0	0	345
Udaiyan	160	141	144	79	81	48	8	2	0	0	0	663
Others	255	156	161	59	50	39	7	2	0	0	0	729
Depressed castes	117	72	66	21	6	5	3	0	0	0	0	290
Occupational titles	16	14	19	8	5	4	0	0	0	0	0	66
Muslim	15	9	6	7	1	0	0	0	0	0	0	38
Christian	41	17	16	6	7	1	0	0	0	0	0	88
Caste unknown, female	189	127	114	48	25	18	2	0	0	0	0	523
Temple	36	29	22	8	14	19	5	2	1	0	1	137
No holder's name	0	1	2	0	0	0	0	0	0	1	0	4
Others	180	73	84	32	37	16	2	1	1	0	0	426
Total	1,355	855	847	354	348	229	47	20	5	3	1	4,064

owned the land in 1895. The result reveals the following features of the transfer.

First, these 20 examples do not include any land which was registered in 1895 as *purambokku* (land for public purposes), *samudayam* (village common land) and plots without a registered *pattadar*. This seems to indicate that the acquisition of land by Depressed-caste members in this village was not a result of any government policy regarding the assignment of uncultivated land but was achieved independently. Though, as we shall examine later, there were instances of land acquisition by Depressed castes through this policy, the total area thus assigned by the government was not very large and it is undeniable that many Depressed-caste members obtained land independently from this government policy. Secondly and more important, the land owned by a Depressed-caste *pattadar* in 1925, in many cases, consisted of plots which had been owned by different persons, sometimes of different communities, in 1895. This also indicates that land acquisition by Depressed castes was in the main not through non-market transactions, such as gifts from landlords, but through buying land bit by bit on the land market. In other words, a considerable number of Depressed-caste families came to own small plots of land through normal market transactions. Supporting this observation is the fact that the ratio between wet and dry land in the area owned by Depressed-caste *pattadars* was not very different from the average for the whole village.[3] Thirdly, a part of the area owned by Depressed castes in 1925 had been in the

[3] See tables in Yanagisawa and Mizushima, *Nijisseiki Hajime Minami Indo niokeru Kasuto to Tochihoyu Kozo*. Some early nineteenth-century sources indicate that *mirasidars* in some districts assigned their Depressed-caste labourers land which the latter cultivated 'like *payacaries*' to secure their subsistence ('Replies from Mr. F.W. Ellis, Collector of Madras, to the Mirasi questions, dated 30th May 1916', in Bayley and Hudleston, *Papers on Mirasi Right*, pp. 336–37). One may interpret the 'acquisition' of land by Depressed castes, as our data shows, merely as a legal recognition of the ownership of land which either they had actually enjoyed for many years or they had once cultivated like *payacaries*. This interpretation may be plausible if there is evidence that a Depressed-caste member in many cases became a *pattadar* of land which, in 1895, had been registered as any one of the following descriptions; village common land, land jointly owned by many landholders and land held by a single large landholder. However, our data demonstrates rather that, as shown above, the land owned by Depressed castes in 1925 had been very often registered in different *pattas* and had been owned by some different persons, often of different communities. Hence, it is safer to think that some Depressed-caste members started owning land by newly purchasing it in the ordinary land market.

possession of *vettiyans* in 1895. In all probability these *pattas* had been given as tax-free land for the services of *vettiyans* and then passed on to the Depressed-caste members through succession.

In spite of the rapid increase in their landholdings, the extent owned by the Depressed castes never exceeded 5 percent of the total cultivated land. In this sense, land transfers to Depressed castes never radically altered the basic pattern of landholdings in village society. However, this fact does not completely minimise the implication of the increase in their holdings. The area owned by the individual member of the Depressed castes was very small. In other words, the number of land-holders in this community was disproportionately large compared to the total amount of land owned. In the 14 villages of the wet zone, the number of *pattadars* belonging to Depressed castes increased from only 2 in 1865 to 36 in 1895, while the number jumped to 208 in 1925. In the intermediate zone villages, this number grew from 10 in 1865 to 55 in 1895, and 290 in 1925. The total number of Depressed-caste *pattadars* in both zones in 1925 therefore was 498, 41 times larger than in 1865.

According to the population data appended to the Settlement Registers, there were 4,914 families in 1925 in the 21 villages in the present study except for one village for which population data is lacking. If we assume that the Depressed castes accounted for one-fifth of the total population as suggested in Chapter 2, the total number of Depressed-caste families works out to about 1,000. The number of Depressed-caste *pattadars* in these 20 villages was 494. If we further assume that the 494 Depressed-caste *pattadars* belonged to different families, we can conclude that as much as half the Depressed-caste families came to own their own tiny plots of land. While the above calculation and assumption are not indisputable, it is possible that the acquisition of land, however small in total extent, by the Depressed communities, may have had a significant importance in their lives and may have encouraged their independence from the dominant higher castes by providing them with the economic means to attempt to emancipate themselves from their landlords.

This new trend in landholding was not limited to the Depressed castes alone but encompassed low-caste Non-Brahmans, such as the Muttiriyars and Udaiyars, whose landownership also increased remarkably. Land held by the Muttiriyars in the wet villages leapt from 131 acres in 1865 to 356 acres in 1895, and again to 522 acres in 1925 (Tables 2.1, 5.1 & 5.3; Figure 5.1). In the intermediate zone, the figures were 107 acres in 1865, 181 acres in 1895, and 443 acres in 1925

Figure 5.1
Index Number of Area Held by Various Communities in Wet Zone Villages in Lalgudi *Taluk*, 1925 (1865=100)

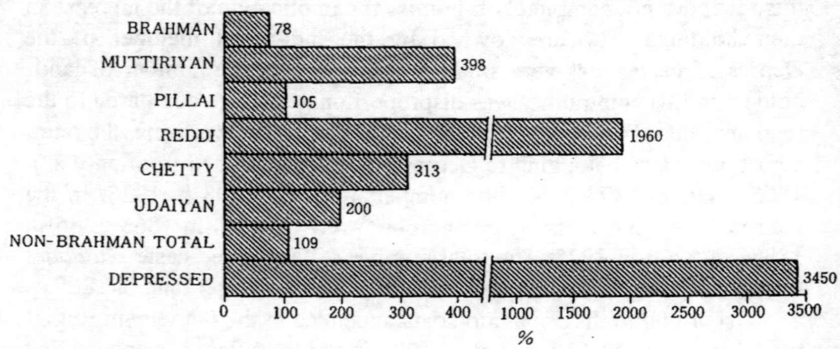

Figure 5.2
Index Number of Area Held by Various Communities in Intermediate Zone Villages in Lalgudi *Taluk*, 1925 (1865=100)

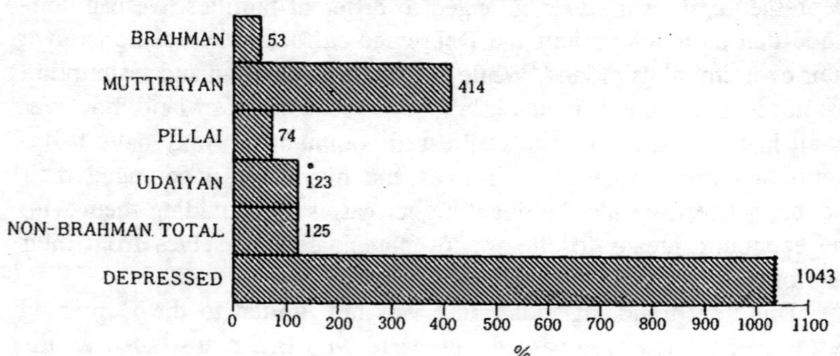

(Tables 2.3, 5.5 & 5.7; Figure 5.2). The Udaiyar landholdings too posted similar increases; from 352 acres of wet land in 1865, they expanded to 432 acres in 1895 and 703 acres in 1925; and in the intermediate zone, 1,045 acres in 1865, 1,102 acres in 1895 and 1,289 acres in 1925. The number of *pattadars* belonging to low-caste Non-Brahmans also increased. For example, in the wet zone, while only 42 Muttiriyars were *pattadars* in 1865, their number increased to 206 in 1895 and to 561 in 1925, almost ten times over the 1865 figure (Tables 2.2, 5.2 & 5.4). As we have already seen, most low-caste Non-Brahmans had been making a living as tenants, agricultural labourers and cowherds, owning no land, or very little, though they were not quite so completely excluded from landownership as the Depressed castes. The acquisition of land by low-caste Non-Brahmans may have stimulated the same growth of independence among them that we saw among the Depressed castes.

The two decades after 1925 seem to have witnessed the working of the same trend in landholdings in Tamil districts, though the evidence available is scanty. Since no Settlement Registers are available for the 21 villages in Lalgudi *taluk* after 1925, we have to depend on a revenue document, called *chitta*, obtained for a wet zone village, Appadurai, in Lalgudi *taluk*.[4] A comparison of the 1925 Settlement Register and the *chitta* for this village reveals that the Depressed castes in the village had held 4.9 acres or a mere 1.2 percent of the total village land (excluding the temple land) in 1925; this had multiplied to 9.1 acres or 2.4 percent of the total in 1952.[5] Though the areas were negligibly small, they did indicate the growing extent of landholding by Depressed castes even after 1925. The data for the low-caste Non-Brahmans exhibits a complex picture. The land owned by the village Muttiriyars, the largest group in the village population, decreased from 7.7 percent to 6.2 percent of the total village land between 1925 and 1952. However, another group of low-caste Non-Brahmans, Padayachis, marked an increase in landholding and other villagers who were low-caste Non-Brahmans also increased their landholdings. Thus as a whole, the area held by low-caste Non-Brahmans remained roughly constant in this period.

The changes the dry villages witnessed after 1865 in their landholding pattern paralleled those in wet and intermediate zone villages. In the five dry villages in Lalgudi *taluk*, the areas held by the Depressed castes rapidly increased. Not only the Depressed-caste members, but low-caste

[4] Yanagisawa, *Socio-Economic Changes*.

[5] Ibid., p. 102.

Non-Brahmans, such as Muttiriyars and Udaiyars, also expanded their landed property after 1865.[6] Along with these points of similarity, the information from dry villages also demonstrates some important differences between the dry zone and the other two zones. Daily coolies were the prevalent form of agricultural labour in the dry area and the general condition of the Depressed castes was not as oppressive as in wet zone villages. In South Arcot district, there were very few *padiyals* or permanent farm servants, and most of the agricultural labourers were day labourers, many of whom either owned or leased small plots of land.[7] We can infer that these differences are attributable partly to the type of agriculture carried out in the dry zone, which tended to demand labour all the year around, providing circumstances favourable for the emancipation of labourers in this region.[8]

Increase in landownership of Depressed castes and low-caste Non-Brahmans in other districts

The increase in the area owned by Depressed castes and low-caste Non-Brahmans has already been pointed out by some scholars.[9] The data

[6] For detailed tables demonstrating the changes in the landholding pattern in the dry zone villages, see Yanagisawa, *Minamiindo Shakai Keizaishi*, Tables 8.1–8.8, 8.10–8.15. The acquisition of land by former landless classes in Salem district was indicated by P.B.R., No. 205, 15 June 1903, p. 20, par. 24; P.B.R., No. 212, 15 July 1905, p. 25, par. 17. For Coimbatore district, see *Manual of Coimbatore District*, p. 179.

[7] Hjejle, 'Slavery and Agricultural Bondage', p. 123; P.B.R., No. 106, 29 May 1918, p. 10, par. 15, p. 21, par. 34. For Salem district, see P.B.R., No. 212, 15 July 1905, p. 30.

[8] *Manual of Coimbatore District*, p. 207; P.B.R., No. 28, 11 Jan. 1912, p.8, par. 25; *MBEC*, Vol. 2, *Written Evidence*, p. 352; 'Results of enquiries made by the Board of Revenue as to the condition of the labouring classes in 1872 (P.B.R., No. 2179, 11 November 1872)', cited in Raghavaiyangar, *Memorandum*, p. lxxxvi.

[9] Kumar, 'Landownership and Inequality', p. 260; Djurfeldt and Lindberg, *Behind Poverty*, p. 62; Michael Moffat, *An Untouchable Community in South India* (Princeton, 1979), pp. 48–50, 174; Baker, *Rural Economy*, pp. 182–83; Sivertsen, *When Caste Barriers Fall*, p. 57; Yanagisawa, *Socio-Economic Changes*, pp. 60–61; Tsuyoshi Nara and Tsukasa Mizushima, 'Neikuramu Mura Chosahokoku I [Social Change in a Dry Village in South India: An Interim Report]', *Studies in Socio-cultural Change in Rural Villages in Tiruchirapalli District, Tamilnadu, India* 4 (Tokyo: ILCAA, 1981), p. 108; Tsukasa Mizushima, 'Changes, Chances and Choices', pp. 75–86; Robert L. Hardgrave, Jr., *The Nadars of Tamilnad: Political Culture of a Community in Change* (Bombay, 1969), p. 53; Bugge, *Mission and Tamil Society*, p. 154. Charlesworth

presented above has statistically confirmed this trend in landownership. Descriptive sources from districts in Tamilnadu also point to the acquisition of land by these lower caste people.

A report of 1893, which supports the above analysis, states:

> Taking the labouring classes as a whole, the improvement in their condition in recent years is manifested, not in any clearly visible rise in the standard of living of the lowest grades or in the comforts that they enjoy, but in the fact of a considerable proportion of the labourers, who, under the old conditions, would have remained in the lowest grade, having been drafted into the next higher grade, while a portion of the latter has gone into the grade which is next higher, and so on. Thus, a percentage of labourers of the pannial class, as will be seen from Mr. Clerk's account, has gone into the grade of porakudies, and a considerable percentage of porakudies has gone into the class of tenants, paying definite rents in cash or kind, while a portion of the latter has acquired landed property and become Puttadars.[10]

The Inspector-General of Registration found in 1906, from inquiries made during his tours of inspection, that several field labourers had acquired land of their own.[11] Census data on the Palli caste, the largest community of the low-caste Non-Brahmans in the Tamil districts, also supports this observation. According to the 1891 Census of India, though the bulk of the Palli were still labourers, many had started to cultivate their own land.[12] The 1901 Census data recorded that two-thirds of the Palli were landholders.[13] Despite doubts about the accuracy of the census records, this may be taken as reflecting the acquisition of small plots of land by low-caste Non-Brahmans in many districts.

In Thanjavur, it was stated that there could be no doubt that the position of the *porakudis* had very considerably improved, several of them having become landholders. The purchase of landed property by lower-caste members was also reported from Chingleput district: 'Judging by general impressions I should say that the lower classes of agriculturists, *i.e.*, the Pallis and Panchamas, are steadily acquiring land in Chingleput. . . . There were many instances of large landholders

---

suggests that labourers bought land to grow cotton in Western India (*Peasants and Imperial Rule*, p. 224). See also Pandit, 'Myths Around Subdivision and Fragmentation of Holdings'.

[10] Raghavaiyangar, *Memorandum,* p. 152.

[11] G.O., No. 468, Judicial, 14 Mar. 1906, p. 5.

[12] *Census of India, 1891*, Vol. 13, *Madras*, Part 1, p. 246.

[13] *Census of India, 1901*, Vol. 15, *Madras* (Madras, 1893), Part 1, p. 230.

selling good land at fair prices to members of the lower castes.'[14] In Tirunelveli also, 'the opening of the market to all classes alike, and giving the low castes as good a title to hold lands obtained by purchase as the high, has thrown no inconsiderable part of the land out of the high caste monopoly in which it was held, and into the hands of the thrifty merchant, artisan or laborer'.[15] As the District Registrar noted, the result was that the higher classes, who had been sole landholders before, had now to give up their land little by little, whereas the poor labouring classes acquired land 'by dint of their economic savings'.[16] The Registrar further stated that 'before the beginning of the present generation', the landowner maintained the cattle, supplied the expenses of cultivation, seed, manure, etc., while all the manual labour was done by the cultivator. The quantity of produce the landlord gave his cultivator was barely sufficient to maintain a family, and the cultivator had to perform menial services for the landlord utterly unconnected with cultivation. However, according to the Registrar, the situation changed.

> The daily increasing independence of the cultivator, his boldness to refuse to give the landlord anything more than his actual due, using his time and labor to more profitable things, his savings, &c., have enabled him to buy cattle of his own to meet the expenses of cultivation from his own pocket without depending on the mercy of his usurious landlord, who, saved of these services, is paid a much less share of the produce.
>
> The said cultivators have gone on further. They began to advance sundry sums to their landlords, and have bought, in most cases, small bits of land of their own, which they cultivate themselves, and obtain all the produce without a sharer.[17]

A large landowner in Tirunelveli also admitted in 1930 that some people who had been formerly agricultural labourers without land were

[14] Raghavaiyangar, *Memorandum*, p. 149; G.O., No. 2765, Revenue, 16 Sept. 1912, p. 4. According to J. Gray, in 1915 the area held by Depressed castes accounted for 8.1 percent and 4.3 percent of the total occupied area in South Arcot and Chingleput districts respectively (G.O., No. 1675, Home [Misc.], 2 Dec. 1919, p. 90).

[15] *Manual of Tinnevelly District*, pp. 30–31.

[16] Raghavaiyangar, *Memorandum*, p. ccxx. In Tirunelveli, 'one of the most noticeable features of the resettlement recently concluded was the enormous increase of Shanan pattas (both in wet and in dry lands) in almost every quarter of the district' (*Gazetteer of Tinnevelly District*, p. 128).

[17] Raghavaiyangar, *Memorandum*, pp. ccxxii–ccxxiii.

now landowners.[18] The Deputy Collector of Coimbatore district, who made personal enquiries into the condition of the labouring classes, concluded that those who had once formed the landless class, the petty traders, the artisans and the weavers, and who had now chosen to work in the fields and elsewhere, 'have now acquired landed property to some extent'.[19]

This change in landholding seems to reflect the transformation in agrarian relations described in previous chapters. From the latter half of the last century, the landed and the landless both became more mobile. First, the emigration of people from lower castes provided some of them with a chance to save money with which to purchase land in their villages, though the extent of the land purchased by lower-caste members in this way may not have been large since 'many of them . . . return[ed] poorer' and an increasing number of Tamil emigrants did not return to their native villages but settled on the estate with their family.[20] Second, as discussed in Chapter 4, the growth of emigration, the intensification of agriculture and the exodus of higher-caste members to urban areas aided the expansion of the tenancy system. Some Depressed-caste members and low-caste Non-Brahmans who had raised their status from mere labourers to that of tenants managed to save money, with which they purchased land. Even though, as I showed in Chapter 2, higher-caste landlords (*mirasidars*) tried to prevent land being transferred to lower-caste villagers especially to Depressed castes, the lower-caste members tried to raise their status and actually some successfully acquired very small landed property, demonstrating their zeal towards independence.

Interestingly, small farmers who had emerged from the labouring class pursued intensive cultivation, growing valuable crops using irrigation wells, at least in some areas. The *Statistical Appendix for the Gazetteer of Trichinopoly District* stated in 1931 that the area under wells had increased and that 'a larger number of erstwhile agricultural labourers have become petty landholders having invested their savings

[18] *MBEC,* Vol. 4, *Oral Evidence* (Madras, 1930), p. 406.

[19] Raghavaiyangar, *Memorandum*, p. 151 n. The report of the Department of Agriculture stated that many of the emigrants returned to India with sufficient money to purchase land on which to maintain themselves by their own labour for the rest of their lives (G.O., No. 2825, Confidential, Revenue, 18 Sept. 1911, p. 10).

[20] G.O., No. 468, Judicial, 14 Mar. 1906, p. 5; Slater (ed.), *Some South Indian Villages,* p. 82; R. Jayaraman, 'Indian Emigration to Ceylon'; Kumar, *Land and Caste*, pp. 141–42.

in small extents of land and, by sinking wells in them, converting them into garden lands which yield such valuable crops as chillies, tobacco and sugarcane'.[21] A report from Tirunelveli district indicates the same trend. Referring to the enormous increase in the number of Shanar *pattas* as one of the most noticeable features of the resettlement conducted around 1910, it noted that in many villages the Shanar labourer was steadily converting himself into a peasant-owner and that cultivation with the aid of wells was his specialty. 'If water exists under the ground a Shanan will find it, and will quickly convert into a luxuriant garden a patch of poor soil which, in the time of its previous owner, had been a dreary waste.'[22] The Shanars were reported to stand out as the most enterprising of garden cultivators in all parts of this district.[23] These pieces of evidence seem to indicate that small farmers who had emerged from the labourer class may have partly contributed to the rapid increase in the number of wells in Tamilnadu as described in Chapter 3.

The Settlement Report of Trichinopoly district offers more evidence regarding the importance of cultivation of garden land for these small farmers. The following statement is very suggestive:

> There is no hard and fast line between the petty ryot and the agricultural labourer and many of the former seek to eke out an existence by themselves and their families working as casual labourers during the busy season. Many of this class are investing their savings in land, and by sinking wells are enabled to take up land which by dint of hard labour can be improved until it produced good crops. It is to garden land that the petty ryot must in most cases turn. It is seldom possible for him to get large areas of dry land while the rents for wet land are usually so high that he might just as well continue to be a labourer. On garden land a man's industry governs his outturn.[24]

Though no explicit explanation was furnished as to the origin of the 'petty ryot' in the above statement, in view of the above quotation from

[21] *Statistical Appendix for Trichinopoly District* (1931), 'Supplement to the "A" Volume of the Trichinopoly District Gazetteer', p. 84.

[22] *Gazetteer of Tinnevelly District*, p. 128.

[23] Ibid., p. 157. In this connection an observation made by Krishna Bharadwaj deserves attention. In considering the reverse relationship between yield per acre and farm size as revealed by the 1954–57 Farm Management Survey, he has found that a relatively greater portion of land was devoted to more lucrative crops on smaller farms (*Production Conditions*, p. 14).

[24] P.B.R., No. 86, 26 Nov. 1923, p. 27, par. 22.

the 1931 *Statistical Appendix* for Trichinopoly District, the 'petty ryot' referred to here can be understood as denoting erstwhile agricultural labourers who had succeeded in obtaining small plots of land. The description reveals a close link between the growth of this type of small farmer and the intensification of agriculture. In garden land, the outturn depended on the industry and effort of the cultivator and an erstwhile labourer who had acquired a small bit of land could increase his yield by devoting intensive and careful labour to cultivation. The intensive cultivation of well-irrigated garden land is, at least in some areas, likely to have been an important economic base for the economic independence of former labourers, though no categorical conclusion is possible from this short reference. In previous chapters, it was noted that both the emancipation of agricultural labourers and the general trend towards intensification of agricultural practice lessened the advantages of large-scale farming. Here I shall add one more channel through which this change in cultivation worked against the advantage of the large scale farmer. The intensification of agriculture provided former agricultural labourers, upon whom large farms had depended, with a basis for economic independence, thus leading to the same result. The source also indicates that, conversely, the growth of small farmers out of the labourer classes strengthened the trend towards intensive agriculture. Thus these two, that is, the intensification of agriculture and the development of the trend towards independence among the agricultural labourers, were closely interlinked processes, stimulating each other.

Market conditions also encouraged the intensive cultivation practiced by small farmers. It will be recalled that there was an increase in the railway trade of some items for which people of lower classes were among the most important consumers, and it was inferred that this expansion of demand for those commodities reflected the emancipation of the lower classes. Interestingly, the kinds of product that were reported as being cultivated by small *raiyats* who had originally been labourers were chillies, tobacco and sugarcane, crops all related to the items that increased their trade by railway. In other words, increases in consumption by lower-caste people seem to have sustained and encouraged intensive cultivation by former labourers who owned garden plots, though the point still needs to be clarified by further research.

Low-caste Non-Brahmans who had been working as tenants or agricultural labourers in the wet zone also tried to raise their status to that of small landowning farmer. This trend is basically same as that of the Depressed castes.

Decrease in landownership of Brahmans

In sharp contrast to the increase in the area owned by Depressed castes and low-caste Non-Brahmans, there was a decrease in the landholdings of the Brahmans, the largest landholding group, between 1865 and 1925. With the exception of 2, all the 14 wet villages studied here evidenced a fall in Brahman landholdings. The 3,713 acres owned by Brahmans in 1865 shrank to 2,884 acres in 1925 (Tables 2.1 & 5.3; Figure 5.1). In this connection, we have to examine the change in area held by female *pattadars*. Most women *pattadars* in a village are likely to have belonged to the dominant landowning castes in the village. Hence a large portion of female *pattadars* probably belonged to Brahman and Vellalar communities. In the wet zone villages, the area owned by female *pattadars* jumped in the period between 1865 and 1925 from 126 acres to 755 acres, an increase of 629 acres, of which a considerable part must have belonged to female *pattadars* in Brahman communities. However, even if we assume that all the increased area was owned by female *pattadars* belonging to Brahman communities, the total area held by Brahmans did decrease in this period.

A similar trend was exhibited in the 7 villages of the intermediate zone, where the land owned by Brahmans nearly halved from 1,124 acres in 1865 to 595 acres in 1925 (Tables 2.3, 5.5 & 5.7). Though the area belonging to female *pattadars* showed an increase, from 341 acres in 1865 to 632 acres in 1925, and even if we assume that all the women landholders were Brahmans, the overall landholdings of Brahmans registered a definite decrease.

Changes in Brahman landholdings prior to and after 1895 exhibit different patterns. In the period between 1865 and 1895, the total holdings by Brahmans posted a marginal increase in the 14 wet land villages, from 3,713 acres to 3,795 acres (Tables 2.1 & 5.1). In this period, the area owned by female *pattadars* increased almost four times, from 126 acres to 439 acres, and hence the increase in the area owned by Brahmans may have been larger. The intermediate zone followed the same pattern, 1,124 acres in 1865 becoming 1,337 in 1895. However, during those 30 years there was no corresponding decrease in the landholdings of Non-Brahmans and Depressed castes and hence it is wrong to conclude that there was any real expansion in Brahmans' landholdings. Two factors would explain this apparent anomaly. The first one is a change in the way *samudayam*, or village common land, was registered in the Settlement Registers. As I shall show later, a large portion of the land registered as *samudayam* in the 1865 registers was registered as land owned by dominant landholders, such as Brahmans, in the 1895 registers. This seems to suggest that the area registered as *samudayam* in 1865 was in reality under the direct control of those dominant landholders. In other words, it may be misleading to take the transfer of *samudayam* land to the holdings of Brahman communities at its face value and to interpret it as indicating a real increase in their property. The second factor is a technical change in the way names of joint *pattadars* were described in the Settlement Registers. As only one of the joint *pattadars*' names was mentioned in the 1865 Settlement Registers and not each of them, a considerable area that was held by Brahman joint *pattadars* cannot be reckoned as such in our data-processing, whereas each of the joint *pattadars*' names was given in the 1895 registers, resulting in a nominal increase in the area owned by the Brahmans.

Thus it can be gathered that the seeming increase in area owned by Brahmans in the period between 1865 and 1895 as indicated by the tables may have been, in the main, only nominal, although it is also undeniable that Brahman landownership did not decrease in this period. As I shall discuss later, K. Gough's study of a village in Thanjavur revealed that Brahman landholdings were already in decline by the 1890s.

For changes after 1925, we have to depend on data from Appadurai village, where Brahmans owned 58.1 percent of the total land, outside that owned by temples, in 1925.[25] The area declined slightly to 56.5 percent in 1952, suggesting that even the period after 1925 witnessed the working of the same trend in Brahman landownership in the wet zone villages.

The gradual decline of Brahman landownership was reported from other districts. Studying a Thanjavur village, K. Gough pointed out a progressive decrease in the land areas held by Brahmans: while 98 percent of village land was owned by the village Brahmans in 1827, the area fell to 80 percent in 1897 and further dwindled to 41.2 percent in 1952. This clearly indicates a mass transfer of land from the hands of Brahmans to other communities.[26] A considerable amount of data is available about the changes in Tirunelveli district, which witnessed a definite decrease in the area owned by Brahmans. 'In the cases in which an appreciable tract of land has passed from one class of owners to

[25] Yanagisawa, *Socio-Economic Changes*, p. 103.

[26] Gough, *Rural Society in Southeast India*, pp. 195–212. See also André Béteille, *Caste, Class, and Power: Changing Patterns of Stratification in a Tanjore Village* (Berkeley and Los Angels, 1965), pp. 193–94.

another, it has almost invariably been from a number of the landlord class to an industrious cultivating proprietor, from a Brahman who does not take direct personal interest in agriculture to a Sevalai Vellalar or Shanar, that is, to men who will work on the land with their families, put labour into it and by sinking a well will grow two crops where one grew before.'[27] To cite another reference from the same district,

> (1) Landholders who do nothing more than let their lands and collect the rents.
> (2) Those who have some lands of their own which they cultivate themselves, and who also take up lands from others on lease, if circumstances would permit it.
> (3) Those who have no lands of their own, but only cultivate the lands of others on different terms of leases.
>
> Those coming under the second and third class have improved their status by yearly fresh acquisition of land, and by converting waste lands into cultivable ones. With the exception of a small percentage who are engaged in trade, the major portion of those falling under the first class are by degrees growing poorer and poorer by selling or mortgaging their property.[28]

With the exception of those engaged in trade, Brahmans thus gradually sold their land.[29]

Chapter 4 delineated changes in large farms managed by members of higher castes. To reiterate the process by which large landowners leased out their land, first, the gradual process of emancipation of labourers made it difficult for Brahman landowners to secure dependable labourers and make them work on the farms as hard as before; second, this change in the agricultural labour market occurred just when agriculture exhibited a trend towards more intensive cultivation and, therefore, more active and motivated participation of the workers was required to augment the yield of crops; and third, many Brahman families emigrated to urban areas in search of salaried jobs and better education, and some Brahmans leased a part of their holdings to tenants, thus

[27] P.B.R., No. 200, 5 June 1909, p. 7.

[28] Raghavaiyangar, *Memorandum*, pp. ccxx–ccxxi. It was also reported that 'the big landed gentries are so heavily involved in debts that their estate is going into the hands of their tenants in small holdings' (*MBEC,* Vol. 2, *Written Evidence*, p. 165).

[29] Dharma Kumar indicates that non-cultivating landlords, especially Brahmans, sold or leased their land to cultivators and moved to the cities or took to trade and money-lending in the village ('Agrarian Relations: South India', p. 232).

weakening their commitment to agricultural management. It is in this context that the decrease in Brahman landholdings should be understood. There is every probability that some Brahmans may even have sold a part of their land to raise funds for investment in their education and to cover other expenses necessary to maintain life in urban areas.[30] The process by which Brahman landlords lessened their personal interest in agriculture and reduced their landownership was well portrayed in the 1936 survey report on Gangaikondan village in Tirunelveli, quoted in Chapter 4.[31]

Of course, shifting to urban areas did not necessarily mean that Brahmans had no other choice but to sell their land. In fact even today there are many cases of Brahman families, though living in urban areas, still owning land in rural areas and leasing it to tenants. However, the trend towards the emancipation from landlords and the growth of disobedience was noticed not only among agricultural labourers but also among tenants. A 1914 survey reported 'complaints by landlords that they experience[d] unusual difficulty in collecting their rents'.[32] Sayana's Report on the Madras Presidency noted that 'the relations between the landlords and tenants were very strained during the depression. . . . There is a continued effort on the part of the tenant to get reduction of rents and to avoid payment of rents on grounds of distress and poverty, while the other frightens him with threats of eviction and civil courts.'[33] Sivaswamy suggested there was a growth in tenant

[30] Baker suggests that education was one of the chief reasons for the indebtedness of the agriculturists (*Rural Economy*, p. 178). A witness in Thanjavur stated that 'they [agriculturists] even sell their lands to educate their children' (*MBEC*, Vol. 2, *Written Evidence*, p. 142).

[31] Chapter 4, pp. 110-11; Thomas and Ramakrishnan (eds.), *Some South Indian Villages: A Resurvey*, p. 61. The emigration of Brahmans to urban areas was probably an important factor determining the extent to which they lost their landholdings. The Settlement Register of Lalgudi *taluk* indicates that the reduction in Brahman landholding was larger in the intermediate zone villages than in the villages of the wet zone. The distance from urban area may have accounted for this to some extent. While Brahmans living in the wet zone villages could work and attend schools in Tiruchirapalli city by commuting there everyday, those living in the intermediate zone had to move to the urban area for the same purpose, leading to a greater loss of land in the intermediate zone villages. In two small towns near Tiruchirapalli, Srirangam and Tiruvanaikovil, there are many Brahman families who had migrated from distant rural villages. It is presumed that this movement to urban areas may have started at the end of the last century (Yanagisawa, *Socio-Economic Changes*, pp. 218–20).

[32] G. O., No. 3594, Confidential, Revenue, 9 Dec. 1914, p. 55.

[33] Sayana, *The Agrarian Problems of Madras Province*, p. 275.

resistance to landlords. In the Madurai in 1947, 'the tenants have been agitating for a half-share of produce',[34] and in Tirunelveli, 'there is an agitation for the reduction of the fixed kind rent by one-eighth'.[35] In Tiruchirapalli district, 'landholder[s] will engage only such tenants who will do housework without murmur and without talking about legal rights'.[36] These reports amply confirm the accelerating resistance of tenants to the landlords.

As we have already seen, some descriptions point to the acquisition of small pieces of land by some tenants. My analysis shows that in the Lalgudi *taluk* of Trichinopoly district, many persons appeared as new *pattadars* from low-caste Non-Brahman communities such as the Muttiriyars, suggesting that many tenant farmers of this community acquired small plots of land. The acquisition of land by tenants would have strengthened their bargaining position with their landlords.

Thus, a study of the scanty evidence suggests that in the first half of the present century, tenants as well as labourers grew less obedient than before to landlords. It would not have been easy for landlords to collect rent from their tenants in a situation where the tenants were demanding rent reductions or refusing to pay it at all. This would have posed particular difficulties for Brahman landlords who lived in remote areas such as towns, and some naturally tended to sell the whole or a part of their holdings. This trend may have been accelerated by another effect of the exodus of Brahmans to urban areas, that is, the weakening of the unity among village landowners (*mirasidars*). This probably resulted in a lessening of the landlords' power to prevent their land from moving to other communities. In other words, the two changes in landholding examined above, the decrease in the area owned by Brahmans and the acquisition of small plots by members of Depressed castes and low-caste Non-Brahman communities, were two sides of the same phenomenon. That the dominance of higher castes in landownership was weakening is suggested in a contemporary document.

> . . . in some villages of the taluks of which I was the Tahsildar, there were one or two big men who paid all the taxes of the ryots of those villages and took possession of all the produce raised by them, lending them again small quantities of produce for their subsistence. Now such men have diminished in number, because the ryots are able to pay their own taxes and keep to themselves the lit-

[34] Sivaswamy, *Tenant*, Part 2, p. 20.
[35] Ibid., p. 23.
[36] Ibid., p. 33.

> tle they could save, instead of sending it to the pockets of the rich men. Thus, wealth is now more spread than it was.[37]

Even in Thanjavur district, a stronghold of Brahman landholders, a witness wrote that 'a number of big mirasdars . . . have already [been] ruined and are still being ruined', and another stated that 'the tenants are well off, but landholders have become impoverished'.[38]

Increase in Landownership by the Newly Rich

In addition to the decline in the domination of higher castes in landownership, the period witnessed another important change in the landholding pattern.[39] Some of the newly rich who had accumulated wealth under British rule expanded their landed property and some even grew into large-scale landholders. At the centre of this new wave were such communities as the Chettiars and Vellalars, two Non-Brahman communities. Data from the Settlement Registers of 1895 and 1925 point to the fact that this phenomenon gained momentum after the 1890s.

Increase in landownership of Vellalars and Chettiars in the wet zone

The traditional occupation of the Chettiars of South India is said to be trade,[40] and many merchants are from this community even today. Studying their landholdings in the 14 wet zone villages from the mid-

[37] Raghavaiyangar, *Memorandum*, p. 261. The Manual of Tinnevelly district suggests: '. . . the social and political results of the changes have been to raise the position of the lower castes and classes, to give them the opportunity of rising to independence and wealth, and to furnish the upper classes with appropriate means of sharing with all the rights which they once enjoyed exclusively. . . . The higher castes, inheriting the qualities developed by the system of monopoly of land by which they so long kept the upper hand, are heavily weighted in the race by their own habits and modes of thought and action when their monopoly is broken up, and are less fitted for a severe competition with the hardier races below them' (*Manual of Tinnevelly District*, p. 32).

[38] *MBEC,* Vol. 2, *Written Evidence*, pp. 125, 153.

[39] The 'Nadan' changed their title to 'Nadavan' between 1865 and 1895 and therefore these two titles denote the same community. Though Tables 2.1 and 5.1 point to a change in landownership by this community, it may be inappropriate to regard this change as indicating a general trend in the wet zone as a whole, since the majority of their land was concentrated only in two villages.

[40] According to the Manual of Trichinopoly district, out of 6,912 Chettiars who were employed, 3,927 were traders (p. 102).

nineteenth century onwards, a sharp increase can be noted. In 1865 they owned 103 acres, 142 in 1895 and 322 acres, more than double the previous figure, in 1925. In the intermediate zone, their landholdings increased more than 20 times, from 7 acres and 47 acres in 1865 and 1895 respectively to 163 acres in 1925. As noted in Chapter 3, South Indian agriculture was integrated into the world market and became commercialised under British rule. Traders and businessmen from this community are likely to have accumulated their wealth making the most of the opportunities offered and invested the funds so accumulated in landed property.

A similar trend is noticed in other communities also. While the Reddiar, an important community of 'agriculturists' who were believed to have come from Telugu districts, reduced their holdings in the dry zone villages, they rapidly increased their land in the wet zone villages. The meagre 20 acres they held in the wet zone in 1865 grew to 56 acres in 1895 and an immense 392 acres in 1925. The Pillais also gained in area by 1925, though they had suffered decreases in landownership between 1865 and 1895.

Increase in the landownership of larger Non-Brahman landholders

It is very important to note that there was a growth of large landholders among the Chettiars, Reddiars and Pillais. The area these communities owned in the 14 wet villages is aggregated for each size group and the rates of change between 1895 and 1925 are shown in Figure 5.3. The vertical axis shows the size of landownership, from the smallest size group ('1') at the bottom to the largest size group ('11') at the top. The graph shows the change in extent as a percentage, the standard year being 1895. The *purambokku* land is excluded from the calculation.

The figure shows that the extent of land owned by the three communities considerably increased in the large size groups, namely size groups 9, 10 and 11, or 25 acres or more, and the increase was particularly remarkable in the largest size group 11, or 100 acres and more. On the other hand, an increase is noticeable in the smaller size groups (size groups 1–4, or less than 3 acres), while the area decreased in the middle size groups. As a whole, the chart indicates a possible concentration of landownership and a growth of large landowners in these communities. Figure 5.4 shows the change in area held by all Non-Brahman communities in the wet villages. It indicates more clearly the growth of stratification among Non-Brahmans in the wet villages during the period.

Figure 5.3
Index Number of Area Held by Pillais, Reddiars and Chettiars in Wet Zone Villages in Lalgudi *Taluk*, 1925 (1895=100)

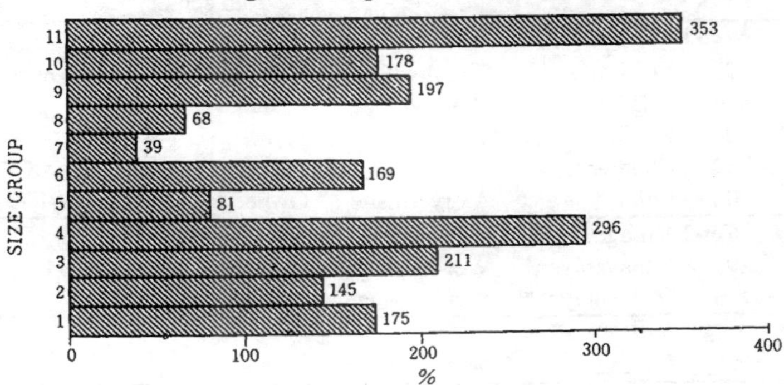

Figure 5.4
Index Number of Area Held by Non-Brahmans in Wet Zone Villages in Lalgudi *Taluk*, 1925 (1895=100)

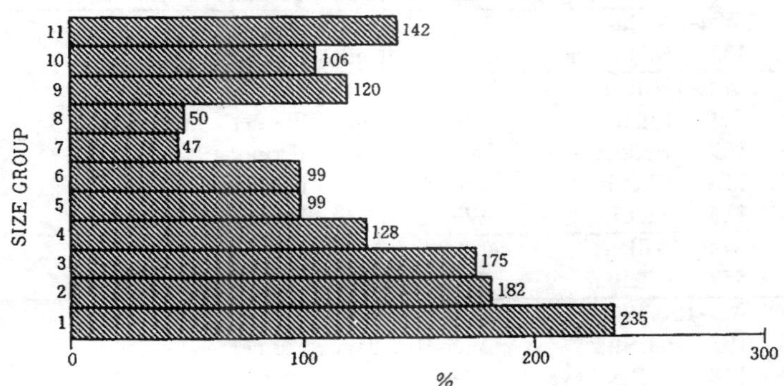

Table 5.9
Large Landholders Who Expanded Holdings between 1895 and 1925 in Villages in Lalgudi *Taluk*

Patta-dar	Land tax(Rs) (1925)	Community (Title)	Residence	Main economic activity at the beginning of the 20th century
	Wet-1 Village			
W-1	775	Muslim	Tiruchy city	Lorry & bus company owner
W-2	676	Udaiyan	Other village	Estate agent
W-3	401	Pillai	Wet-1 village	Farmer
W-4	264	Chettiar		(No information)
W-5	108	Pillai	A dry village	Owned tea estate in Ceylon
	Wet-2 Village			
W-6	296	Malavarayan*	Wet-2 village	Farmer
W-7	113	Malavarayan*	Wet-2 village	Farmer
	Wet-4 Village			
W-8	907	Pillai	Wet-4 village	Farmer
	Wet-5 Village			
W-9	206	Ayyangar	Srirangam	Farmer
W-10	155	Pillai	Tiruchy city	Owner of timber depot
	Wet-6 Village			
W-11	1170	Reddiar	Wet-6 village	Given land by W-12
W-12	1007	Reddiar	Rangoon	Worked for the British Army
W-13	383	Reddiar	Other village	Given land by W-12
	Wet-7 Village			
W-14	133	Muttiriyar	Wet-7 village	Farmer
	Wet-8 Village			
W-15	4520	Pillai	Wet-8 village	Farmer
W-16	169	Reddiar	Wet-8 village	Farmer
W-17	116	Chettiar	Wet-8 village	Farmer
W-18	115	Muttiriyar	Wet-8 village	Farmer
	Wet-9 Village			
W-19	857	Chettiar	Tiruchy city	Saree merchant
	Wet-10 Village			
W-20	193	Chettiar	Wet-10 village	Farmer
W-21	118	Pallavarayan*	Wet-10 village	Farmer
W-22	116	Cervaikaran**	Wet-10 village	Farmer
	Wet-11 Village			
W-23	252	Ayyangar	Wet-11 village	Farmer
W-24	152	Ayyangar	Srirangam	Vakil
W-25	134	Kalattuvandan*	Wet-11 village	Farmer

Table 5.9 (Contd.)

	Wet-12 Village			
W-26	235	Kangiyan*	Wet-12 village	Farmer
W-27	167	Kangiyan*	Wet-12 village	Farmer
	Wet-13 Village			
W-28	414	Reddiar	Wet-6 village	Same person as W-11
W-29	291	Reddiar	Rangoon	Same person as W-12
	Wet-14 Village			
W-30	687	Pillai	Tiruvanaikovil	Contractor (bridge construction)
	Intermediate-1 Village			
I-1	98	Raju	Int.-1 village	Farmer
	Intermediate-2 Village			
I-2	152	Chettiar	Sriramgam	Farmer
	Intermediate-3 Village			
I-3	276	Kavundan	Ceylon	Kangany of tea estate (Native of this village)
I-4	201	Kavundan	Int.-3 village	Farmer
I-5	195	Pillai	Ceylon	Kangany of tea estate (Native of Turaiyur *taluk*)
I-6	120	Temple	Srirangam	Temple
I-7	176	Kavundan	Ceylon	Kangany of tea estate
I-8	111	Chettiar	Manachanallur	Rice mill owner
I-9	101	Chettiar	Manachanallur	Rice mill owner
	Intermediate-5 Village			
I-10	80	Kavundan	Int.-5 village	Farmer
I-11	66	Chettiar	Manachanallur	Rice mill owner
	Intermediate-6 Village			
I-12	64	Paraiyar	Int.-6 village	Farmer
I-13	56	Vangar*	Int.-6 village	Farmer
	Dry-2 Village			
D-1	42	Depressed caste	Dry-2 village	Farmer
	Dry-3 Village			
D-2	32	Muttiriyar	Dry-3 village	Farmer
D-3	31	Muttiriyar	Dry-3 village	Farmer
	Dry-4 Village			
D-4	30	Pillai	Tiruchy city	(No information)
	Dry-5 Village			
D-5	29	Pillai	Dry-5 village	Farmer
D-6	27	Chettiar	Other village	Moneylender

Note: * Title of Kallar caste; ** Title of Muttiriyar caste

Int.: Intermediate

Economic background to the growth of Non-Brahman large landholders

In order to clarify the economic background to the growth of large landholders of Non-Brahman communities, I conducted interviews with village accountants and other aged villagers in each of the 26 villages and collected information about the large landholders. The names of the large landholders about whom information was being collected were selected from the computer-processed landholders' lists for 1895 and 1925. First, I calculated the caste-wise number of the large landholders paying more than Rs. 100 (in the case of wet villages) and of the top ten largest landholders (in intermediate and dry zone villages) for each village for each of the two years; then I selected the communities in which the numbers of larger landholders had increased during the period; last, I determined the large *pattadars* who not only belonged to the selected communities but also considerably increased their holdings between 1895 and 1925. In the course of my fieldwork, I gathered information on these selected landholders, especially on their economic activities at the beginning of the twentieth century through interviews with the villagers. The economic activities and place of residence of these landholders are tabulated in Table 5.9. Naturally, the villagers did not remember clearly the economic situation of these *pattadars*, and sometimes they had no idea even of their names, but the data shown in Table 5.9 remains useful in clarifying changes in landownership during the period.

The table shows, first, that a considerable number of the large landholders expanding their landed property holdings were Non-Brahman outsiders living in Tiruchirapalli city, Srirangam town, Ceylon, Rangoon, etc., and were engaged in commercial activities, in transportation, in the construction of a bridge over the River Kollidam, in managing tea estates in Ceylon, in service with the British Army at Rangoon, etc. Needless to say, many of these non-agricultural economic activities were facilitated and developed by the socio-economic transformation of Indian society under British rule. In this sense this class of people were the newly rich who had grown under colonial rule. My findings lead me to conclude that some Non-Brahmans accumulated their wealth through commercial activities and other non-agricultural activities, purchased large plots of land in the wet villages and developed into large landholders during the period.[41]

[41] Though I call them 'the newly rich', this neither implies that they originated from social classes different from those who had been engaged in trading

Second, the table shows that there were many Non-Brahman resident farmers who became large landholders during the period. One may interpret this change as suggesting a growth in the number of 'rich farmers' among the Non-Brahmans. This point, however, remains to be clarified by future research, since we lack accurate information that may reveal certain aspects of their land management, such as whether their main source of income was from their farm or from such non-agricultural activities as money-lending to neighbours.

Since the Settlement Register data for the 26 villages in Lalgudi *taluk* is not available for the period after 1925, we shall examine cases of land transfer in Appadurai village. In this village, there were many cases after 1925 of non-local people acquiring land. A Naidu family, for example, had no land in this village in 1925 but purchased 7 acres of village land after 1925. An interview with their descendants revealed that their grandfather was a merchant in Tiruchirapalli city, dealing in paddy and millet in the biggest market in the city. His son, who was also engaged in the grain trade and ran a tannery business, bought the land in this village because it was fertile.[42] In another example, a Christian, who had worked as a supervisor in an estate in Ceylon for about thirty years, returned to Tiruchirapalli in 1930, started a rice mill there and bought land in Appadurai village.[43] Available data suggest that the area owned

---

and money-lending nor that traders and moneylenders appeared only in the colonial period. Rather, it is well known that the pre-colonial period witnessed a considerable development in trading and money-lending activities. However, as I discuss in this chapter, the integration of South Indian agriculture in the world trade network and the consequent expansion in the commercialisation of agriculture offered greater opportunities for traders and moneylenders. Furthermore, the new colonial rule provided many new spheres of economic activity, such as the management of plantations, transportation, rice mills, civil constructions, the activities relating to the armed forces and lawyers. The term 'the newly rich', as used here, denotes all those who seized the new favourable opportunities to accumulate wealth, regardless of their origin.

Though moneylenders and traders increased their holdings, the area they acquired was not necessarily the land owned by the person to whom they had given a loan or with whom they had traded. They may often have invested their accumulated funds to purchase rich land in wet zone villages, regardless of the place of their economic activity.

[42] Yanagisawa, *Socio-Economic Changes,* p. 240.

[43] Ibid., pp. 240–43. An important change in landholding in Uttar Pradesh has been revealed by Eric Stokes. There, the old elite who had owned 60 to 65 percent of the land in the province lost their land, whereas in Kanpur district money-lending castes extended their hold from 15.7 percent of the land in 1802 to 41.7 percent in 1900 (Stokes, *The Peasant and the Raj,* pp. 213–14). Changes

in this village by Tiruchirapalli traders did not decline after 1925 but rather increased. It can be surmised, therefore, that the trend of acquiring landed property in the wet zone by the newly rich was not reversed but remained discernible even after 1925.

Data from other districts also point to the acquisition of land in the wet zone by the newly rich. A memorandum notes the acquisition of land by traders and professionals in 1902. Stating that there had been an increase in the numbers and wealth of traders, moneylenders, factory-owners, lawyers and other professionals compared to 1891, it revealed that 'the demand for good land is increasing; much of the land newly irrigated by the Periyar has been taken up by professional men, and the legal profession has so increased its properties that whereas in 1891 only one pleader or vakil in five was a land-owner, in 1901 the proportion was one to three—a fair commentary on the value of land. About 11 percent. of the whole land in the Presidency is held by all classes of trading and professional men and by officials.' Together with 2.5 percent of land owned by moneylenders, a total of 13.5 percent of the land was held by traders, moneylenders and professionals by 1902.[44] My

---

in the landholding pattern in colonial Andhra also deserves attention. According to D. Rajasekhar, while Brahman landholders lost their land, traders and moneylenders were the net gainers. D. Rajasekhar, 'Commercialization of Agriculture and Changes in Distribution of Land Ownership in Kurnool District of Andhra (c.1900–50)', in Bhattacharya et al. (eds.), *South Indian Economy,* pp. 92–96.

[44] G.O., No. 711, Revenue, 11 Aug. 1902, p. 26.

The Inspector-General of Registration examined the figures on sales of land and concluded, 'in no district in the Presidency is there any reason to fear that lands are passing from the hands of agriculturists to the trading or other classes' (Kumar, 'Landownership and Inequality', p. 257 n. 33. See also Kumar, *Land and Caste*, pp. 178–79). This statement, however, needs to be qualified. First, 'the bulk of the lending is done by ryots' (*MBEC* Vol. 1, p. 81). Hence, if the amount of land purchased by professional moneylenders was not large, a considerable extent of land may have been transferred to those *raiyats* who lent money to their neighbours. My data from Lalgudi *taluk* also suggests that not all the newly rich belonged to 'non-agriculturist castes' like Chettiars, but rather many were members of those castes whose traditional occupation was supposed to be agriculture, such as Pillais and Reddiars. (The difficulty in determining the status of the purchaser or seller was discussed in 'Notes Connected with G.O., No. 468, Judicial Department, 14 Mar. 1906', p. 2.)

Second, apart from the above problem regarding the definition of 'non-agriculturist', the amount of land that passed out of the hands of agriculturists to those of non-agriculturists cannot be considered to have been totally insignificant, if cases of mortgage are taken into account. Though it is difficult to assess how many of the cases of mortgage represented or resulted in the real transfer of

analysis of the Settlement Registers for villages in Lalgudi *taluk* yielded quantitative evidence for this type of land transfer. Later, in 1929, the Madras Provincial Banking Enquiry Committee issued a questionnaire, in which witnesses were questioned whether 'a large number of people who are efficient farmers, are being turned into tenants for a period, or tenants at will through the process of the enforcement of the old debts and the landed property passing on into the hands of creditors'. Most witnesses who replied to this question answered in the affirmative.[45] Tsukasa Mizushima's examination of the case studies done by this committee in Madurai confirms this by pointing to the transfer of village land to moneylenders in Madurai town.[46] K. Gough seems to provide us with another example. In her analysis of land registers for a Thanjavur village, she indicates that a considerable portion of the land the Brahman landholders lost was gained by traders from outside the village between 1897 and 1952.[47]

This trend in landholding was confirmed in 1934 by the *Report on Agricultural Indebtedness*, which noted that in the period between 1903

---

landed property, the Inspector-General of Registration considered mortgage as a type of land transfer. He stated in 1911 that 'the net extent of property that passed out of the hands of agriculturists each year on mortgage in ryotwari villages forms an insignificant portion of the total holdings, viz., 0.7 *per cent.* of dry lands and 1.0 *per cent.* of wet lands'. Since the net extent annually transferred to 'non-agriculturists' by sale amounted to about 0.2 percent of the total wet holdings, the net wet land which annually passed out of hands of agriculturists to non-agriculturists either by sale or mortgage accounted for about 1.2 percent of the total wet land in the Madras Presidency. Though the Inspector-General considered this rate to be insignificantly small, the cumulative result after a period of say 30 years could be very significant, if the land transfer continued at the same annual rate of 1.2 percent (G.O., No. 2825, Confidential, Revenue, 18 Sept. 1911, Enclosure A, p. 8). Thus the registration statistics seem to accord with, rather than invalidate the above observation that land was passing into the hands of traders and moneylenders.

[45] For the affirmative replies, *MBEC*, Vol. 2, *Written Evidence*, pp. 19, 40, 145, 165, 190, 280, 296, 398, 407, 437, 494, 512, 514, 584, 590, 611, 878, 882, 887, 890, 959, 1144; for the negative replies, pp. 109, 337, 505, 1244.

[46] Mizushima, 'Minami Indo Noson no Ruikeika' p. 8. In his survey report of a village in Madurai, a professor of a College stated in 1918 that 'the moneylender and his exorbitant rates of interest were the veritable bane of the poorer ryots' (G.O., No. 1779, Revenue, 7 May 1918, p. 6).

[47] Gough, *Rural Society in Southeast India*, pp. 195–211. According to M.S.S. Pandian, a large extent of landed property was alienated by small peasants to non-agrarian classes in Nanchilnadu (presently included in Kanyakumari district) in the 1920s and 1930s. M.S.S. Pandian, *The Political Economy of Agrarian Change: Nanchilnadu, 1880–1939* (New Delhi, 1990), pp. 157–62.

and 1931, a great deal of money had been invested in land, particularly in wet land, by people who were not cultivating *raiyats*.[48] It stated:

> So, from 1931 to 1934, the area of ryotwari land which went to non-agriculturists, excepting that in Malabar and South Kanara, is 2,070,000 acres. Of the 10,362,000 acres of ryotwari land which changed hands during these years, I should say a very large proportion went to big absentee landlords particularly agriculturist moneylenders. This shows that many small and medium landholders were and are being rendered landless and destitute because of foreclosure on their debts.[49]

It would be wrong to interpret this accumulated wealth through money-lending and trade as being confined to the members of such Non-Brahman communities as the Chettiars and Pillais. There are instances of Brahmans also expanding their landed property and being engaged in such activities as money-lending and trade. Gough pointed out that in the latter half of the nineteenth century some Brahmans who became traders bought paddy from the local villages, sold it in Pudukkottai and bought back merchandise to sell in Thanjavur.[50] In 1916 in Dusi village, where all the landowners were Brahmans, 'almost all the landlords have made savings. About 20 per cent of the savings is utilised as agricultural capital, about 10 per cent in savings banks, about 50 per cent on loans to neighbours.'[51] In Gangaikondan village, Tirunelveli district also, 'there are about ten principal moneylenders in the village who have lent Rs. 275,000 among the villagers . . . 80 per cent. of moneylenders are Brahmins'.[52]

Thus, even though some Brahmans may have enlarged their holdings as a result of trading and money-lending, for example, a larger amount of land left Brahman hands as a result of the decline of Brahman dominance in village society; this resulted in a net reduction in the area held by the Brahman communities.

[48] G.O., No. 41, Revenue, 6 Jan. 1934, p. 4. A survey of rural indebtedness conducted in 1935 in two villages in South Arcot district revealed that a banker had come to own a large amount of land in one of the villages simply because of his money dealings (B.V. Narayanaswamy Naidu and V. Venkataraman, *The Problem of Rural Indebtedness* [Anamalainagar: Annamalai University, 1935], p. 14).

[49] Sathyanathan, *Report on Agricultural Indebtedness*, p. 33.

[50] Gough, *Rural Society in Southeast India,* p. 187.

[51] Slater (ed.), *Some South Indian Villages*, p. 91.

[52] Thomas and Ramakrishnan (eds.), *Some South Indian Villages: A Resurvey*, p. 105.

Changes in the Distribution of Land among Various Size Groups

As discussed in Chapter 1, the conventional view about the changes in Indian rural society under British rule has it that the British revenue policy and the development of commercial agriculture and a money economy led to the impoverishment of agriculturists and the growth of stratification in rural society; farmers' debts increased and considerable numbers of farmers lost a part or all of their landholdings, whereas moneylenders, merchants and some rich farmers increased their holdings. This view assumes an increase in the number of landless agricultural labourers and pauper farmers and, on the other side, an increase in the area held by larger landowners at the expense of deteriorating numbers of middle-class farmers. Dharma Kumar has aggregated the land revenue statistics for each district in the Madras Presidency, drew Lorenz Curves for each district and concluded that a clear tendency for the concentration of land did not exist in South Indian districts between 1853 and 1946, though a slight concentration in landownership can be noticed in some of the irrigated districts.[53]

However, as I have shown in the previous section, one of the findings from the analysis of the Settlement Registers and other sources was that a group of Non-Brahmans, engaging in such businesses as trade, money-lending, transportation, construction and the management of plantations, accumulated wealth and purchased landed property, some of them even growing into large landowners. This, in contrast to the conclusion drawn by Dharma Kumar, points to a trend towards a polarisation of the Non-Brahman society. How should this be reconciled with the results of Dharma Kumar's analysis?

Figure 5.5 shows the size-wise change in landownership in the period between 1895 and 1925, for all 26 villages from the three ecological zones in Lalgudi *taluk* and for all communities. The *purambokku* land and *samudayam* (village common land) are excluded from the calculation. As the chart indicates, while the area in the smaller size groups expanded, a reduction in area is discernible in the larger size groups (size groups 7 and more). This accords well with Dharma Kumar's view that landholding was not concentrated in fewer hands.

Figure 5.6 demonstrates the changes for the 14 wet zone villages. Here, we find an increase in the area belonging to size group 11, or 100 acres and more, which seems to indicate a slight tendency towards differentiation in landownership. However, if account is taken of the facts

[53] Kumar, 'Landownership and Inequality'.

Figure 5.5
Index Number of Area Held by Various Size Groups in Villages in Lalgudi *Taluk*, 1925 (1895=100)

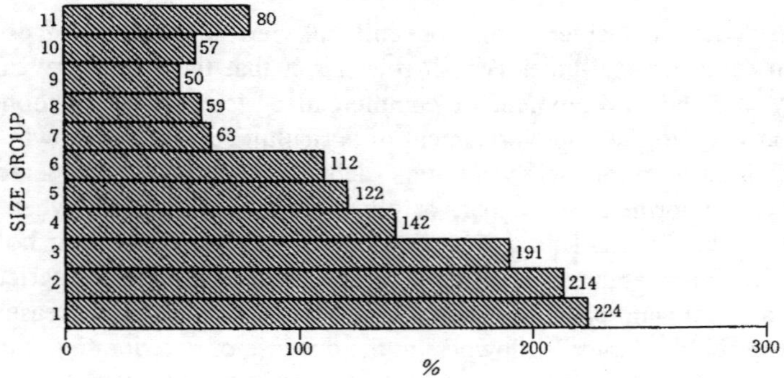

Figure 5.6
Index Number of Area Held by Various Size Groups in Wet Zone Villages in Lalgudi *Taluk*, 1925 (1895=100)

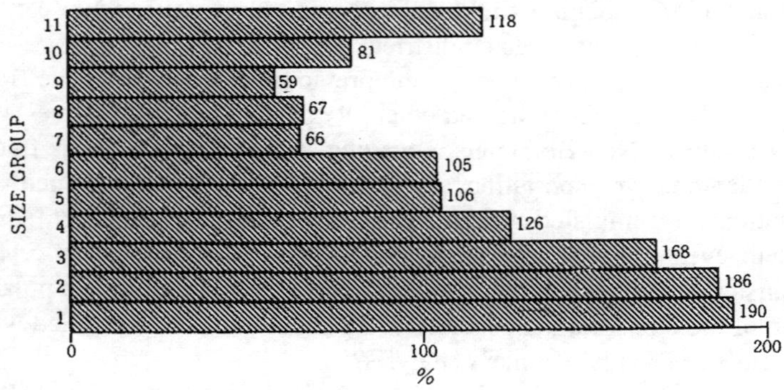

Figure 5.7
Index Number of Area Held by Various Size Groups of Brahman Communities in Wet Zone Villages in Lalgudi *Taluk*, 1925 (1895=100)

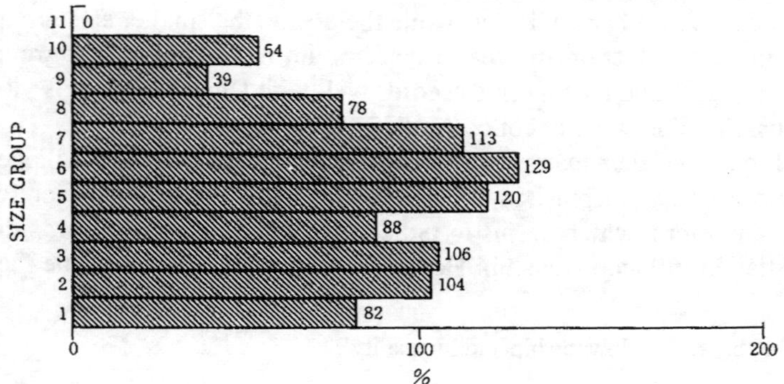

that the rate of increase in this size group was as low as 18 percent and that the area belonging to the other large size groups (size groups 7 to 10) nearly halved in the same period, it is difficult to identify a clear trend of land concentration in the hands of larger landholders. Thus this chart also supports Dharma Kumar's view, which admits a slight concentration in some of the wet districts.

The seeming absence of a trend towards a concentration of landholdings in the wet zone can be attributed to changes in Brahman landholdings in the zone. Figure 5.7 shows changes in the extent of land owned by Brahmans, the largest landowning community, in the wet zone. It shows a remarkable decrease in the larger size groups. Landholders owning more than 15 acres (size groups 8 to 11) decreased their holdings to a large extent. The larger the size of ownership, the greater the rate of reduction. Landownership in the middle size groups expanded, but it decreased in the smaller size groups.

What seems most important is that this change in Brahman landownership, as demonstrated by Figure 5.7, is the complete reverse of changes in the area owned by the Chettiars, Vellalars and Reddiars as shown in Figure 5.3, where the area of both the larger size groups and the smaller size groups considerably increased. Thus, the period between 1895 and 1925 witnessed two opposite processes taking place simultaneously in the wet zone villages of Lalgudi *taluk*. If the data is analysed without taking into account the difference between the Brahman and Non-Brahman communities (Figures 5.5 and 5.6), the growth of larger size landownership among Non-Brahmans may not be noticed, since it is shadowed by the counter-balancing changes in Brahman landownership (Figure 5.7).

These findings lead me to conclude that, with progress in the commercialisation of agriculture and other economic changes under colonial rule, a group of newly rich people from Non-Brahman communities probably acquired landed property, with some of them growing to large landholders, and that a trend towards polarisation was noticeable in Non-Brahman communities.[54]

In addition, the Depressed-caste members and low-caste Non-

[54] Polarisation among the landowners is suggested by the Manual of Tinnevelly district. It reports that there was wild speculation in the extension of cultivation, which led often on one hand to the aggrandisement of single landholders, and on the other to the ruin of the unsuccessful speculator in land, in either case widening the degrees of difference in wealth and power among individuals of the landowning class (p. 30).

Brahmans exhibited another type of change in landholding. Figure 5.8, which shows the changes in the landholdings of the Depressed-caste members, Muttiriyars and Udaiyars in the wet zone villages, indicates that the landholdings of these communities increased in almost all the size groups. The increase was particularly remarkable in the smaller size groups. The aggregate picture of changes in landholding in wet villages, demonstrated in Figure 5.6, results from a merging of these three types of change into one.

I shall now briefly examine changes in the intermediate and dry zones in comparison with those in the wet zone. The charts for the intermediate and dry zones (Figures 5.9 & 5.10) show that landownership decreased in the larger size groups and increased in the smaller size groups. It is important to add that Vellalar communities generally decreased their landholdings in the larger size groups in these zones. My findings in the intermediate and dry zones seem to support the notion that the supposed polarisation in landownership did not proceed in these zones.[55] However, data from my fieldwork reveal that some villagers in intermediate and dry villages purchased land in wet zone villages (Table 5.9). The *pattadar* signified by the code number W-5 in that table lived in a dry village but owned a tea estate in Ceylon and ten acres of newly purchased land in a wet village. Another case is that of the Reddiars shown by code numbers W-11, W-12 and W-13, who were originally the natives of an intermediate zone village but lived in the Wet-6 village to look after land purchased there. A merchant, a native of a dry village but living in Lalgudi town at the time, told us that it was not uncommon for rich villagers in dry villages to purchase land in more fertile areas in the wet and intermediate zones. It is not unlikely that villagers in the dry and intermediate zones who accumulated wealth through various economic activities invested their funds in purchasing more valuable land in villages with better irrigation rather than purchasing land in their own dry villages. In support of this observation, a cotton merchant in Coimbatore district testified before the Banking Enquiry Committee that 'monied classes and merchants purchase only irrigated wet lands, but not dry lands'.[56] Though they did not expand their landed property in the dry and intermediate zone villages, the possibility that the number of

[55] Washbrook, 'Economic Development and Social Stratification in Rural Madras: The "Dry Region" 1879–1929'; Bruce Robert, 'Economic Change and Agrarian Organization'.

[56] *MBEC,* Vol. 4, *Oral Evidence*, p. 522.

Figure 5.8
Index Number of Area Held by Various Size Groups of Muttiriyars, Udaiyars and Depressed Castes in Wet Zone Villages in Lalgudi *Taluk*, 1925 (1895=100)

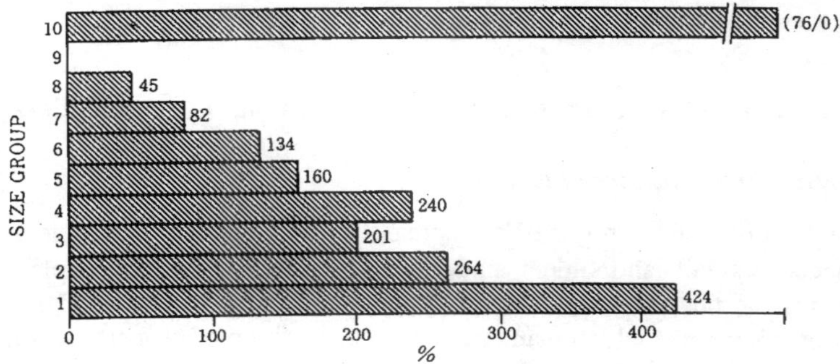

Figure 5.9
Index Number of Area Held by Various Size Groups in Intermediate Zone Villages in Lalgudi *Taluk*, 1925 (1895=100)

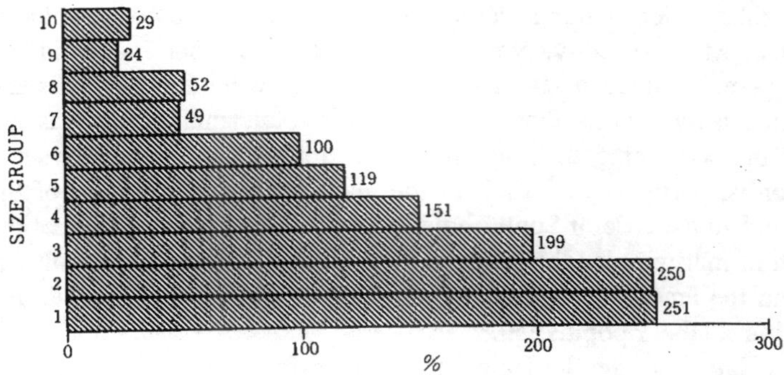

Figure 5.10
Index Number of Area Held by Various Size Groups in Dry Zone Villages in Lalgudi *Taluk*, 1925 (1895=100)

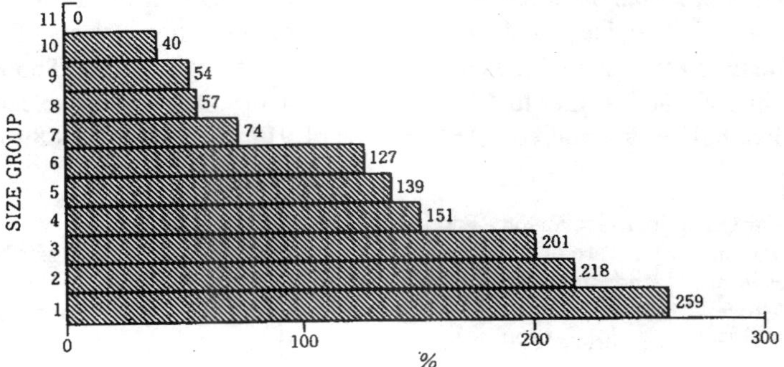

rich villagers in these zones grew cannot easily be ruled out and should be carefully examined in future research work.

An Interpretation of the Increase in the Number of Landholders

Increase in the number of landholders

Many scholars have reported an increase in the number of landholders, especially small landholders, under British rule. The popular explanation for the fact finds the cause in population increases and the Hindu law of inheritance which mandates an equal partition of property among sons.[57] I have already presented, in Chapter 1, some criticisms that have been made against this popular view. In the case of western India, Dhairyabala Pandit analysed the genealogies of several landowning families in South Gujarat and concluded that, contrary to the popular view, subdivision among descendants was not as considerable as expected. More recently, Neil Charlesworth noted that India did not enter the realm of rapid aggregate population growth until the 1920s and presented a hypothesis that an individual's total landholding was not falling but was being split into smaller and more geographically separated plots, partly as the result of the market-oriented response of the farmers.[58] In the case of South India, Bruce Robert has assumed that the growth of marginal landholdings in part reflects both extensive cultivation and the emergence of new landholders from the small farmer and agricultural labour population.[59]

My data from the Settlement Registers offers some clues to test the validity of the various interpretations regarding the increase in the number of landholders. In Lalgudi *taluk* also, the number of landholders increased to a great extent during the period. In the wet zone villages the number more than doubled between 1865 and 1895, from 1,361 to 2,921, and further increased to 4,862 during the next thirty years. The intermediate zone also witnessed a rapid increase, from 1,160 in 1865 to 2,115 in 1895 and further to 4,064 in 1925. The dry zone was no exception; landholders numbered 1,161 in 1865, 1,917 in 1895 and 3,689 in

[57] For example, Macpherson, 'Economic Development in India'.

[58] Pandit, 'Myths around Subdivision and Fragmentation of Holdings'; N. Charlesworth, 'Trends in the Agricultural Performance', pp. 130–31.

[59] Bruce L. Robert, J., 'Structural Change in Indian Agriculture: Land and Labour in Bellary District, 1890–1980', *IESHR* 22, 3 (1985), p. 289.

1925. The increase was especially remarkable in the smaller size groups. For example, in the wet zone villages the total number of landholders increased between 1865 and 1895 by 1,560 persons, of which 821 were in the smallest size group 1, 308 were in the second smallest size group 2 and 201 were in size group 3.[60] The increase in number of landholders witnessed during the next thirty years was also mainly in the two smallest size groups. The intermediate and dry zones were no exception, in that the number of smaller landholders increased very sharply.

Increasing population pressure?

Can the increase in the number of landholders be fully explained by population increase and land division under Hindu law? The population increase in the 26 villages was in fact much less than the rate of increase in the number of landholders for our 60 year period. The figures in Table 5.10 are derived from the population data attached to the Settlement Registers for 1895 and 1925 and from the 1871 Census data for

Table 5.10
Changes in Population in Villages in Lalgudi *Taluk*

Year	1871 Persons (Houses)	1895 Persons (Houses)	1925 Persons (Houses)
14 Wet villages	14,260 (2,214)	15,555 (2,651)	16,585 (3,445)
Persons per house	6.44	5.87	4.81
6 Intermediate villages	6,660 (1,042)	6,507 (1,096)	7,222 (1,469)
Persons per house	6.39	5.94	4.92
5 Dry villages	7,129 (1,178)	8,158 (1,628)	9,025 (1,937)
Persons per house	6.05	5.01	4.66

Source: Figures for 1895 and 1925: From *Resettlement Registers of Villages in Lalgudi Taluk, Trichinopoly District.*
Figures for 1871: The village names corresponding to those of 1895 are identified by the description about changes in village boundaries in the 1895 Settlement Register for each village. The 1871 figures for thus identified villages are compiled from *Census Statement of Population of 1871 in Each Village of the Trichinopoly District* (Madras, 1874).

[60] For the detailed tables, see Yanagisawa, *Minamiindo Shakai Keizaishi,* Tables 7.16–7.19

the corresponding villages. In the intermediate zone, six villages were studied (one was omitted due to lack of information). A glance at the table reveals that the rate of population growth in each of the two 30 year spans, from 1865 to 1895 and from 1895 to 1925, was around 10 percent or less, which seems too low to explain the great increase in the number of landholders, an increase of 200 percent in each 30 year span.

Second, there is evidence that, in the whole of South India at least till the 1910s, the expansion of cultivated land kept pace with the increase in population. According to a report of 1893, there was a 30 percent increase in the population of Madras Presidency between 1852 and 1891, with a parallel increase in the cultivated land—25 percent in dry land, 40 percent in land under government irrigation and 138 percent in private land irrigated by wells. It concluded 'that the increase in the cultivated area, making allowance for the increased productiveness of irrigated as compared with unirrigated lands, is quite on a par with it if it does not exceed the increase in population'.[61] If we consider the effect of improved irrigation facilities and wells on agricultural production, 'the percentage of increase in production cannot be less than 3 or 4 times the increase in population'.[62]

C.J. Baker, examining population growth after the 1890s, has shown that the cultivated area per head of population changed very little between 1880 and 1910 in Tamilnadu except some districts such as Coimbatore; however it decreased sharply after 1930.[63] Data available from the 1923 Settlement Report of Trichinopoly district also supports his argument about the period before 1930. In this district between 1891 and 1921, while the population posted an increase of 20 percent, the area cropped with paddy expanded to a larger extent, from 190,000 acres to 260,000 acres, or by 38 percent. 'The rate of increase of areas under staple crops is far greater than the rate of increase of the population.'[64] 'Still, a large area remains and the reason for the non-occupation of this seems to be lack of population. The population in the villages where there is a large extent of waste is not sufficient to cultivate it.'[65]

My data thus supports the criticism put forward by Charlesworth and Pandit regarding the conventional view that attributes the increase

[61] Raghavaiyangar, *Memorandum*, pp. 47–48.

[62] Ibid., p. 48.

[63] Baker, *Rural Economy*, p. 167, Graph 6. See also Kumar, *Land and Caste*, pp. 15–17.

[64] P.B.R., No. 86, 26 Nov. 1923, pp. 26–27, par. 22.

[65] Ibid., p. 15, par. 11.

in the number of landholders to population increase and the resultant subdivision of land.

An examination of Charlesworth's hypothesis

This being so, does Charlesworth's hypothesis sufficiently explain the increase in the number of landholders? He emphasises the importance of distinguishing the subdivision and the fragmentation of landholdings. While the former, subdivision, was a process in which the real number of landholders increases, with fragmentation, the individual's total landholdings were not falling but were being split into smaller and more geographically separated plots. Charlesworth argues that what actually happened to the holdings was not subdivision but fragmentation. Partly as a result of a market-oriented response on the part of the farmers, a landholder came to own a larger number of smaller plots spreading over different villages and, therefore Charlesworth argues, the total area held by a landholder did not actually diminish.[66]

If Charlesworth's argument is right, then each village should have registered a large increase in the number of plots. However, data from the Settlement Registers go against his supposition and indicate only a negligible increase in the number of village plots.[67] For example, in village No. W-5, there were 599 plots in 1865, 621 in 1895 and 590 in 1925. In village No. W-6, the total number of plots was 932 in 1865, reduced somewhat to 844 in 1895 and slightly recovered to 983 in 1925. Neither of these instances point to any noteworthy increase in plot numbers. In the intermediate village No. I-4 too, the data were not very different: 945 plots in 1865, 1,005 in 1895 and 1,424 in 1925. Except for the last figure, no rapid increase in the number of plots was noticed in these cases. These facts cast doubt on the validity of Charlesworth's contention.

Acquisition of land by Depressed-caste members and low-caste Non-Brahmans

My examination of the Settlement Registers of the Lalgudi villages reveals that increases in the number of *pattadars* belonging to the

[66] Neil Charlesworth, 'The Origins of Fragmentation of Landholdings in British India: A Comparative Examination', in Peter Robb (ed.), *Rural India: Land, Power and Society under British Rule* (London, 1983), p. 182.

[67] Yanagisawa and Mizushima, *Nijisseiki Hajime Minami Indo.*

Depressed and low-caste Non-Brahman communities accounted for the largest part of the total net increase in the number between 1895 and 1925. For instance, in the wet zone villages, the small *pattadars* in size group 1 increased in number by 1,166 people, of which more than half were Non-Brahmans, including 228 Muttiriyars, and 101 were Depressed-caste members. As we have seen already, though these communities formed a large proportion of the population, they had either a negligible or very small amount of land in their possession, as per the data of 1865. Their landholdings as a whole rose steeply especially after 1895. In the process, those low-caste Non-Brahmans and Depressed-caste members who had owned no land in 1865 acquired tiny plots and became very small landholders.

A careful examination of the 1925 Settlement Registers reveals many new caste-titles not seen in the 1895 Settlement Registers. The *pattadars* with these new titles also formed a portion of the new small *pattadars*. This also indicates that the increase in the number of landholders can be, to a considerable extent, explained by the acquisition of land by the members of the communities which had a negligible extent of land in their possession at the time of the previous settlement.

Thus, together with the weakening of the traditionally dominant Brahman landownership, a considerable number of persons belonging to the landless communities, such as the Depressed and lower-caste non-Brahman castes, came to own tiny plots of land. This offers a highly plausible explanation for the unprecedented increase in small landholders recorded.[68]

Changes in the number of Brahman landholders

However, before we draw any conclusion about the issue, we must examine the problem posed by changes in the number of Brahman landholders between 1865 and 1925. The number of Brahman *pattadars* seems to have changed in two phases; the first between 1865 and 1895, and the second between 1895 and 1925.

[68] The Settlement Report of Tinnevelly district stated: 'Thus, in spite of disintegrating action of Hindu Law the number of the larger pattas is only very slowly decreasing. The large increase in pattas is due rather to the splitting up of the already small holdings and the creation of new holdings by taking up new land than to the disappearance of the fairly large holdings' (P.B.R., No. 94, 1 Apr. 1907, p. 13, par. 20). This observation accords well with the findings obtained by an analysis of Lalgudi village data.

A. Changes between 1895 and 1925

We shall first examine the change in the second period, since it was simpler than that of the earlier period. Between 1895 and 1925, the number of Brahman *pattadars* in the wet zone increased by just 32 persons, or only 4 percent of the 866 Brahman *pattadars* in 1895, which accounted for only a marginal part of the increase in the total number of landholders. The situation was similar in the intermediate zone villages, where even a reduction in the number of Brahman *pattadars* was recorded. Thus for this period, we cannot identify any sign of the fragmentation of land being caused through multiple inheritance, occurring as a result of population growth. This conclusion is in accord with my previous findings regarding population data.

This is confirmed by a study of individual cases of large Brahman landholders. In village No. I-5, a large landholder belonging to the Brahman Ayyar caste held *patta* No. 4 over a vast area of 96 acres in 1895. I have examined names of *pattadars* who appeared in the 1925 registers as owners of the plots that had been owned by this Brahman landholder in 1895.[69] The result reveals that while the largest portion of his land, 32 acres in extent and consisting of 22 plots, was transferred to a Mu. Kalyandaramayyar, probably as a form of inheritance, the remaining portion was divided into many small parts, each consisting of one or two plots, and was transferred to many different persons separately. Among the new *pattadars* were members of several Non-Brahman communities such as Chettiars and Muttiriyars, and even members of Depressed communities appeared as new owners. This, without doubt, indicates that a large portion of the area once included in *patta* No. 4 was sold to unrelated people, including members of other communities, and that this process created a number of small landholders. It is quite obvious that what happened here cannot be explained as the result of the partition of property among sons.

B. Changes between 1865 and 1895

Changes in the number of Brahman landholders in the period between 1865 and 1895 were more complex. The Brahman *pattadars* in the wet zone rose sharply in number, from 370 persons in 1865 to 866 in 1895. Several factors were responsible for this phenomenon.

First, the increase of small landowners of less than one acre is perhaps mostly nominal, caused by a technical change in the way of noting

[69] See Haruka Yanagisawa, 'Mixed Trends in Landholding in Lalgudi Taluk: 1895–1925', *IESHR* 26, 4 (1989), p. 434, Table 10.

joint *pattadars'* names in the Settlement Registers. Since, as mentioned before, each of the joint *pattadars'* names was not listed in the 1865 Settlement Registers, the majority of probable Brahman joint *pattadars*, unless they had single *pattas* of their own, cannot be reckoned among Brahman landholders in our data-processing, whereas each of the joint *pattadars'* names was given in the 1895 registers, resulting in a large nominal increase in the number of Brahman landholders.[70]

Second, joint *pattas* were more numerous in the 1895 Settlement Registers than in the 1865 Registers. This was noted in Appadurai village, Lalgudi *taluk*, as well as in many other villages.[71] For instance, in the case of village No. W-5, the 1865 Register recorded only 4 joint *pattas* out of 37 *pattas*, whereas the number rose to 23 out of a total of 68 *pattas* in 1895, and 48 out of 142 in 1925. A similar trend was noticed in the intermediate zone villages. While there was no joint *patta* in 1865 in the intermediate village No. 1-4, the village witnessed a spate of joint *pattas* in 1895, 152 out of 251. The increase in the number of small Brahman holders in this period was partly attributable to this augmentation of joint *pattas*.[72]

As I shall discuss later, the area that was registered as *samudayam* or village common land in the 1865 Settlement Registers very often came under joint *pattas* in 1895. This change in the registration of the village common land probably resulted in the entry of a large number of new small Brahman landholders in 1895. Though the implication of this

[70] In order to assess the effect of this technical difference in the manner of registration of joint *pattas* between the two Settlement Registers, we have analysed the cases of W-1 and W-6 villages. In 1895, the number of Brahman *pattadars* was 21 and 50 respectively for two villages. However, the majority of small Brahman *pattadars* owning less than one acre did not own single *patta* but held only joint *pattas* jointly with other *pattadars*. Therefore, if the names of joint *pattadars* had been registered in the 1895 Settlement Registers in the same manner as the 1865 registers, many of these small *pattadars* would not have appeared and the number counted as Brahman *pattadars* would have been only 7 and 20 respectively. This seems to suggest that probably more than 60 percent of the seeming net increase in the number of Brahman *pattadars* was nominal, simply created by the technical change in the manner of registration.

[71] Yanagisawa, *Socio-Economic Changes*, p. 53.

[72] The case of Appadurai village reveals that joint *pattas* were of three types. The first were joint *pattas* owned by two or three co-holders belonging to the same community. The second were those issued for house-sites where the villagers lived. In this case, the co-holders were large in number for a *patta* and were villagers. The third type was issued for the land which had been registered as *samudayam* in 1865 but was registered as area held jointly by many influential landholders, such as Brahmans (ibid., pp. 53–56).

change in registration remains to be examined by further research, there is no doubt that it did not indicate any increasing partition of landed property as a result of population growth. The two factors relating to joint *pattas* would account for the majority of the increase in the number of small holders owning less than one acre, who formed about 70 percent of the net increase in the total number of Brahman holders in this period.

Third, however, these two factors cannot explain the increase in medium-sized landholders owning between 1 and 50 acres, because most owners in this group held single *pattas* and, therefore, had nothing to do with the above differences between two registers relating to joint *pattas*. The rate of population growth between 1865 and 1895 was only about 9 percent, which was not large enough to explain the increase in the number of Brahman landowners in this size group.

A report quoted in the previous section seems to offer an explanation, hinting at a possible correlation between the intensification of cultivation and the change in family size. It goes: 'My enquiries tend to show that, under the stress of necessity and the additional incentives to individual exertion promoted by *the break up of the joint family system*, greater care is now bestowed on cultivation of lands in Tanjore district than in times past; and this is to some extent the case in other districts also (emphasis added)'.[73] In this connection, a change suggested by population data in these villages is worth noticing. Table 5.10 shows the population and numbers of houses in some villages in this *taluk* in 1871, 1895 and 1925. Though the definition of 'house' in the statistics remains obscure, the data seem to indicate a decrease in family size in this period and, thereby, endorse to some extent the above cited statement that joint families were breaking up.[74] It may not be too bold to presume that the breaking up of the joint family may have influenced the increase in the number of Brahman landholders, though the data we have is too limited to make any general conclusion.

[73] Raghavaiyangar, *Memorandum*, p. 56. Manual of Tinnevelly district also wrote that the recognition of a right to divide had done much towards breaking up the system of family holdings. *Manual of Tinnevelly District*, p. 30.

[74] Dharma Kumar has already pointed out the break-up of large landholdings and related it to the break-up of joint families (Kumar, 'Agrarian Relations: South India', p. 234).

Changes in the number of Vellalar, etc., landholders

There was an increase in the number of landholders belonging to the Pillai, Chettiar and Reddiar communities. The three factors we considered in examining the situation of Brahman landholders would account for some of the increase in Vellalar landholders. In addition, we have to take into account the effects of the disintegration of their communities. As we have already seen, during the period between 1895 and 1925, large landholdings in these communities increased while medium-sized holdings decreased slightly. As a result, the number of landholders increased both in the larger and smaller size groups and decreased in the medium size groups, suggesting that some medium-sized landholders from these communities may have declined to smaller landholders and that this resulted in an increase in the number of smaller landholders. However, the extent to which this possible decline of medium-sized farmers changed the whole structure of landownership by these communities should be further examined.

To summarise, a total of five possible factors worked to change the number of landholders. (1) Many Depressed-caste members and low-caste Non-Brahmans, who had owned either a negligible or a very small amount of land in 1865, gradually came to possess small plots of land, (2) a large part of the land that had been recorded as *samudayam* or village common land in 1865 was registered in the 1895 Settlement Registers as land held jointly by many small *pattadars*, resulting in a large increase in the number of small registered landholders, and (3) a technical change in the way joint *pattadars* were listed also brought about a phenomenal rise in the number of small holders. These three factors account for the majority of the increase in the number of small landowners during the period. In addition, (4) between the years 1865 and 1895, some Brahman joint families seem to have broken up and consequently divided their landed properties, which resulted in an expansion of medium-sized landholder groups in this community. (5) A decline in medium-sized landholders among Non-Brahmans is also likely to have influenced the change in the number of holders. While these two additional factors also are likely to have contributed to the increase in landholders in this period, more research needs to be done in order to assess their effect correctly.

Thus my examination of the Settlement Registers confirms that the sharp rise in the number of landholders for the 60 year period from 1865 to 1925 cannot be explained by population growth under the equal inheritance system. Rather a large part of the increase, in the numbers of smaller landholders in particular, was the result of the weakening of the pattern of landownership dominated by a small number of large landholders belonging to high castes. Interestingly, this process of decline in the traditional pattern of landholding was accompanied by an intensification of agricultural practice, as we saw above. This implies that it is wrong to interpret the increase in the number of small holdings as either simply reflecting or necessarily resulting in a deterioration of agricultural production.[75] Rather the tendency towards smaller units of landholding was accelerated by the intensification of agricultural practices. The above quotation regarding the break-up of the joint family system of Brahmans in Thanjavur also points to the same conclusion. Charlesworth considers land fragmentation to have been conducive to the maximum utilisation of the landholders' own family labour. Though, as we have seen, his hypothesis about the fragmentation and subdivision of land is not supported by the evidence, he must be applauded for his questioning of the conventional wisdom that looks on the subdivision of land only as a counter-productive process working against agricultural progress.[76]

Other Changes in Landownership

Increased landownership by women

The Settlement Registers reveal some other important changes in landholding in villages in the Lalgudi *taluk*. Remarkable among them is the rise in both the number of female *pattadars* and the area owned by them, particularly in the wet and intermediate zone villages. From 1865 to 1925, the area held by the category 'caste unknown, female' jumped from 126 acres to 755 acres in the wet zone (Tables 2.1 & 5.3). In addition, in 1925, 391 acres were held by female *pattadars* whose caste affiliation we can identify, giving a total amounting to 1,146 acres or more than 12 percent of cultivated land. In the intermediate zone also,

[75] Stokes, *The Peasant and the Raj*, p. 229.

[76] As we shall see later, the changes in South India have their parallels in agrarian change in seventeenth- to nineteenth-century Japan. In Japan also, the trend towards intensification of agriculture was accompanied by a trend towards fragmentation of the landholding and towards the scattered location of plots of a farm.

the area held by women expanded from 341 acres in 1865 to 450 acres in 1895 and again to 632 acres in 1925 (Tables 2.3, 5.5 & 5.7).

The factors behind this expansion are not very clear. We shall examine some cases of female *pattadars* in order to clarify certain aspects of land transfers to female *pattadars*.

First, landed property seems to have been transferred to women only when there was no male successor to the land. To illustrate this point, we shall analyse cases in village No. W-5. A large area of 97 acres had been owned by a male Brahman named Periya Venkata-subbayyan in 1865. According to palm-leaf records kept by a landlord in a neighbouring village, he was a son of Kodandaramayyan, residing in Angarai.[77] During the thirty year period since 1865, a large portion of Periya Venkatasubbayyan's land moved to two Brahmans, Venbuvayyan and A.K. Venbuvayyan. The naming system in Tamil-nadu commonly uses the first letters of the father's and grandfather's names and of the place name of residence as initials preceding a person's name. If we can infer that 'A' of A.K. Venbuvayyan stood for the place name, Angarai, and 'K' for the father, Kodandaramayyan, then he was a brother of Periya Venkatasubbayyan. As to the second landholder, Venbuvayyan, there is no such indication, but thirty years later again, in 1925, the majority of the land owned by Venbuvayyan in 1895 was owned by P.V. Ramasami Ayyar. It is highly probable that 'P' and 'V' of P.V. Ramasami Ayyar stood for the grandfather, Periya Venkata-subbayyan, and the father, Venbuvayyan, respectively, and therefore, that Venbuvayyan of 1895 was Periya Venkatasubbayyan's son. Thus A.K. Venbuvayyan and Venbuvayyan are inferred as having been a brother and a son of Periya Venkatasubbayyan respectively and they probably inherited a considerably large area of Periya Venkata-subbayyan's land in 1895. On the other hand, five female *pattadars* appeared in 1895 among the 34 *pattadars* who were the new owners of part of the land previously owned by Periya Venkatasubbayyan; interestingly though, none of these female *pattadars* became the owner of a large amount of land. The maximum area held by a female *pattadar* was only 0.8 acre, hardly large enough to indicate any inheritance of land by her. It was obviously rare for a woman to inherit anything when a male inheritor existed.

In contrast, a female *pattadar* in the same village named T.M.S. Vengammal owned a large area of land amounting to 13.5 acres in 1895. Of this, 11.4 acres had, in 1865, been owned by a Brahman, M.

[77] Subbarayalu, *Palm-Leaf Records*, nos. 5, 21, 27, 28, 29.

Appasamiyyan, who owned a total of 19.4 acres. Of his 19.4 acres 9.5 acres came into the hands of a Seshachala Naidu, who probably was a Non-Brahman and therefore acquired the land in a manner other than inheritance. Thus it seems that M. Appasamiyyan did not have any male inheritor and except for a part sold to the Naidu and a small area transferred to male *pattadars*, his land is likely to have been inherited by his female relative, Vengammal.

Though not comprehensive, the above case study indicates that only in the absence of a male heir did women have a chance of an inheritance. Several other instances analysed so far seem to support this conclusion.

Changes in village common land

In 1865, a large area was registered as *samudayam* or village common land. By 1895, much of it was registered as land under joint *pattas* held jointly by many *pattadars*.

To cite a few examples, in village No. W-6, there were 4.66 acres of *samudayam* land in 1865. A part of this, 2.88 acres, surfaced in 1895 as joint *patta* No. 116 held by 83 joint *pattadars*. In village No. W-5, 14.86 acres were *samudayam* land in 1865. Out of these, 9 acres came into the joint possession of 45 people as joint *patta* No. 32 in 1895. The majority of the *pattadars* were Brahmans, and the rest were persons with the titles of Muttiriyan and Rao. This leads us to speculate that in 1865 *samudayam* land was not actually used jointly by the majority of the village population, including those belonging to lower castes, but were controlled by a few higher-caste landowners.[78] This is another point that needs further clarification.

Expansion of temple land

The data from the Settlement Registers point to a remarkable increase in the area owned by temples between 1895 and 1925. In the wet zone villages, temples owned 322 acres in 1865, increasing to 720 acres in 1925. To understand the source of the newly added land, I traced the previous owners of the land located in village No. I-2, as I did in the previous section.

[78] Interestingly, the Collector of South Arcot district suggested that the influential *raiyats* used the waste land as their private grazing ground (G.O., No. 2435, Revenue, 26 June 1918, p. 15).

We can identify three types of origin of temple land. The first type is that which was already in the possession of temples by 1895. The second type is land which had been owned in 1895 by the dominant landowning communities in the village such as the Pillais. Influential large landlords in this village probably donated their land to temples. The third type is former joint *patta* land held by good number of joint landholders in 1895. The results of the examination of village No. I-5 also points to the same conclusion. Though it is necessary to examine the reasons why some of the dominant landowners donated their land to temples in this period, the question is beyond the scope of this study.

Changes in landownership by village servants and artisans

The Registers also offer interesting data for the clarification of changes in landownership by village servants and artisans.

First, in the 14 wet zone villages in 1865, there were ten *kavals* or village guards, who are supposed to have been traditionally responsible for village security, each owning an average of two acres of land. However, the number decreased to five in 1895 and in 1925 just one man was on record. In the 7 villages of the intermediate zone, there were ten *kavals* including 'watchman' in 1865, three people in 1895 and none in 1925. This probably reflects the abolition of the *kaval* system under British rule, when a new system of village security was established.[79]

Second, there was a marked increase in the land owned by some providers of village services, such as *navitans* (barbers) and *kottans* (stonemasons). Further research needs to be done here to understand the process.

The Findings: Tamilnadu Agrarian Change in a Comparative Perspective

The findings

Chapters 4 and 5 show that the period between the 1860s and the 1920s

[79] For the government policy towards village officials, see Christopher Baker, 'Madras Headman', in K.N. Chaudhuri and Clive J. Dewey (eds.), *Economy and Society* (Delhi, 1979); D. Arnold, *Police Power and Colonial Rule: Madras 1859–1947* (Delhi, 1986).

witnessed two different processes going on at the same time in the wet and intermediate zone villages.

The first process represents the decline in the dominance of higher-caste landowners in landownership and agrarian relationships. Growing emigration by members of lower castes to overseas estates stimulated a sense of independence among them, with the result that higher-caste landowners had difficulty in securing labourers and making them work as hard as before. On the other hand, a considerable number from the higher castes migrated to urban areas, lessening their interest in agriculture, at the very time agriculture was tending towards more intensive cultivation, which diminished the advantage of large-scale farming.

These changes encouraged the higher-caste landowners to let their land to tenants, and some previous labourers raised their status to small tenants though they had still to supplement their income by working as hired day labourers. Some among them even raised their status to small landholders by purchasing small plots of land. In this way new landholders emerged from among low-caste Non-Brahmans and Depressed-caste members, who had previously worked as agricultural labourers or tenants in fields held by members of higher castes. On the other hand, higher-caste landowners not only leased their land to tenants but some of them reduced their holdings, selling a part of their land. Though they tried to prevent land being transferred to the lower-caste villagers, especially to Depressed-caste members, the landownership of the Brahman community decreased during the period and the decrease was sharper in the larger size groups. These changes indicate that traditional landowners from the higher castes could not successfully retain the same powerful influence as formerly to control landownership in the village, though they still owned the largest share of the land. This trend may be understood as representing the tendency in agrarian relations towards a system in which small peasants dominate agricultural production.

The second process was the growth of large landholdings and stratification among Non-Brahman communities. As South Indian agriculture became more commercialised and farmers were integrated into the world trade network, growing debts in the agricultural sector probably led some small holders to decline to the status of tenants. The same developments under British rule led, at the same time, to the acquisition of landed property by traders, moneylenders and others who became rich by exploiting the economic opportunities offered under colonial rule. Thus some Non-Brahmans grew into large landholders, and this led to a stratification among people belonging to Non-Brahman communities.

The growth of stratification among Non-Brahman communities is not readily apparent, since it is shadowed by a sharp decrease in large landholdings within the Brahman communities. By identifying these two different trends in South Indian society, we can envisage a reconciliation between the Nationalist view on rural change and Dharma Kumar's findings regarding changes in landholding.

Is it possible to identify different trends in different periods in South Indian agrarian change after the 1860s as Charlesworth did in his study of Western India?[80] My examination of the data from Appadurai village and Gough's village survey, as well as the Settlement Registers for the villages in Lalgudi *taluk*, suggest that the situation in Tamilnadu was different from that in Western India, in that a general uniformity in trend is discernible across the period though with differences in the extent of change. To summarise the findings for each period: (1) As the data from the Settlement Registers demonstrate, the period between 1895 and 1925 saw the most remarkable progress both in the increase in landholding by lower castes and in the decrease of landholdings by higher castes. The rapid expansion of the area held by the newly rich and the growth of large landholders among Non-Brahmans is also clearly discernible during this period. (2) The period between 1865 and 1895 witnessed a clear trend towards an increase in the area held by Depressed-caste members and low-caste Non-Brahmans, as well as towards the transfer of land to the newly rich. While it was not possible to confirm the decrease in Brahman landholdings prior to 1895, no evidence indicates any clear tendency towards an increase in landholdings by Brahmans in this period. (3) For the period after 1925, we have to

[80] In analysing the agro-economy of Western India, Charlesworth categorised the changes into three time periods, 1880–90, 1900–1930 and after 1930. According to him, in the 1880s and 1890s, linking up with expanded modern communications and new market opportunities could give the rich peasant pioneer a major, windfall advantage over the bulk of the villagers. Thus, he argues, historical conditions in this period favoured stratification. After 1900, a major new stimulus to cash crop production came from price increases. Though this created intensified geographical stratification, the economic expansion of this period may have brought widely distributed benefits within agrarian society. The period after 1930 witnessed a new trend. While conditions for labourers were good because the reduction in the rates of wages had been smaller than the fall in prices, the large cultivators employing hired labourers on a large scale suffered most. Thus he found different trends among the three periods in Western India (Charlesworth, *Peasants and Imperial Rule*, p. 224).

depend on the data from Appadurai village and Gough's survey, which roughly confirm both the fact of acquisition of land by Depressed-caste members and the newly rich and that of a tendency towards a decrease in Brahman landholding. While there is no evidence available for the acquisition of land by low-caste Non-Brahmans after 1925, the data does not suggest that there was any trend towards a decrease in their landholding.

No one period, therefore, clearly exhibits trends clearly different from those of the others. To reiterate, the increase in the area held by lower-caste members and the weakening of the dominance of higher-caste members on one hand, and the growth of large landholdings by the Non-Brahman newly rich on the other, were the two main streams of change that flowed uninterruptedly from 1865 to the time of Independence, with a peak between 1895 and 1925.

I have so far highlighted various aspects of change in the pattern of landholding in the wet districts of Tamilnadu. It is, however, important to reiterate that there are no indications that these changes brought about a radical transformation of agrarian relations in the region. In spite of these changes, the majority of those engaged in agricultural work did not become independent landowning peasant farmers but basically remained either with the status of labourer or tenant.

Though the area owned by the Brahmans decreased in the period, they were still, even in 1925, the largest landholding group in the wet villages in Lalgudi *taluk*. The majority of the Non-Brahman newly rich who enlarged their landholdings were from the higher castes. All in all, more than half of the land revenue collected in the wet zone villages in this *taluk* even in 1925 was from land owned by people of higher castes such as the Brahmans, Pillais and Reddiars. In Appadurai village, about which we have detailed information, 80 percent of the arable land up to the time of Independence was in the hands of landlords living outside the village.[81] Though we can perceive a weakening of the dominance in landholding by the higher castes, it was not to such an extent that it might have radically eroded the basic structure of the landholding pattern. Nor do we see any radical change in the size-wise distribution of land. As discussed above, the growth of the large ownership by the Non-Brahman newly rich offset the decline of large landholdings by the Brahmans, with the result that there was no considerable change in size-wise distribution.

Although the area owned by low-caste people expanded after 1865,

[81] Yanagisawa, *Socio-Economic Changes,* p. 102.

it accounted for only a small percentage of the total in terms of absolute acreage; even in 1925 the Depressed castes contributed only 1 percent to the land revenue collected in the wet villages of Lalgudi *taluk*, while the Muttiriyars and Udaiyars jointly contributed a little more, but not more than 10 percent. Even though a considerable number of former agricultural labourers acquired or leased land, many Depressed-caste families remained landless and had to work as full-time agricultural labourers. Those Depressed-caste families owning some area of land probably did not exceed 40 percent of the total of this caste in Lalgudi *taluk*. The remaining families, owning no landed property, must have remained mere agricultural labourers without any operational holdings, except some who had raised themselves to tenant cultivators. Still a considerable number of them were permanent labourers such as *pannaiyals*, as evidenced by Gray, who stated in 1918 that farm servants or *padiyals* in Chingleput were almost invariably Depressed-caste members and estimated that the total number of *padiyals* in the district was probably one-half to two-thirds of the number of male agricultural daily coolies.[82]

In addition, those small farmers of the Depressed castes who had emerged from the status of agricultural labourer either by leasing or buying land still had to supplement their incomes by working as coolie labourers. In the 14 wet villages of Lalgudi *taluk* in 1925, the extent of land owned by Depressed-caste *pattadars* was generally less than one acre per *pattadar*, scarcely ever exceeding two acres (Table 5.4). Since the income they earned from their own farms was, in most cases, too small to maintain their families, they and their family members had no choice but to hire themselves out as day labourers on other farms to earn supplementary income, which often may have been larger than the income from their own farms. As a whole, the majority of Depressed-caste families had to work either as daily coolies to supplement the income from their farms, or as permanent labourers. Thus they still remained agricultural labourers.

The lot of the low-caste Non-Brahmans followed a path very similar to that of the Depressed-caste members. For example, in the wet zone of Lalgudi *taluk* in 1925, 418 out of 561 Muttiriyar *pattadars* owned less than one acre. As was the case of the Depressed castes, these small holdings could not assure the holders a livelihood through the income they earned by cultivating their own land. Thus they still had to hire themselves out as day labourers.

[82] P.B.R., No. 106, 26 May 1918, pp. 12, 15.

We have also observed that some small landholders may have lost a part or whole of their holdings because of an increase in their debts and may have been reduced to the status of either mere labourers or tenants who usually had to hire themselves out as daily coolies, creating a new inflow of labour supply to the agricultural labour market.

These observations provide us with clues to understand why the ratio of agricultural labourers in terms of the total agricultural population neither decreased nor clearly increased in South India in the colonial period, as indicated by the census data.[83] As I have shown above, the majority of Depressed-caste members and low-caste Non-Brahmans, even if they obtained small plots of land or became tenant cultivators, had to hire themselves out as labourers. Of course, a small number of Depressed-caste members probably grew to independent farmers as the result of the acquisition of land and would have stopped working as agricultural labourers. But this possible reduction in the labour supply would have been offset by a new flow of labourers from families who had declined from the status of independent farmer by losing a part of their land.

[83] The following table compiled from census data indicates changes in the share of agricultural labourers in the agricultural working force.

Table 5.11
The Share of Agricultural Labourers in the Agricultural Working Force in the Madras Presidency

(thousand)

	Adult male	Male workers	Population supported		Male workers		
	1871	1881	1891	1901	1911	1921	1931
Agricultural working force	7,021	6,637	11,667	8,445	9,099	9,473	9,082
Cultivators, etc.	4,938	4,465	8,617	6,092	6,445	6,680	5,714
Agricultural labourers	2,083	2,172	3,050	2,353	2,654	2,793	3,368
Proportion of agricultural labourers	29.7%	32.7%	26.1%	27.9%	29.2%	29.5%	37.1%

Source: *Census of India.*

Note: 'Cultivators, etc.' includes the following census categories; 'Cultivators', 'Land proprietors', 'Landholders', 'Planters', 'Landlords', 'Farmers', 'Permanent leaseholders', 'Farm bailiffs', 'Pattadars, Ryots', 'Agriculturists', 'Tenants', 'Growers of special products', etc.

'Agricultural labourers' denotes such census categories as 'Agricultural labourers', 'Ploughman', 'Farm servants', 'Field labourers', 'Labourers and workmen otherwise unspecified' and 'General labourer'.

Though the total number of agricultural labourers did not decrease, permanent labourers such as *pannaiyals* were gradually displaced by day labourers. Small farmers of the Depressed castes hired themselves out as day labourers instead of being hired as permanent workers, since they now needed to have time to cultivate their own farms. The development of a sense of independence among these classes also stimulated this trend. The 1921 Settlement Report of Tanjore district reported: 'The tendency will probably be towards a further rise [of grain wage] owing to the growing fluidity of labour caused by the facilities for emigration and to some extent also to the replacing of pannaiyals by free labourers as the result of the present movement for the acquisition of house-sites for Panchamas.'[84] The report suggests that this replacement of *pannaiyals* by day labourers was a result of the emancipation of the labourers. In Vadamalaipuram village in Ramnad district, there were 53 permanent labourers and about 100 casual labourers in 1916, whereas in 1958 out of 140 resident agricultural labourers, only three were attached workers and the rest were all casual workers.[85]

In addition to this change in the composition of the Depressed-caste labourers, the newcomers to the labour market who had been reduced from the status of independent farmers were probably employed not as permanent labourers but as day labourers. Gray reported in 1918 that while a caste-Hindu *padiyal* or farm servant was comparatively rare, a caste-Hindu agricultural daily labourer (male) was very common. This implies that caste-Hindus were rarely employed as permanent labourers if they, having lost their landed property, had to be employed as labourers.[86] These factors all led to an increase in the proportion of day labourers in the agricultural labourer population.

[84] P.B.R., No. 28, 12 Feb. 1921, p. 49.

A similar change was noted in the 1890s in the Nellore district, where, according to M. Atchi Reddy, a large section of farm servants were transformed into day labourers as well as tenant cultivators. Atchi Reddy seems to attribute this change to the fact that a large number of annual farm servants were thrown adrift and that the *raiyat* had no necessity to maintain annual farm servants in hard times since he could employ seasonal workers at the time of sowings and harvest, indicating that this transformation was advantageous to the employers (M. Atchi Reddy 'Commercialization of Agriculture', p. 180). Though Tamilnadu also witnessed the same kind of transformation of annual farm servants, there was a difference in the basic attitude of *mirasidars*, who, in Tamilnadu, as Gray observed, tried to keep their farm servants rather than changing them for freer labourers even in 1918 (P.B.R., No. 106, 29 May 1918, p. 19).

[85] Athreya, *Vadamalaipuram*, p. 93.

[86] P.B.R., No. 106, 29 May 1918, p. 12, par. 20.

This change in the composition of agricultural labourers was observed by Baker, who says, 'The extraordinary glut of labour, from the depression years onwards, gave the employing mirasidars considerable opportunity to alter the pannaiyal system. It became ever easier to rely on the supply of casual labour to cover the workload during the peaks of the cultivation system, and this made it possible to dispense with a large number of pannaiyals who were maintained underemployed for most of the year simply in order to ensure a labour supply at the critical times.' However, it is very doubtful whether Baker's statement is supported sufficiently by evidence.[87] Sivaswamy's statement, to which Baker has referred, rather reveals that the replacement of permanent labourers by day labourers was neither a simple result of the glut of labour created by the agrarian depression nor was it promoted completely by employers against the preferences of labourers. Rather, one of the main factors causing this change in employment was the labourers' own preference for independent daily labour over working as tied permanent servants of traditional type.

The Government Order I cited above already pointed to the

[87] Baker, *Rural Economy*, p. 196. Baker based his view on two sources: Government of Madras, *Scheme of Road Development for the Madras Presidency* (by A. Vipan, Madras, 1935); and K.G. Sivaswamy, *Caste and Standard of Living Versus Farm Rents and Wages* (p. 13). For the former, he did not refer to the page number on which he found the information, and I cannot find anything relating even approximately to his account.

For the latter source, several points should be considered. First, nothing on page 13 of the source indicates the existence of a glut of labour. Second, what Sivaswamy stressed is as follows: With the growth of the cultivation of commercial crops and food crops for export, the organisation of large farmers working with the aid of semi-feudal labourers changed its character. There was a growth of a class of independent and occasional labour and a class of servants engaged for a few months or for a year, who were different from the old tied-labourers. 'The semi-feudal servants wanted to become independent and free labourers' (p. 11). Those who cultivated garden land wanted a large number of farm servants. In the Godavari and Kistna deltas, he reported, the Depressed-caste members preferred to be casual workers rather than permanent farm servants. 'The Panchamas who were once satisfied with being engaged as Palerus are today extremely reluctant to work as such.' It is in this context that Sivaswamy cited the case of the replacement of permanent labourers by day labourers.

The Report of the Economic Enquiry Committee (Madras, 1930), on which Sivaswamy partly based his argument, emphasised that the Depressed-caste members preferred to be casual workers in almost every deltaic place and that 'there has been a steady and even very marked decrease in the last twenty years in the number of people who are willing to work as palerus' (Vol. 1, pp. 62).

replacement of permanent labourers as early as 1921, that is, before the start of the agrarian depression and only three years after Gray reported how eagerly *mirasidars* were trying to maintain their farm servants, as mentioned above.[88] This also confirms that it is wrong to relate directly the growth of day labourers with the glut of labour caused by the agrarian depression. Even by 1930, there seems to have been no radical change in the stance of Thanjavur *mirasidars* towards their *pannaiyals* since the Gray report. A landlord owning 60 acres of home farm and employing 20 *pannaiyals*, in this district testified to the Madras Provincial Banking Enquiry Committee in 1930 that while he leased a part of his own land to tenants, all of them were originally labourers and, he said, 'the object of making lessees is to create an interest in them so that they may not give up the land and go away'.[89] Another piece of evidence for this may be found in the result of a survey done in a village in 1950s. In Vadamalaipuram village, 32 out of 42 casual workers who answered the question on whether they wished to be permanent farm servants answered in the negative, mainly citing the absence of freedom and of any limitation on the hours of work for permanent workers.[90]

Of course, surveys do not completely agree here. K. Gough has reported that by 1952 in Kumbapettai village, there had been a reduction in the number of *pannaiyals* and an increase of coolie labourers, though most labourers preferred *pannai* to coolie work. She seems to attribute the change mainly to a growth of a pool of marginal, coolie labour, as a result of which landowners could dismiss their *pannaiyals*. This statement, however, should be qualified by the other important facts she has revealed. According to her, 39 percent of the Depressed-caste population of the village had become *kuttagai* tenants.[91] This acquisition of

[88] It was stated already in 1926 that in wet villages in Guntur district, the competition among *raiyats* for agricultural labourers grew year by year and enabled the Panchamas who had till then been serfs to become independent, leading to a decrease in the number of annual labourers (Ranga, *Economic Organization*, Vol. 1, p. 181).

[89] *MBEC,* Vol. 4, *Oral Evidence*, p. 330.

[90] Athreya, *Vadamalaipuram,* p. 94.

[91] Gough, *Rural Society in Southeast India*, pp. 194, 260–61. Their farm size would not have been too meagre, though smaller than that of Non-Brahmans, as inferred by the fact that the average holding of eighteen Pallar tenant farmers came to 3.8 acres. These Depressed-caste tenants were hardly able to serve as *pannaiyals* but could only hire out their labour as coolies, since they had to make time for the cultivation of their own farms. In fact, of 22 Pallar *pannaiyals* those holding any leased land amounted to only one, whereas a large portion (40 percent) of Pallar male coolies held some leased land (ibid., pp. 271–72).

tenancy land by the Depressed castes was one of the factors that led to the reduction of *pannaiyals* among Depressed-caste members. She also reveals that young men often preferred coolie to *pannaiyal* work, since if they were strong and diligent they could be fairly confident of working at least six months of year and sometimes up to 270 days.[92] Thus it is probably fair to assess that nearly half of the Depressed-caste households in this village had no need to depend upon *pannaiyal* employment but rather preferred coolie to *pannai* work if they needed wage income. This demonstrates that some progress had been achieved in the economic independence of Depressed-caste members from Brahman landowners. Thus, it is misleading to understand that the reduction of the percentage of *pannaiyals* in this village simply implies a strengthening of landlords' bargaining power and that it was achieved solely on their initiative. Rather it reflects too the progress towards the economic independence by Depressed-caste members from their landlords.

I do not intend to infer that the emancipation of labourers was the only factor that led to the replacement of permanent labourers by day labourers. To reiterate, some small peasants may have declined to the status of a mere agricultural labourer. This, together with the increase in the number of Depressed-caste day labourers, led to a growth in the coolie labour market, which in some cases probably underpinned the replacement of *pannaiyals* by day labourers. What seems most important, however, is the fact that even when there was no glut of labour and, furthermore, even where landowners felt a shortage of labourers, the number of *pannaiyals* declined, as demonstrated above. The common feature observed in most cases is the emancipation of labourers from dominant landholding classes.[93]

A comparison with East Asian experience

Of the two trends in South Indian agrarian change as outlined above, the process representing the decline in the dominance of high-caste landowners in agrarian relationships seems to have its parallel in agrarian change in seventeenth- to nineteenth-century Japan. Both areas witnessed the intensification of agricultural production, the acquisition of land by erstwhile agricultural labourer classes and the decrease in the number of permanent servile labourers. The general trend in agricultural

[92] Ibid., p. 281.

[93] In this connection, the discussion by Dharma Kumar is suggestive ('Introduction to Reprint', in *Land and Caste*, repr., p. xl).

progress in Japan and in Tamilnadu was towards a smaller rather than a larger farm.[94]

In the period before the Tokugawa Era (1603–1868), and also early in this era, the size of a farm was generally large, and there were many large farms, mainly cultivated by permanent servile labourers, who were expected to serve their masters throughout their lifetime and were in turn supported by their masters. In this period, the seasonal fluctuation of labour input was so large that a large working force was needed to cultivate the land, especially at the time of transplanting and harvesting, and for collecting the green manure from the forest. The plough was drawn by animal power, which only a large farmer could afford to purchase and maintain. The forest was important for feeding the draft animals and for the collection of manure.[95]

Several important changes occurred in the agricultural practices in the late medieval and the Tokugawa periods, particularly in the seventeenth and eighteenth centuries.[96] The introduction of the hoe enabled even small peasant farmers owning no draft animals to cultivate their land. Changes in fertilisers also supported small peasant farming. The introduction of soy-bean fertiliser decreased the large demand for labour for collecting green manure in the forest and thereby reduced the importance of the forest. In a later period, such fertilisers as dried sardines became available in the markets. Improvements in the art of soil enrichment also involved an increase in the amount of fertiliser applied and the meticulous care given to the timing of its application.[97] An invention of a new-type thresher drastically reduced the amount of labour required in threshing. The development of early-, middle- and late-ripening rice varieties with different dates of maturation enabled peasants to even out the periods of heavy labour demand, especially periods of planting and harvesting, and enabled them to introduce more extensive double cropping. A red Indica variety of rice, which could be

[94] For a fuller discussion, see Haruka Yanagisawa, 'A Comparison with Japanese Experience', in Peter Robb, K. Sugihara and H. Yanagisawa (eds.), *Local Agrarian Societies in Colonial India: Japanese Perspectives* (London, 1996).

[95] Teisaku Hayama, 'Shono Noho no Seritsu to Shono Gijutsu no Tenkai [The Development of Small Peasant Cultivation Method and Technique]', in Sasaki Junnosuke (ed.), *Zairai Gijutsu no Hatten to Kindai Shakai* (Tokyo, 1983).

[96] Hayama, 'Shono Noho'.

[97] Chie Nakane and Shinzaburo Oishi (eds.), *Tokugawa Japan* (Tokyo, 1990), p. 71.

cultivated in less fertile land, was supposed to have been grown by small poor farmers in newly-reclaimed land and thus promoted the process whereby the poor peasants became independent farmers.[98]

These technical innovations promoted the expansion of the areas under double cropping during the period. The trend towards fragmentation of a farmer's landholding and the scattered location of the farm plots was not necessarily a regression in agriculture. The fact that a farm consisted of several plots under different irrigation conditions, receiving water at different times, was rather advantageous for those small farmers who could disperse the risk of farm management and mitigate the concentration of labour demand in the peak season by cultivating different varieties of rice among the scattered plots.

The new agricultural techniques and the new method of production were more labour-intensive in character and required much more careful management than before. A smaller labour force was needed to cultivate land, and even a small farmer could manage a farm successfully. Thus the new farming system was suited to a small farmer who depended on his own family members as his main labour force, as they tended to cultivate land with meticulous care. This new system of agriculture can be called the 'family farm' or 'peasant farm' system.

This change in agricultural techniques in Japan accompanied the gradual establishment of the peasant farm system.[99] The change proceeded in two ways: first, there was a tendency for servile labourers to become independent small peasants; second, a small nuclear family increasingly became an independent farming unit. Along with this change, the number of small farmers increased and the size of an average farm decreased.[100] On the other hand the importance of large farms hiring permanent servile labourers decreased considerably. For example, in a Kyushu district, the tendency for servile labourers to become small peasants started in the late medieval period. One study also points to a considerable increase in the number of cultivators, in particular to a big increase in the number of small cultivators, as well as the growth of the number of plots, reflecting the fragmentation of farm land into sepa-

[98] Hironori Yagi, *Suiden Nogyo no Hatten Ronri* [The Logic of the Development of Irrigated Rice Agriculture] (Tokyo, 1983), p. 90; Shuichi Miyakawa, 'Daitomai to Teishitsuchi Kaihatu [Great China Rice and Reclamation of Damp Lowlands]', in *Ine no Ajiashi* (Tokyo, 1987), Vol. 3, p. 280.

[99] Kanji Ishii, *Nihon Keizaishi* [Economic History of Japan], 2d ed. (Tokyo, 1991), pp. 53–56.

[100] Akira Hayami and Matao Miyamoto (eds.), *Nihon Keizaishi* [Economic History of Japan], Vol. 1 (Tokyo, 1988), p. 49.

rate plots.[101] A decrease in the number of persons registered as dwellers in a living unit was also reported.[102]

An important change occurred in the type of agricultural labourer hired by large farmers. In the Kansai area, the most common type of agricultural labourer in the early seventeenth century was a *fudai-genin*, who was obliged to serve his master throughout his life (as generally were his children after him, for generations). After the middle of that century, the number of such life-long servile labourers decreased, and instead there was an increase in the number of *chonenki-hokonin*, who served a master for eight to ten years, generally from childhood until the beginning of adulthood.[103] This change has been understood to indicate the emergence of many small farmers from the former agricultural labourer class, whose farms were too small to engage all of their family members in the work of cultivation, and to provide them with subsistence, so that parents were obliged to send their sons to work as *chonenki-hokonin* for other big farmers. After about 1740, the most common type of agricultural labourer in this area was the worker hired on a one-year contract.[104] The number of day labourers also increased at this time.[105] Thus the term of labour contract gradually shortened in the Tokugawa period. In addition to the general tendency for servile labourers to become peasants, the development of labour demand from outside the rural society, particularly in urban areas, contributed to the disappearance of the long-term labour contract of the old type.[106]

This observation leads us to conclude that in both colonial Tamilnadu and seventeenth- to nineteenth-century Japan, the development in agricultural techniques was generally towards intensive agriculture, which was more efficiently managed by small peasant families and which promoted the emergence of small farmers with small landholdings, and thus diminished the importance of the large farms which hired

[101] Yagi, *Suiden Nogyo*, pp. 126–28, 132–34.

[102] Ishii, *Nihon Keizaishi*, p. 55.

[103] Ryuzo Yamazaki, 'Settsu niokeru Nogyo Koyo Rodo no Hatten [Development of Hired Agricultural Labourers in Settsu Area]', in Takamasa Ichikawa, Nobuo Watanabe, and Toshio Furushima (eds.), *Hoken Shakai Kaitaiki no Koyo Rodo* (Tokyo, 1969), p. 202. Dharma Kumar has compared the *pannaiyal* and *padiyal* in South India with *fudai* and *genin* of seventeenth-century Japan (Kumar, *Land and Caste*, p. 190).

[104] Rintaro Imai and Akihiro Yagi, *Hoken Shakai no Noson Kozo* [The Structure of Rural Villages in Feudal Society] (Tokyo, 1955), pp. 152–53.

[105] Ibid., p. 157.

[106] Hayami, *Nihon niokeru Keizaishakai*, p. 99.

permanent servile labourers. In the case of paddy cultivation, which has been the main crop both in wet areas of Tamilnadu and in Japan, the direction of agricultural progress was towards the family farm system. The decline in farm size and the 'fragmentation' of landholdings did not necessarily mean a deterioration in agricultural production, but rather reflected the progress of agrarian society in paddy-cultivating districts.

Progress in agriculture does not necessarily mean a change towards a larger farm cultivated by hired wage labourers. It is plausible that at least in the wet rice-producing areas in East Asia, including Japan and China,[107] and in the wet districts in Tamilnadu, the main trend in these periods was towards a smaller farm.[108] As the Japanese case outlined above clearly indicates, the main lever that propelled the change was the development of agricultural productive power in the form of intensification of agricultural practice. The external impact played an insignificant role in this transformation. Therefore, the pattern of the change thus identified can be considered as an outgrowth of the internal force of change inherent in agriculture in these areas. This probably suggests that the series of changes discerned in Tamilnadu, namely a decline in the dominance of large high-caste landowners, the acquisition of small amounts of land by the labourer class and the decrease in the number of permanent bonded labourers, should be understood as basically representing a development of an internal force of change. The extent to which the external impacts, including that of British rule, contributed to the changes may not have been very large.

I do not imply that small family farms have such advantages over larger size farms in all circumstances. It is very doubtful that small farms are generally more highly competitive even when they cultivate crops other than rice in different ecological conditions. Even in rice cultivating areas, a family farm probably proves the superior unit of production only when agrarian production is at a certain stage of technical as well as socio-economic development. It may not be easily ruled out that further development, for example, in the form of mechanisation of agricultural production, may weaken the competitive edge of family farms and even make a larger farm more advantageous.[109]

[107] As to the case of Chinese agriculture, see Francesca Bray, 'Rice Economies: The Rise and Fall of China's Communes in East Asian Perspective', in Jan Breman and Sudipto Mundle (eds.), *Rural Transformation in Asia* (Delhi, 1991).

[108] See also Bray, *Rice Economies*.

[109] In this connection, a series of debates over the inverse relationship discovered by the Farm Management Surveys between farm size and output per

It is of course misleading to overemphasise the aspects of similarity between the case of Tamilnadu and the Japanese experience. The most noticeable difference between the two is the fate of agricultural labourers. In Japan, the number of agricultural labourers rapidly decreased in the latter half of the nineteenth century and they actually disappeared by the beginning of the twentieth century.[110] This contrasts with the case of South India, where the number as well as the proportion of hired labourers in the agricultural population, if not having rapidly expanded, have never shown a clear trend to decrease even in the twentieth century, though their dominant form changed from that of permanently attached labourer to coolie labourer. In other words, the family farm system has not been established as a dominant form of agrarian management in the wet districts of Tamilnadu, though the trend towards the family farm system was witnessed in Tamilnadu agriculture between 1865 and 1925.

This difference may be attributable to several factors. First, though Tamilnadu agriculture exhibited signs of a change towards intensive agriculture, it lacked the kind of improvements which might have reduced the labour demand in peak seasons, such as were achieved in Japan over a long period of at least three centuries. Second, in the latter half of the Tokugawa period, there was a widespread development of rural small-scale industry, which led to a reduction in the labour supply to the agricultural labour market from the small farmers' families.[111] In contrast to this, in nineteenth-century South India, there was little development of subsidiary industry among farmers in rural areas in the same way as Japan. The colonial condition was probably one of the factors that set an important limit on the expansion of subsidiary industry.[112] Third, what contributed most to the disappearance of agricultural labourers in Japan was the expansion of labour demand in the industrial sector after the Meiji Period, particularly in the 1910s and 1920s.[113] The

---

acre particularly in paddy agriculture deserves attention (Bharadwaj, *Production Conditions,* p. 31). For a brief summary of the debate, see V.B. Athreya, G. Djurfeldt and S. Lindberg, *Barriers Broken, Production Relations and Agrarian Change in Tamil Nadu* (New Delhi, 1990), Chapter 8.

[110] Satoru Nakamura, 'Kindai Sekai niokeru Nogyo Keiei, Tochi Shoyu to Tochi Kaikaku [Agricultural Management, Landownership and Land Reform in the Modern World], no. 1', *Keizai Ronso* 143, 1 (1989), pp. 30, 29–30.

[111] Hiroshi Sinbo and Osamu Saito (eds.), *Nihon Keizaishi* [Economic History of Japan], Vol. 2 (Tokyo, 1989), p. 54.

[112] Yanagisawa, 'Handloom Industry and Its Market Structure'.

[113] Yoji Shimizu, 'Chuno Hyojunka Keiko to Nomin Keiei [A Trend towards

importance of the serious limit set on the development of industry under the colonial condition in India cannot be too strongly emphasised. The major demand for labourers came only from plantations; labour demand from the industrial sector in India was too limited to cause a general rise in the agricultural wage level in South India and to reduce the number of labourers in the agricultural sector. Colonial rule further impeded the decrease in the number of agricultural labourers in Tamilnadu. As was mentioned in this chapter, in the process of stratification among the Non-Brahmans, a considerable number of small farmers may have sunk to the status of smaller farmers, tenant farmers or agricultural labourers. The possible decrease in the labour supply from erstwhile agricultural labour classes may have been offset by a new inflow of daily labourers from the declining farmer families. Fifth, Hideyoshi's national cadastral survey attempted to identify a single taxpayer for each plot of land and officially to deny multi-layer ownership. The Tokugawa government supported the independence of the small peasant farm, trying to prevent the appearance of large-scale production and landless agricultural labour. By contrast, as we shall see in the next chapter, in the *raiyatwari* settlement in the Madras Presidency, those large landholders (*mirasidars*) who owned servile labourers or leased out their land to tenants were not precluded from being identified as taxpayers. There was actually no prohibition against the hiring of debt-bonded labourers, no positive policy having been adopted by the Madras government at least up to 1892, and even after then the measures taken by the government were very limited. The stance of the government policy as a whole continued to be pro-*mirasidar* at least up to World War I.

To summarise, my comparison of South Indian and Japanese agricultural changes seems to indicate an important similarity in agrarian progress between the two regions. We notice a change in agricultural methods towards intensive cultivation, an emergence of small family farms from the former agricultural labourer class, and a gradual deterioration of large farms cultivated by non-family servile labourers. It is plausible that at least in the wet rice-producing areas in seventeenth- to nineteenth-century East Asia (including Japan and China) and in colonial Tamilnadu, the main trend in agriculture was towards smaller farms, though the evidence produced in this study is too limited to fully support my conclusion.

It is also very important to note that the South Indian case differs at

---

Middle Peasants and Their Farm Management]', in Shigeaki Shina (ed.), *Famiri Famu no Hikakushiteki Kenkyu* (Tokyo, 1987).

a crucial point. A large section of the agricultural population remained agricultural labourers in South India. The family farming system has not been established as a dominant form of agrarian management in South India, as was the case in Japan, though the trend towards the family farming system was present in Tamilnadu agriculture. The difference can be attributed to many factors, of which at least some seem to have been closely connected with the colonial conditions in India: the decline of some indigenous industries, the serious limit set on industrial development, the growth of stratification among Non-Brahman communities and the resultant decline of some farmers into the status of tenants and agricultural labourers, and the basic stance of government policy. Thus, though it is difficult to judge the impact of colonial rule on the growth of agriculture as a whole, it may not be denied that colonial rule and structural changes in society resulting from colonial conditions placed some important obstacles in the way of the inherent growth of Tamilnadu agriculture.

6

Government Policy towards Agricultural Labourers and Tenants

No assessment of historical change in the agrarian societies of South India can be complete without measuring the impact of government policy. Though wide-ranging policies of the Madras government had both a direct and an indirect influence on the changes, I will consider here only those policies that had a direct bearing on the lower classes. It is particularly important to assess the extent that government policy contributed to the emancipation of the lower castes and to the deterioration in the pattern of landholding seen in the 1860s. With this focus, this chapter will trace those basic trends in policies that may have influenced the conditions of the lower castes and lower classes in Tamilnadu.

When the *Statement Exhibiting the Moral and Material Progress and Condition of India* reviewed the problems of the Depressed Classes in 1920, most cases referred to concerned the Madras Presidency, suggesting that this Presidency had formulated and implemented the most systematic policies for Depressed castes in the whole of India.[1] Government policy towards these castes was a hot issue in local politics.[2] Since the 1891 Tremenheere report on 'Chingleput Pariahs' marked an epoch in the history of government policy towards Depressed castes, I shall examine that policy using 1891 as a watershed.

Economic Policies Relating to Labourers and Tenants before 1891

Government attitude towards mirasi rights

The main feature of the Tremenheere report was to identify the causes

[1] *Statement Exhibiting the Moral and Material Progress and Condition of India during the Year 1920* (London, 1921), pp. 155–59.

[2] C.J. Baker and D.A. Washbrook, *South India: Political Institutions and Political Change, 1880–1940* (Delhi, 1975), pp. 49–51.

of the plight of the Depressed-caste members (he uses 'Pariah' [Paraiyar] as a term denoting Depressed castes) in Chingleput district. Tremenheere saw the key to its solution to be the acquisition of land by Depressed-caste members. He argued that the main obstacle to the Paraiyars owning land was the prevalence of *mirasidars'* rights and their recognition by the administration. Excellent studies exist concerning the attitude of the Madras government towards the rights of *mirasidars*, and so here I will deal with the question only briefly.[3] In this chapter, I examine the policy towards *mirasidars* only to judge whether it encouraged the acquisition of land by members of lower castes.

After a series of twists and turns, the government selected, from the early 1820s onwards, the class of *mirasidars* as the persons responsible for the payment of land taxes. This decision was documented by the Proceedings of the Board of Revenue, dated 4 December 1820, in which the Board replied to an inquiry made by the Collector of South Arcot district, with regard with whom they should make revenue settlements, either with the occupant *raiyats* or with the head inhabitants called *mirasidars*.

> With respect to the particular farms and fields, where an ancient meerassidar can clearly establish a legal right to the land on any ground, and is at the same time to be depended on for the rent, his claims should of course be attended to by the collector: the *oolcoodies* [*ulkudis*] and *poracoodies* [*parakudis*], and other tenants, were in some cases, or might have become freeholders, and therefore meerassidars themselves, and the *pottahs* should in general be continued in their names, but in cases where it is evident that they are rightfully only the subtenants of the old meerassidars, and the old meerassidars are to be depended upon for the rent, the collector should settle with the old meerassidars, and leave them and their subtenants to settle together. . . .
>
> It never was intended that the ryotwar settlement should go lower than the landholders or meerassidars; it never could have been meant that their cultivating subtenants should be immediately included in the engagements with the circar; it would appear, however, that in some cases this mistake has been actually made, and it seems to have been supposed that under a *ryotwar* settlement the collector is to settle with the actual cultivators, although only sub-

[3] Nilmani Mukherjee, *The Ryotwari System in Madras* (Calcutta, 1962). For a fuller understanding of the policy in different contexts, see Bandopadhyay, *Agrarian Economy of Tamilnadu.*

> tenants, and to leave the landholders to get what they could from their tenants, as a recognition of their landlord's right.[4]

Thus the general principle of the Board was for the Collector to choose *mirasidars* as the tax paying *pattadars* and to settle with them, wherever *mirasidars* were present, though, as pointed out by Mukherjee, *mirasidars*' rights were not unconditional, since they had to cultivate the land and pay revenue,[5] and the neglect of these duties would lead to the forfeit of their rights. If there were no *mirasidars*, *pattas* were issued to the occupants of the land, such as *ulkudis*.[6]

The claim of *mirasidars* over uncultivated waste land remained unsettled till the 1840s. In the early 1820s, the Collectors of Madras, Tinnevelly and Madura stated that the right of *mirasidars* extended to 'waste lands' but they did not particularly define what this right was.[7] The Collector of Madras observed that though the *mirasidars* possessed the exclusive right of cutting firewood, working quarries, etc., they had no right of cultivation, much less could they claim any to break up common used for pasturage or to cut down productive trees. It was also stated that the consent of the government was necessary regarding any change being made in the appropriation of the land.[8]

It was in 1841 that the *mirasidars*' preferential right to cultivate and occupy waste land was officially approved. In a despatch dated 28 July 1841, the Court of Directors ordered:

> Without entering upon a discussion of the respective rights of Government, and the Meerassidars, over the waste lands, (a point still under the consideration of the superior Tribunal to which the case has been appealed), it will be enough for us to state our opinion, that it is desirable that, in all cases where Paycarries propose to cultivate the waste lands of a Meerassy Village, their proposal should be, in the first instance, communicated to the Meerassidars, to whom, in the event of their being willing to cultivate, or to give security for the Revenue assessable on the lands, the preference

[4] 'Extract from Proceedings of Board of Revenue, dated 4th December 1820, on a reference from Mr. Hyde, Collector of South Arcot, as to the parties with whom he was to make the Settlement of the Government demand', in Bayley and Hudleston, *Papers on Mirasi Right*, p. 417.

[5] Mukherjee, *Ryotwari System in Madras*, pp. 218–19.

[6] Ibid., p. 219; Bayley and Hudleston (eds.), *Papers on Mirasi Right*, pp. 347, 416, 424–25.

[7] 'Extract from the Proceedings of the Board of Revenue, under date 11th December 1823', in ibid., p. 428.

[8] Ibid., p. 429.

> should be given. We consider that the Government has a clear right to the Revenue to be derived from the conversion of waste lands into arable, but we at the same time think it preferable that this object should be attained, whenever practicable, without causing the intrusion of strangers into the Village community.[9]

Thus, as the Collector of Chingleput district wrote in 1843, while in this district formerly the Collector had been undoubtedly vested with the right to grant waste land in *mirasi* villages to 'Paycarry cultivators' without the consent of the *mirasidars*, this practice of long standing was announced illegal.[10]

In the early 1850s, the Dittum system was adopted in Chingleput district, the *mirasidars*' stronghold, and was in effect till 1855.[11] Under this system, the *mirasidars* could cultivate just as much as they wanted of the assessed land and so much only was entered in their *pattas*. They allotted a portion of the remaining land to *payakaris* for cultivation. These fields were entered in one common (*samudayam*) *patta*. The government did not charge tax on the remaining waste, however great, even though the land remained uncultivated because of negligence of the *mirasidars*. Considerable areas of land thus still evaded tax payment under the guise of waste land, and this led to the abolition of the Dittum system.[12]

Under the new system which followed the abolition of the Dittum system, the *mirasidars* had to declare the amount of land they wanted entered in their *pattas* and had to pay tax for that amount, regardless of whether the land was cultivated or not. If a *mirasidar* wanted to give up a part or the whole of his *patta* land, he had to give notice of his intent before August 15th that year. On the other hand, the government had the power to issue fresh *pattas* for land not taken up by the *mirasidars* to *payakaris* (cultivators holding no *mirasi* right) who wished to cultivate the land and applied for it. This would result in the *mirasidars* losing not only a part of their land permanently to the *payakaris*, but also the tenancy rent or *swatantram* they used to collect from them as well.

[9] 'Extract from a despatch of the Court of Directors, dated 28th July 1841, No. 8', in ibid., pp. 455–56. See also Kumar, *Land and Caste*, p. 87; Board of Revenue, Vol. 1767 (TNA), 8 Sept. 1841, pp. 11329–30.

[10] Board of Revenue, Vol. 1849 (TNA), 2 Mar. 1843, pp. 3291-92.

[11] For government policy in Chingleput district, see Eugene F. Irschick, *Dialogue and History: Constructing South India, 1795–1895* (Berkeley and Los Angeles, 1994), Chapter 4. The Dittum system was adopted also in South Arcot district. Bandopadhyay, *Agrarian Economy of Tamilnadu*, p. 123.

[12] G.O., No. 590, Revenue, 13 Apr. 1875, p. 1377.

Inevitably, they took various measures to prevent the *payakaris* from obtaining land *pattas*. Too numerous to catalogue, the Collector of Chingleput recorded a few examples of these.[13] When a *payakari* applied for land he wished to cultivate, the *mirasidar* quickly included it in his *patta*, even if he had no intention of cultivating it or paying the land revenue. When the land was later taken over by the government due to tax arrears or default and auctioned, the *mirasidar* connived with his relatives to buy it back at a cheap price, so that it would return to his possession. Being powerful landlords, 'and being usually the influential inhabitants of each village, with friends at taluq head-quarters, they have been, to a great extent, successful, and managed to keep large areas waste which might profitably have been cultivated by Poyakaries, thereby giving rise to increased ill-feeling'.[14] The government, on its side, lost a part of its land revenue. According to the data, in 1871, more than half of the whole revenue realised by the sale of land was recovered in the single district of Chingleput.

In 1875, the Madras government redefined the rules for the payment of *swatantram* by the *payakaris* to the *mirasidars*, in the event of the government issuing *pattas* to the *payakaris*. The government expected that the *mirasidar*, assured of his fees to the land, 'will no longer intrigue to keep it all in his own hands'.[15]

In this way, the government selected *mirasidars* as *pattadars* of the land, recognised their preferential right over waste land and reinforced the responsibility of non-*mirasidar pattadars* to pay land rent to the *mirasidars*. Tremenheere's remark in 1892 is far from unreasonable: 'We have permitted ancient privileges to survive until they have become anachronisms, and we have created new privileges.'[16]

It may not be totally wrong to interpret the policy of partiality towards the privileged *mirasidars* as being a projection of the fact that the British colonial administration in Tamilnadu had to depend on the *mirasidars*' power to control local society. As Washbrook correctly indicated, 'Village officers, clerks, revenue and police inspectors and *tahsildars* were of far greater consequence in deciding the vital questions of who paid what and whose grievances were redressed than the

[13] Ibid., p. 1378.

[14] Ibid.

[15] Ibid., p. 1391–93.

[16] G.O., Nos. 1010–1010A, Revenue, 30 Sept. 1892, p. 635. See Hjejle, 'Slavery and Agricultural Bondage', p. 87.

Governor or departmental Secretaries'.[17] Of course, this did not imply that the rights of *mirasidars* were unconditionally supported by the government. They were recognised so far as they did not harm the collection of the land revenue by the government. The guiding principle of the government was to secure revenue from rural society.[18] In other words, at least in the period prior to 1892, when dealing with *mirasi* rights, the government never seriously considered protecting the interests of the Depressed-caste members and low-caste Non-Brahmans.

As we saw in Chapter 2, *mirasidars* aggressively impeded the acquisition of any land by members of lower castes to ensure that their labour would be available to cultivate the *mirasidars*' own land. It was vital for the *mirasidars* to establish exclusive rights over uncultivated land so that the lower castes would not have a chance to occupy it. A statement of the Collector of Tanjore district suggests explicitly that the object of the *mirasidars*' claim over waste land was to prevent members of other castes from owning the land in the village: 'There appears to be no objection to allowing to the Meerassidars the privilege of transferring their right by sale or otherwise, as a means of protecting themselves from the intrusion into their community of persons distasteful to them whether by caste or otherwise, which could not but be a fruitful source of dissension unfavorable to the prosperity, if not to the peace of the community.'[19]

Even in other districts where the *mirasidars*' rights over waste land were not recognised, *pattadars* already owning land were given priority of claim to arable waste land. No land was given to any applicant till it had been offered to the *pattadars* and refused by them.[20]

The Madras government officially endorsed the advantageous position of *mirasidars*, fully aware of the fact that recognition of their

[17] Washbrook, *The Emergence of Provincial Politics*, Chapter 2; Ludden, *Peasant History*, p. 177. Kamala Ganesh argues that the government policy was to accommodate local interest groups which held superior positions in the traditional agrarian structure. Kamala Ganesh, 'Jajmani Relations in Tirunelveli District: A Case Study of the Kottai Pillaimar, 1839–1979', *IESHR* 22, 2 (1985), p. 199. Tanika Sarkar also indicates that the *mirasi* tenure system was even reinforced in some places. Tanika Sarkar, 'Bondage in the Colonial Context', in Utsa Patnaik and Manjari Dingwaney (eds.), *Chains of Servitude: Bondage and Slavery in India* (Madras, 1985), p. 117.

[18] Mukherjee, *Ryotwari System in Madras*, p. 220.

[19] 'From Mr. Kindersley, Principal Collector of Tanjore, to the Secy. to the Board of Revenue, dated 26 August 1841', in Bayley and Hudleston (eds.), *Papers on Mirasi Right*, p. 471.

[20] G.O., Nos. 1010–1010A, Revenue, 30 Sept. 1892, p. 617, par. 14.

preferential rights would hamper the acquisition of land by the lower castes. As I discussed in Chapter 5, low-caste Non-Brahmans and Depressed castes started acquiring landed property after 1865. What is important is that this phenomenon evolved, not because of any support given by the government, but rather in spite of the pro-*mirasidar* government policy.

Abolition of slavery

The Abolition of Slavery Act of 1843 was meant to have a direct bearing on the condition of the Depressed castes.[21] At the beginning of the nineteenth century, the British Collectors co-operated with each other in catching and bringing escaped slaves back to their owners. In fact, in the Malabar district, the government itself owned slaves.[22] In 1833, when the East India Charter came up for renewal, the Charter Act incorporated a clause saying that slavery in India should be abolished as soon as practicable. The India Law Commission was established under the Charter Act of 1833 and the slavery abolition law (Act V of 1843) was passed.[23] As Benedicte Hjejle has quite rightly suggested, this law was only effective on paper. It merely meant that no claims to the services of slaves could be upheld in a British court.[24] Owning a slave became a punishable criminal offense only in 1861, when the Penal Code was passed.

Even this Penal Code did not create a significantly changed situation in the state of servitude, which in reality continued in a veiled form, as I have discussed in Chapter 2, under the pretext of repayment of loans. Thus in spite of the legal abolition of slavery, hardly any active steps were taken to bring a radical change to the condition of servitude in Tamilnadu. As Dharma Kumar points out, 'Essentially the Government solved the problem of slavery by ignoring it.'[25] Such a passive attitude to this social problem was a natural consequence of the government's dependence on the dominating rural elites, such as slave

[21] For the abolition of the slavery, see Nancy Gardner Cassels, 'Social Legislation under the Company Raj: The Abolition of Slavery Act V 1843', *South Asia*, n.s., 11, 1 (July 1988).

[22] Kumar, *Land and Caste*, p. 68.

[23] Cassels, 'Social Legislation under the Company Raj'; Hjejle, 'Slavery and Agricultural Bondage', pp. 96–102.

[24] Hjejle, 'Slavery and Agricultural Bondage', p. 98.

[25] Kumar, *Land and Caste*, p. 74.

owners, to control rural society. 'The slave owners were simply too powerful and it would be dangerous to antagonize them.'[26]

Policy towards tenants

Towards the latter half of the nineteenth century, most of agricultural labourers were Depressed-caste members, as were a large proportion of the tenants working for the *pattadars*.[27] The government's attitude towards these tenants needs also to be examined.

To reiterate the treatment of tenant cultivators under the *raiyatwari* settlement operations in the first half of the last century, the government officially recognised the *mirasidars* as the *pattadars* responsible for the payment of land revenue, whereas the *parakudis* and *ulkudis* were excluded from any kind of landownership in villages where *mirasidars* dominated.

In 1875, in an attempt to protect tenants in these villages, the Collector of Chingleput suggested that the names of tenants or *payakaris* cultivating *samudayam* land be registered in the *pattas* and sub-receipts be issued to each *samudayam* occupier for the assessment due on his individual holding. His proposal was turned down by the Government of Madras, for the reason that landlords would resent the registration of tenants as undue interference and the result would be a great increase in litigation.[28]

After a lapse of five years, the issue of the protection of tenants was revived and brought under active consideration by the Indian Famine Commission. In 1881 the Government of Madras was urged to consider various possibilities in order to solve the problem: whether the subletting of land by *raiyatwari pattadars* should be discouraged or forbidden; whether the status of tenants should be recognised and the rent, area of land and the conditions of tenure be recorded if land was allowed to be rented to tenants; and whether it was desirable to improve the position of tenants-at-will so that they could secure occupancy right of the land.[29] However, the Government of Madras totally rejected the adoption of any such steps. It states that, in the first place, the number of *raiyat* proprietors who did not take part in cultivation themselves was

[26] Hjejle, 'Slavery and Agricultural Bondage', p. 100.

[27] In Chingleput district, the bulk of sub-tenants were reported to be 'Pariahs' (G.O., Nos. 1010–1010A, Revenue, 30 Sept. 1892, p. 657).

[28] G.O., No. 590, Revenue, 13 Apr. 1875.

[29] G.O., Nos. 437–438, Revenue, 29 Apr. 1882, pp. 387–91.

comparatively very small; secondly where they had sub-tenants, they treated them well; thirdly, if, by 'bona fide cultivator', the Famine Commission meant only the person who actually held the plough or personally laboured in the fields, the measures which the Commission recommended 'would be subversive of property in land throughout the country, and would, by depreciating the value of land', result in a reduction of the wherewithal for the improvement of land.[30]

In 1885, the Collector of Tanjore district proposed protecting actual cultivators (whether tenants or *pannaiyals*) by law so that they might be assured of a fixed percentage of the produce and not be liable to summary eviction as long as they cultivated the land properly and paid the share due to the landholder. This was also turned down by the Madras government on various grounds, one of which was that any artificial restriction placed on the share of the *raiyats* might necessarily have the effect of driving the *raiyats* to the adoption of the *'pannei'* system of cultivation, a result which the Collector himself very much deprecated.[31] As a result, no steps were taken till 1892 to safeguard tenants under *raiyatwari pattadars*, and the government sanctioned unlimited rights to the *pattadars*, as long as they paid land revenue to the government.

Increase in the tax burden of the lower strata

In addition to the indifference of the government towards the protection of the lower classes, we should take into account the effect of the change in composition of government revenue in the nineteenth century. From the 1840s to the 1880s, the share of land revenue as a percentage of the total revenue or taxation of the Madras government decreased from 68 percent to 47 percent,[32] but this loss in share was compensated by an increase both in salt receipts and income from *abkari* farms and excise.

From 1805 the Madras government had the sole monopoly of salt production throughout the Presidency. This monopoly was relaxed in 1882 permitting private parties to produce and sell salt on paying a certain amount of excise duty. At first, when the government monopoly

[30] Ibid., pp. 401–8.

[31] G.O., No. 1195, Revenue, 29 Oct. 1885; G.O., Nos. 1304–1304A, Revenue, 23 Nov. 1885.

[32] The share of land revenue of the total revenue of Madras government further declined after the 1880s. See Christopher John Baker, *The Politics of South India: 1920–1937* (Delhi, 1976), p. 16.

Figure 6.1
Changes in the Share of Important Sources of Revenue and Taxation in the Madras Presidency

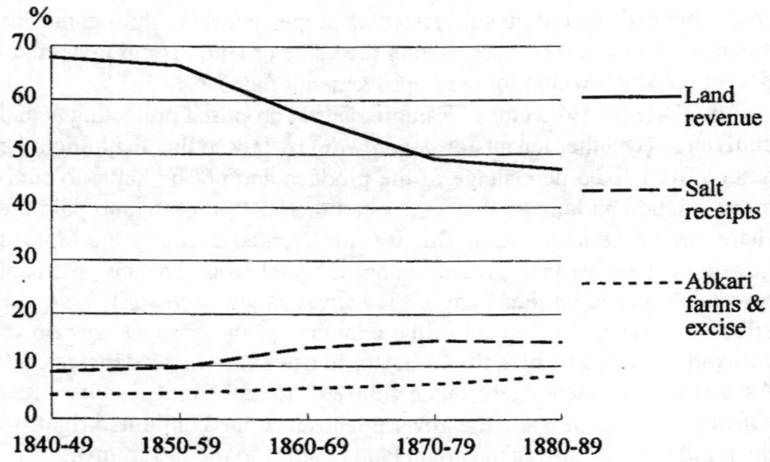

Source: Compiled from Raghavaiyangar, *Memorandum*, pp. cxxvi–cxxxii, Statement showing the growth of Revenue or Taxation in the Madras Presidency from 1800–01.

was created, the price of salt at government factories was fixed at 9 1/3 annas per *maund* (82 2/7 lbs.) and it was continually increased till it amounted to 2 rupees 11 annas in 1888. Meanwhile, the salt revenue jumped 13.5 times from Rs. 130 thousand in 1809–10 to Rs. 1,760 thousand in 1889–90. Since the total quantity of salt exported and sold increased only 1.6 times, the increase in salt income was almost wholly due to price increases.[33] As the 1892 report pointed out, 'There can, however, be little doubt that the salt tax presses with severity on the poorer classes.'[34] The diet of the poorer classes was such that they had to use a much larger quantity of salt than the richer classes, who used considerable quantities of sugar and of vegetables containing salt. The salt tax, taking the consumption per head in the Presidency at 16 lbs. per annum, amounted from 2.5 to 5 percent of the income of a poor family, which was barely sufficient in many cases for sustenance.[35] That salt formed an indispensable ingredient in the labourers' diet was noted, as

[33] Raghavaiyangar, *Memorandum*, p. 116.
[34] Ibid., p. 117.
[35] Ibid., p. 118.

early as the beginning of the last century, by Buchanan, who stated that in Coimbatore 'a servant with these wages can once or twice a month procure a little animal food. Milk is too expensive. His common diet consists of some boiled grain, with a little salt and capsicum, and perhaps some pickles. His drink is the water in which the grain was boiled.'[36]

Another important source of revenue for the government, and one that was to increase considerably, was liquor (local liquor, *toddy*, from palmyra and foreign liquor) and opium. Drinking was common among low-caste people,[37] especially the Depressed castes, who consumed more than any other group, as noted in Chapter 3. Very often, a part of the wages of agricultural labourers was paid in the form of *toddy* money. A 1914 report stated: 'They [*parakudis* and *pannaiyals*] pay a not inconsiderable contribution to the Government treasury, since it is from them that the toddy revenue realised in the district upwards of seven lakhs is chiefly collected.'[38]

On the other hand, as we saw in Chapter 2, the core of those who paid land revenue in the latter half of the last century was a group of rich landholders, who rented their land to tenants, or hired Depressed-caste labourers. As we have observed, the share of the produce paid as land revenue declined sharply in this period. Thus the total effect of the change in the composition of the government revenue was to lighten the tax burden imposed on the upper classes in the village, enabling them to secure a part of agrarian surplus, at the cost of the labourers and low-caste farmers, who groaned under a heavier load of taxation.

To sum up the government policy in the period up to 1891, no positive steps were taken to ameliorate the condition of the Depressed castes and of other lower castes, except the abolition of the slavery, which actually proved ineffective in raising the socio-economic status of bonded labourers. Changes in taxation only added to their hardship. Step by step, the preferential rights of *mirasidars* were officially recognised by the government. This government attitude, quite favourable to the dominant classes in the villages, reflected the government's dependence on those classes for the control of rural society.

[36] Francis Buchanan, *A Journey from Madras through the Countries of Mysore, Canara and Malabar* (London, 1807), Vol. 2, pp. 315–16.

[37] Raghavaiyangar, *Memorandum*, p. 121.

[38] 'Notes to G.O. Nos. 3594–95, Revenue, 9 December 1914', p. 68.

Tremenheere's Proposals in 1891 for the Amelioration of Depressed Castes

In the 1891 report on the Depressed castes ('Pariahs') in Chingleput district, J.H.A. Tremenheere, Collector of Chingleput, put forward his proposals for the amelioration of their condition.

A. Grant of Land to Depressed Castes and Amendment of Land Application Rules

Tremenheere firmly believed that the pivotal point of the whole issue of the Depressed castes was landownership: 'I regard the direct connection of the Pariah with the land as the main lever with which we can raise his material condition.'[39] He proposed the following measures.[40]

1. An amendment of the Land Application Act of the Madras Presidency so as to put all residents of a village on the same footing as the existing *pattadars* (Proposal A-1): While in a *mirasi* village *mirasidars* had preferential rights over waste land, in a non-*mirasi* village, when an application for the cultivation of waste land was made, priority was given to those *pattadars* who already owned land in the village. In particular, the first preference went to those who already owned land adjoining the waste land concerned. This rule thus prevented people like the Paraiyars who owned no land at all from acquiring land for cultivation. Tremenheere proposed to amend this rule, to clear the way for equal rights for all.

2. In *mirasi* villages, the preferential right of *mirasidars*, which, he thought, was the main obstacle to the acquisition of land by the Paraiyars, should be required to be exercised either once and for all or in the first month of each year (Proposal A-2). Since 1875, the State had been collecting fees from non-*mirasi pattadars* who acquired waste land and paying them to the *mirasidars*. This, he proposed, should be abolished (Proposal A-3) [G.O., Nos. 1010–1010A, Revenue, 30 Sept. 1892 (in this chapter, hereafter the same), 'Note on the Pariahs of Chingleput', Sections IV, V, VI].

3. According to Tremenheere, the State had at its disposal the following four kinds of land not affected by the *mirasi* preference. (1) It had 19,500 acres in non-*mirasi* villages in Chingleput district which it could throw open to resident Paraiyars. (2) Some *mirasi* land was

[39] G.O., Nos. 1010–1010A, Revenue, 30 Sept. 1892, p. 619. Hjejle has already examined the Tremenheere report in detail ('Slavery and Agricultural Bondage'). Our discussion owes much to her work.

[40] G.O., Nos. 1010–1010A, Revenue, 30 Sept. 1892, p. 635.

acquired every year by the government though arrears in revenue. The *mirasi* preference no longer existed regarding such land. (3) A similar remark could be made about land held by non-*mirasidars*, relinquished by them or acquired by the government through arrears. The *mirasi* preference did not exist over such land, provided it was held before the previous settlement when *mirasi* fees were recognised regarding newly occupied waste land. (4) Wherever large blocks of arable waste existed, the Forest Department was authorised to constitute them into reserved forests, provided that the land had not been occupied for 18 months. In this district, 18,000 acres came under this category. Tremenheere recommended that out of the areas in (1) and (4), some favourable localities should be set apart for Paraiyar settlement. The rest, and the scattered plots in (2) and (3), should be available for the first resident applicants, whether castemen or Paraiyars (Proposal A-4) [Section VI].

B. Protection for the Tenants

The *zamindari* system functioned in parts of the Madras Presidency. To protect the Paraiyars as *raiyats* under *zamindars*, Tremenheere recommended the speedy passing of a Madras Tenancy Act (Proposal B-1). Steps should later be taken to amend the position of tenants cultivating land under *raiyat pattadars*. He suggested that if a tenant under a *pattadar* occupied the land for more than 12 years, he should be given occupancy rights for the land (Proposal B-2) [Sections VII, VIII].

C. Recasting of the Breach of Contract Act

As we have seen already, even after the legal abolition of slavery, permanent agricultural labourers 'mortgaged' themselves and worked in a state of servitude. 'Unable to check their master's calculations, their debts before long amount to three or four times the original sum.'[41] The only way they could leave their master was to find a new master who would repay their debts. If they tried any other method, they were sued in court, or subject to the penal provisions of the Breach of Contract Act.[42] Tremenheere pointed out that most of these bonds were not enforceable by law. But 'the padiyal does not know this', and lived in dread of legal action. Tremenheere therefore suggested enacting a proper and intelligible Breach of Contract Act, which should include provisions directed against quasi-slavery and limiting all labour

[41] Ibid., p. 622.

[42] For the Workmen's Breach of Contract Act, see Kumar, 'Introduction to reprint', in *Land and Caste*, pp. xxvii–xxviii.

contracts to one year, and perhaps requiring their registration (Proposal C) [Section IX].

D. A Free Home for Depressed-caste Members
As we have seen in Chapter 2, in some districts *mirasidars* claimed proprietary rights over even the house plots of the Depressed-caste members. If a Paraiyar disobeyed or acted against the wishes of the *mirasidar*, he was threatened with eviction. Tremenheere recommended that Paraiyars be given the unquestionable ownership of their homes (Proposal D) [Section X].

E. Other Measures
Tremenheere further suggested that state-aided emigration be considered (Proposal E-1), that the number of liquor shops be reduced to discourage labourers from drinking too much (E-2), that the government make concentrated efforts to spread education among the Paraiyars (E-3), and that the sanitation of Paraiyar hamlets be improved (E-4) [Sections XII, XIII, pp. 635–36].

The Tremenheere report and its proposals were epoch making in that the policies recommended were much more comprehensive and would be more effective, if implemented, in elevating the socio-economic conditions of the Depressed castes than any of the policies that had been framed by the government so far. In particular, based on his observations in Chingleput district, Tremenheere regarded the acquisition of land by Paraiyars as the main lever to raise their status. As we shall see later, the government slowly started implementing plans to ameliorate the lot of the Depressed castes. The actions later carried out never went beyond the sphere of Tremenheere's suggestion though they were partial implementations of his programmes.

The emancipation of the Depressed-caste people and the acquisition of land by some of them, formed, as I have pointed out in previous chapters, the background against which Tremenheere proposed his new programme. His report acknowledged such a trend among this section of the population, noting, for example, that a son returning from Natal or the salt factories on the coast would, from his savings, enable his father to buy a small patch of ground.[43] 'The battle in the past has always between mirasidars and caste non-mirasidars; the possibility of the Pariahs acquiring land was hardly in the minds of district officers, . . . In many parts, at present, the possibility is a new idea to the Pariahs

[43] G.O., Nos. 1010–1010A, Revenue, 30 Sept. 1892, p. 618.

themselves.' The Paraiyar 'is keenly eager to get land, and when the soil is suitable digs a well and improves the holding rapidly. So eager is he in fact that he constantly enters upon Government waste without authority.' It was also noted that in Chingleput and Thanjavur districts, 'the bulk of such applicants for unoccupied land in those districts are undoubtedly the lower castes'.[44]

It is also important to note that Tremenheere's proposals never attempted to emancipate the Depressed-caste members completely but aimed to ameliorate their condition to a limited extent. Tremenheere himself was well aware of the magnitude of the changes his proposals would effect if implemented. 'I am not unprepared to hear my proposals spoken of as revolutionary and as involving the abolition of mirasi right. In one form at least they can hardly be revolutionary in any bad sense, unless the Chief Justice of Madras can be supposed to have recommended revolution. Nor have I proposed to abolish mirasi right.'[45] He recognised the *mirasidars*' claim to waste land and only protested against its exercise for the purpose of obstruction. Much less did he propose to act against the *mirasidars*' dominance in landholding, that is, the economic background of their control over the Depressed castes. In this sense, his proposals never aimed at ultimately solving the Depressed-caste problem by means of, for example, a radical land reform transforming landless labourers into independent landholding farmers. The Madras Missionary Conference sent a memorial to the Governor, in which it proposed steps to be taken to ameliorate the condition of the Depressed castes, stating that 'your memorialists confidently hope that these five millions will soon prove a strength to the Government which has befriended them'. It further noted that 'such an allotment of waste lands to Pariah pattadars would also be a financial gain to Government. . . .'[46] This memorial was close in stance to Tremenheere's proposals and shared much the same political and financial points of view.[47]

[44] Ibid., pp. 633, 630, 681.
[45] Ibid., p. 634.
[46] Ibid., p. 613.
[47] Ibid., p. 637, Appendix B.

Examination of Tremenheere's Proposals by Government and Government Order

Criticism by the Board of Revenue

The Board of Revenue reacted negatively and raised objections to almost all the proposals submitted by Tremenheere.

A. Regarding Land Procurement
As to the amendment of the land application rules in the way proposed by Tremenheere (A-1), the Board averred that the preferential rights enjoyed by *pattadars* over waste land had been in vogue for fifty years without any special evil alleged or proved to have resulted from their operation, and hence, no amendment was warranted [p. 652]. Thus the rule, which, the Board of Revenue itself later considered, 'unduly favours richer men and excludes the poor',[48] remained unchanged.

Secondly, the Board argued that it was impossible to question the *mirasidars*' rights to all the waste land in their villages and to the levy of *swatantram* or fees from non-*mirasidars* [pp. 644–45]. In *mirasi* villages, the *mirasidars* had preference over all comers, while in non-*mirasi* villages the preference was confined to those who owned land adjoining that applied for and to those *pattadars* who owned any land in the village over those who did not hold land. Since, in the majority of cases, waste land fit for cultivation was to be found generally in the vicinity of existing holdings, the practical effect of the two sets of rules was similar in that they excluded non-*pattadars*. Therefore, the Board considered, the Paraiyar in Chingleput was hardly under any greater disadvantages than his co-labourer in any district where the *mirasi* system did not exist. Referring to the fact that non-*mirasidars* actually acquired land in Chingleput district, the Board concluded that the *mirasi* privilege was not a very effectual bar to the acquisition of land by non-*mirasidars*. As the assessment on all land taken up was always rigidly exacted, traditional *mirasidars*' tactics to exclude outsiders could not be repeated [pp. 646–50]. Tremenheere's proposals relating to *mirasi* rights (Proposals A-2, 3) were, thus, totally dismissed by the Board.

The Board's reaction to Tremenheere's recommendations in regard to the settlement of Paraiyars (Proposal A-4) was also negative. The total extent of available waste being small and much of it comprising poor soil, the Board was doubtful whether it would be possible to form

[48] G.O., No. 2435, Revenue, 26 June 1918, p. 4.

Paraiyar settlements in such localities with any chance of success. Any attempt to bolster up the Paraiyar or any other labouring classes following Tremenheere's proposals would, the Board argued, only lead to an increase in pauper holdings without any advantage either to the cultivator himself or to the government. However, the Board stated, where Paraiyars were willing to start cultivation on their own account, the possibility of giving them land might be favourably considered [pp. 653–54].

B. Regarding the Protection of Tenants

The Board declined to accept Tremenheere's suggestions relating to Paraiyars under *zamindars* (Proposal B-1), stating that most of the proposals had been anticipated in the new Tenancy and Zamindari Kurnam Bills, which were under consideration in the Legislative Department. Regarding the issue of protection for tenants working under the *pattadars* of the *raiyatwari* system (Proposal B-2), the Board endorsed the 1882 denial of protection [pp. 654–55].

C. Regarding Amendments to the Breach of Contract Act

Referring to labourers working under a master to repay their debts, the government considered that 'there seems nothing intrinsically objectionable in such contracts; and, in the absence of any special causes, there is no reason why the relations between master and servant—the mirasidar and the Pariah—should not be left to be regulated by the ordinary law of demand and supply. Mr. Tremenheere himself states that most of these bonds are not enforceable by law. They are illegal already—that seems to be enough' [pp. 657–59].

D. Regarding Housing Amenities

Acknowledging that the State had the complete right to control the appropriation of vacant village-sites in *mirasi* villages as well as in non-*mirasi* villages, the Board stated that government should interfere as little as possible and that there seemed no necessity to take legislative action. The only action that the Board considered to be necessary was 'to set apart, wherever the necessity is proved, separate village-sites for the Pariahs, out of lands reserved for public purposes or bought in by Government' [pp. 666–67].

E. Regarding the Other Proposals

The Board found no necessity for any scheme of state-aided emigration of the poorer classes (Proposal E-1), since the possibilities of emigration were very well known among the people. According to the Board, the government had endeavoured to reduce the consumption of liquor by raising the duty and reducing the number of *toddy* and *arrack* shops and therefore, the Board considered, the complaint of an excess number of liquor houses was groundless. The only sphere in which the Board positively supported the proposal was education. The Board suggested that special measure should be taken for the Pariahs' education [pp. 668–71].

Government Order of the Revenue Department

After a scrutiny of the Board's view on the Tremenheere report, the Revenue Department issued a Government Order in 1892, in which the Department concurred with the Board's view except in the following issues. First, the government did not admit the absolute right of the *mirasidars* to all the land in their villages nor did it agree with the Board in considering that this right had been established by the High Court Judge. The State had the right to appropriate 'immemorial' waste land in *mirasi* villages for State purposes without any preference to the *mirasidars* [pp. 676–77]. Second, as regards the provision of village-sites for the Paraiyars, when tenants were expelled from their houses by *mirasidars* and were left homeless, the government would direct the Collector to provide them with housing plots either by assigning them as *purambokku* from the waste or by acquiring by purchase. Such cases of eviction should be reported to the government for court action [p. 677]. Third, the government should be prepared to give opportunities to the Paraiyar and other non-*mirasidars* to obtain land for cultivation by making small allotments available to them out of areas which had been freed from preferential rights by purchase at sales for arrears of revenue and which were at the absolute disposal of government [p. 681].

The reaction of the Madras government to Tremenheere's proposals implies first, that the government did not discern any sign of non-economic bondage which restricted the freedom of labourers and tenants, rather insisting that they were 'bound by no restrictions'.[49] This is in sharp contrast to the observations made by Tremenheere and other contemporaries, which demonstrate that labourers and tenants were far from free agents but were strictly bound by non-economic as well as economic restraints. Second, the Madras government interpreted any proposal to interfere in employer-employee relationships or tenant-landlord relationships and to limit the exertion of the rights of land-holders and employers as a total denial of their rights. In the view of the

[49] G.O., Nos. 1010–1010A, Revenue, 30 Sept. 1892, p. 674.

government, Tremenheere's report was 'creating a social revolution and confiscating private property' and 'depriv[ing] the mirasidars of the ownership of the soil in every case in which a Pariah has paid rent for twelve years'.[50] Needless to say, the protection of the occupancy right of tenants does not necessarily imply a denial of the right of landownership in a modern society. It should be pointed out that what the Madras government was keen to retain, under the pretext of the protection of property rights, was not property rights in a modern sense but the 'traditional' agrarian relationship dominated by the *mirasidars*. Third, though the government's basic stance towards the issue did not alter, the 1892 Government Order was a new departure in the sense that it contained a directive to Collectors to take some steps to ameliorate the lot of Depressed-caste members, an instruction which had been lacking before 1892, and this served as the base from which later schemes for the Depressed castes, such as those framed in the twentieth century, developed. It seems important to note, particularly in view of the development of the policies at a later period, that the government order opened the way to assign land to Depressed castes. However, it would be misleading to interpret it as implying that the government aimed at transforming the Depressed-caste members into independent small farmers. The Revenue Department was in complete agreement with the Board of Revenue in that Tremenheere's view that the acquisition of land by Paraiyars would be the main lever to raise their material condition was a fallacy and that policies based on this would lead to an increase of pauper holdings.[51] In contrast to Tremenheere, the Madras government considered that the greatest and most lasting benefits to Paraiyars might be effected through their education.[52]

New Policy of the Madras Government

Assignment of land to the Depressed castes

The 1892 Order of the Madras government, which included the assignment of land acquired by the government to the Paraiyars, served as the guideline for ensuing policies towards the Depressed castes. Thus directed, the Collector of Chingleput formulated a plan of action, asking

[50] Ibid., p. 673.
[51] Ibid., p. 676.
[52] Ibid., p. 677. See Hjejle, 'Slavery and Agricultural Bondage'.

the district officers to prepare a list of all the land in each village bought by the government; to report if any Paraiyar settlements could be formed; and to publish in all villages that a large area of land irrigated by the Kurnool-Cuddapah canal was available for cultivation.[53] The government decided in 1902, with regard to the assignment of waste land throughout the Presidency, to reserve for Collectors the right to waive the ordinary rule of preference in favour of the Depressed-caste members.[54] The preferential rights of *mirasidars* suffered a further blow in 1909, when the government stopped its support for the collection of *swatantram*,[55] and again in 1911 from the Supreme Court judgment that it did not support the rights enjoyed by the *mirasidars* over all the unoccupied land of the Presidency.[56]

The most important change was made in the land application rule in 1918, when the Madras government ordered that in dealing with applications for the assessed waste land, the claim of the adjacent *pattadars* should be abolished and that preference should be first given to residents in the village. The order further agreed with the Board of Revenue in that specific areas might be reserved for assignment to the depressed classes, subject to necessary safeguards.[57] Thus, the claims of the *mirasidars* and adjacent *pattadars* over waste land were gradually restricted after 1893, slowly opening up the way for the Depressed-caste members to procure land, and were finally abolished in 1918.[58]

However, the amount of land assigned by the government in this policy did not amount to such an extent as to create any significant change either in the landholding pattern in Tamilnadu or in the economic status of the Depressed castes. By 1918, the government had made several grants of waste land to Depressed castes for dwelling and cultivation. Extensive tracts had also been made over in favour of missionary groups for the formation of agricultural settlements for these castes, for which more than 4,000 acres of land had been allotted.[59] As the government admitted, however, not much had been done by 1920 in

[53] P.B.R., No. 92, 17 Feb. 1894, p. 1.

[54] Government of India, Public Proceedings, Vol. 10842, Enclosure, No. 319A, Aug. 1920, p. 747.

[55] G.O., No. 2868, Revenue, 19 Oct. 1909, p. 16. See Hjejle, 'Slavery and Agricultural Bondage', pp. 121–22.

[56] P.B.R., No. 10, 12 Jan. 1920, p. 86.

[57] G.O., No. 2435, Revenue, 26 June 1918. For Chingleput district, see G.O., No. 686, Revenue, 21 Mar. 1919.

[58] Baker, *Rural Economy*, p. 185; G.O., No. 2435, Revenue, 26 June 1918.

[59] P.B.R., No. 60, 18 Mar. 1918, p. 6.

most districts to carry out the Government Order for the assignment of the land. Almost a decade later, George Paddison, the Commissioner of Labour, gave evidence in the Royal Commission on Agriculture in India that a total of 180,000 acres had been assigned to the *Adi Dravidas* (Depressed castes) in the Presidency.[60] According to the annual reports of the Labour Department, the amount assigned rose to 237,000 acres by 1927–28 and to 343,000 acres by 1930–31, indicating a rapid progress in the implementation of the policy in the 1920s.[61]

However, it should be stated that the 180,000 acres assigned by 1926 accounted for only 0.7 percent of the total *patta* land in the Presidency and even the 340,000 acres for 1931 accounted for only 1.2 percent.[62] It seems particularly important to note that the main part of the areas assigned was dry land and concentrated in some of the dry districts of the Presidency. Table 6.1 shows that, among Tamil districts, two districts, North and South Arcot, accounted for more than 60 percent of the total area assigned in Tamilnadu. In other districts, in particular in wet districts such as Thanjavur, Tiruchirapalli, etc., the percentage of the assigned areas was very low, generally not exceeding 0.6 percent of the total *patta* land even in 1930–31. As we have noted before, the acreage held by Depressed-caste *pattadars* in the two districts of Chingleput and South Arcot in 1915 accounted for 4.3 and 8.1 percent of the total *patta* land respectively.[63] Since the assigned areas in the above two districts formed only 0.5 and 0.9 percent respectively of the total *patta* land in 1928 (Table 6.1), the contribution made by government policy to the holdings of Depressed castes was very small, accounting for only about 10 percent of the total area held by these communities. This observation fits well with my contention, based on the analysis of the Settlement Registers of Trichinopoly district, that the acquisition of land by Depressed-caste members was, for the most part, not attributable so much to government policy as to ordinary market transactions.

The ameliorating effect of the land assignment policy was further lessened by the poor quality of the land assigned and the lack of the necessary funding for cultivation. 'Failures of land schemes are in many

[60] *Royal Commission on Agriculture in India,* Vol. 3, p. 319.

[61] G.O., No. 2778L., Public Works and Labour Department, 5 Nov. 1928, p. 62, Statement VII; G.O., No. 3218L., Public Works and Labour Department, 21 Dec. 1931, p. 30, Statement VII.

[62] *Jamabandi Report for Fasli 1335 (1925–26)* (Madras, 1927), pp. 46–47.

[63] Chap. 5 in this volume, p. 142 n. 14.

Table 6.1
Statement Showing the Extent of Land Assigned to *Adi Dravidas*
(acres, %)

District	*Patta* land total (1930–31)	Area assigned (percentage)	
		Up to 1927–28	Up to 1930–31
North Arcot	1,235,913	38,696 (3.1%)	56,560 (4.6%)
South Arcot	1,615,961	15,202 (0.9%)	22,968 (1.4%)
Chingleput	696,187	3,575 (0.5%)	5,683 (0.8%)
Coimbatore	2,290,833	6,473 (0.3%)	9,003 (0.4%)
Madura	1,185,803	8,226 (0.7%)	6,748 (0.6%)
The Nilgiris	228,456	46 (0.0%)	27 (0.0%)
Ramnad	324,490	476 (0.1%)	573 (0.2%)
Salem	1,163,567	7,115 (0.6%)	9,456 (0.8%)
Tanjore	1,163,567	965 (0.1%)	980 (1.0%)
Tinnevelly	1,229,294	3,224 (0.3%)	4,386 (0.4%)
Trichinopoly	1,481,844	4,096 (0.3%)	6,882 (0.5%)
Total	12,615,915	88,094 (0.7%)	123,266 (1.0%)

Source: G.O. No. 2778L., Public Works and Labour Department, 5 Nov. 1928, p. 62, Statement VII; G.O. No. 3218L., Public Works and Labour Department, 21 Dec. 1931, p. 30, Statement VII; *Jamabandi Report for Fasli 1340 (1930-31),* p. 79, No. 20.

cases due to the fact that land given them is so often largely such as others do not want because it is poor.'[64] In the majority of instances, it was observed, they lost their land because they did not have the capital required to carry out cultivation.[65] The opposition of *mirasidars* to the assignment would also have been a factor obstructing the progress of the implementation, as indicated by reports that in some cases *mirasidars* dissuaded their Paraiyars from taking up land, though, as we shall shortly see, some *mirasidars* or landlords seem to have accepted the assignment of land to their labourers.[66]

While the assigned land considered above included house-sites allotted to the Depressed castes, the majority of the assignments were for cultivation. Let me add here a few words about the results of the government policy of allocating house-plots to Depressed-caste people. Here also, rapid progress was made in the 1920s; the total number of sites provided since the inception of the Labour Department was 22,000 by 1928 and it jumped to 67,000 sites by 1931.[67] In 1919, the Board of

[64] P.B.R., No. 10, 12 Jan. 1920, p. 23; P.B.R., No. 92, 17 Feb. 1894.
[65] P.B.R., No. 10, 12 Jan. 1920, p. 42.
[66] P.B.R., No. 92, 17 Feb. 1894, p. 2.
[67] G.O., No. 2778L., Public Works and Labour Department, 5 Nov. 1928,

Revenue estimated the Depressed-caste population to number about 4,700,000.[68] The number of Depressed-caste families in the Presidency must therefore have been around 1,200,000, of which about 5 percent benefited from this house-site scheme.

Other measures for the amelioration of Depressed castes

It was education that showed the greatest progress during the period between 1893 and 1920. The number of pupils went up from 30,000 to 150,000 between 1892–93 and 1919, and the number of educational institutions from 1,400 to 5,000. Special concessions were given to people of Depressed castes by the government to encourage their education: they were admitted into elementary schools under public management without payment of fees and were granted special scholarships to secondary schools.[69] In spite of these efforts to raise the educational level of the Depressed castes, only 2 percent of the total Depressed-caste population attended school, while the percentage for the general population was more than 3 percent.[70] What was more, even this limited success was mainly the result of the contribution made by Christian missions and other societies and not by the government itself. Almost two-thirds of Depressed-caste schools in the Madras Presidency were run by missionary establishments; they had 3,500 schools with about 100,000 pupils attending.[71]

The government also attached importance to the cooperative movement among this section of the population. Cooperative movements were started at the beginning of the twentieth century, and by 1920, about 14,000 persons from Depressed-castes had become members of various cooperative societies and 233 societies claimed more than 25 persons of these castes as members. In 1920 societies for Depressed castes alone numbered 118; by 1931 there were 2,000.[72]

---

p. 10; G.O., No. 3218L., Public Works and Labour Department, 21 Dec. 1931, p. 12.

[68] G.O., No. 1675, Home (Misc.), 2 Dec. 1919, p. 54.

[69] Government of India, Public Proceedings, Vol. 10842, Enclosure, No. 319A, Aug. 1920, pp. 769–70; G.O., No. 1675, Home (Misc.), 2 Dec. 1919, pp. 34–35.

[70] Government of India, Public Proceedings, Vol. 10842, Enclosure, No. 319A, Aug. 1920, p. 769.

[71] Ibid., p. 768–70.

[72] Ibid., Enclosure, No. 319A, p. 770; *Census of India, 1931*, Vol. 1, Part 1, p. 487; G.O., No. 875, Confidential, Revenue, 19 Apr. 1916, p. 29.

The need to amend the Breach of Contract Act, a proposal recommended by Tremenheere but rejected by the government in 1892, was finally recognised by the Board of Revenue. It stated that 'the Board considers it necessary to enact that no agreement to discharge a debt by labour shall have effect for more than one year, that in every such agreement the period of labour shall be stated, and that labour for the period therein specified which may not exceed a year shall extinguish not only the interest but also the principal of the debt evidenced by the agreement.'[73]

Lastly, the post of Labour Commissioner was created in 1919 to ameliorate the condition of the depressed classes. George Paddison, the first Commissioner of Labour, was put in charge, not only of the Depressed castes but also the 'aboriginal tribes' and labourers in urban industries.[74]

The new policy in a changing historical context

A consideration of government policy towards the Depressed castes will not be sufficient without an appraisal of it from an historical perspective, one which focuses particularly on clarifying both the background and the underlying tone of the policy.

Several elements that would have motivated the government can be distinguished in the background of the policy, particularly regarding the accelerated development and progress of the scheme and its implementation after World War I. A paragraph from the *Statement Exhibiting the Moral and Material Progress and Condition of India during the Year 1920*, provides us with a key for understanding the government stance towards the depressed classes.

> At the end of May an All-India Conference of the depressed classes was held at Nagpur, in which vehement protests were made against the humiliation to which these classes are subjected and a firm determination enunciated to be free from it at any cost. A notable feature of the gathering, which of itself suffices to lend it a unique character, was a strong expression of gratitude towards government for its impartial treatment of all classes, combined with bitter criticism against the attitude of social intolerance assumed by certain

[73] P.B.R., No. 10, 12 Jan. 1920, p. 110.

[74] Government of India, Public Proceedings, Vol. 10842, Enclosure, No. 319A, Aug. 1920, pp. 749–52. See also G.O., No. 748, Confidential, Revenue, 29 Mar. 1919.

> members of the Nationalist Party. This growing class consciousness of the depressed castes in India is a feature which is full of hope; but if not properly guided it will cause anxiety in the future. In places where these classes have tangible economic grievances, the tendency to disorder resulting from the growth of class solidarity is marked. Reference has been made in another place to the increasing importance of the Tenants' Union movement in Northern India, which, if its direction should fall into unscrupulous hands, may easily lead to trouble of a serious kind throughout a large portion of the rural areas affected.[75]

What emerges from this is first, the prerequisite to this change in government attitude was the recognition of the 'growing class consciousness of the depressed castes' in India. No further elaboration is necessary, since I have already spoken in detail about the process through which the members of Depressed and other lower castes endeavoured to emancipate themselves and raise their status from mere agricultural labourers to that of small farmers. Some Depressed-caste members in South India organised the Depressed Classes Conference similar to the All-India Conference in Nagpur.[76] Second, the government was very keen to prevent this large group of people from joining the Nationalists, particularly after World War I, when the nationalist movement expanded and became a serious threat to the government. The government highly appreciated 'a strong expression of gratitude towards government' and the 'bitter criticism against' members of the Nationalist Party. The government had come to share the view expressed by the Madras Missionary Conference in 1891: 'Your memorialists confidently hope that these five millions will soon prove a strength to the Government which has befriended them.'[77] The rapid development of the policy after World War I may well be understood in this context. Third, the government was also aware that the growing class consciousness of the depressed classes would lead to disorder if not properly guided, particularly where those classes had serious economic grievances.

Notwithstanding a discernible advance in the government policy towards Depressed castes after 1892, there are reasons to believe that not only was the net effect of the government policy on existing agrarian relations limited, as we have seen already, but the basic stance of

[75] *Statement Exhibiting the Moral and Material Progress and Condition of India during the Year 1920*, p. 160.

[76] They held the third session of the Conference in 1912. See G.O., No. 1739, Revenue, 11 June 1913.

[77] G.O., Nos. 1010–1010A, Revenue, 30 Sept. 1892, p. 613.

the government towards the landholding and labourer classes, though modified, remained virtually unchanged. The sources suggest that government policy never aimed to create a radical alteration of the landholder-labourer relationship. In order to understand the objectives of the government and how it aimed to situate the Depressed-caste members in the contemporary agrarian setup, the following oral evidence given by George Paddison, the Commissioner of Labour of the Madras government in charge of implementing government policy for the amelioration of the Depressed castes, at the Royal Commission on Agriculture in India is suggestive.

> 12353. Are most of these lands so situated that the depressed classes can cultivate them and at the same time earn a wage as agricultural labourers from owners of other lands?—Yes, as a general rule I should say they are. . . .[78]
>
> 12463. *Professor Gangulee*: I desire to ask you one or two questions about the settlement work you are doing. When you settle agricultural labourers, what area of land do you give them?—I think three or four acres is the ideal for those going to remain as labourers, because there is practically no irrigated land to be assigned; it is all dry land.
>
> 12464. In the dry tracts have you any definite areas for particular localities? Do you try to find out what could possibly be called an economic holding for a particular tract?—No, we do very little in that way, because this again is done by the Revenue Department, not by us.
>
> 12465. The allotment is done by the Revenue Department?—Yes. The idea is that the labour supply should not be depleted, that they should be working labourers with land to fall back upon. Of course, when we start a colony on a disafforested area we should try and give an economic holding. . . .
>
> 12467. Who is the guiding spirit in settling these labourers on the land? For instance, if they want good seed, manures and things of that sort, to which agency would they go? In actually settling these labourers on the land, they do require some assistance by way of manure or seed? What agencies can they fall back upon to supply them with those requirements?—They get that from their employers generally, the caste ryots.
>
> 12468. There is no official agency working in that direction?—No.[79]

[78] *Royal Commission on Agriculture in India,* Vol. 3, p. 319.
[79] Ibid., p. 327.

Though some of the replies are not very clear, they do suggest that the land assignment policy of the government did not aim at transforming the landless people of Depressed castes into landowning independent farmers, but rather intended on keeping them as agricultural labourers, by allotting them plots too small to allow them to be independent farmers. As Paddison explicitly stated, the basic idea was that the labour supply should not be depleted and that they should remain working labourers with land to fall back upon. When a colony on a disafforested area was started, the government tried to provide 'an economic holding' with which a farmer could live as an independent farmer, but such cases would not have been frequent.[80] Paddison's statement was endorsed in 1928 by S.H. Slater, the Commissioner of Labour, who wrote that 'it is no real advantage to turn good domestic servants or industrial labourers into indifferent ryots. . . . the possession of an acre or two of land is a real advantage'.[81]

Having no intention of encouraging them to become independent farmers, the government did not create any official agency to support the Depressed-caste members in their cultivation of their assigned land, forcing them to depend on caste-Hindus for the supply of manure and seed. The purpose of their education, stated by the government as follows, was in accord with this aim: 'The depressed classes now provide a large portion of the unskilled labour of the country. . . . The object of education should be to increase the usefulness of the community in its own sphere, . . .'[82] It was also stated that 'the reconciliation of these two points of view seems to lie in adjusting teaching at each school to the needs of the labour market in the locality. If a Panchama school is in a purely agricultural district, the endeavour should be to teach the boys to read, write and understand simple accounts and there-after to be agricultural labourers'.[83]

It may not be completely misleading to say that Paddison considered his policy as a positive measure aimed at securing Depressed-caste members as agricultural labourers in a changed socio-economic condition. He cited an interesting case regarding the guarantee of housing plots to them:

> . . . though the landowners objected most strongly when this work

[80] For a case of disafforested land in Bellary district, see G.O., No. 1469, Revenue, Press, 28 June 1916.

[81] G.O., No. 1555, Revenue, 16 July 1928.

[82] P.B.R., No. 60, 18 March 1918, pp. 7–8.

[83] 'Notes to G.O., Nos. 1675–76, Home (Misc.), 2 Dec. 1919', pp. 42–43.

> was begun and sometimes refused to employ their own labourers for some time, they soon found that the labourer who has a house of his own is much less liable to run away, has more self-respect, has acquired a habit of thrift, has frequently, in order to repay his instalments of the loan, given up drinking and is a much more valuable asset to his master than he was when he had no hope of improvement.[84]

There is some evidence to support his view. The Special Deputy Collector, Tanjore, also stated that 'theoretically speaking there is greater danger of a Panchama having no stake in the village running away from the village altogether than one who owns a site there and has some inducement to remain there'.[85] Actually, 'in some instance the higher classes have put forward men of the depressed classes to get the lands for themselves'.[86] To quote another example, 'recently, in the village of Damal, in the Conjeeveram taluk, the Ayangars, a sect well known in the mofussil for its conservative habits and for contempt, if not oppression, of the poor, constructed a well in the paracheri at their own cost for the sole domestic use of their servants. This was, as I gather, more due to the fear of losing their service than to better motives, but the result however obtained is good.'[87] Thus, it is probably not incorrect to understand government policy as aimed at securing the Depressed-caste people as stable agricultural labourers and at making them work harder by allotting them house-plots and small plots of land, since Depressed-caste labourers tended to run away if they had no stake in their villages. How far the government succeeded in its object, is of course, a different question.

The fact that the government had to take measures to secure an obedient labour force implies that the policy was a reaction to the growth of a tendency towards emancipation among the members of Depressed and other low castes.

Conclusion

To sum up, till 1892, no positive measures were adopted by the gov-

[84] *Royal Commission on Agriculture in India,* Vol. 3, p. 315.

[85] 'Letter from the Special Deputy Collector, Tanjore,' in G.O., No. 1740, Revenue, 25 July 1919, p. 7.

[86] P.B.R., No. 10, 12 Jan. 1920, p. 42.

[87] P.B.R., No. 92, 17 Feb. 1894, p. 4.

ernment to ameliorate the condition of the members of Depressed and other lower castes, except for the abolition of the slavery. The need to protect the rights of tenants working under *raiyat pattadars* was completely ignored. On the contrary, government policy benefited *mirasidars* by recognizing their preferential rights over waste land. Changes in the taxation system also favoured the landowning classes over the lower classes. The existing land application rule gave preferential rights to *pattadars* who already owned land in the village, and so hampered the acquisition of waste land by landless classes. The procurement of plots of land by landless people belonging to the Depressed and other low castes was not, as my analysis of the Settlement Registers of Lalgudi villages shows, a result of the government policy but achieved despite it.

The 1891 Tremenheere report was a new departure in that, for the first time, comprehensive and constructive proposals were submitted to improve the socio-economic condition of the lower castes. It was in this report too that the acquisition of landed property was considered the main lever in raising the state of Depressed castes. While the immediate response of the government was to reject the majority of Tremenheere's proposals, the government recognised the need for catering to at least the minimum necessities of these castes, such as allotting limited areas of land and guaranteeing housing plots. After World War I, these policies began to be rapidly implemented. The Depressed-caste members were beginning to benefit, though to a limited extent, through land assignments and educational facilities, with a new Commissioner of Labour in charge.

The implementation of the policy of amelioration towards the Depressed castes, particularly after the 1910s, was accelerated by the government's concern over the expanding nationalist movement and the subsequent need to foster a pro-British mood among the Depressed castes, now developing their 'class consciousness' and solidarity. The government expected the policy to prevent Depressed-caste class consciousness and serious economic discontent leading to the eruption of social disorder.

The land assignment policy was not aimed at transforming landless people from Depressed castes into landholding independent farmers. On the contrary, land assignment guidelines were that, with the exception of the creation of a new settlement, the labour supply should not be depleted and Depressed-caste members should remain labourers though owning their house-plots and small plots of land. The growing tendency towards the emancipation of the Depressed-caste labourers made it increasingly difficult for landowners to secure the labourers needed to cultivate their land. The policy of assigning small plots of land and house-sites to labourers may be understood as a measure to secure labour in the new socio-economic climate. This implies that the government never aimed at reversing the relationship between the class of dominant landowners, the main group of land-tax payers, and the class of labourers and tenants. The government had been dependent upon the dominant landowning groups in the village for the collection of revenue and the control of rural society. This basic stance remained unchanged though the means to achieve the aim may have been modified. The government was too careful to destroy an existing system, which, they thought, was vital for agricultural production and revenue collection.

The strong influence the dominating landowning classes had is well illustrated by the following remark by A.G. Cardew on the difficulty in passing a tenancy bill in the Legislative Council.

> The difficulty, which was experienced in passing the Land Estates Bill was child's play compared with the difficulties which will have to be encountered in passing a Tenancy Bill. While there were only two or three representatives of the proprietor class then in the Legislative Council, probably 75 per cent. of the native members own land which they cultivate by tenants, so that the opposition to any provisions in the interests of the tenants is likely to be rather formidable.[88]

The real problem, however, was not simply passing the law through the Legislative Council. Since the British administration in South India heavily depended on the rich and powerful landholders in the villages, it could not take any measures that would radically infringe on the economic advantages enjoyed by these local powerholders.

[88] 'Letter from A.G. Cardew to Atkinson, C.S.I., dated 6 January 1910', in 'Note to G.O. Nos. 3594–95, Revenue, 9 December 1914', pp. 32–33.

7

Rural Change after Independence: A Case Study of a Village in Tiruchirapalli District

While there are a good number of survey reports on the economic structure of Tamil villages, generally the focus of these works has been to clarify either the structure of the rural society at the time of the survey or the changes that have occurred since Independence. The findings of these surveys have been generally interpreted as demonstrating the impact of recent agrarian changes, in particular of the 'Green Revolution'. Very few scholars have tried to locate them in the longer historical perspective. Between 1979 and 1982, I surveyed a village named Appadurai as a member of a group of Indian and Japanese scholars who were studying a group of villages in Lalgudi *taluk*, Tiruchirapalli district. Our fieldwork revealed that there is a remarkable similarity between some of the changes in the post-Independence period and part of the agrarian transformation which took place in the colonial period, suggesting that there is a need to consider the post-Independence changes in a longer historical perspective. In this chapter, I discuss the results of my fieldwork as well as the findings obtained by other surveys of Tamil villages in the context of the historical changes in South Indian rural society over the past one hundred years.[1]

The survey of Appadurai village was conducted in two phases: the first between October 1979 and February 1980 and the second between October 1981 and February 1982. The information was collected mainly through interviews with both the villagers of Appadurai village and the absentee landlords owning land in this village. I visited every household, with a few exceptions, in the village to collect data during the two periods. The information was collected through conversation, and I did

[1] For details of the research area, see Yanagisawa, *Socio-Economic Changes*; Hara, 'Introduction'; Yoshimi Komoguchi, *Agricultural Systems in Tamil Nadu: A Case Study of Peruvalanallur Village* (Chicago, 1986).

not use any uniform questionnaire to be filled in. In addition to the interviews, I analysed village documents kept by the village accountant or in the *taluk* office at Lalgudi. Data relating to the employment of the villagers was also collected at some of the important factories located in Tiruchirapalli and its suburbs.

The Sample Village

The River Kaveri is one of the biggest rivers in South India and its delta is the largest paddy cultivating area in Tamilnadu. The village Appadurai is located on the banks of the River Kollidam (Coleroon), a tributary of the Kaveri. A typical wet village, the land belonging to Appadurai is irrigated by the Ayyan Channel, which gets its water from the Kaveri. Tiruchirapalli city is the largest urban centre in the vicinity, having grown to be an important industrial centre in Tamilnadu. In its suburbs is one of India's largest factories, manufacturing heavy electric equipment. The village is within a ten kilometre commuting distance from Tiruchirapalli, and many villagers who work in Tiruchirapalli as factory workers or bus drivers, commute by bus, train or cycle. In this sense, Appadurai can be called a suburban village of Tiruchirapalli. In between the village and Tiruchirapalli, there are two large religious centres with two famous temples, Srirangam and Thiruvanaikoil.

The revenue village of Appadurai consists of three hamlets, Appadurai, Melavaladi and Akilandapuram. The village is separated into two parts by a broad metalled road, lining which there is a commercial centre with vegetable shops, barbers, tea shops, tailors, fertiliser shops, rice mills, potters, etc.

Along the road, but between the two parts of Appadurai village, is another village, called Terukuchattram, which had been an *inam* village (land held wholly or partially free of revenue) before the 1960s, and as such the land had been exempted from the survey and revenue settlement. Though Terukuchattram had become an ordinary independent *raiyatwari* village after the abolition of the *inam* system, the *karnam* (village accountant) of Appadurai held the *karnam* post of Terukuchattram also. From the view point of the villagers' everyday social life, these two villages should be considered as one unit, and therefore, I interviewed people from both. In this chapter, I shall treat Terukuchattram as a part of the sample village and references to 'this village' or 'the village' will include both Appadurai and Terukuchattram except when I deal with historical data, because no Settlement Register was compiled for Terukuchattram before the 1960s.

The number of households belonging to Appadurai and Terukuchattram villages in 1981 was 408 and 62 respectively, totalling 470. The people of Appadurai village lived in several hamlets, namely Appadurai, Akilandapuram and Melavaladi. The localities were demarcated roughly caste-wise. For example, of the 270 households in Melavaladi hamlet, 67 lived in the Non-Brahman area, 117 on the two streets where the Scheduled Castes (Depressed castes; hereafter 'SCs') mainly lived, and 86 in the commercial area along the road. While almost all the inhabitants of Appadurai and Akilandapuram hamlets were of the Muthuraja (Muttiriyar) caste, the inhabitants of Melavaladi living in the Non-Brahman street were mainly Pillais, Chettiars and Muthurajas. The Muslims lived mainly in the commercial area along the road. One of the two streets in the SC quarter was for Pallar households, and the other for Paraiyar households. The households in Terukuchattram village were mostly Muthurajas.

Table 7.1
Sample Households

Community	Number of households	Community	Number of households
Pillai	32	Asari	13
Chettiar	26	Pallar	93
Muthuraja	199	Paraiyar	18
Muslim	35	Others	35
Nadar	19	Total	470

As shown by Table 7.1, the Muthuraja was the largest community in these two villages, followed by Pallars, Muslims, Pillais and Chettiars. The major religion of the villagers was Hindu. Out of 470 households, 35 were Muslim while about ten Muthurajas and several Paraiyar households were Christians; the rest were all Hindus. The main occupation of the villagers was agriculture, on which 268, or about 57 percent, out of a total of 470 households, depended. Forty-two households, or 9 percent, had their main occupation in the urban area; the remaining 33 percent either ran small businesses such as small factories and shops or were employed as hired labourers in the non-agricultural sector of the village.

Changes in Agricultural Production since the 1960s

Introduction of HYVs into paddy cultivation

Paddy was the main crop cultivated by the villagers even in the nineteenth century. Similar to other wet zone villages, paddy cultivation had increased in area at the cost of dry crops after 1864, and after 1925 the area under double cropping had further increased owing to the construction of the Mettur Dam, etc. Although the area under sugarcane and plantain (banana) cultivation increased recently in the 1970s, paddy continued to be the most important crop in the village and, therefore, the village economy deeply depended upon it.

Changes in paddy production in the 1960s and 1970s in this village seem hardly any different from those reported by surveys of other wet villages in Tamilnadu.[2] The cultivation of high-yielding varieties (hereafter 'HYVs') in this village started in 1967. Villagers recollected that by 1975 nearly 70 percent of the farmers had adopted the HYV seeds and almost all by 1980. At the time of our survey, the variety called ADT 3, with a duration of 120 days, was cultivated as the first crop, the *kurvai* crop, and IR 20 and Ponni varieties, with a duration of 140 to 150 days, were cultivated as the second crop, the *thaladi* crop.

With the increasing adoption of HYVs in the village, the consumption of chemical fertiliser had multiplied, as had been the case in other villages. The villagers remembered that the manure used some twenty-five years before had been mainly natural, such as cow dung, oil cakes, and straw waste, and sometimes cattle urine and ammonium sulphate mix. According to an old farmer, people had applied mainly cow dung to the first crop, oil cakes to the second crop and after that sulphate had been applied. People had started using chemical fertilisers in the latter half of the 1960s. A fertiliser-shop owner suggested, comparing 1967 and 1980, that the consumption of fertiliser had increased sharply, three times during the last five years. Although it is not easy to assess the change quantitatively, fertiliser consumption had definitely increased steeply in the 1970s. There was a difference in the amount of fertiliser

[2] For the Green Revolution in Tamilnadu, see Kathleen Gough, *Rural Change in Southeast India, 1950s to 1980s* (Delhi, 1989), pp. 49–81; B.H. Farmer (ed.), *Green Revolution? Technology and Change in Rice-growing Area of Tamil Nadu and Sri Lanka* (London, 1977); S.S. Sivakumar, 'Aspects of Agrarian Economy in Tamil Nadu: A Study of Two Villages', *EPW*, 6, 13, & 20 May, 1978; Madras Institute of Development Studies, *Tamilnadu Economy: Performance and Issue* (New Delhi, Bombay and Calcutta, 1988), Chapter 5.

applied per acre between the large and small farmers: the larger farmers generally applied more fertiliser than the small farmers, except the farmers in the smallest size group, who applied the largest amount per unit.[3]

Owing to the introduction of HYVs and the greater application of fertiliser, the yield of paddy had increased considerably. Villagers claimed that the yield around 1980 was about 50 percent more than that of fifteen to twenty years before and 20–40 percent more than five years before. This is confirmed by the village records, *adangal*, maintained by the village accountant (*karnam*), which indicate that the average yield had increased by about 50 percent during these fifteen years.[4] It may be important to note that farms of different sizes showed differences in the average yield per acre: the yield per crop per acre was about 37 *kalams* on the large-size farms of 5 acres and more, 38.7 *kalams* on 3–5 acres, 33.9 *kalams* on 1–3 acres, and 31 *kalams* on less than 1 acre, demonstrating that farmers operating 3 acres and more were getting a larger outturn per unit than the smaller farmers and suggesting that the impact of the introduction of the HYVs on the crop yield differed with farms of different sizes. This however is a topic beyond the main scope of this study.

The agricultural calendar of the village was connected with the supply of irrigation water from the River Kaveri. In a normal year, the supply of water from the Kaveri started in June or July and stopped around February. The harvesting of the second crop finished in March. After the second crop, blackgram (*ulundu*) might be cultivated as the third crop, if the second crop was harvested earlier. Almost all agricultural operations were conducted manually without using any agricultural machinery. The demand for labour fluctuated seasonally, being high at the time of harvesting and transplanting. The demand reached its peak when the first crop was harvested in October and November. This was because farmers wanted to finish this harvesting as quickly as possible, first to avoid possible damage to the crop by the monsoons, second to sell their crop before the price of paddy fell sharply in October and November due to a glut in the markets, and third to plant the second crop as early as possible.

Although irrigation for cultivation mainly depended on the channels that provided water from the Kaveri, the importance of well irrigation cannot be overlooked. The number of irrigation wells had increased

[3] Yanagisawa, *Socio-Economic Changes*, p. 69, Table 11-A.

[4] Ibid., p. 72, Table 13.

sharply after 1970 and by 1980 had reached 49 wells in Appadurai village and Terukuchattram. All were bore-wells with oil engines for pumping water, except two which were pumped by electricity. Wells were indispensable in the cultivation of plantain and sugarcane. Water was available from the irrigation channels till the end of January. After that, farmers depended on pumpsets from February to May, if they needed irrigation water. As I shall mention later, the cultivation of sugarcane and plantain started in January and, therefore, had to rely on well irrigation between February and May. Out of the total of 49 wells, 29 were installed where plantain or sugarcane were cultivated at least once in several years. Ten wells in particular were on plots which had been cropped with plantain or sugarcane for three years or more. In addition, paddy cultivation too benefited from the presence of wells. Out of the 49 wells, 12 were installed on land cultivated solely with paddy. A farmer with a pumpset could start preparing the nursery one month ahead of the release of channel water and could harvest one month earlier to avoid the rainy season and could also sell the paddy at a better price. The wells were also utilised for the cultivation of a third crop. Some villagers cultivated pulses and oil seeds with the help of pumpsets after harvesting the second crop. Finally, some farmers owned pumpsets in the dry land, where they cultivated coconut trees.

The cost of an oil engine and bore-well amounted to Rs. 10,000. Small farmers owning less than 2.5 acres of wet land might be given a government subsidy covering one-fourth of the cost, and marginal farmers owning less than 1.25 acres of wet land might be subsidised at one-third of the cost. In spite of this, the majority of the bore-wells, 27 out of the 49 irrigation wells, were on farms of 5 acres or more. The larger farmer managing more than 10 acres often owned two wells or sometimes more.

It should be remembered that an improvement in paddy cultivation and the introduction of new varieties had been discernible even in the period before Independence, though these changes had been accelerated after the middle of the 1960s. My examination of South Indian agriculture after the 1870s points to an intensification of cultivation, which suggests that the South Indian farmers were innovative enough to achieve steady agricultural improvement and had a well-developed ability to adapt new technology. K. Gough has also already stated that an increase in the yield and total production of rice occurred even before the start of the Green Revolution.[5] This implies that such technical

[5] Gough, *Rural Change in Southeast India*, pp. 66–71; Athreya,

innovation as achieved in the process of the Green Revolution was not something completely new and alien to South Indian farmers but was in a sense a further development of the improvement in agriculture that had started in the period before the Green Revolution. Here is one aspect of continuity between the period of the Green Revolution and the time before it.

At the same time, some aspects of the Green Revolution were different from previous changes. As I have already indicated, there was apparently a difference according to the size of farm in such indexes as the amount of manure applied, the rate of those holding wells and the yield of crop. As we shall see below, plantain and sugarcane were cultivated mainly by larger farmers. These pieces of evidence seem to suggest that the larger farmers had an advantage over smaller farmers in the process of the Green Revolution, though this issue of vital importance remains to be examined by further research.

Increase in plantain, sugarcane and coconut tree cultivation

Village cultivation records (*adangal*) show the name of the crop cultivated on each plot of land for each year. I have calculated the total area cultivated for each crop from the data available in the *adangal* since 1966. One remarkable change in the cropping pattern was the sharp increase in plantain and sugarcane cultivation. The cultivation of these two crops had gradually increased during the 1960s and showed a jump after 1975, amounting to about 59 acres or about 11 percent of the total wet land in Appadurai village in 1981. These two crops were concentrated mainly in Appadurai hamlet, where they accounted for about 20 percent of the cropped area.

Plantain was cultivated as follows. It was usually planted in January. In February and March, the field was weeded, dried leaves were removed and chemical fertiliser was applied. In May–June farmers weeded and irrigated the field every 15 days, using pumpsets. After June, weeding was not needed but irrigation should have been continued. In November and December, the trees bore fruit and sulphate was applied. In December–January, the trees needed support to prevent falling. From February to March, farmers cut the plantain, according to

---

Vadamalaipuram, p. 65. For Punjab also, Neeladri Bhattacharya suggests that many of the conditions for the transformation as witnessed in the 1960s and 1970s had started developing earlier (Bhattacharya, 'Agricultural Labour and Production', p. 151).

its maturity. The process was almost the same with sugarcane cultivation. Usually, planting was done in January and harvesting the following January.

The cultivation of sugarcane and plantain was not as stable and easy as paddy cultivation. First, the land should have been well drained. The soil in the Melavaladi hamlet side was not suitable for the cultivation of these two crops as it was ill drained and, therefore, only a small area was cultivated with these two crops in this part of the village. Second, cultivation was risky, as a strong wind or a cyclone could easily damage the plants seriously. Third, rotation of crops was essential when land was cultivated with sugarcane. If sugarcane was cultivated on the same land continuously for several years, soil fertility tended to get depleted. For example, a farmer who started sugarcane cultivation in 1977 also cultivated the same crop the next year, namely, 1978 with a yield of 47 tons. In 1979, however, the yield decreased to 27 tons and he had to switch to paddy cultivation in 1980. Fourth, a sufficient supply of water was essential. Irrigation from wells was necessary after February when channels stopped supplying water and farmers with no wells had to rely upon bore-wells owned by rich farmers.

Though the cultivation of sugarcane and plantain yielded a bigger return per acre than paddy cultivation, the two crops were cultivated mainly by those farmers who not only owned suitable land with good drainage and a pumpset but also operated a farm large enough to bear the risk. The location of these cultivators from the *adangal* records reveals that 50–60 percent of them were large farmers running 5 acres and more.[6]

Responding to the increasing demand for coconut, some rich farmers were expanding their coconut topes (groves) too.

Changes in the cropping pattern in this village were discernible in other villages also. Gough points out the expansion in the cultivation of crops other than paddy, such as sugarcane, groundnuts and cotton,[7] and a report from a Ramanadapuram village also points to the diversification of crops produced.[8]

[6] See Yanagisawa, *Socio-Economic Changes*, p. 82, Table 16.

[7] Gough, *Rural Change in Southeast India,* p. 79.

[8] Athreya, *Vadamalaipuram*, pp. 59, 73. In Dusi village, with the advent of well irrigation, there has been some shift towards cash crops such as groundnut, chillies and vegetables (Guhan and Bharathan, *Dusi,* p. 37). For the increase in the area under sugarcane cultivation, C.K. Kurien, *Dynamics of Rural Transformation: A Study of Tamil Nadu: 1950–1975* (New Delhi, 1981), p. 27. See also V.K. Ramachandran, *Wage Labour and Unfreedom in Agriculture: An*

Socio-Economic Change in Major Communities

The economic relationship between the social groups in the village had undergone a remarkable change since the 1950s. We shall proceed to examine the patterns of transformation for each community in the village.

Changes in landownership after 1952

The change in the land distribution pattern among the communities seems to have reflected the basic direction of the social transformation of the village. We have clarified the share of each community in the ownership of cultivated land in the village in 1952, 1961 and 1979.[9] The data for 1952, 1961 and 1970 have been calculated from an old *chitta* record (record of landowners) kept by a previous village accountant, and the figures for 1979 have been collected from the present *chitta* record. The data thus collected have been cross-checked against the interviews with the landholders and the village accountant.

We have seen in Chapter 5 the changes in landholding that had occurred in this village before 1952. Though the village, like other villages in wet Tamil districts, had witnessed a decrease in the area owned by outsiders, particularly of Brahmans in the first half of this century, the landholding pattern of the village was still characterised by the dominance of Brahman outsiders even in 1952: these outsiders owned 82 percent of the land, of which the largest part, 52 percent of the wet and dry land, was held by Brahmans. The majority of these Brahmans, as previously stated, lived in Thiruvanaikoil and had special connections with the Akilandeswari Temple there, while the remaining Brahmans lived in Srirangam town or in some other remote places. Most likely, these outsiders did not cultivate the land themselves but let tenants or agricultural labourers do it.

However, the period after 1952 witnessed important changes. First, the area owned by Brahmans decreased from 209 acres (about a half of the village land) in 1952 to about 170 acres (about 38 percent of the total) in 1979. Other absentee landholders, like Muslim landlords living in Tiruchirapalli city, also more or less reduced their ownership. Second, the land owned by the villagers increased: in 1952 villager-owned

---

Indian Case Study (Oxford, 1990), pp. 35–38.

[9] Detailed data are given in Yanagisawa, *Socio-Economic Changes*, pp. 100–103, Tables 18-A, B, C, D.

land accounted for about 18 percent (excluding temple land); by 1979 it jumped to about 29 percent. The increase of landownership by the Muthurajas and people of the Scheduled Castes is noteworthy: the Muthurajas nearly tripled their landholding from about 23 acres in 1952 to 68 acres in 1979, while that of people from the Scheduled Castes increased from 9.1 acres in 1952 to 16.63 acres in 1979. However, the Pillais' and Chettiars' holdings did not change conspicuously.[10] Third, despite these changes, the villagers owned only 29 percent of the arable land in Appadurai village in 1980. The basic structure of landownership had not completely changed in the sense that absentee landlords dominated landownership even in the 1980s as in the nineteenth century. As I shall discuss later in detail, the pattern of change in land distribution after 1952 in this village was basically similar to that observed in the wet villages both in Lalgudi *taluk* and other districts in the period before Independence, suggesting an element of continuity in social change.

To clarify the background of the changes in the landholding pattern, I shall examine the socio-economic transformation for each of the main communities in the village after the 1950s.

Pillais and Chettiars

The Pillai and the Chettiar communities not only lived on the same street in the village but also more or less shared the same socio-economic characteristics in village society as well. Though they formed only a small portion of the village population, their socio-economic standing in the village was high and many families in these two communities derived from the landowner class. We collected through interviews the data on the main occupations of the previous generation, that is, the fathers of the present villagers. About 54 percent of the Chettiar and about 47 percent of the Pillai households answered that their fathers had owned land.[11] Since these two communities contained a relatively large number of families who had immigrated from other villages, the percentage of those whose fathers owned land was fairly high compared with the other communities.

Two directions of development were conspicuous in the economic activities of these two communities. First, in addition to managing their farms, they tended to start and manage small enterprises like rice mills

[10] Ibid., p. 113.
[11] Ibid., pp. 114–15, Tables 20-A.

or match factories. Second, they were strongly oriented to urban employment in tandem with farm management.

The first trend was well demonstrated by the high percentage of those engaged in non-agricultural occupations in these two communities; 41 percent and 54 percent of the Pillai and Chettiar families respectively were engaged in non-agricultural occupations in the village as their main occupations. To take the example of rice mills, a Chettiar managed one of the two rice mills in the village, which he had inherited from his father, and the other mill was owned and run by a Pillai living in another village. Another villager, a Pillai, was managing on lease a rice mill in Thiruvanaikoil town which was owned by a machine broker. A Pillai and a Chettiar had started match factories just before our survey. Others ran tea shops and a fertiliser shop.

Interestingly, most of these small entrepreneurs also managed more than 5 acres of farmland. Conversely, two-thirds of the Chettiar and Pillai families running 5 acres and more were involved with some kind of enterprise, while the percentage of such cases was much smaller in the same size group in other communities. Although they generally earned a larger profit from the business, they maintained their connection with the land by employing *pannaikarans* (labourers on a yearly contract) to cultivate it for them.

The strong orientation to urban jobs in these two communities was reflected in the percentage of urban workers, which was larger in the Pillai and Chettiar communities than any other communities except the Muslims. About 47 percent of the Pillai and 27 percent of the Chettiar households in this village had one or more family members who worked as urban employees.[12] The percentage was larger in families who operated large farms: about two-thirds of Pillai farmers managing 5 acres or more had urban employees in their families, while in the Chettiar community also, 67 percent of households operating 5 acres or more, and 60 percent of households in the 3–4.99 acre size group had urban employees. Although they were employed as labourers in factories, they also managed their farms in the village.

The main urban jobs sought were bus drivers and conductors, policemen, and skilled workers in the factory manufacturing heavy electric equipment and in an ordnance factory, etc. The bigger farmers generally sent their sons out to higher salaried jobs. For example, two-thirds of the Pillai farmers operating 5 acres or more had at least one employed person in their family who earned more than Rs. 500 per

[12] Ibid., p. 131.

month. Such people accounted for 21 percent of the total working population in the families of this size group. The percentage of the employed people getting lower salaries was low among these size group families. By contrast, the job category in which members of the families of smaller farmers operating less than 3 acres were generally employed carried lower salaries.

The difference in educational level probably accounted for this variation in salary of employed people according to the farm size of the employed person's family. The level of education in these two communities was high: 43.8 percent of the Pillai households and 30.8 percent of the Chettiar households had members who had passed the Secondary School Leaving Certificate (SSLC) examinations or entered Industrial Training Institutes (ITI). The larger landowners generally gave higher education to their sons: there was no Pillai or Chettiar farmer household working 5 acres and more which did not contain an SSLC or ITI certificate holder among its family members. Those educated up to these levels accounted for 35.7 percent and 54.5 percent of the working population in this size group of farmers in the Pillai and Chettiar communities respectively. There were several government primary schools in and around the village and a government high school within walking distance of the village. Although the majority of the village children went to these near-by schools, well-to-do Pillai and Chettiar families sent their children, especially their sons, to the non-governmental schools in towns even far away, spending a lot on tuition, transportation, boarding expenses, etc., and therefore, only the wealthy farmers could bear this monetary burden. The boys educated at non-government schools were said to pass the SSLC examination easily, often with a high score and, when they scored well, they were more likely to enter ITI, polytechnics and colleges. An SSLC or ITI certificate was the minimum qualification required for well-paid urban employment drawing a monthly income of more than Rs. 500. The sons of the larger farmers had an obvious advantage and got the best of both worlds.

Even after getting salaried jobs in urban areas, they lived in their village and tended to continue managing their farm as long as possible. A typical instance was a Chettiar farmer who was a skilled labourer in Bharat Heavy Electrical Limited (BHEL), drawing a monthly salary of Rs. 800. While he commuted to the factory everyday, he managed about 5 acres of agricultural land, employing a *pannaikaran* to cultivate the land and took a vacation to supervise day labourers during busy farming seasons such as harvesting time. The Chettiars and Pillais intended to purchase new land and expand their landed property when they accumulated funds in the future. Thus, they were partly urban employees and partly farmers. The Chettiar and Pillai families placed their hopes on their sons getting good urban jobs and also managing the farms, even if they had land exceeding 5 acres. Working the farm and nothing else was an undesirable choice which they were obliged to make if they failed the SSLC examination.

I have so far examined the groups of people who were the natives of this village and were more or less managing farms. In addition, the two communities contained a large number of people who had no agricultural holdings at all; about 50 percent of the Pillai and 54 percent of the Chettiar households had no farms, with some of them being immigrants from other areas. Most of them either operated small businesses or were employed in the town. This is in accord with the fact that in spite of the large number of those without any farms to operate, the percentage employed as agricultural labourers for these two communities was around 10 percent of the total working population, which was much smaller than the corresponding figures for other communities in the village, for example 27 percent for Muthurajas and 50 percent for SCs.

Muthurajas

The Muthuraja (Muttiriyar) community, officially registered as one of the backward classes, was the largest in the village population. Most of their ancestors had probably been tenants: 82 percent of the fathers of the Muthuraja households were reported to have managed farms and 70 percent cultivated land as tenants.[13] As previously stated, the absentee landlords owned a large extent of the village land, which the Muthurajas had cultivated as the most important tenant community in the village.

As we have already seen, after the 1950s, the Muthurajas had gradually increased their landholdings, from 23 acres in 1952 to 68 acres in 1979. Furthermore, the total area operated by them, either as owners or tenants, was remarkably large, amounting to 339 acres out of the total of 452 acres, though cultivation as tenants formed the major part of their management. Thus, the Muthurajas had raised their socio-economic position in this village since the 1950s and appeared to be concentrating their efforts on improving their position as agricultural producers. In this context, the following facts are noteworthy.

First, the percentage of those in agricultural occupations was high

[13] Ibid., p. 140, Table 22-A.

in the Muthuraja community compared with the others: about 70 percent of the working population and 72 percent of the households turned out to be mainly engaged in agriculture, which was the second highest after the SCs.[14] By contrast, the proportion engaged in business was extremely small. Second, they were the least concerned of all the communities with urban employment, again with the exception of the SCs, and the rate of SSLC or ITI certificate holders among their family members was lower than the Pillais and Chettiars. Such employees living in remote places were particularly few in number. The occupational patterns of the family members of the large-scale farmers operating 5 acres and more most clearly reflected the difference between the Muthurajas and the Pillais and Chettiars: while in the Muslim, Pillai and Chettiar communities, more than half of the farmers in the largest size group had urban employees in their families, only 29 percent of the Muthuraja farmers in this size group had any.

In this connection, the attitude of indifference shown by some rich Muthurajas towards urban jobs deserves consideration. Government offices, public enterprises and some private companies recruited workers mainly through employment exchange offices. Except for the Muthurajas, almost all of those who had passed the SSLC examination or finished the tenth standard education registered their names with employment exchange offices and waited for an employment opportunity. Eleven sons belonging to Muthuraja families did not register their names even though they had obtained an SSLC qualification, but opted for full time farm management. This reflected the fact that for well-to-do Muthurajas who had sharply increased their landownership and raised their status as farmers, agriculture was the most important concern.

A somewhat different tendency existed among Muthuraja farmers operating between 3 and 4.99 acres: in this size group, 38 percent had urban employees in their family, a figure higher than any other size group in this community. This is probably because while the farmers of this size group could afford to provide their children with the good education necessary for attaining urban employment, the extent of land they owned was too small to accommodate all their sons. However, the difference in trend among the different size groups within this community was a relative one. The rate, though relatively higher than those of the other size groups in the Muthuraja community, was lower compared with the same size group in other communities. In this sense, the farm-

[14] Ibid., p. 143.

ers of this size group among the Muthurajas also shared the distinguishing trait that marked this community.

However, it is misleading to think that every member of this community had raised his status as a farmer. While the Muthuraja community as a whole had increased its landownership, the rate of increase was not equal for every stratum of the community. Our interviews indicated that a disintegration of the economic situation of the Muthuraja community had started in the 1950s. The process seems to have been in two phases.

First, the holding of tenancy land had been polarised. Though I have been unable to trace the quantitative changes in the distribution of tenancy rights since no statistical data is available for the period before 1972, the information from many villagers pointed to a polarisation in the tenancy holdings. For example, the ex-*karnam* stated that while almost all Muthurajas in Appadurai had had tenancy rights before 1950, some very big tenants from among the Muthuraja community had acquired tenancy land from tenants with tiny leases by offering landowners higher rents during the 1950s. To verify this, I collected information on the transfer of tenancy rights from 119 Muthuraja households: 23 households replied that they had gained tenancy rights, 40 turned out not to have experienced any considerable change, and 56 answered that they had lost tenancy rights. Of the latter 56 households, 46 gave the period when the right was lost: 14 before 1950, 20 in the 1950s, and 12 in the 1960s and 1970s. As the information was completely dependent upon my informants' memories, it is not completely reliable but may be enough to act as a rough guide to clarify trends in the transfers. The figures indicate that a considerable number of tenants lost their tenancy holdings in the 1950s. This is in accord with other information gained from interviews with the villagers, who said that in the 1950s they had returned their tenancy land to the landlords on demand, since there had been no legal protection for tenants and social consciousness had been low.[15] After the mid-50s, tenancy laws had come into force and the social and economic movements of labourers and tenants had started to evolve. After the 1960s, they said, it had become difficult for landlords to change tenants at will. They had to pay money (several thousand rupees per acre) to the tenant if they wanted to withdraw the tenancy rights. Though about 70 percent of the Muthuraja families had had tenancy holdings in the past,[16] a considerable number

[15] Ibid.; pp. 148–49.
[16] Ibid., p. 140, Table 22-A.

of them had lost their holdings to influential Muthurajas. Poor Muthurajas with no tenancy rights complained that the landlords had given the tenancy rights only to wealthy people.

Second, the rate of increase in landholding had been far from uniform for every Muthuraja, the inequality among Muthurajas having widened since 1970. While about three-fourths of the Muthurajas had increased their landholdings, only a small number of them could have expanded their land by more than 3 acres and the majority in fact had done so to an even smaller extent.[17] I have drawn Lorenz curves based on data from the Settlement Register of 1925 and Chitta records. The curves for 1925 and 1952 are similar to that of 1961. While the curve for 1970 falls slightly nearer to the diagonal, indicating a reduction in the extent of inequality, the curve for 1979 is far from the diagonal again, indicating a sharp increase in relative inequality during these ten years. The Gini coefficients, which indicate the extent of inequality, for the corresponding years are 0.41 for 1925, 0.42 for 1952, 0.42 for 1961, 0.39 for 1970 and 0.47 for 1979. The large coefficient figure for 1979 confirms the increasing inequality of land distribution among the Muthuraja landowners.

Two factors should be considered in this context. First, the polarisation of tenancy holdings had preceded the changes in landownership. Large amounts of tenancy land accumulated by influential Muthurajas seem to have formed the basis of the later expansion of their landownership. Most of the nine Muthuraja families who increased their landownership by more than 3 acres had cultivated a large area of land as tenants before. The second factor we should consider is the impact of the introduction of the HYVs, which seems to be particularly favourable to larger farmers capable of taking advantage of technical innovations. They were probably able to use profits from agriculture to buy new land. The relationship between the size of farm and the impact of the HYVs remains an important issue that needs to be examined by further research.

Thus while some Muthuraja families had become large farmers either by purchasing or leasing large areas, a large section of this community had been reduced to the status of agricultural labourer when they had lost whole or part of their tenancy land. Out of the 199 Muthuraja households in the village, 66 can be categorised as farmers: 9 as owner-cultivators, 11 as tenant-cum-owner cultivators and 46 as tenants. On the other hand, 44 households depended mainly upon day labour

[17] Ibid., p. 149, Table 22-E.

(coolie) and 32 were tenants-cum-coolies. In total, 76 families, or about half of Muthuraja households engaged in agriculture, were more or less employed as day labourers.

Scheduled Castes and the agricultural labour market

There were two types of agricultural labourers in this area: labourers on yearly contract called *pannaikaran* and day labourers or coolies. The first type is supposed to have originated from the attached labourer of the previous century. The socio-economic condition of the Depressed-caste members in this village in the nineteenth century may not have differed much from the general condition of those in the delta area. The *pannaikarans* and day labourers accounted for 64 percent of the fathers of the SC families, the corresponding figures of which were much smaller in other communities. Particularly remarkable is that 31.5 percent of the fathers of the SCs turned out to have been *pannaikarans*,[18] whereas the corresponding figures for other communities were almost zero. Thus, the vast majority of the SCs in this village had been agricultural labourers and a considerable number of them had been employed as *pannaikarans* before the 1950s.

The socio-economic condition of the SCs had changed remarkably during the past few decades. First, they had acquired tenancy rights, second, they had increased their landownership and third, the conditions for *pannaikaran* employment had changed.

A. Acquisition of Tenancy Rights

The acquisition of tenancy rights by the SCs seems to have preceded the later changes. Some SCs acquired tenancy land from the landlords they had served for a long period as *pannaiyals*. The number of such cases, however, was very small, amounting to only 5 or 6. The majority of SCs in this village obtained tenancy rights through the activity of an agricultural labourers' union.

As is generally known, an anti-Brahman and anti-religious Dravidian movement started in South India in the 1920s.[19] As early as 1944, a branch of the *Dravidar Kazhagam* (Dravidian Federation) was

[18] Ibid., p. 156, Table 23-A.

[19] Saraswathi Menon indicated that the Kisan movement developed in Thanjavur district, challenging the structure of social barriers erected by caste between the caste-Hindu peasantry and the Depressed-caste labourers. 'Historical Development of Thanjavur Kisan Movement: Interplay of Class and Caste Factors', *EPW,* Annual Number, February 1979.

established in this village. After Independence, in 1956, the Dravida Agricultural Labourers' Association (*Dravida Vivasaya Thozhilalar Sangam*) was organised as part of the *Dravidar Kazhagam* movement, and its branch was established in this village in the same year. All the Pallars (Scheduled Caste) in this village joined the association. Soon after its establishment, the association began pressurising the Brahman landlords to invest the association with tenancy rights over their land and succeeded in acquiring tenancy rights for about 60 acres of land, which were then distributed among the members of the association: a family was assigned 0.5 acres on an average and a widow was given 0.25 acres. The association also demanded a reduction in rent; according to the villagers, the landlords required 30 *kalams* of paddy as yearly rent per acre, whereas the association required a reduction to 24 *kalams*. However, things took a new turn after one or two months. The landlords made an attempt to take back the tenancy rights they had given the association, reporting duress in an unsuccessful attempt to have the police arrest the members of the association. Though the relationship between the landlords and the association became strained, a conference was held by the two parties, in which police officers and revenue officials also participated. The landlords finally accepted the claim of the association at the conference. At that time, according to Brahman informants, the Pallars were strongly united and they permitted neither the Pallars in the village nor the outsiders to work in the field. The landlords were, the Brahmans said, forced to accept their claim because the landlords could not cultivate their fields without their labour force.

The 60 acres of tenancy holdings thus newly acquired in 1956 were distributed to about eighty Pallar families, out of whom about 20 families returned the tenancy rights to the landlords due to a lack of funds necessary for cultivation. Of the 60 acres of tenancy land 75 percent was owned by the Brahmans, 20 percent by Non-Brahmans and 5 percent by the SCs.

The activities of the association organised mainly by the SCs had exerted a great influence on the whole of village society. First, the number of SC tenants and the extent of their holdings had increased as the result of the movement. SCs holding tenancy rights had increased from only 8 households before 1956 to 67, and the extent of tenancy land cultivated by SCs amounted to 79 acres. In 1980s, of the total of 93 Pallar households in the village, 74 percent or 69 households more or less managed farms, though the average area was extremely small. The percentage of tenants in the SC households was higher than in other communities. It is especially remarkable that about 81 percent of the tenancy land cultivated by the SCs was owned by Brahmans. The corresponding figure for Muthuraja tenants was only 23 percent, indicating the key role played by the activity of the association in the acquisition of tenancy holdings by the SCs.

Second, the increase in landownership by the SCs was also related to their movement. While none owned their own land in the previous century, by 1925 they owned a little, reflecting steady progress towards the economic independence of the Depressed-caste members. The SC movement against the landlords in this village was probably stimulated by this gradual growth in landownership. Conversely, at the same time the tenancy holdings they acquired through the movement may have served as an economic base for the expansion of their landownership.

Third, the movement had awoken the SCs to their own combined power and its socio-economic ramifications. They stated, 'We lived as slaves in the past but after the establishment of the *Dravidar Kazhagam*, the situation largely changed. The landlords began to accept our demands'. The SC movement had not only stimulated their self-respect as the mainstay of agricultural production but also strengthened their socio-economic position vis-à-vis the landlords, thus creating a factor which, as I shall examine later, had worked towards reducing the area owned by absentee landlords, such as Brahmans.

B. Increase in Landownership

SC landownership had increased sharply over the years, in the number of people owning land and the amount they owned. In 1925, six persons from Depressed castes owned land in Appadurai, only two of whom lived in the village while the remaining four belonged to a neighbouring village. Apart from these, two persons of Depressed castes in the neighbouring village were granted land as a reward for their services to the village. At the time of our survey, excluding those living in other villages, 13 SC households owned a total of 16.63 acres in this village, 6 times in number and 25 times in extent compared with the 1925 figures.

I should perhaps mention two points here. First, obtaining tenancy holdings had served as an indispensable stepping stone for the acquisition of land. People said that it was very difficult for an agricultural labourer like a coolie or a *pannaikaran* to save money to purchase land. In fact, all the SC landowners had spent several years as tenants before their first acquisition of land. Not a few SCs purchased the land which they had cultivated as tenants. Second, before the 1950s, a close association with people of non-Depressed castes had been vital for a SC to purchase land, because, according to the villagers, only people who had belonged to communities other than Depressed castes had had a chance of getting information about a Brahman wanting to sell his land. The situation had changed since then; in 1980, people said, Brahmans conveyed their intentions directly to the SCs, reflecting the improved social condition of the SCs after their social movement had got underway.

Hence, as a result of the acquisition of tenancy holdings and landownership during the last five decades, the SCs had been emerging from their condition of mere labourers to become farmer-cum-labourers operating a total of one hundred acres of village land, and as well enjoying slightly better socio-economic status than before in village society.

C. Changes in the Employment Condition of *Pannaikaran*

As previously stated, many village SCs had worked as *pannaikarans* in the past. However, the relation between village SCs and *pannaikaran* service, as well as other aspects of employment conditions of *pannaikarans*, had considerably changed during the last several decades.

First, we notice a shortening in the term of *pannaikaran* service. While a *pannaikaran* had generally served under the same landlord for many years, this was not common by 1980 and only a few *pannaikarans* worked under the same landlords continuously for several years. A landowning villager said that in his father's day, the same *pannaikaran* had worked under him for many years but now he employed different *pannaikarans* every year; the *pannaikarans* were not sincere and were usually careless after one year because they were able to get day labour employment and, what is more important, they had some tenancy holdings allotted them by the *Sangam* (Association). Though there was no general agreement on when the change occurred, the villagers generally agreed that, in contrast to past custom, the landlords in many cases employed different persons each year.

Second, it had been getting more difficult to recruit *pannaikarans* from the village and its vicinity, since, according to local farmers, many of local SCs preferred daily coolie labour to working under one man for a year or two. Recruiting them from remote villages seemed a common alternative, although most landlords preferred not to recruit *pannaikarans* from remote areas as they would not know the nature of the land, the system of irrigation, the diseases of the crops, etc., in this area. Information collected from the SC street affirms this: about 30 SCs had once worked as *pannaikarans* in the past, but only 8 did so in 1980.

Third, employers of *pannaikarans* were said to be annoyed with frequent demands by their *pannaikarans* for higher wages and for improvements in their condition. A Chettiar farmer in Melavaladi hamlet said that though he had employed *pannaikarans* two years before, he could not employ them in 1980 because they demanded higher wages. Another farmer indicated that his *pannaikaran* required a cup of coffee as a gift; that had not been necessary some ten years before.

The labourers' demand for higher wages had, however, not necessarily resulted in a significant increase in remuneration. The average remuneration obtained by 23 *pannaikarans* for 1980 was 21.74 *kalams* of paddy, whereas the figures for 14 cases averaged 19.77 *kalams* ten years before, and 18.52 *kalams* some twenty years before. On the other hand, the 1960s and 1970s witnessed a rapid increase in the paddy yield per acre, which should have resulted in an augmentation in the amount of labour input per acre and the intensification of labour of *pannaikarans*. Considering the intensification of labour, the increase in the remuneration of *pannaikarans* during these twenty years had been only trifling. While the wage increase itself may have mattered little to the employers in terms of the economy of farm management, the problem they were confronting was probably the dearth of loyal and obedient *pannaikarans*. As farmers said, employing a *pannaikaran* was troublesome as he might quit his job at any time and join another landowner. Another complained that a *pannaikaran* might not hesitate to leave at a peak time. Both landlords and SCs admitted difficulties in dealing with *pannaikarans*.

These pieces of evidence point to an increasing difficulty in securing obedient *pannaikarans*, both quantitatively and qualitatively. The direct cause of this difficulty may be found in the fact that the people in the lower strata of the villages, such as SCs, had increasingly preferred to be employed as coolie labourers rather than as *pannaikarans*. The following three developments seem to have underpinned the preference exhibited by these people. The first was the development of the desire for socio-economic independence and the spirit of self-respect in the SCs. Their desire and spirit had grown in general as a result of their movement towards socio-economic independence after the end of the nineteenth century and were especially encouraged by the *Dravidar Kazhagam* movement of the 1950s in this village. The second was the acquisition of tenancy holdings and landownership by the SCs, which formed the economic basis for the realisation of their desire. But for these holdings, many SCs would prefer working as *pannaikarans*, as they would otherwise have to depend upon the unstable earnings from daily coolie labour. The situation may differ completely however if a SC has 0.5 acres of tenancy holding. He can secure at least a portion of the paddy necessary for home consumption from his tenancy land. Cultivating this and working as a coolie, he may manage to make a living without being employed as a *pannaikaran*. In addition, if a person has an acre of operational holding, a considerable amount of labour is required for the cultivation of that land, which may keep the cultivator from being employed as a *pannaikaran*.[20] Third, in addition to the acquisition of small holdings, there had been an increase in the number of days on which daily coolie labour was in demand, specially in the slack seasons, as we shall see below. Though the income a coolie labourer earned was not sufficient to maintain a family, this increase had enabled SCs with small farms to make a living by combining income both from their own farms and work as a coolie without serving as a *pannaikaran*.

D. Changes in the Employment Conditions of Day Labourers

Apart from a few (only 8) persons employed as *pannaikarans*, the bulk of SCs worked as day labourers. Out of the 111 SC households, 90 households (195 persons) were engaged in agriculture, of whom 28 households (113 persons) were mainly day labourers and 42 households (48 persons) were partly in coolie labour and partly in farm management. A total of 70 households (161 persons) or 83 percent of the agricultural population were thus engaged in day labour.

In this section, we shall examine changes in the day labour market in general without limiting our scope to that of SC labourers. The first change was an increase in labour demand during the slack season. The three developments witnessed in the 1960s and 1970s had contributed to this increase in labour demand at this season: the expansion of sugarcane and plantain cultivation, the growth of the straw business and seasonal emigration. The cultivation of sugarcane and plantain had expanded since the 1960s, as seen above. While in the case of paddy cultivation, hardly any farm work was required after the second harvest finished in March until June or July, when the preparation of new seedlings started, the cultivation of sugarcane and plantain started in

[20] The findings revealed by Sudipto Mundle in his survey of a Bihar village deserves attention. Acquisition of minimum assets by SCs in this village made them economically and socially independent from their employers ('Notes from a Palamau Village', in Arvind N. Das and V. Nilakant [eds.], *Agrarian Relations in India* [Delhi, 1979]). See also Gyan Prakash, *Bonded Histories: Genealogies of Labour Servitude in Colonial India* (Cambridge, 1990), p. 225.

January and demanded coolie labour even between March and July, that is, the period which previously had been the farmer's slack season. Second, the coolie labour market had been affected by the growth of the straw business, which I shall examine later in detail. A large amount of excess straw was collected in rural areas and brought to and sold in Tiruchirapalli, etc. The trade had developed particularly after the 1960s and was pursued mainly by the SCs. The amount of excess straw collected from rural areas was very large, providing SCs and other lower classes with a considerable amount of employment: 14 persons (11 households) carried on this business (it was the main occupation of 8 families), and 34 persons (31 families) were employed as coolies in this business. Of these 42 households, 32 were SCs. This means that out of the 111 SC households, 29 percent (32 households) depended upon the straw business. Since farmers usually stored the straw for a few months after harvest, the straw trade was carried on all the year round. Third, the emigration of labourers to other villages had reduced excess labour in slack seasons. With the advent of the Green Revolution, the cultivation of high-yielding varieties augmented the demand for labour in the harvesting season. To fill the gap between the demand and the local supply of labour, groups of labourers temporarily migrated to and from remote areas, working on contract. SCs were the sole emigrants from this village. Since 1970, two groups had been emigrating regularly from this village, to particular villages twice a year. To cite an example, a group of village SCs went to a village in Tiruchirapalli district. The group leader first went to the village, where he met some landlords and made contracts with them. Returning to Appadurai, he collected about 20 persons and then the group went to the village to work in the fields. The leader received the pay in a lump sum, and distributed wages to each labourer. In 1980, they stayed for 15 days in August in that village, where they worked in transplanting. They left Appadurai again in January for the same village and stayed there for about one month. Usually the group consisted of much the same members wherever they went. The two groups had started this type of migration in 1970. Totally about 40 SCs participated in this type of migration in 1980.

A second change observed in the day labour market was an increasing inflow of migrating labourers from other villages during the busy seasons. As with villages where the villagers of Appadurai migrated to work, a large number of immigrant labourers from other villages flew into the village to fill the gap between demand and local supply of labour during the harvesting season. In the same manner as the SCs of this villagers did, they came in groups of 20–25 people each during the harvesting seasons and worked on a contract basis. They stayed in the accommodations provided by influential farmers and worked in the fields which belonged on the whole to the owner of the accommodation and his relatives.[21] In 1981, about 40 percent of the coolie labourers engaged in harvesting the first crop were outside labourers.[22] The conditions of inside labourers had no doubt been influenced by the inflow of outsiders. Some SCs said that the landlords tended to give work to outsiders because the latter contracted with them at a lower wage than the local labour groups. The negative influence on the coolie wage level was also suggested by other SCs. Thus the inflow of the migrating labourers had worked to limit the rise in coolie wage level, as seen below.

Third, wage levels had changed. The wage in kind for harvesting had increased from 1.5 *marakkals* to 2 *marakkals* between 1975 and 1980, and this is confirmed by the statistics of Lalgudi *taluk* office. However, the cash rate of wages for other kinds of labour had risen only by a small extent in this period. Since the consumer price of paddy had risen by 1.5 times, the real wage level paid to the coolie labour other than at harvesting and transplanting had hardly risen or may have possibly fallen during the period. This finding in the village coincides with the statistics for the whole state, which show that the general coolie labour wage had risen by only 20 percent since 1960, and that the harvesting wages had marked a relatively larger increase.[23] The slow

[21] For the case of outside labourers, see Yanagisawa, *Socio-Economic Changes*, pp. 172–73.

[22] The sharp increase in migrating labourers reflects not only the increase in labour demand but also important changes in the villages the labourers left. Visiting some of the native villages of the immigrant labourers, I collected information about the background of this migration. In one village, while in the past the land had been irrigated mainly by wells and raising the well water had been done manually with the help of cattle, the manual power used in raising water has been replaced by pumpsets, resulting in the creation of a redundant labour force. In another village, as sugarcane has sharply increased in place of paddy cultivation, a part of the labour force which had been used in harvesting the paddy has been thrown out of employment. In addition to this, a drought which occurred a few years before in the dry areas, compelled a number of the villagers to migrate. For the contract gang labour system, see Athreya et al., *Barriers Broken*, pp. 139–46.

[23] Government of Tamil Nadu, Department of Statistics, *Season and Crop Report of Tamil Nadu for the Agricultural Year 1978–79 (July to June) (Fasli 1388)* (Madras, 1981), pp. 112, 114; Yanagisawa, *Socio-Economic Changes*, pp. 175–81.

growth in labourers' wages may perhaps have been partly due to the inflow of the migrating labourers.

E. The Composition of the SCs Engaged in Agriculture

The structure of the agricultural population belonging to SCs was different from that of the Muthurajas. Out of the 144 Muthuraja households engaged in agriculture, 46 percent or 66 households were engaged mainly in agricultural management and 31 percent were mainly coolies. The percentage doing both coolie labour and farm management was only 22 percent or 32 households. By contrast, out of the 90 SC agricultural households, only 14 percent were engaged in farm management, and pure coolie families accounted for 31 percent. The largest portion of the SC agricultural population, accounting for 47 percent of the total, was engaged both in farm management and coolie labour. This implies that the SCs were not so polarised as the Muthurajas, but had a large intermediate group between the top and the bottom groups and the variation in the community was rather continuous, except for a few rich farmers. A large majority of the SCs more or less shared the common interests of agricultural labourers.

Table 7.2
Distribution of Households Engaged in Agriculture

(%)

	Owner cultivator	Owner-cum-tenant cultivator	Tenant	Tenant-cum-day labourer	Day labourer	Pannai-karan	Total
Pillai	20.0	20.0	30.0	10.0	20.0	0.0	100
Chettiar	60.0	0.0	10.0	10.0	20.0	0.0	100
Muthuraja	6.3	7.6	31.9	22.2	30.6	1.4	100
SC	2.2	2.2	10.0	46.7	31.1	7.8	100

Brahmans

The largest group of non-resident landholders was the Brahman community, the majority of whom lived in the North Street in Thiruvanaikoil, as stated above. A considerable number of them belonged to families with inherited rights to perform *puja* in the Akilandeswari Temple. The *mirasi*, or the right to perform *puja*, passed on from father to son, and those inheriting *puja* rights and owning landed property naturally used to earn income both by performing *puja* in the temple and by receiving rent from tenants.

Besides those who had lived on North Street for generations, some Brahmans had immigrated from remote villages and settled in this town. Brahmans in various villages had been gradually leaving their original villages and tended to move to urban areas. Thirteen percent of the fathers of the Brahman sample households turned out to be natives of other areas. To cite an example, the father of an Ayyar Brahman was a native of a village in another *taluk* of the district, where six Brahman families had lived, performing *puja* in a temple there and ceremonies for non-Brahmans. Out of the six families, four had left the village to live in Thiruvanaikoil, disposing of their land, and only two families remained there in 1980. The information on the migration of Brahman families collected in this village accords well with the historical records examined in the previous chapters.

As shown above, during the three decades after 1952, the area owned by Brahmans had decreased by about 20 percent. About 60 percent of the Brahman sample households had decreased their land, while 20 percent had experienced no remarkable change and 20 percent had increased their land. Several factors had worked to this end. First, under the influence of the movement and activities of tenants and other people in lower strata like SCs as mentioned above, it had been getting difficult for Brahman landlords to collect rents as regularly from their tenants as they would have liked. Many Brahmans interviewed complained that 'the tenants were not faithful to their landlords' and 'the tenants in Tamilnadu were very bad. They tended to pay only a smaller amount of rent or neglect to pay any rent using various pleas as excuses'. In fact, some landlords had not been able to collect rent for several years. Setting aside any judgment about whether the complaints against tenants were reasonable or not, the evidence indicates that there had been an increasing difficulty in controlling tenants and collecting rents. Underlying the problem was the development of movements and an increased consciousness among the people of the lower strata in the village.

Secondly, Acts protecting tenants had legally reinforced the trend mentioned above. These Acts, which were enacted after the 1950s as part of land reform in Tamilnadu, set the rent limit at 40 percent of the gross product in wet land, restricted the eviction of tenants from the land, and stipulated complicated procedures necessary to evict a tenant if the latter failed to pay rent. After the 1960s, Tenancy Registration had been compiled for each village, which officially confirmed the name of the tenant for each plot.[24] However, the Acts seem not to have created

[24] K.V. Rao, *Tamil Nadu Land Reforms* (Madras, 1975).

satisfactory results unless agitation by tenants and people in the lower strata enforced their realization. It is reported that in Thanjavur, actual rents ranged from 60 to 65 percent of the produce as against the legally fixed rent of 40 percent of the produce, and K. Gough indicates that under the threat of a general strike, the landlords were induced to pay all the tenants and labourers shares only slightly less than those stipulated in the Acts.[25] As mentioned already, the Dravida Agricultural Labourers' Association in Appadurai village required a rent reduction to 24 *kalams*, which may have corresponded to 40 to 50 percent of the produce. These facts reveal that the protection of tenants, which the Acts aimed to provide, may have been achieved only when they were enforced by the tenants themselves. Even under the pressure of the movement, the rent paid by tenants in this village often amounted to nearly 50 percent of the produce.

This circumstance had induced some landlords to convert their leased-out land into farms under their direct management, out of fear that they might lose their land if it was not cultivated directly but leased out to tenants. For instance, a Brahman landlord, who had recovered his tenancy land by paying money (Rs. 5,000–7,000 per acre) to his tenants in 1973, stated that if the land were leased to tenants, he would lose his right of ownership to it.

The third factor causing a reduction in Brahman landholding was escalating urban employment. As we have seen, an increasing number of Brahmans had been employed in urban white-collar jobs since the end of the last century. This trend had accelerated after Independence and a considerable number of Tamil Brahmans lived in remote cities such as Madras, Bombay and Delhi. Naturally, it was hardly possible for such families to keep their land under owner-cultivation. They had no choice but to lease out their land to tenants. On the other hand, we have already seen that it was becoming difficult for landlords to control their tenants and collect rent from them. As a result, some Brahmans had disposed of the whole or a part of their landed property, increasing their dependence on earnings from urban jobs.

Fourth, the so-called land ceiling acts had also influenced landown-

[25] Mythily Shivaraman, 'Thanjavur: Rumbling of Class Struggle in Tamil Nadu', in Kathleen Gough and Hari P. Sharma (eds.), *Imperialism and Revolution in South Asia* (New York & London, 1973), p. 254; Joan P. Mencher, *Agriculture and Social Structure in Tamil Nadu* (New Delhi, 1978), p.112. Research in Tiruchirapalli district also suggests that a precondition for the relative success of land reform was the movement of tenants (Athreya et al., *Barriers Broken*, pp. 103–4).

ership by large landlords to a slight extent. In 1961, the Fixation of the Ceiling on Land Act was enacted, and at the time of our survey 15 acres was the standard maximum limit for a family. Two Brahman families and a Mudaliar family, all very large landlords, had sold a portion of their land because of the act. But this probably accounted for only about 10 percent of their total holdings.

However, it would be wrong to think that all Brahman families were moving in the same direction. Brahmans owning land in Appadurai had gradually differentiated into three categories as they adjusted to these circumstances: (1) priests who had been disposing of their land, (2) urban employees, and (3) those specialising in farm management, not engaged as priests or urban employees.

A typical example of the first category was the case of a Pandidar Brahman who owned through inheritance the *mirasi* right to perform *puja* in the Akilandeswari Temple. Though his ancestor had owned 12.63 acres of land in 1925, the family had sold a large portion of it, and had been left with only 5.25 acres in 1952 and with just 3.68 acres in 1979. Now he and his son were working as *gurukkals* at the temple. Most of the families in this category used to draw their income not only from their service as priests but also from their own land, which had been leased out to tenants as well. During the two or three decades after 1950, they had gradually disposed of their land and had increased their dependence on income from the temple, feeling the difficulty in controlling their tenants in the intervals between their service. The resultant decrease in income from the land seems to have been compensated for by an increase in the income they derived from *puja* service, which had grown considerably, mainly due to a sharp increase in the number of people who were devotees of large and famous temples in preference to local village temples. Villagers concurred that people had been increasingly visiting large and famous temples in big religious centres instead of visiting village temples. This trend had been accelerated by the pilgrimage tours that had come into fashion. The most famous destination of such tours was Iyappan Malai in Kerala State, on the way to which a large number of people visited the Thiruvanaikoil and Srirangam temples. The Brahmans interviewed estimated that the number of devotees visiting the Akilandeswari Temple had increased by ten times in the 1970s and, as a result, the income a *gurukkal* received had increased considerably. Out of a total of 38 Brahman families, 18 families were *pujaris*, belonging to this category.

The second category consisted of families dependent on urban employment. They preferred educating their sons for a government job rather than for the priesthood, considering that a university degree and a government job were more conducive to a comfortable future. Of the 38 Brahman households, 14 households, or 37 percent of the total, depended on urban employment as their main occupation. The number of those employed in urban jobs totalled 23, of whom only one belonged to a family of the first category; the remaining were all from the second category. Out of the 23 urban employees, 16 were employed in higher paid jobs earning Rs. 500 and more. The rate of the Brahman sample households which included these highly salaried employees amounted to 37 percent, an outstanding figure if compared with the figures for the other communities in Appadurai village. A considerable number of Brahmans were in the officer or supervisor class of workers. Families in this category, even if they had inherited the right to perform *puja*, preferred not to work in the temple but to lease the right to do so to other persons.[26]

The third category consisted of families specialising in farm management.[27] Though only six families belonged to this category, their share in the agricultural production of this village was significant. A typical family was that of an Ayyar Brahman, a native of Erode, who had come to Thiruvanaikoil to marry and had settled down there. Though he had held no land in 1925, with the exception of one acre owned by his wife in Appadurai, the Ayyar and his family members had acquired about 21 acres of land in Appadurai and 28 acres in Terukuchattram during the fifty years after 1925. As mentioned above, the Akilandeswari Temple itself was registered as the *patta* holder for more than 60 acres of land in Appadurai, of which about 14 acres were occupied by the Ayyar and his family members free of rent to the temple. They, therefore, owned or enjoyed nearly 63 acres. This large area was held separately by several family members and relatives, such as the Ayyar, his son, his wife, his daughter, his grandsons, etc., so far as the registration of ownership is concerned. However the majority of the land seems in practice to have been controlled by the Ayyar and his son, so far as its management was concerned.

The family's land management was distinguished by the following outstanding features. First, they were specialised farmers, neither

[26] Yanagisawa, *Socio-Economic Changes*, pp. 226–30.

[27] According to K. Gough, there were some Brahman landlords who had prospered as modern style capitalist farmers (Gough, *Rural Change in Southeast India*, p. 126).

engaged in the duties of the priesthood nor in urban jobs. The Ayyar's son had been diverted to agriculture by his father, and had left his studies in the middle of a B.A. course because his father had not been able to look after all the land. A further illustration of this comes from another Ayyar family in this category. In this family the Ayyar and his brother each owned more than ten acres of land in Appadurai. The Ayyar, 30 years old, had been fully engaged in agriculture since he had completed a pre-university course. Though he had inherited the right to perform *puja* in the Akilandeswari Temple, he never worked as a priest but supervised his farm every day. The right was lent to a substitute who performed *puja* in his place. His brother, after completing his education up to SSLC, had been mainly engaged in agriculture. Though he had also inherited the *mirasi* to perform *puja*, he served in the temple only for about three or four months in the year when he was free from the demands of agriculture. For the remaining months, he went to the field every day and the *mirasi* right was lent to a substitute.

Second, they cultivated a large portion of their holdings themselves. In the case of the Ayyar in the first instance, 10.7 acres or about 50 percent of the 21.6 acres owned by the Ayyar family in Appadurai village were cultivated by the owner. This contrasts to the average rate of land under owner-cultivation in the whole Brahman landownership, which was only 35 percent. The management of a large area necessitated a system of farm management. He appointed two managers, both Muthurajas, who supervised several *pannaikarans* and managed the agricultural work. He had two large bungalows in Appadurai village, in one of which a *pannaikaran* family lived. His son went to the bungalows everyday by scooter to make arrangements about the farm work and directed what had to be done. The cultivation of sugarcane on a large amount of the land was one important feature of his management; half of the operational holding was covered with sugarcane, from which the family earned a good profit.

Third, they made efforts to keep the tenants on the remaining area of land, which was leased out, faithful to them. The tenants admired the landlord for his kindness, saying that he lent money to them at a nominal interest when it was needed. On the other hand, the tenants were aware that such financial aid was accorded only when the tenant was faithful to the landlord. Thus financial aid seems to have played an important role in keeping the tenants faithful to the landlord.

The Brahmans in the third category were progressive and specialised farmers, converting as much land as possible to their direct management, cultivating profitable crops and working to keep their tenants faithful by giving them financial aid. Though the Brahmans as a whole had decreased the extent of their landholding, the Brahmans in this category had enlarged not only their operational holdings but also their ownership, at the cost of the families belonging to the other two categories.[28]

The structure of agricultural production in the village: an overview

I shall summarise the foregoing sections in regard to changes in landownership and agrarian relations.

First, the greatest characteristic of the changes after 1952 was the increase in the extent of land owned by villagers, especially by those communities directly engaged in agricultural manual labour, and the considerable decrease in the landholdings of absentee landlords. Second, the growth of a sense of independence among the SCs, a trend witnessed since the end of the last century, had been accelerated after Independence by the development of the trade union movement in the village. As a result of the acquisition of tenancy rights and the increase in the demand for coolie labour in the former slack season, people from the SCs could afford to support themselves from income from both their tenancy land and their coolie wages, and so refuse to work as *pannaikarans*. Third, this trend in SC communities, together with the enactment of the tenant protection Acts, had underlain the changes in landownership. Landlords had experienced difficulties in collecting rents and controlling tenants. The increasing employment of Brahmans in urban jobs had accelerated the trend, inducing absentee landlords to dispose of their land. Fourth, to combat this situation, some Brahmans had specialised in farm management and land administration and increased their landownership as well. They tried to cultivate as much land as possible under their own management and to attract tenants who would be faithful. Fifth, while a small number of well-to-do Non-Brahman farmers had sharply increased their holdings, many others had been left behind. This inequality, especially within the Muthurajas, widened in the 1970s.

These transformations imply a departure in the relationships among the agrarian strata from those of the nineteenth century. As a result of their movement to raise their status, their acquisition of small parcels of land and the land reforms, labourers and tenants were in a relatively

[28] Yanagisawa, *Socio-Economic Changes*, pp. 235–38.

better position with respect to landlords than in the past, and the landlords and large farmers could no longer arbitrarily make use of them as in the past.

The connection between the hierarchy of caste and that of economic status had also weakened. While the Brahmans had reduced their ownership, the SCs, previously employed mainly as *pannaikarans* or daily coolie labourers, had gradually increased their operational holdings and some had even grown into rich farmers. The Muthurajas, who had been mostly tenants in the past enjoying a slightly better socio-economic status than the SCs, had disintegrated into two groups: some families had emerged as rich farmers, while a large section of people had lost their tenancy right and become mere day coolie labourers. Of the latter group of Muthurajas, in the 1980s the majority did not live in circumstances easier than those of the SCs, as far as their economic condition was concerned. The social influence of caste on the relationships among the strata in village society seems to have gradually weakened, and mere economic factors had now become more important as determinants of the relationships among the classes and strata.

It is very important to reiterate, however, that in spite of these changes, the structure of the agrarian relationships had not been radically transformed from what it had been in the nineteenth century in the sense that both landownership and agricultural production were concentrated in a small section of people and, as a result, the majority of the villagers continued to be agricultural labourers and tenants, as shown below.

First, the cultivation by tenants still remained the dominant form of agriculture in this village. An analysis of such sources as the Tenancy Registration, documents relating to a court case, and others[29] reveals that in the early 1980s about 277 acres or about 60 percent of the arable land in Appadurai village was cultivated by tenants, indicating that the landlord-tenant relationship was of primary importance in agricultural production in this village. The majority of the owners of tenancy land were Brahmans. Brahmans owned about 170 acres, of which 110 acres or 65 percent were leased out to tenants. Of the area leased out, the largest portion, 45.5 acres or 41 percent, was cultivated by SC tenants. The area registered as temple land was all leased out, and the Muthurajas in Appadurai hamlet cultivated most of it. The Mudaliars and Muslims living in Tiruchirapalli also leased out almost all of their land and most of their tenants were Muthurajas. Thus, the landlord-

[29] For the sources on tenants, see ibid., pp. 247–50.

tenant relationship in this village was still of the 'traditional' type in the sense that landlords lived in remote places and villagers cultivated the land as tenants.

Second, nearly half the land was cultivated by big farmers operating 5 acres and more. Thirty-four farmers belonging to this size group, accounting for about 13 percent of the total families engaged predominantly in agriculture, cultivated 226.43 acres or 40 percent of the total 561.55 acres run by the villagers. In addition, some large Brahman landowners did not lease out all their land but cultivated some of it with the help of *pannaikarans*. Though the exact extent of such direct cultivation by Brahmans is not clear, it was at least 60 acres. In sum, the total area cultivated by larger farmers from both Brahman and non-Brahman communities amounted to more than 50 percent of the total agricultural land. More than two-thirds of these large farmers employed *pannaikarans* and one-third of them had installed pumpsets on their farms.

The remaining land was mainly cultivated by farmers cultivating between one and four acres, accounting for about 40 percent of the total number of farmers. The farmers of this size group seldom employed *pannaikarans* but depended on their own family labour force and daily labourers.

Third, agricultural labourers numerically dominated the agricultural population of the village. Seventy-six households (90 persons), accounting for 28 percent of the total number of households supported by agriculture, were engaged both in coolie labour and cultivation as tenants. Eighty households (240 persons) were mainly coolies and 12 households (15 persons) were employed as *pannaikarans*, making the total number of those engaged as hired labour 92 households (255 persons), accounting for 34 percent of the households engaged in agriculture or 48 percent of the total working population. Thus in total, 62 percent of agricultural households had members who were employed as agricultural labourers.

To sum up, the villagers engaged in agriculture consisted of the following four classes: first, a group of larger farmers operating five acres and more, accounting for 13 percent of the total households; second, a group of tenants (or one portion of the farmers operating between one acre and five acres) forming about 30 percent; third, about 30 percent of the households which cultivated small plots of land as tenants and also were engaged in coolie labour at the same time; and fourth, the remaining 30 percent of families consisting of hired labourers.

It may be gathered from the above that the majority of those engaged in agriculture had two problems of a differing nature: the problem of the landlord-tenant relationship, and relations between rich farmers and labourers. To reiterate, first, since about 60 percent of the land was cultivated under a landlord-tenant relationship, nearly 30 percent of the total agricultural product was skimmed off from the village by absentee landlords as rent, and second, since the operational holdings, either in the form of landownership or tenancy holdings, were unequally distributed among the villagers, much of the agricultural population remained lowly paid agricultural labourers.

Change in Non-Agricultural Occupations in the Village

Two hundred and seventy persons belonging to 155 households, accounting for 33 percent of the sampled households in the village, were engaged in non-agricultural occupations in the village. In addition, 19 persons living in other villages ran small shops, etc., on the main bus route in Appadurai village. Small businesses had undergone a major change during the decades before 1980. I shall classify the non-agricultural occupations into three categories according to the type of change during the period.

Deteriorating occupations

Some 'traditional occupations' exhibited clear signs of deterioration, such as a decline both in the number of persons engaged in them and in the income from them. The direct causes for the decline were competition with machine-made products, the introduction of machinery, changes in the trading system in the commodity, and changes in the tastes or preferences of consumers.

Pot making was a typical declining occupation. Five households of the Vellar caste, 'traditional' potters, lived in this village, but only three of them were engaged in this profession in 1980. Even so, one of the three made pots only as a side job when not employed as an agricultural day labourer. Of the two families not engaged in this occupation, one was employed as a coolie and the other was a beggar. The main reason for this decline was the competition with aluminium utensils and the resultant decrease in the demand for pots.

Another example was oil crushing (called *checkku*), which used to be the traditional job of Chettiars. The industry had faded away because of the emergence of the motor-powered crushing industry. Three Chettiars had owned oil crushing units in this village, and the fathers of two Chettiars had been also engaged in this industry in other villages. However, none of the five Chettiar families was in oil crushing in 1980, but three ran tea shops, one was employed as a hired labourer (coolie) and the last worked in the artificial gem stone polishing industry.

Many descendants of former goldsmith families had abandoned their traditional occupation because, according to them, villagers preferred purchasing gold ornaments from jewelry shops in Tiruchirapalli rather than buying them in the village. Only one old goldsmith still worked in the village, mending the ornaments of villagers and earning a meager income. Masons also had been reduced in number. The ancestors of seven Muthuraja families had been masons, carving temple statues and making grinding stones. However there was no demand for grinding stones by 1980, due to the introduction of electric grinding machines and the emergence of flour mills, and no one in this village was engaged in this occupation any more. Temple priests, *pusaris*, were struggling too, as the people's faith in the village temples had weakened and they preferred visiting famous temples such as those at Samayapuram, Thiruvanaikoil, etc. The number of temple festivals during the year had decreased also: the village celebrated three main festivals, of which one used to be celebrated every year in the past but occurred only once in two or three years in the late 1970s. Though three priest families still were looking after the village temples, they all admitted that their incomes had been declining for many years.

New opportunities in the non-agricultural sector

In contrast to these declining traditional occupations, the decades had witnessed an expansion of some non-agricultural economic activities. The synthetic gem polishing industry had grown in and around Tiruchirapalli and, according to the Assistant Director of Industry and Commerce, the district met 95 percent of the total demand in India. The chief raw material for the industry, *dhalam* or corundum, was produced in Coimbatore district and was cut, coned, faceted and polished in Tiruchirapalli district. This had grown into a very important cottage industry in the district: about 40,000 workers living in and around Tiruchirapalli city were engaged in it.[30] Large merchants controlled this

[30] The Synthetic Gem Cutters Industrial Co-operative Society Ltd., Tiruchy,

industry. They bought corundum and sold it to small producers, who cut them into cubes by employing cutters with power-operated machines. These cut stones or cubes were purchased by small middlemen or master workmen who got them coned, faceted and polished by employing other workers. Such a merchant generally controlled at least twenty workers and paid wages according to the number of stones polished. While the cutting work was usually done in Tiruchirapalli city, the other three processes, coning, faceting and polishing, were mostly carried on in the workers' houses themselves as a cottage industry in surrounding villages. The worker had to pay to hire the machine when it was loaned by the merchant. In Appadurai village, the synthetic gem polishing industry developed rapidly after Independence. In 1980, 46 persons (5 percent of the total working population in the village) from 30 households worked in it. The industry provided job opportunities for the largest number of villagers after agriculture. Interestingly, these workers were mainly drawn from those families who had neither land of their own nor tenancy rights. Although the industry provided important job opportunities for poor villagers, the workers were generally under the control of merchants who aimed to make full use of cheap rural labour.[31]

The paddy-straw trade had developed considerably in the 1960s and 1970s and had provided another avenue of earning for villagers. The majority of the 47 villagers engaged in this business were SCs and had come to be engaged in the trade within the last ten years. There were two reasons for this rapid development. With changing food habits, urban people drank more coffee and tea, consuming more milk than before. This had caused an increase in cattle population kept by urban households, expanding the demand for straw as feed. Secondly, while the yield of paddy straw had increased due to the introduction of the HYVs, the consumption of straw as manure for cultivation had reduced because of the replacement of straw by chemical fertilisers, resulting in a rapid increase in the excess straw that was available for trade. Each straw dealer in the village owned one cart and a pair of bullocks and generally hired one or two coolie labourers for the business. He purchased the straw not only from his own village but also from the villages located between Appadurai and Lalgudi town. The number of

---

History and Note on Gem Industry (Tiruchirapalli, n.d.).

[31] Yanagisawa, *Socio-Economic Changes*, pp. 269–72; Karin Kapadia, 'The Profitability of Bonded Labour: The Gem-Cutting Industry in Rural South India', *The Journal of Peasant Studies* 22, 3 (April, 1995).

cart-loads dealt with by a dealer was said to range from 100 to 200 per year. It is important to note that the trade was not confined to any limited period in the year but was carried on throughout the year because landowners usually kept straw in their gardens for some time after the harvest. I have already mentioned that the straw business, which provided job opportunities for people of the lower classes throughout the year, may be mentioned as one of the factors that had enabled the SCs to live without being employed as *pannaikarans*.

The village in the thirty years before 1980 had also witnessed many changes in the service sector. The consumption of 'mutton' had increased during the last two decades. According to an old 'mutton' seller, the number of people who consumed 'mutton' had increased ten times compared with his father's time, when the only 'mutton' stall in the village had dealt with just one goat weekly. In 1980, there were three stalls, each dealing with four to twenty goats weekly. The increase in 'mutton' consumption may have been partly due to a change in people's cooking habits and partly due to the improvement of the socio-economic condition of the villagers.

The hire cycle shops, which owned several cycles for hire, had increased from two shops thirty years before to five in 1980 in Appadurai. They were also engaged in repairing the villagers' cycles, which sometimes yielded a better income, as an increasing number of villagers used their own cycles. Three cycle shops owned loudspeakers for hire. When a family solemnised a marriage, they hired a loudspeaker for broadcasting music from morning to night. During December and January, people broadcast devotional music early in the morning from 4 A.M. to 6 A.M. The broadcasting of devotional music, according to the villagers, had become popular in the past fifteen years.

Running a tea shop can be included in this category. The village had seven tea shops in the commercial centre of the village, engaging 14 persons. According to villagers, tea consumption of villagers had grown significantly compared with thirty years before, when there had been only two tea shops in the village. They said that only 10 percent of the villagers habitually had drunk tea some thirty years before; in the 1980s almost all the villagers did so.

The number of tailors had been increasing as the people had changed their tastes in clothes. The village had 12 tailor shops and 15 tailors were engaged in the work, including those employed outside the village. The interviews reveal that the majority of their fathers had been in different occupations, and many had started their work in the 1960s and 1970s. This reflects the increase in tailoring work in this period. They said that while some twenty-five years before people had worn only *dhotis* and shirts, many wore pants also in 1980s and the wearing of shirts had also increased. Though some fashionable villagers preferred having their pants and shirts made in tailor shops in the town, orders for village tailors had also increased.

Other occupations

In contrast to the above two categories, some of the traditional services had neither seriously declined nor prospered. There were four carpenters of the Asari caste making ploughs and repairing carts and houses in the village. People indicated that an increase in the number of bullocks had led to an increased use of ploughs. They had managed to survive in this changing situation. The village had six blacksmiths, four Asaris and two Muslims. The four Asaris made and repaired grain-sickles (*aruval*), whereas the Muslims manufactured and mended horse-shoes, and repaired iron belts on cart wheels. The villagers did not concur about the change in demand for their services: some asserted that as a result of the introduction of the tired wheeled cart, work orders had decreased slightly but others claimed that their income was not worse than before, because people were using a larger number of sickles as a result of the introduction of HYVs.

Factors underlying the changes

The above observation regarding occupations enables us to identify some factors underlying the changes. The first was technical changes in production and services. A typical instance was the growth of rice mills, which had made grinding stones obsolete and caused many masons to quit their traditional jobs. The potters and oil crushers in the village had been ruined, losing to the competition of machine products. By contrast, people engaged in new occupations, such as pipe fitters, electricians and rice mill workers, had appeared and increased in number. Technical developments in agriculture had led to the expansion of the straw business. Some in the traditional occupations, such as blacksmiths and carpenters, had managed to maintain their economic status by adapting themselves to the changing technologies.

Second, the changes in consumption habits had also influenced the village industries and services. The increase in the number of tea shops, 'mutton' shops and tailors had been the result of the changes in people's consumption patterns. The growth of the straw trade had likewise been stimulated by the increased consumption of milk in urban areas. The urban-oriented change in taste among villagers had ruined the village goldsmiths, and the shift of villagers' faith to the famous temples had negatively affected the village priests.

A third factor may be a small improvement in the socio-economic condition of the villagers, especially those of the lower classes, as reflected in the limited increase in the extent of their landownership and tenancy holdings. The improvement had contributed to the relative growth of the purchasing power of villagers as compared with the past. The increase in the consumption of 'mutton' and tea and in the demand for pants and shirts and the development of the cycle shops not only reflected changes in the mode of living in the village but also had been supported by an increase in the purchasing power of villagers as well. It is, however, misleading to overemphasise this. The purchasing power of the majority of villagers still remained very low, even though it had improved somewhat, since it was regulated by an agrarian structure that was characterised by the dominance of outsiders in landownership and the concentration of farm production in the hands of a few large farmers. The types of occupations available matched the level of the purchasing power. Only a small number of villagers owned their own cycles, with many hiring them from a shop. If the income of the villagers increases and a larger number of villagers become rich enough to purchase their own cycles in the future, the number of hire cycle shops may decrease.

It is very difficult to assess the overall effect of these changes in the non-agricultural occupations on the general situation of employment in the village. While some traditional occupations had seriously declined during the three decades following Independence, the development of new job opportunities, such as the straw trade, the synthetic gem polishing industry, the tea shops and the 'mutton' shops, seems to have been large enough to increase the percentage of those engaged in non-agricultural occupations, though no statistical evidence is available for this. These occupations formed an indispensable part of the village economy, providing jobs for 270 persons from about one-third of the total number of households.

However, the increase in the percentage of those engaged in non-agricultural occupations does not necessarily imply that a wider variety of occupational choice was offered for the villagers in the 1980s.

Rather, for many villagers, these jobs were not such as to be selected as first choice. In this connection, the non-agricultural occupations in the village society may be classified into two broad categories: businesses which required a considerable amount of capital investment and those needing very little. Grouped under the first category were rice mills, match factories, fertiliser shops, large- and medium-size grocery shops, homeopathy clinics, etc. These required more than Rs. 10,000 as an initial investment. Many of those engaged in businesses in this category ran farms of several acres.[32]

The second category can be divided into two types: (1) the traditional and (2) the non-traditional. (1) Potters, goldsmiths, carpenters, blacksmiths, basket makers, masons, tree climbers, land diggers, barbers, washermen, etc., were of the traditional type. These were mostly inherited family-wise or caste-wise, and quite a few from other communities had newly entered these occupations. Interestingly, the majority of these traditional artisans had no landholdings and were rarely employed as agricultural labourers. Those employed in urban jobs were much fewer. In other words, the extent to which those belonging to the traditional artisan castes had diversified their occupations was extremely limited. (2) The non-traditional type of small business engaged people from various communities. Generally speaking, salaried jobs in government offices or big factories were preferred first. When they could neither get an urban job with a good salary nor operate large farms, they had no choice but to be engaged in these non-traditional occupations. Naturally those engaged in occupations of a non-traditional nature were not generally satisfied with their own jobs. They wished to purchase land or give their children a higher education whenever they had money to spare. Generally, however, they were too poor to purchase land.

Except for those businesses requiring a considerable amount of investment, most non-agricultural occupations, both traditional and non-traditional, were mainly confined to the poorer classes of villagers. Out of 270 villagers engaged in non-agricultural occupations, about two-thirds had no operational holdings at all.[33] Non-agricultural occupations of the second category and employment as agricultural labourers were the sources of the meagre income of poor villagers with no land.

[32] For detailed information, see Yanagisawa, *Socio-Economic Changes*, pp. 258–62, Table 29.

[33] See ibid., pp. 94–96.

Urban Employment and Village Society

The considerable number of villagers employed in urban areas served as an important channel through which the village economy was combined with the economy of the outside world.

Employees in large factories and government offices

Workers employed in urban areas in and around Tiruchirapalli city can be classified into two categories: permanent employees in large factories and government offices, and workers in small factories and shops, etc., in the town. The categories differed both in the conditions of employment and in the socio-economic background of the labourers.

The most prominent factory in Tiruchirapalli city and its surrounding area was the state-operated Bharat Heavy Electricals Limited (BHEL), which employed about 14,000 permanent labourers and 1,200 temporary labourers. The Southern Railway Workshop in Tiruchirapalli had 6,367 employees, Dhalmia Cement Plant 1,557 and the Ordnance Factory 1,575. Seven other factories, though smaller than the above, had more than 100 employees each. Government offices, especially the Electricity Board and the state-operated bus companies, provided important employment opportunities for the villagers.

The permanent workers employed in these large factories and government offices are distinguished from the second category of workers by the following features. First, they were generally paid better wages. Most earned more than Rs. 500 per month, while the majority of those employed in shops or commercial concerns drew less than Rs. 300 in 1980.[34] Second, workers in a factory or an office were ranked into classes and could expect to be promoted not only to a higher grade within the same class but also to a higher class. In the case of BHEL, the workers consisted of four classes: (1) executive (officer) class, (2) supervisor class, (3) skilled worker class and (4) unskilled worker class. Skilled workers, for example, were first posted at the lowest rank of the skilled worker class, that is, Grade IV. They usually spent three years in Grade IV, five years in Grade III, six years in Grade II and six years in Grade I. Third, employees of large factories and government offices were generally in continuous service. The villagers seldom resigned from these factories or offices except to retire or unless they were

[34] The jobs of urban employees and the number of villagers employed are listed in ibid., p. 298, Table 30.

discharged due to strikes.[35] The relatively better payment, the system of a regular increase in wages and the generally better labour conditions in big factories and government offices induced workers to continue their service as long as possible.

Fourth, the large factories and government offices generally recruited workers who had the necessary qualifications.[36] For example, the minimum qualification necessary for eligibility was stipulated for each of the four classes (executive officers, supervisors, skilled workers and unskilled workers). In BHEL, those holding a B.A., a B.Sc. or a higher degree were eligible for the executive class. Candidates for the supervisor class had to have a diploma acquired at a polytechnic, and skilled workers were employed from the graduates of ITI. Many offices and large factories required even candidates for unskilled workers to have the SSLC or to have attained the eighth standard. In BHEL those engaged on probation were confirmed as regular workers after working as trainees for one year and they were then posted to offices. If a worker was employed as an executive class employee, he might be appointed to a rank in the executive class from the beginning, usually at the lowest rank of the class, say engineer. Those employed as supervisor and skilled worker class employees were posted at the lowest ranks of the supervisor class and skilled worker class respectively and were promoted to higher grades within each class every several years.

It is clear, therefore, that a worker's career was to a large extent decided by his qualifications and the kind of employee class in which he was first employed. This observation may be endorsed by an examination of the promotion system and the structure of the basic wage. Besides recruiting new workers for each class from the external labour market, companies filled vacancies by promoting workers from a lower

[35] See ibid., p. 303, Figure 10.

[36] The education system in Tamilnadu in the 1980s was as follows. Primary education was a five-year course, followed by five years at high school ending with an examination to get a Secondary School Leaving Certificate (SSLC). The results of this examination were important for the future of the student. The minimum mark required for passing the examination was 35 percent. Depending on the marks scored, a student might choose one of several courses: a) a higher secondary school (2 years) followed by an undergraduate course for a bachelor's degree in a college (3 years). After this, some might proceed to postgraduate courses, namely, the M.A. (2 years), the M.Phil. (1 or $1\frac{1}{2}$ years) and the Ph. D. course (3 years); b) three years of education at a polytechnic institute leading to a diploma; c) entering the Industrial Training Institute (ITI) for vocational courses of 1 or 2 years' duration to obtain certificates as fitters, welders, turners, electricians, wiremen, etc.

class within the company. However, workers had to spend many years before they had a chance to be promoted to the higher class. A skilled worker in BHEL became a candidate for promotion to the supervisor class only after twenty years of service in the skilled worker class. Considering the years spent in waiting for entrance to these jobs, they might be in their middle forties by the time they succeeded. Furthermore, in some factories it was very difficult for a candidate to succeed in getting promotion, which was usually merit-based and very competitive. Only one-tenth of the candidates were said to be promoted. The salaries in big factories were directly proportionate to the qualification and level of the employee. To cite an example, the basic salary paid to a Grade IV skilled worker started at Rs. 395 per month. This increased by Rs. 10 per month every year and after a few years, the worker might be promoted to Grade III, where his basic salary increased as before. It took about fifteen years for him to draw a basic salary of Rs. 580, which corresponded to the basic salary of a supervisor on appointment. Supervisors started with this amount and executives got Rs. 750 as their initial basic salary.

Employees in small factories and shops

Villagers hired in this category of employment were of three groups: (1) drivers and conductors in private bus transportation companies and lorry drivers; (2) salesmen in shops in Tiruchirapalli and workers in small factories, such as an ice factory, rice mills, a metal factory, etc.; and (3) daily labourers and watchmen in big and small factories and offices and cleaners in bus companies, etc. This category had the following characteristics.

First, wages and other labour conditions for these jobs were much poorer than those in the big factories and government offices. Even drivers and conductors in private bus companies (Group [1]), though relatively better paid, drew only about Rs. 300 or Rs. 400 and workers in (2) and (3) groups were paid even less than Rs. 300. According to a villager, it was not possible to live in an urban area with a monthly income of less than Rs. 350. An agricultural labourer in the village was paid on an average Rs. 10 per day and many village artisans earned just about the same. As such, therefore, the income level of an urban employee in this category was not much different. Second, in contrast to the big factories and government offices, these small factories and shops generally lacked a graded service system and workers did not enjoy regular salary raises or promotions. Third, due to the poor labour conditions and the lack of the legal protection for small factory workers, the length of their service was usually short, not exceeding five years. The workers often quit their jobs when they came across better employment opportunities.

The workers were of two kinds: those who had neither land nor any possibility of being employed in the big factories and government offices due to their low educational level; and those who had passed the SSLC examination and had registered their names at the employment exchange office, but were employed in these small factories or shops for an interim period awaiting recruitment by the big factories, etc.

Village economy and urban employment

The number of urban employees in the village was 141, accounting for about 15 percent of the total working population. Though the figure did not exceed the number of those engaged in the non-agricultural occupations in the village, urban employment had an importance qualitatively different from that of the non-agricultural occupations in the village. It had an economically weighty role in the life of the upper classes of villagers, especially those who owned a considerable amount of land. Of the households operating 5 acres and more, 32.4 percent had urban employees in their families and the percentage reached 45.2 in the case of households operating 3–4.99 acres.

The importance of urban jobs was particularly remarkable in the Brahman sample families, 42.1 percent of whom had urban employees as family members and 36.8 percent of whom depended on urban employment as their main source of income. Except those Brahman families who specialised either in farming or the priesthood, Brahmans were becoming increasingly dependent on urban jobs, particularly on white-collar jobs. Among the villagers, this inclination was remarkable in the Pillai and Chettiar communities. Families with urban employees accounted for two-thirds of those operating 5 acres and more and 50 or 60 percent of those operating 3–4.99 acres in those two communities.

The average income of an urban employee was also quite different from what people could earn through non-agricultural occupations in the village. Except for some businesses like rice mills, the income from non-agricultural occupations in the village was generally low, being around Rs. 10 per day. In contrast, 35 percent of the urban employees were paid Rs. 500 and more monthly and some were paid even more than Rs. 800. While about 38 percent of the urban employees were paid less than Rs. 300 per month, a considerable number of them expected to be employed in the big factories or the government offices with a salary exceeding Rs. 500 in the future, accepting these poorly paid jobs at the time as a preliminary step to future employment. A regular monthly income exceeding Rs. 500 was roughly equivalent to the earnings of a farmer operating more than two acres. Farmers operating several acres of land generally wished to have one or two of their sons become urban employees and have the rest engage in agriculture in order to prevent further subdivision of their holdings among the sons. Since a higher education was required to get better jobs, expenditure on education was regarded by those farmers as a long-term paying investment.

A remarkable correlation is discernible between the size of operational holdings and urban employment. The socially and economically upper classes of villagers had a greater possibility of being employed in urban jobs, especially in the big factories and the government offices. While 32.4 percent of the households in the size group of 5 acres and more and 45.2 percent of those in the size group of 3–4.99 acres had urban employees in their families, the corresponding figure for villagers operating less than 1 acre was only 17–18 percent. The difference was especially remarkable in the percentages of households with urban employees drawing Rs. 500 and more: 28.6 percent and 20.6 percent of the households in the size groups 3–4.99 acres and 5 acres and more respectively had urban employees drawing Rs. 500 and more; whereas the corresponding figures for households operating less than 3 acres were only 6 or 8 percent. The difference existed among the various communities also. The percentage of urban employees drawing Rs. 500 and more to the total working population in each community was as follows: Brahman 29.6, Pillai 13.0, Muslim 10.8, Chettiar 7.9, Muthuraja 4.5, SC 2.1 and others 4.7. The percentage with the highest wages, exceeding Rs. 800, was especially high in the Brahman community. Since, as mentioned already, higher qualifications gained through higher education were essential for getting jobs with a better income, a considerable number of children were sent to private schools. The socially and economically upper classes could afford to bear the expenditure for a higher education, with the result that they had a larger number of urban employees among their families.

It is, however, misleading to overemphasise the dominance of the upper classes in urban jobs. A considerable number of youths from the lower classes had passed the SSLC examination and were presently employed in urban jobs. According to informants, more than 30 percent of the skilled workers in BHEL and the Southern Railway Workshop were SCs. Some SCs from Appadurai, though small in number, were employed in BHEL and the Southern Railway Workshop. The government reservation policy as effected in 1980 stipulated that government offices and public enterprises should reserve a fixed percentage of posts for the Scheduled Castes. BHEL, Tiruchirapalli, reserved 18 percent. However, the advance of the SCs in the urban employment had not been simply a result of government policy, though it no doubt had contributed to that end. First, in order for an SC to apply for a reserved post, the candidate was required to have completed secondary education, or at least the eighth standard. Second, the share of SCs among skilled labourers in some of the big factories was, as seen above, larger than the stipulated rate of reservation. They had to compete with candidates belonging to other communities when they applied for posts beyond the reserved portion. As previously discussed, the people in the lower strata, including SCs, had gradually acquired tenancy rights and landownership, and had raised their socio-economic position through their movement for independence. These changes had no doubt encouraged them to improve their level of education and aspire for a better future. The headway they were making in urban employment is an indication of that.

The Findings

To summarise, the three decades after 1952 witnessed a change in the pattern of landownership as well as various changes in the basic socio-economic structure of Appadurai village. First, the trend towards independence among the Depressed-caste members, agricultural labourers and tenants, which began in the nineteenth century, had accelerated since 1950. The greater unity and activity of people in the lower strata, especially of the trade union organised by the SCs, had contributed to a raising of their socio-economic position. The acquisition of tenancy rights, the increase in demand for coolie labour in the former slack seasons and the growing consciousness of freedom placed them in a stronger position to dictate terms than before and induced them to refuse work as *pannaikarans*. Second, the increasing commitment of landlords to urban employment and the development of movements by the people of the lower strata, along with the enactment of laws protecting tenants, underlay the changes in landownership. Landlords, particularly absentees, were not able to collect rents from their tenants as easily as before, finding it difficult to control them. This had led to a reduction in the amount of land owned by outsiders, especially by the Brahmans, and to a rapid increase in villager landholding. Third, while the area owned by the Muthurajas and other villagers as a whole had increased considerably, the Muthuraja community had tended to disintegrate: some Muthurajas had increased their holdings, both as owners and tenants, but many had been reduced to labourers upon losing their tenancy land. Fourth, though some non-agricultural occupations of a traditional type had declined, the three decades witnessed the growth of new industries, such as the straw trade, and there seems to have been an expansion of job opportunities for those villagers with no operational holdings. Fifth, urban employment was an important source of income for higher-caste families, particularly for Brahmans. On the other hand, the lower classes had also made headway in urban employment, which not only reflected but also accelerated their independence and an improvement in their social status.

These changes in Appadurai village were, in some essential aspects, common with those in several other villages surveyed in the early 1980s. Let us first consider the transfer of land from Brahman and those of other high castes to people of lower castes. Some villages that had been surveyed by the University of Madras twice, in 1916 and 1936, were again surveyed in the early 1980s. V.B. Athreya, who examined the changes in Gangaikondan village in Tirunelveli, reports that though in 1916 Brahmans used to be the major landholders, followed by Pillais, the major landholding castes in the 1980s were Maravars (Thevars), Hindu Pallars, Konars and Christian Pallars,[37] indicating a sharp decline in Brahman landlordism. Athreya also noticed a sharp decline in the area of land under tenancy cultivation after 1958–60; this he attributed to the emigration of Brahmans to towns.[38] The village thus witnessed a process of transition from Brahman (and Pillai) landlordism to owner cultivation by the 'agricultural castes' including the SCs.[39] The decrease of landownership by non-resident Brahmans and the acquisition of land by castes other than Brahmans, particularly by the dominant Vannia

[37] Athreya, *Gangaikondan*, pp. 9–10, 32, 97.
[38] Ibid., pp. 98, 129.
[39] Ibid., p. 10.

Naickers, was also noted in the survey of Dusi village.[40] Tenancy was in the early 1980s significantly less than in 1937. This trend was reported to be in part related to the transfer of land from non-cultivating Brahman landlords to self-cultivating resident owners and in part reflecting the resumption of tenancies in the 1950s consequent on tenancy legislation.[41] A similar change was observed in a village surveyed by S.S. Sivakumar and Chitra Sivakumar and others.[42]

Some village surveys point to a trend towards independence among Scheduled Caste and other lower-caste members. In Reddimangudi, a village in Tiruchirapalli district, Tsukasa Mizushima observed a shortage of *pannaiyals* or permanent labourers as well as a decrease in landholding by the dominant Reddiar caste. He attributes this shortage to an increasing self-consciousness among them, and to the increase in both alternative work opportunities like sheep and goat herding and the demand for labour in wet area as a result of the Green Revolution.[43] Hisashi Nakamura's survey of a village in the dry zone of Tiruchirapalli district also suggests the importance of livestock herding for the economic independence of Scheduled Caste members. There, a conflict between the dominant Vellalars and the Paraiyars over the rearing of black goats led to a refusal by the Paraiyars to render such traditional *adimai* service to the Vellalars as the tom-tom beating for funerals, disposal of dead animal carcasses, etc. When the landholding Vellalars counteracted by refusing to employ them as labourers in their fields, the Paraiyars began to support themselves by goat rearing.[44] P.B. Mayer has

[40] Guhan and Bharathan, *Dusi*, pp. 3, 47, 51.

[41] Ibid., pp. 54, 165.

[42] 'Class and Jati at Asthapuram and Kanthapuram: Some Comments Towards a Structure of Interests', *EPW,* Annual Number, February 1979. See also Athreya et al., *Barriers Broken*, p. 110; Peter B.R. Hazell and C. Ramasamy, *The Green Revolution Reconsidered: The Impact of High-Yielding Rice Varieties in South India* (Baltimore and London, 1991), p. 72. K. Gough reports cases in which the Brahmans and Vellalars declined in wealth, but while a very small amount of land was bought by Pallars, most of the lost land was purchased by traders, bureaucrats and industrialists, resulting in a more concentrated pattern of landownership (Gough, *Rural Change in Southeast India*, pp. 276, 524). See also the case of a Madurai village where Maravar owners were losing their traditional place of preeminence in landownership (Ramachandran, *Wage Labour and Unfreedom*, p. 232).

[43] Mizushima, 'Changes, Chances and Choices', p. 173.

[44] Hisashi Nakamura, 'Disintegration and Re-integration of a Rural Society in the Process of Economic Development: The Second Survey of a Tank-based Village in Tamil Nadu', in *Studies in Socio-Cultural Change in Rural Villages in Tiruchirapalli District, Tamilnadu, India* 5 (Tokyo: ILCAA, 1982), pp. 56–

also stressed the relative inability of most landlords to control their tenants and their labourers.[45]

The decrease in the number of permanent farm servants and the preference for daily labour by agricultural labourers is also an aspect of change often reported by village surveys.[46] In Vadamalaipuram village, the system of *padiyals* had disappeared by 1958 and the number of permanent labourers has further decreased since then. As I have already mentioned, even in 1958, the majority of the workers interviewed expressed no wish to be permanent farm servants because of the absence of freedom and the lack of limits on the hours of work.[47] There was an increase in the demand for agricultural labour as a result of the increase in the intensity of cropping between 1958 and 1983, and, furthermore, the non-agricultural employment opportunities created by nearby spinning mills and match factories tended to draw labour away from agriculture. These developments made casual labour a more attractive proposition for workers.[48]

In this connection, the growth of non-agricultural employment opportunities and the contribution of these opportunities to the independence of lower-caste members is another finding reported by many surveys. Athreya asserts that in Vadamalaipuram, 'the emergence of employment opportunities in manufacturing has been a positive aid to the Thevar households in breaking out of their servitude to Naidu landlords'.[49] In addition to the spinning mills and the match factories, the

---

58. For the case in Thanjavur district, see Gough, *Rural Change in Southeast India,* p. 320. Ramachandran observes that 'the kind of subordination and code of conduct that landlords used to expect of the irrigation workers is quickly going out of date' (Ramachandran, *Wage Labour and Unfreedom*, p. 232).

[45] 'Is There Urban Bias in the Green Revolution? Report on a Field Trip to North Thanjavur', *Peasant Studies* 2, 4 (1984). See also, Sivertsen, *When Caste Barriers Fall*, pp. 85–87.

[46] In Kumbapettai village in Thanjavur district, the percentage of *pannaiyals* decreased between 1952 and 1976 from 37 percent of the male agricultural labourers to 9 percent (Gough, *Rural Change in Southeast India,* pp. 296, 525). Examining a village in Madurai district, Ramachandran denied the existence of any general tendency for methods of control in agricultural tasks to change in the direction of long-term contracts, whereas in a village in North Arcot district the number of *padiyals* is reported to have increased (Ramachandran, *Wage Labour and Unfreedom in Agriculture*, p. 237; Hazell et al., *Green Revolution Reconsidered*, p. 65).

[47] Athreya, *Vadamalaipuram*, p. 94.

[48] Ibid., pp. 94, 24, 34–35.

[49] Ibid., p. 115.

increase in the demand for labour from other industrial units, which emerged rapidly in nearby Sivakasi and Thiruthangal during this period, led to a relative labour shortage. 'This created a situation where the landowners could not muscle the labourers into submission when the Thevar households managed to move out of the cattle-sheds of landlords to huts near the main road. . . .'[50] The case of Dusi village is another example. Located close to Kanchipuram, a famous weaving centre, the village witnessed the emergence of weaving as a major secondary, and alternative source of, livelihood from the early 1960s. There has been a widespread growth of other non-agricultural occupations such as *beedi* manufacturing, tailoring, etc., reflecting the growth of income earned in agriculture and in weaving. A shortage, particularly of boys, for minding cattle has been observed, presumably because many boys were employed in weaving.[51] In Dusi, 'mobilising labour becomes difficult because a number of agricultural labourers come from outside the village and unskilled labourers in Dusi have an outlet for alternative casual employment in Kancheepuram'.[52] A survey of a village in Tirunelveli has also noted the growth of non-agricultural employment. The most striking feature was the growing demand for labour created by modern manufacturing industries: a cement factory, a chemical factory, a textile mill and other industrial units were established in and around the village[53] and offered employment opportunities to the villagers. There was also a significant development in livestock, wood cutting, charcoal making, brick making and construction,[54] though their impact on agricultural employment is difficult to assess because of the lack of basic data supplied by the survey.[55] S. Guhan and Joan P. Mencher's survey of Iruvelpattu village yielded similar results: more employment in agricultural and non-agricultural sectors and a growth in the self-reliance of SCs.[56]

[50] Ibid.

[51] Guhan and Bharathan, *Dusi*, pp. 3, 42, 68–69, 163.

[52] Ibid., p. 56.

[53] Athreya, *Gangaikondan*, p. 28.

[54] Ibid., pp. 132–33.

[55] Ibid., p. 116, p. 32; J. Harriss makes a suggestive consideration on how the availability of employment outside villages influences the labour relations in rural areas (J. Harriss, *Capitalism and Peasant Farming*, pp. 268–70). See also John Harriss, 'Agriculture/Non-agriculture Linkages and the Diversification of Rural Economic Activity: A South Indian Case Study', in Jan Breman and Sudipto Mundle (eds.), *Rural Transformation in Asia* (Delhi, 1991).

[56] S. Guhan and Joan Mencher, 'Iruvelpattu Revisited (I) (II)', *EPW*, 4 & 11 June 1983.

In addition to these, livestock and animal husbandry also provided an independent economic base for landless agricultural labourers and small cultivators in some villages. In Vadamalaipuram village there was a significant increase in the number of milch cattle, from 86 in 1958 to 170 in 1983. Particularly important is the fact that while in 1958 landless and small cultivator households owning up to five acres possessed less than one-sixth of the total milch cattle kept in the village, the same group, by the early 1980s, accounted for more than half of the cows and nearly 70 percent of the she-buffaloes in the village. The Pallars' share was not insignificant; they owned 17 out of 67 cows and 35 out of 103 she-buffaloes. The sale of milk has been increasing remarkably.[57] Of 424 goats and sheep, an overwhelming proportion, 365, were held by landless households.[58] It is also reported from this village that the significant employment of Pallars in the mills, and their exposure to and involvement in union activities, led them to assert their democratic rights. They, especially the youth, were less subservient to the dominant landowners belonging to the Naidu and Konar castes.[59]

John Harriss has already stated that many village surveys note the growth of non-agricultural employment.[60] In testing Kurien's assertion that there has been a tendency of small farmers to leave the land and farming to join the ranks of the rural proletariat in Tamilnadu,[61] Harriss examined various surveys of villages in Tamilnadu, including those mentioned above. His conclusion is that there has not been a trend towards increased landlessness but rather a proliferation of very small

[57] Athreya, *Vadamalaipuram*, pp. 104–5.

[58] Ibid., p. 88. In Vadamalaipuram, the duration of employment for men's casual labour seems to have decreased during the period between 1958 and 1983, while that for female workers increased. Athreya attributes this decline for male workers to the tractorisation of ploughing work, and the increase for female workers to the outcome of more intensive cropping and higher yields arising therefrom (ibid., p. 96). The reduction in the number of working days of male agricultural labourers, however, has not resulted in a surplus of male labourers because, as pointed out earlier, the increased demand for labour from the mills and small factories and the growing livestock economy were already drawing them away from the fields. The tractorisation can be viewed as a countermove adopted by farmers to overcome the labour shortage.

[59] Ibid., p. 115.

[60] John Harriss, 'Chapter 6: Knowing About Rural Economic Change: Problems Arising From a Comparison of the Results of "Macro" and "Micro" Research in Tamil Nadu', in Pranab Bardhan (ed.), *Conversations Between Economists and Anthropologists* (Delhi, 1989).

[61] C.T. Kurien, 'Dynamics of Rural Transformation: A Case Study of Tamil Nadu', *EPW*, Annual Number, February 1980.

holdings, and that there are also indications of a marked increase in the number of persons engaged in non-agricultural activities, an increase in demand for agricultural labour and a tightening of the labour market.[62] This observation coincides with the findings of Peter Mayer's survey of Tamilnadu village studies.[63]

While the results of the village surveys are not uniform enough to be conclusive, it may be safe to say that in more than half, though not all, of the villages surveyed in Tamilnadu, (1) there has been an increase in agricultural and non-agricultural labour demand, (2) that landownership by the Scheduled Castes and other lower-caste people increased along with the growth of both a sense of and an economic basis for self-reliance and (3) that as a result the landowners have difficulty in mobilising agricultural labourers and so have decreased their landholdings. Thus in many villages in Tamilnadu we can identify the same trends as we have observed in Appadurai village.

Though it is undeniable that these changes have occurred concurrently with the Green Revolution, what seems to be most important is that most of the above-mentioned changes in agrarian structure were already in progress during the colonial period, in other words, considerably before the Green Revolution. This implies that it is wrong to consider the changes observed by the recent surveys as being wholly attributable to the impact of the Green Revolution. Rather they should be viewed as a part, or a developed form, of a long-standing process which started in the latter half of the last century. Changes witnessed in the colonial period, such as the trend of lower castes to be emancipated from landholders and the decline of the dominance of higher-caste landholders in terms of both landholdings and control over labourers, were not only the predecessors of the changes observed in the later period but were also the pre-condition on which their further development was achieved in the post-Independence period. The non-Brahman move-

[62] Ramachandran's recent report, which J. Harriss's review article was not able to take into consideration, asserts that, like in Kumbapettai village of Thanjavur, there was a decline in the average number of days of employment available to a landless agricultural labourer in a village in Madurai district from 1977 to 1988 (Ramachandran, *Wage Labour and Unfreedom*), whereas Marshall Bouton's research on Thanjavur rural change points to an increase in demand for agricultural labour as a result of the new technology (Bouton, *Agrarian Radicalism*, pp. 244–50).

[63] Peter Mayer, 'Has India's Self-Sufficiency in Agriculture been Achieved at the Expense of Social Justice? Reflections on Recent Village Studies in Tamil Nadu', *South Asia Bulletin* 12, 2 (Fall 1992).

ment, which started in the 1920s and later served as the political basis for the development of the SC movement in some villages like Appadurai, was no exception.

As we saw in the previous chapters, the decline in the dominance of higher-caste landholders in the colonial period was caused by such factors as the emancipation of the lower castes stimulated by their emigration, the exodus to urban centres by higher-caste landholders and the intensification of cultivation. The socio-economic conditions after Independence have been such as to promote this tendency. To reiterate, the exodus to urban centres by members of the higher castes, particularly of Brahmans, has been further accelerated. The growth of the sense of independence among the SCs has been stimulated in the post-Independence political and social situation. Further, though labourers no longer emigrate to foreign plantations, demands for the labour of the lower classes, both from agricultural and non-agricultural sectors, seem to have expanded in Tamilnadu, as village surveys suggest. As to the intensification of cultivation, a similar development can be witnessed after the 1960s. No doubt the new technology introduced by the Green Revolution brought about such a leap. Thus an aspect of Green Revolution technology has worked to promote a tendency observed since the end of the last century.

However, it may be misleading if we interpret the Green Revolution as simply encouraging small farmers and landless labourers. The new technology developed by the Green Revolution seems in part to benefit larger farmers more than smaller ones, unlike the previous growth in intensified cultivation. This is an important question which needs further examination though it is beyond the main scope of this study.[64]

The study of Appadurai village definitely suggests that even with the growth in economic and social independence of the lower strata in the village, the majority of the villagers are still either agricultural labourers or tenants. More than half of the village land in Appadurai village is still held by non-resident landowners and, in terms of agricultural production, more than half of the land is managed by large farmers operating more than five acres. While job opportunities in urban areas has been increasing, the better ones are generally enjoyed by Brahmans and other higher-caste members. The future socio-economic development of the village will depend on various elements, both inside and outside the vil-

[64] See also Athreya et al., *Barriers Broken,* Chapter 8.

lage. However, my examination suggests that one of the most important factors is how the basic agrarian structure characterised by the domination of the landlord-tenant relationship and the concentration of production under larger farmers can be changed and reformed. This process of transformation will be deeply influenced by technical changes, the development of job opportunities and changes in government policy. Probably more crucially, it will depend partly on how quickly and effectively the lower strata of agricultural labourers and poor tenants can grow into an influential group in rural areas and partly on how reforms aiming to change the present basic pattern of landholding might be implemented in the future.

8
Conclusion

In the 1860s, the wet villages in Tamilnadu were far from being an egalitarian society. My analysis of the Settlement Registers for villages in Lalgudi *taluk* has revealed a highly concentrated pattern for landholdings in wet villages. More than half of the land was owned by members of higher castes, such as Brahmans and Vellalars, usually comprising a handful of large landowners, whereas the majority of the villagers, mainly consisting of low-caste Non-Brahmans and Depressed-caste members, held no land or at most a negligible area. Such a concentration in landownership was quite common in other wet areas such as Thanjavur and Chingleput districts. The land owned by people from the higher castes was mainly cultivated either through a sharecropping system or by using permanent labourers like *pannaiyal*. Landowners had to rely for the cultivation of their land principally on permanent labourers and under-tenants either of low-caste Non-Brahmans or from Depressed castes. An examination of a village survey of Chingleput district done in the 1760–70s discloses that agricultural labourers accounted for more than half of the total workforce actually engaged in agriculture. The high-caste landowners obstructed the acquisition of land by those of lower castes, particularly of Depressed castes, since the higher castes would have lost their advantage if the members of lower castes became landholders.

Agrarian society in Tamilnadu, as described above, underwent a marked change after the 1870s. Three developments seem to have most strongly stimulated this change in agrarian society: the intensification of agricultural production, the emigration of lower- and higher-caste members to estates and urban areas respectively, and the integration of the South Indian agricultural economy into the world trade network under the colonial system.

My scrutiny of the Settlement Registers for Lalgudi villages as well as other descriptive sources has revealed that two different kinds of transformation proceeded in wet and intermediate zone villages in the British period. The first change was the gradual deterioration of the pattern of landownership, as seen in the 1860s, characterised by the dominance of landowners of the higher castes. The growing emigration of agricultural labourers and other members of the lower castes to overseas estates, etc., not only provided them with alternative job opportunities but also stimulated the growth of their sense of independence. The available evidence indicates that, as a result, the higher-caste landowners felt increasing difficulty in securing labourers and making them work as hard as before. On the other hand, a large number of higher-caste people left their villages for urban areas to get employment in white-collar jobs and a higher education, lessening their concern with agriculture and land management just at a time when agriculture was tending towards more intensive cultivation. Farmers increasingly felt that more careful cultivation would yield a better crop, and so the advantage large-scale farming may have enjoyed in the past diminished.

These changes induced the higher-caste landowners to lease a part or the whole of their land to tenants, instead of cultivating the land with the help of permanent labourers, while some of the previous labourer class raised their status to small tenants though they had still to supplement their income by working as hired day labourers. There is evidence to show that some of them even raised their status to small landholders by purchasing a small plot of land. Thus, as the Settlement Registers demonstrate, there was an emergence of new landholders from among the low-caste Non-Brahmans and Depressed-caste members. On the other hand, some of the higher-caste landowners not only leased their land to tenants but reduced their holdings, selling a part of their land. As the case of the Lalgudi villages clearly shows, the Brahman community reduced the extent of land held, particularly after the 1890s, and the reduction was sharper in the larger holdings. This reflected the inability of high-caste traditional landowners to retain their former powerful influence by controlling the ownership of land in villages, though they still owned the largest share of the land.

This transformation was accompanied by an important change in the type of agricultural labourer. Though the total number of agricultural labourers did not decrease, permanent labourers such as *pannaiyals* were gradually displaced by day labourers. Those former agricultural labourers who had been able to raise their status to small farmers by acquiring either small tenant holdings or small plots of their own land hired themselves out only as day labourers instead of permanent workers, since they now had to give some of their time to cultivating their own farms. A developing self consciousness among these classes also promoted this trend by stimulating a sense of aversion to servile employment. Thus the replacement of *pannaiyals* by day labourers probably reflected in part the progressive emancipation of these labourers from dominant landowners. In addition, those newcomers to the labour market who had fallen from the status of independent farmer were probably employed not as permanent labourers but as day labourers.

These changes in Tamilnadu had their parallels in agrarian changes in seventeenth- to nineteenth-century Japan. Both areas witnessed changes such as the intensification of agricultural production, the acquisition of land by the erstwhile agricultural labourer classes and the consequent increase of small farmers, and the decrease in the number of permanent bonded labourers. This indicates that the general trend in agriculture both in Japan and Tamilnadu in the period before mid-twentieth century was towards a smaller rather than a larger farm. This type of change seems to represent the growth of an internal force for change inherent in agriculture in Asian paddy-cultivating areas. The change towards smaller units of cultivation does not imply an agricultural retrogression but rather reflects agricultural progress in paddy-growing areas.

The other form of transformation in Tamilnadu under British rule was the growth of Non-Brahman large landholders and the stratification of the Non-Brahman population. This change was mainly stimulated by the commercialisation of South Indian agriculture and the integration of farmers into the world trade network, which probably led to the spread of rural debts and the resultant decline of some small landowning farmers into the status of tenant. The other side of this process was the transfer of land to the newly rich, such as traders, moneylenders and others who had gained wealth by exploiting the economic opportunities created and developed under colonial rule. Some Non-Brahmans considerably expanded their landed property in this way, growing into large landholders, and this led to stratification among people belonging to Non-Brahman communities.

The Settlement Registers for the Lalgudi villages demonstrate statistically the development of these two trends in the period between 1865 and 1925. The two types of change seem to have continued even in the period between 1925 and 1947, though data we have is scanty. If the data used does not identify the caste affiliation of landholders, the growth of large landholders from Non-Brahman communities is not easily noticed as it is offset statistically by a sharp decrease in large landholdings among Brahman communities. The identification of these two different trends in South Indian society enables us to reconcile the two views on rural change under British rule, namely that of the Nationalists, which emphasises the disintegration and polarisation of peasant society, and that put foreword by its critics, who denied the progress of polarisation.

It is, however, important to reiterate that though we can perceive a weakening in the dominance of the higher castes in landholding, it is not to such an extent that it might have radically eroded the pattern of the basic structure of landholding. Nor do we see a radical change in the size-wise distribution of land. The growth of large holdings by the Non-Brahman newly rich offset the decline in the large landholdings owned by Brahmans, resulting in no considerable change in the size-wise distribution. Although the area owned by the Depressed-caste members and low-caste Non-Brahmans expanded after 1865, it was too small to create a radical change in the landholding pattern, since it accounted only for a small percentage of the total in terms of absolute acreage. Even though a considerable number of former agricultural labourers acquired or leased land, many Depressed-caste families remained landless and had to work as full-time agricultural labourers. In addition, many small farmers of the Depressed castes, who had emerged from the agricultural labourer class either by leasing or buying land, still had to supplement their income by working as coolie labourers. Low-caste Non-Brahmans did not differ much from the Depressed-caste members: they still had to hire themselves out as day labourers or cultivate land as tenants.

The above consideration of the colonial period, as well as the findings presented by many surveys of Tamil villages done in the 1980s, give us a new insight into the changes that occurred in post-Independence villages, pointing to an aspect of continuity through one hundred years. The growth of a sense of self-reliance among the lower classes, and the resultant difficulty felt by large landowners in mobilising agricultural labourers has been a feature commonly perceived by most surveys of Tamil villages. Other common features witnessed in many villages surveyed have been a decrease in the landholdings of higher castes or the previously dominant castes, an expansion of the area held by low-caste Non-Brahmans and Depressed-caste members, and the development of other economic bases for their independence. An increased demand for both agricultural and non-agricultural labour has been observed also in many villages in Tamilnadu.

These observations encourage us to consider that while, with the decline of the colonial regime, the economic basis that had underpinned the progress of the second type of transformation hardly remained, the first type of social transformation, namely the gradual decline of the dominance of higher castes, further proceeded in the period after Independence. In particular, the self consciousness among people of lower castes, which was fed in the colonial period, grew further, stimulated by movements among them after Independence. Though these changes occurred concurrently with the progress of the Green Revolution, it is misleading to attribute the changes observed by the recent village surveys solely to the economic effect of the Green Revolution. Rather, many of them should be considered to be developments of a process which started in the colonial period. This is one of the major points I would like to emphasise in this study.

The study has also highlighted the importance of the growth of self consciousness among the lower classes, which has been one of the most important agents behind the structural change in agrarian relations since the 1880s, though many aspects of change are closely interlinked with each other.

My study of Appadurai village also suggests that even with the growth of the economic and social independence of the lower strata of the village, the majority of the villagers are still either agricultural labourers or tenants. Even in the 1980s, more than half of the land in the village was still owned by non-resident landowners and, in terms of agricultural production, more than half of the land is under the management of large farmers. Therefore, a radical transformation in the landholding pattern of rural society is still an important issue regarding the future development of agrarian society in Tamilnadu.

APPENDIX 1

The Proportion of Agricultural Labourers in Fifty Villages Surveyed by Barnard

In the 1760s, Barnard surveyed about 2,200 villages in Jagir (presently belonging to Chingleput district) and recorded a detailed account of each village.[1] The records furnish us with invaluable data which enable us to calculate the proportion of agricultural labourers in both the agricultural population and the total agricultural labour force. I will analyse a sample of 50 villages in one area (Vol. 56A, Nos. 427–94), the records of which are relatively legible.

These villages had a total number of 1,827 houses, of which 370 'landholders', 102 'farmers' and 43 'servants' are considered to have been directly concerned with agricultural production, even if all of them were not actually engaged in agricultural labour. The breakdown of these three groups is shown in Table A.1. Apart from the categories recorded, there were groups who were classified according to caste without any indication of their specific occupation. Among them, the six groups shown in Table A.2 may have played a role in agricultural production. A total of 1,042 households were thus more or less connected with agriculture as landholders, farmers, cow keepers or agricultural labourers. Other households were artisans and providers of services, like weavers, village clerks, dancers, carpenters and barbers, while 68 houses of Brahmans were not shown as having any specific occupation and so may be considered part of the non-agricultural population.

[1] The records are kept in the Tamil Nadu State Archives. Tsukasa Mizushima's work is the first attempt to systematically analyse these huge records. Tsukasa Mizushima, 'Mirasi System and Local Society in Pre-Colonial South India', in Robb et al. (eds.), *Local Agrarian Societies.* I am most indebted to Mizushima for giving me access to the photocopy of the records, which have been used as data in this appendix.

Table A.1
Breakdown of Agricultural Population in 50 Villages in Jagir, 1760s

(houses)

Landholders		Farmers		Servants	
Vellara	201	Reddi	41	Pally	43
Brahmin	143	Commawar	18	Total	43
Pally	18	Vellara	17		
Cow keeper	5	Brahmin	14		
Cavaries	3	Cow keeper	5		
Total	370	Pally	3		
		Cavaries	3		
		Pandaram	1		
		Total	102		

Table A.2
Supposed Agricultural Population without Specified Occupations in 50 Villages in Jagir, 1760s

	(houses)
Pariar	304
Pally	127
Cow keeper	47
Vellara	25
Reddi	14
Commawar	10

Let us consider first the number of households among the agricultural population which did not manage a farm on their own account but worked as hired labourers and cow keepers. It is probably safe to assume that the 'Pally (Palli) servants' were primarily hired agricultural labourers. The 'Pariar' (Paraiyar) population poses a problem, as the report provides no information on their economic positions. If we assume that the Paraiyars in this district were agricultural labourers, as indicated by a source of later period,[2] the 43 Palli servants and the 304 Paraiyars, that is, a total of 347 households or 19 percent of the total number of households were agricultural labourers. In addition, the 47 'cow keepers' who had no other indication of occupation may not have been farmers. The main occupation therefore of 394 households was not

[2] Collector of the Chingleput to Board of Revenue, 9 August 1819, P.B.R., Vol. 829 (TNA), pp. 6890–93. See also Chitra Sivakumar and S.S. Sivakumar, *Peasants and Nabobs*, p. 22; Kumar, *Land and Caste*, p. 55; Eugene F. Irschick, 'Peasant Survival Strategies and Rehearsals for Rebellion in Eighteenth-Century South India', *Peasant Studies* 9, 4 (Summer 1982).

the operation of a farm but rather hired labour for agriculture or cow keeping. This figure represents 38 percent of the total number of households concerned with agriculture, much higher than the 17–25 percent suggested by Dharma Kumar.

Next we shall calculate how many households may have been farmers directly managing the land. As Mizushima indicates, Barnard's 'landholders' and the 'farmers' probably denoted the classes later called '*mirasidars*' and '*ulkudi*' respectively by the colonial administration.[3] This hypothesis can be confirmed. Ellis observed, based on Place's data about Jagir around the end of eighteenth century, that the ratio of *mirasidars* to the whole population was 1 to 6.5.[4] This accords well with Barnard's report, where 'landholders' comprised about one-fifth of the total population. Examining *mirasidars* in 52 villages of the Jagir, Ellis found that out of every 100 *mirasidars*, 53 were Vellalars, 20 Brahmans and 27 were other castes.[5] The caste composition of Barnard's 'landholders' shows 'Vellaras' (Vellalars) as comprising 54 percent, which is in accord with Ellis' figures. While some *mirasidars* may have not managed their land but leased it out to tenants, as we shall see later, it is undeniable that a considerable number of *mirasidars* were engaged in farm management.

The 102 households of 'farmers', accounting for about 6 percent of the total houses, may have managed their own farms, though with some exceptions, as we will see later.

The point in question is the position of those who had no occupational designation—127 Palli houses, 25 'Vellara' houses, 14 Reddi houses, and 10 Commawar houses. What was the status of these households in relation to agricultural production of the village? In view of the fact that one set of households from these castes was explicitly defined as 'landholders' or 'farmers', we cannot automatically regard those with no occupational standing as self-employed cultivators. It may be safer to suppose that these castes included people of different occupational standings, including cultivators and agricultural labourers. Of them, the position of the Palli caste seems to have been the most complicated. Though the Pallis did not belong to the Depressed castes like the

[3] Tsukasa Mizushima, *Minami Indo Zaichishakai no Kenkyu* [A Study of Local Society in South India] (Tokyo: ILCAA, 1987), p. 59.

[4] 'Replies from Mr. F.W. Ellis, Collector of Madras, to the Mirási questions, dated 30th May 1816', in Bayley and Hudleston (eds.), *Papers on Mirasi Right*, p. 248.

[5] Ibid., p. 251.

Paraiyars, many of them may have been agricultural labourers.[6] In this area too, though 18 Palli households were grouped as 'landholders', 43 were specified as being servants. It would be wrong therefore to assume that the 127 Palli households with no occupational designation were all farmers. At the very least they would have included a good number of agricultural labourers.

Let us consider, by way of summary, the number of households which may have managed farms. (1) If we assume that all 'landholders' and 'farmers' were actually managing farms, the total comes to 472 houses. (2) If the 'Vellara', Reddi and Commawar without any occupational designation are also assumed to have managed farms, the total comes to 521 houses. (3) If we further add the 127 Palli houses with no occupation tag, the total becomes 648. This last figure projects the maximum number of households that could have been engaged in managing a farm, but this would appear to be an overestimation, since a number who must have been just labourers were included in the description of the Pallis.

Third, let us consider how many could have both managed their own farms and cultivated the land with their own labour. Of the total number of landholding houses, 143 were Brahman families, while of the farmers 14 were Brahman houses. 'Bramins, . . . being forbid to cultivate the lands themselves, must employ servants for that purpose.'[7] If we subtract the number of Brahmans from the total number of households which may have managed their own farms, then the figures would be 315 in case (1), 364 in case (2), and 491 in case (3). In other words, in cases (1) and (2), the number of agricultural labourers and cow keepers (amounting to 394) is larger than the number of those who managed their farms using family labour.

A further problem is posed by the Vellalar caste. Many of the Vellalars did not work the land themselves but relied on employed labour. Concerning the *mirasidars* of Thanjavur, 'The lower or poorer classes of Soodra meerassadars alone follow the plough. The Brahmin meerassadars cannot, and the upper classes of Soodra meerassadars will not, personally engage in the labours of agriculture.'[8] It has also been

[6] For Palli, see Kumar, *Land and Caste*, pp. 58–59.

[7] 'Extract from Mr. Place's final report on the Jaghire, dated 6th June 1799', in Bayley and Hudleston (eds.), *Papers on Mirasi Right*, p. 47; Kumar, *Land and Caste*, p. 30.

[8] 'Extract from the Report of Mr. Wallace on the Settlement of Tanjore, for Fusly 1214, dated 1st May 1805', in Bayley and Hudleston (eds.), *Papers on Mirasi Right*, p. 96.

reported from areas near Madras that 'in the villages held by the Vellaler or Agamudeiyar they possess a certain number of slaves: each plough at work requires one man, and when the number of slaves, therefore, is not sufficient for the whole cultivation, hired laborers are employed'.[9] The majority of *mirasidars* belonging to the Brahman or Vellalar castes, therefore, did not cultivate the land themselves. As a result, 'there are some meerassadars, but still far fewer even than those engaging slaves, whose land is cultivated by their own labour, and by that of their relations'.[10] In the 50 villages considered here, there were 201 houses of 'Vellara' landholders. If we can assume that these 'Vellara' landholders did not work in their fields, those who managed their farms with their own family labours would be (1) 114; (2) 163; and (3) 290. As we have reiterated, 347 households in these 50 villages were agricultural labourers, and 47 cow keepers. These two groups together total far more than the number of households that could have directly managed their land by means of family labour.

In other words, agricultural labourers and cow keepers accounted for more than half of the total agricultural work force in Chingleput district at the end of the eighteenth century. The data analysed so far places low-caste agricultural labourers in the area now known as Chingleput at the centre of the agricultural labour force at the end of the eighteenth century.[11] This conclusion, however, remains tentative. Since no information is available in the Barnard report regarding the economic conditions of Paraiyars in the area, our calculation has partly depended upon an early nineteenth-century source. As continuity in their economic positions between the 1760s and the 1810s can be a debatable point, a further consideration may be needed to qualify my conclusion.

[9] 'Translation of Answer to the Questions enclosed in Mr. Secretary Hill's Letter to the Board of Revenue, dated 2nd August 1814, by B. Sancaraya, late Sheristadar to the Collector of Madras', in Bayley and Hudleston (eds.), *Papers on Mirasi Right*, p. 225; *Manual of Trichinopoly District*, p. 187.

[10] 'Extract from the Report of Mr. Harris, Collector of Tanjore, to the Committee, dated 9th May 1804', in Bayley and Hudleston (eds.), *Papers on Mirasi Right*, p. 86.

[11] The vital importance of agricultural labourers is also discernible in the example of 71 villages in Chingleput district analysed by Mizushima. Mizushima, *Minami Indo Zaichishakai no Kenkyu*. This was probably the case too in other paddy cultivating Tamil districts like Thanjavur and Tiruchirapalli.

APPENDIX 2

Change in Paddy Yield per Acre in Tamilnadu: A Consideration of Statistics

In a suggestive review article on changes in agricultural productivity, Sumit Guha has recently attempted to assess changes in yield per acre in India including various parts of the Madras Presidency, using data obtained by crop-cutting experiments.[1] Though changes in agricultural productivity are generally beyond the scope of the present study, I shall briefly consider the data available for Tamilnadu pertaining to it. As Guha states, crop-cutting experiments were carried out in some districts as a part of settlement operations in the latter half of the nineteenth century. He has compared the yield per acre thus obtained in the latter half of the last century (hereafter '1870 data') with the sets of yield figures attained by two later crop-cutting experiments; the first is that of experiments done by the Indian Council of Agricultural Research (ICAR) in 1945–49 (hereafter '1945–49 data') and the second is a set of figures for 1955–57 shown, in *Season and Crop Reports* for these years, as 'results based on crop cutting experiments' conducted by the Department of Statistics (hereafter '1955–57 data').

In addition to the above-mentioned crop-cutting experiments, similar experiments were undertaken three times between 1895 and 1920 either by the Revenue Department or by the Agricultural Department, but data from these experiments have not yet been examined by previous studies, including Guha's. The first set of experiment was in the five years ending 1901–2 (hereafter '1901 data'), the second during the quinquennium 1906–7 to 1911–12 (hereafter '1911 data'), and the third in 1917 (hereafter '1917 data'). Since, as we shall examine later, these four sets of experiments before the 1920s were carried out basically in

[1] Sumit Guha, 'Introduction', in Sumit Guha (ed.), *Growth, Stagnation or Decline? Agricultural Productivity in British India* (Delhi, 1992), p. 46.

the same manner, their results can be used for assessing changes in the productivity of paddy cultivation.

Table B.1 lists the results of these experiments. I shall add some words about the compilation of data in the table. In the processing of the 1901 and 1911 data, the government reduced 38 percent of the yield of paddy (unhusked) to obtain the yield of rice.[2] However, in the statistics of a later period the government assumed rice to be 67 percent of the weight of the paddy, and, therefore, to compare the figures collected by these three experiments with those from others, I have revised the 1901 and 1911 experiment figures on the assumption that paddy yields 67 percent of its weight in rice. The rate of converting a Madras Measure of paddy into pounds poses another problem. Since a Madras Measure is a unit denoting volume, how much a Madras Measure of paddy weighs may differ by area and the variety of rice cultivated. According to the 1883 Manual of Tanjore district, a *kalam* of paddy may be taken as 63.82 lbs. Sources do not agree on how many Madras Measures a *kalam* in Thanjavur corresponded to; according to one source it was 24 Madras Measures, whereas another indicates that it was equal to 27.75 Madras Measures.[3] Hence a Madras Measure of paddy in this area may be calculated as having weighed either about 2.66 lbs. or 2.3 lbs. The 1880 Settlement Report for North Arcot district lists a table showing average yields of paddy both in Madras Measures and in pounds, demonstrating that the average weight of a Madras Measure of paddy was 2.25 lbs. in this district.[4] On the other hand, data from Tinnevelly district indicates that it weighed about 2.48 lbs.[5] Therefore, in Table B.1, I have listed two figures for 1870, one converted by 2.6 and the other by 2.3.

A comparison of yields obtained by crop-cutting experiments before 1940, as shown in Table B.1, reveals, first, that in all districts, the yield increased between 1901 and 1917. Second, except for Ramnad district, which did not exist in the last century, six districts out of nine witnessed a rise in the yield of rice between the 1870s and the 1910s. The data thus can be said to suggest that the paddy yield per acre steadily rose during the period between the 1870s and 1917 in a majority of the districts in Tamilnadu.

[2] G.O., No. 3374, Revenue, 20 Nov. 1913.

[3] Raghavaiyangar, *Memorandum*, p. cvii, and P.B.R., No. 719, 1 Nov. 1892, p. 71, respectively.

[4] P.B.R., No. 1495, 11 Oct. 1880, p. 6892.

[5] G.O., No. 716, Revenue, 3 May 1872, p. 1233.

Table B.1
Yields of Rice per Acre Obtained by Crop-Cutting Experiments before 1940

(lbs.)

	1870A	1870B	1901	1911	1917
Chingleput	919	813	1,011	1,165	1,136
North Arcot	1,776	1,571	1,206	1,478	n.a
South Arcot	1,149	1,016	1,201	1,406	1,624
Salem	1,488	1,316	1,378	1,633	2,149
Coimbatore	1,931	1,707	1,405	1,554	1,794
Trichinopoly	1,097	970	1,366	1,569	n.a.
Tanjore	1,046	925	1,022	1,006	1,132
Madura			1,352	1,677	1,872
Ramnad				1,331	n.a.
Tinnevelly	1,770	1,566	1,428	1,649	n.a.

Sources: 1870A: Taken from Guha, 'Introduction', p. 46, Statement III, except the following. For Coimbatore, I have adopted my calculation from the Settlement Report of the district (P.B.R., No. 1760, 26 June 1878, p. 5759), instead of the yield given by Guha, who adopted Ratnam's data for this district. For Tanjore, I have calculated the yield from G.O., No. 719, Revenue, 1 Nov. 1892, pp. 23–24.

1870B=1870A ÷ 2.6 × 2.3.

1901: G.O., No. 2025, Revenue, 22 Aug. 1903.
1911: G.O., No. 3374, Revenue, 20 Nov. 1913.
1917: G.O., No. 2687, Revenue, 31 Aug. 1917.

Normal (it is also called 'standard' or 'average') yields (or 'outturn') were fixed for different tracts empirically on the basis of past experiments, but it was stipulated that they should be revised every five years on the basis of actual crop-cutting experiments conducted by the staff of the revenue and agricultural departments on the fields judged by them to bear an average crop.[6] In fact, in the period before 1919 the 'normal outturn of the crop per acre' for each district was revised shortly after each of the crop-cutting experiments, whereas it remained unchanged between 1919 and 1954 since no such experiments were conducted by any department of the Madras government in this period. Though no 'normal outturn of the crop' was given in *Season and Crop Reports* for the period before 1905–6, a similar set of estimated yields is available for 1892: a provisional return of the yields of the principal

[6] Indian Council of Agricultural Research (ICAR), *Sample Surveys for the Estimation of Yield of Food Crops* (Delhi, 1951), p. 3; G.O., No. 880, Revenue, 27 Mar. 1911.

crops was compiled for this year from various statistical publications including Settlement Reports.[7] The change in 'normal yield' listed in *Season and Crop Reports* and the 1892 estimated yield, as shown in Table B.2, generally accords with the above-mentioned observation that the paddy yield per acre in Tamilnadu steadily rose from the 1870s to 1917.[8]

Table B.2
Normal Yield of Rice per Acre as Shown in *Season and Crop Reports*
(lbs.)

	1892	1905–9	1911–17	1918–54
Chingleput	694	704	1,005	1,039
North Arcot	1,106	1,106	1,206	1,273
South Arcot	905	905	1,139	1,240
Salem	1,078	1,072	1,273	1,273
Coimbatore	897	905	1,206	1,273
Trichinopoly	999	972	1,206	1,273
Tanjore	928	1,072	1,072	1,173
Madura	676	670	1,340	1,307
Ramnad			1,206	1,206
Tinnevelly		905	1,340	1,340

Sources: 1892: Assessed yields recorded in G.O., No. 2025, Revenue, 22 Aug. 1903.
1905–9, 1911–17 and 1918–54: *Season and Crop Reports.*

Assessing changes in rice yield per acre for the period after 1918 poses a serious problem. No crop-cutting experiments were conducted in the 1920s and 1930s. Though such experiments were carried out by ICAR in 1945–49 as noted before, the manner in which the data was collected in the latter experiments radically differed from that adopted by the experiments before 1920. The main purpose of the 1945–49 survey was to replace the old official method of crop estimation by the random sampling method. While in the previous system the selection of the fields for conducting experiments had been left to the personal discretion of the officials and the results had represented the simple average of experiments, that is, the total yields of all the experiments divided by the number of experiments, ICAR adopted a sampling method known as stratified multi-stage sampling in order to arrive at an objective estimation of yield.

[7] G.O., No. 2025, Revenue, 22 Aug. 1903.

[8] My observation for the change up to 1918 agrees with the finding of George Blyn for the Madras Presidency (*Agricultural Trends in India, 1891–1947: Output, Availability, and Productivity* [Philadelphia, 1966]).

The defect of the sampling method taken in the experiments before 1918 was noticed by the department itself. It noted that in many places the land selected for these experiments was superior to the average class of land in the Madras Presidency. For the results of the 1901 experiments, the Revenue Department remarked that 'the average assessment on the land on which the crops experimented with were grown, is higher than the average assessment for the Presidency' and that, therefore, 'it would be altogether unsafe to adopt averages such those now reported as representing the normal outturn in a year of average crop, which when multiplied by the average area cropped, may give as near an approximation as possible to the outturn in an average year'.[9] The memorandum accompanying the returns of the yields attained by the 1911 crop experiments pointed to a similar feature of the experiments, remarking that in many places the land selected for experiments was apparently superior to the average class of land.[10] Though, as Guha notes, there may have been some other factors which tended to give a downwards bias to crop-cutting data, the most serious defect of these experiment data was deemed to be the overestimation of the true yields.

That the results of the crop-cutting experiments were considered as higher than the real level of normal yields of crops may be confirmed by the way in which a normal yield for each district as shown in *Season and Crop Reports* was estimated and decided. A comparison of these two series of data, as shown in Tables B.1 and B.2, suggests that 'normal yields' of crops was fixed generally at a considerably lower level than the results of the crop-cutting experiments conducted just before. This no doubt reflects that the results of crop-cutting experiments were deemed to be higher than the actual average yield in each district. The same may be said of the data before 1900. The data obtained by the crop-cutting experiments in the settlement operations (the 1870 data) seem to have been dealt with in the same manner as the results of the experiments conducted between 1895 and 1917 were: the 1892 assessed yield was fixed at a lower level than the 1870 crop-cutting data, indicating that the land selected in the 1870 experiments was considered superior to the average class of land.

This crucial difference in the method of sampling between the experiments conducted before 1940 and the 1945–49 ICAR survey leads us to conclude that it is misleading to draw any conclusion on changes in agricultural productivity by comparing the 1945–49 data

[9] G.O., No. 2025, Revenue, 22 Aug. 1903.

[10] G.O., No. 3374, Revenue, 20 Nov. 1913.

with the previous crop-cutting experiment data.[11] In fact, though ICAR compared the results of its 1945–49 survey with 'normal yields' shown in *Season and Crop Reports* in order to assess the accuracy of the latter,[12] it did not compare its data with the results of previous crop-cutting experiments for the Madras Presidency.

The framing of an estimate of total production of a crop for a particular year involved a consideration of three factors: the acreage under crop, normal (standard) yield and seasonal factor (or condition figure). The practice generally followed in *Season and Crop Reports* after 1905 was to express seasonal factor for a year as a percentage of yield per acre attained in that year as compared with the normal yield.[13] If the comparison of the data from 1917 crop-cutting experiments with those of 1945–49 ICAR experiments should be considered inappropriate, figures for seasonal factors would be the only one serial data for judging changes in paddy yield per acre for the period between 1919 and 1954, when 'normal yield per acre of paddy' remained unchanged. Since the reliability of the seasonal factors has long been a matter of debate, I shall briefly compare these seasonal factors with other data in order to assess their reliability.

Table B.3 lists average yield of rice per acre as obtained by multiplying 'normal yields' by percentage figures for seasonal factors, and

[11] Sumit Guha has pointed to a tendency towards a decline in productivity of paddy in Tamil districts after the 1870s on the basis of a comparison of the 1870 data with the results of 1945–49 ICAR and 1955–57 crop-cutting experiments, as noted before. However, in view of the difference in the methods of sampling among experiments, this conclusion should be re-examined.

[12] While ICAR found a difference between ICAR survey estimates and the 'normal yields', they never took the difference as indicating any change in the productivity of crops but attributed it to either the over- or under-estimation of 'normal yields'. For example, for Madras State, it stated that in 12 out of 14 districts, 'normals' were seen to be over-estimated (ICAR, *Sample Surveys*, p. 47).

[13] In Madras, each village accountant estimated the yield for a particular year in comparison with the yield he thought 'normal' in his village. To put it another way, he was not asked to calibrate his judgement on the season with a particular 'normal yield' fixed for each district. District figures for seasonal factor were based on the sum of such small observations. G.A.D. Stuart, 'The Seasonal Factor in Crop Statistics: A Method of Correcting for the Inherent Pessimism of the Farmer', *Agricultural Journal of India* 14, 2 (1919); Alan W. Heston, 'Official Yields per Acre in India, 1886–1947: Some Questions of Interpretation', *IESHR* 10, 4 (1973) (Guha [ed.], *Growth, Stagnation or Decline?* pp. 103–4).

Table B.4 shows yield obtained by the 1945–49 and 1955–57 crop-cutting experiments.

Table B.3
Average Yields of Rice per Acre as Obtained by Multiplying Normal Yields by Seasonal Factors

(lbs.)

	1917 –19	1920 –24	1925 –29	1930 –34	1935 –39	1940 –44	1945 –49	1950 –52	1953 –54
Chingleput	1,053	1,049	1,006	1,020	869	984	652	662	966
North Arcot	1,175	1,181	1,181	1,161	1,110	1,184	896	942	1,248
South Arcot	1,169	1,121	1,141	1,141	1,104	1,125	870	773	1,166
Salem	1,235	1,186	1,186	1,258	1,298	1,379	1,069	1,018	1,235
Coimbatore	1,235	1,235	1,227	1,199	1,189	1,146	1,026	1,002	1,235
Trichinopoly	1,213	1,176	1,214	1,186	1,204	1,218	998	1,018	1,254
Tanjore	1,032	1,046	1,091	1,016	1,100	1,091	988	1,036	1,132
Madura	1,359	1,317	1,286	1,331	1,281	1,324	1,098	1,046	1,248
Ramnad	1,520	1,252	1,134	1,247	1,059	1,154	719	563	1,152
Tinnevelly	1,179	1,257	1,235	1,198	1,179	1,233	1,061	1,089	1,327

Source: *Season and Crop Reports.*

Note: The figures for 1940–44 are the average of only three years, 1940, 1941 and 1944.

Table B.4
Yields of Rice per Acre as Obtained by 1945–49 and 1955–57 Crop-Cutting Experiments

(lbs.)

	1945–49	1955–57
Chingleput	676	958
North Arcot	948	1,470
South Arcot	893	1,362
Salem		1,541
Coimbatore		1,589
Trichinopoly	1,051	1,317
Tanjore	876	1,121
Madura	1,123	1,454
Ramnad	655	864
Tinnevelly	1,163	1,498

Sources: 1945–49: ICAR, *Sample Surveys for the Estimation of Yield of Food Crops*, Table 9.4.

1955–57: For Tanjore, Madura and Ramnad districts, my calculation from *Season and Crop Reports for Madras State for 1955–57.* For other districts, from Guha, 'Introduction', p. 46, Statement III.

Comparing the 1945–49 figures in Tables B.3 and B.4, the average yields for 1945–49 obtained from seasonal factors are generally in accord with the results of the 1945–49 ICAR experiments. Though the former marked generally below the latter figure, the difference was within 10 percent of the latter for all but one district. The average yields for 1953–54 also associate with the 1955–57 crop-cutting data particularly for wet districts. Though we do not have detailed information about how the 1955–57 data were compiled, it is highly probably that they were collected in the same manner as the 1945–49 ICAR experiments[14] and, therefore, can be considered the most reliable indexes for the real yield. Thus for the period of the 1940s and 1950s seasonal factors and real yields synchronized their movements, though there were gaps in absolute level of yields between them.

It may be inferred from these two comparisons that changes in seasonal factors as listed in *Season and Crop Reports* well reflected the changes in the real yields so far as the Tamil districts are concerned. If we can thus assume that changes in seasonal factors mirrored real changes in the yields of paddy, we may be allowed to take Table B.3 as indicating that the rice yield per acre in Tamil districts remained stagnant in the 1920s and 1930s and sharply fell by the middle of the 1940s but recovered to the pre-war level in the first half of the 1950s. This observation partly agrees with the findings of a Director of Agriculture, who in 1946, as Baker reveals, noticed a sharp decline in the yields of paddy, though he indicated that the decline had started in the mid-30s.[15] As has been shown in Chapter 3, some other sources also indicate that there seems to have been either stagnation or decline in agricultural production in the 1920s and 1930s in Tamilnadu, particularly in some wet districts.

[14] According to V.G. Panse, after the 1945–49 crop-cutting surveys carried out by ICAR based on random sampling method, the coordination of these large scale surveys was transferred to the Crop Survey Wing of the National Sample Survey, but the pattern of work continued unchanged and a reliable series of comparable data became available (V.G. Panse, 'Recent Trends in the Yield of Rice and Wheat in India', *The Indian Journal of Agricultural Economics* 14, 1 [Jan.–March 1959]). The figures presented by him as the yields of rice in Madras for 1955 (ibid., Table 10) are almost same as those listed in *Season and Crop Report* for this year as the results of the crop-cutting experiments. This suggests that the 1955–57 yield data listed in *Season and Crop Reports* were compiled in the same manner as those of the ICAR crop-cutting experiments. See also C.R. Rao (ed.), *Data Base of Indian Economy* (New Delhi, 1972), Vol. 1, pp. 248–51.

[15] Baker, *Rural Economy*, p. 177.

This observation regarding changes in yield after 1918, however, needs to be qualified by further examination. On the basis of a comparison of seasonal factors with the 1945–49 and 1955–57 crop-cutting data, we have assumed that the series of seasonal factors can be a good index for assessing changes in yields. Because the results of ICAR and other experiments were available to the provincial governments before the department released the figures of seasonal factors, it is entirely possible that the seasonal factors were not decided independently from the results of the experiments.[16] The above examination of the crop-cutting data also suggests that my observation on the changes in the productivity before 1918 should not be taken as conclusive. Though the series of crop-cutting data before 1944 are comparative in the sense that their samples were selected without any adoption of random sampling and the data can be commonly regarded to have been upwards biased, the extent of the bias may have differed among the different experiments.[17] Many points remain still to be confirmed by future research

[16] R.C. Desai, *Standard of Living in India and Pakistan: 1931–32 to 1940–41* (Bombay, 1953), p. 18 n ('Crop Production', in Guha [ed.], *Growth, Stagnation or Decline?* pp. 82–83 n. 38); ICAR, *Sample Surveys,* p. 31.

[17] Witnesses appearing in the Royal Commission on Agriculture in India were also divided in opinion as to the changes in productivity in Tamilnadu. For example a farmer in Madurai suggested a decline in yield per acre during this period (*Royal Commission on Agriculture in India,* Vol. 3, pp. 432, 445).

Glossary

abkari	Revenue derived from duties levied on the manufacture and sale of inebriating liquors, etc.
adangal	An account recording the cultivation of village lands
Adi Dravida	'Original Dravidian', the lowest castes known as Untouchables or Scheduled Castes
adimai	Slavery, bondage in general
al-varam	System of farm management under which the worker provides only labour, and the land owner provides all other inputs
arrack	Liquor
aruval	A grain-sickle
beedi	Cheep cheroot
cambu	Bulrush or spiked millet
chitta	Register of land records kept for each village, in which information is listed according to *patta* number
cholam	Sorgam, jowar
chonenki-hokonin	A farm servant who served a master for a limited number of years, in Japan
dhotis	Lower cloth
Dravidar Kazhagam	Dravidian Federation
firka	A subdivision of *taluk*
fudai-genin	A farm servant who was obliged to serve his master throughout his life, as were generally his children after him, for generations, in Japan
gur	Unrefined brown sugar
gurukkal	A subcaste of Brahman priests in a Saivite temple
inam	Grant of land wholly or partially free of land revenue

Jagir	Old name of Chingleput district which was originally granted as a *jagir* (assignment of land) by the Nawab of Carnatic
jamabandi	Annual settlement of revenue with cultivators
kalam	A dry measure, equal to 12 *marakkals*
kanji	Rice-water
karnam	A village accountant
kaval, kavalkar	Guarding; a protector, the village watchman
kist	Land revenue payment
kottan	A stonemason
kotta[*i*]	A measure of grains, varying in different places from 21 to 24 *marakkals*.
kurvai	Rice crop harvested in October
kuttagai	Lease on fixed rent
maniyam	Free grant or perquisite held in hereditary right by members of a village
mattu-varam	System of land-tenure under which the tenant provides oxen for cultivation
maund	A measure, the standard Indian maund is 82.2858 lbs.
mirasi	Inheritance, inherited property or rights
mirasidar	The holder of hereditary lands or offices in a village
nattar	The leaders of a *nadu* (a territorial division)
navitan	A barber
padi	A measure of capacity, one-eighth of a *marakkal*
padiyal	A hired servant, especially one paid with grain
pannai	A field, a rice-field
pannaikaran	A labourer on a yearly contract
pannaiyal	An attached farm labourer
parakudi	Tenant not residing in the village
patta	An official certificate given to a landholder specifying the land revenue, area, etc., of the land
pattadar	Holder of a *patta*
payakari	A tenant, a temporary tenant
pisanam	A variety of paddy
puja	Worship, adoration

purambokku (poramboke)	Uncultivated land including roads, house-sites, etc.
pusari	A temple priest
ragi	A kind of millet (*eleusine coracana*)
raiyat	A peasant, a cultivator
raiyatwari system	A system of land tenure under which assessments are made directly on individual landholdings
samudayam	The tenure by which the members of a village community, or *mirasidars*, hold land in common
swatantram	Fee or perquisites claimable by a proprietor from a cultivator of proprietary land
tahsildars	The chief administrative officer of a *taluk*, in the Madras Presidency
taluk	Administrative subdivision of district
thaladi	A second cultivation on the same ground
toddy	Country liquor
ulkudi	A permanent tenant, who has settled in the village
ulundu	Black-gram
varam	Share; sharecropping
vettiyan	A village servant who discharged the lowest offices, such as those of scavenger, etc.
zamindari	An estate; a system of land settlement under which the estate of the *zamindar* was assessed as a whole

Bibliography

1. Unpublished Government Records

Proceedings of the Board of Revenue, Madras.
Proceedings of the Revenue Department, Madras.
Proceedings of the Development Department, Madras.
Proceedings of Public Works and Labour Department, Madras.
Settlement Registers, Lalgudi Taluk, Trichinopoly District, c.1865, c.1895 and c.1925.
Village Maps, Lalgudi Taluk, Trichinopoly District, c.1895 and c.1975.

2. Official Publications

A. Censuses

Census of India, 1871, Madras (Madras, 1874), Vol. 1.
Census Statistics of Population of 1871 in Each Village of the Trichinopoly District Arranged according to Area, Caste, and Occupation (Madras, 1874).
Census of India, 1881, Madras, 2 vols. (Madras, 1883).
Census of India, 1891, Vol. 13, *Madras,* Part 1 (Madras, 1893).
Census of India, 1901, Vol. 15, *Madras* (Madras, 1893).
Census of India, 1921, Vol. 13, *Madras* (Madras, 1922).
Census of India, 1931, Vol. 14, *Madras* (Madras, 1932).
Census of 1931, Village Statistics, Trichinopoly District, Madras Presidency (Madras, 1932).

B. Reports of Committees and Commissions

Indian Industrial Commission, Minutes of Evidence, Vol. 3, *Madras and Bangalore* (Calcutta, 1918).
Madras Provincial Banking Enquiry Committee, Vol. 1, *Report*; Vols. 2 & 3, *Written Evidence*; Vol. 4, *Oral Evidence*; Vol. 5, *Reports of Investigators*; Vol. 6, *Coorg Sub-Committee's Report* (Madras, 1930).
Report of the Indian Taxation Enquiry Committee 1924–25 (Madras, 1926).

Royal Commission on Agriculture in India, Vol. 3, *Evidence Taken in Madras* (London, 1927).

Royal Commission on Labour in India, Evidence, Vol. 7, *Madras Presidency and Coorg, Written Evidence* (London, 1931).

C. Publications of the Government of India

Statement Exhibiting the Moral and Material Progress and Condition of India during the Year 1920 (London, 1921).

Report on the Marketing of Sugar in India and Burma (Delhi, 1942).

D. Publications of the Government of Madras

(1) Annual reports

Administration Report of the Madras Presidency.

Emigration and Immigration in the Madras Presidency (1899–1941).

Report of the Department of Agriculture (1933/34–1947/48).

Report on the Settlement of the Land Revenue of the Districts in the Madras Presidency (1853/54–1946/47).

Review and Returns of the Rail-Borne Trade of the Madras Presidency (1900/1901–1920/21).

Season and Crop Reports (1902/3–).

(2) Manuals

Chingleput, Late Madras, District: A Manual, by Charles Stewart Crole (Madras, 1879).

Madras District Manuals, North Arcot, compiled by Arthur F. Cox, new edition revised by Harold A. Stuart (Madras, 1895, 1894), 2 vols.

Manual of the Coimbatore District in the Presidency of Madras, by F.A. Nicholson (Madras, 1887).

Manual of Salem District, by H. Le Fanu (Madras, 1883).

Manual of the South Arcot District, by J.H. Garstin (Madras, 1878).

Manual of the District of Tanjore in the Madras Presidency, by T. Venkasami Row (Madras, 1883).

Manual of the Tinnevelly District in the Presidency of Madras, by A.J. Stuart (Madras, 1879).

Manual of Trichinopoly District in the Presidency of Madras, by Lewis Moore (Madras, 1878).

(3) Gazetteers

Madras District Gazetteers, Statistical Appendix for Coimbatore District (Madras, 1915, 1933 & 1933).

Madras District Gazetteers, Statistical Appendix for Chingleput District (Madras, 1915, 1928 &1933).

Madras District Gazetteers, Madura, by W. Francis (Madras, 1906).

Madras District Gazetteers, South Arcot, by W. Francis (Madras, 1905).

Madras District Gazetteers, Statistical Appendix for South Arcot District (Madras, 1915 & 1932).

Madras District Gazetteers, Tanjore, by F.R. Hemingway (Madras, 1906).

Madras District Gazetteers, Gazetteer of Tinnevelly District, by H.R. Pate (Madras, 1917).

Madras District Gazetteers, Statistical Appendix for Tinnevelly District (Madras, 1905, 1915 & 1934).

Madras District Gazetteers, Trichinopoly, by E.R. Hemingway (Madras, 1907).

Madras District Gazetteers, Statistical Appendix for Trichinopoly District (Madras, 1905, 1931 & 1933).

(4) Miscellaneous official publications

Papers Relating to the Revision of the Land Revenue Assessment in South Arcot, Selection from the Records of the Madras Government, No. XIV (Madras, 1869).

Papers Relating to the Survey and Settlement of the Chellumbrum and Manargoody Talooks of the South Arcot District, Selection from the Records of the Madras Government, No. XIV (Madras, 1869).

Papers Relating to the Survey and Settlement of the Salem District, Selection from the Records of the Madras Government, No. LXV (Madras, 1879).

Papers Relating to the Survey and Settlement of the Trichinopoly District, Selection from the Records of the Madras Government, No. XXII (Madras, 1855).

The Report of the Economic Enquiry Committee (Madras, 1930), 3 vols.

Report of the Famine in the Madras Presidency during 1896 and 1897 (Madras, 1898), 2 vols.

Report Regarding the Possibility of Introducing Land and Agricultural Banks into the Madras Presidency, by F.A. Nicholson (Madras, 1895), 2 vols.

Report of the Tanjore Commissioners: A.D. 1799 (Tanjore, 1905).

(5) Reports listed under individual authors

Bayley, W.H., and W. Hudleston (eds.). *Papers on Mirasi Right* (Madras, 1862).

Brown, Charles Philip (ed.). *Three Treatises on Mirasi Right* (Madras, 1852).

Dykes, J.W.B. *India Board, Salem, an Indian Collectorate* (London, 1853).

Raghavaiyangar, S. Srinivasa. *Memorandum on the Progress of the Madras Presidency during the Last Forty Years of British Administration* (Madras, 1893).

Sathyanathan, W. R. S. *Report on Agricultural Indebtedness* (Madras, 1935).

Rao, D. Narayana. *Report on the Survey of Cottage Industries in the Madras Presidency* (Madras, 1929).

3. Secondary Sources

Amin, Shahid. *Sugarcane and Sugar in Gorakhpur: An Inquiry into Peasant Production for Capitalist Enterprise in Colonial India* (Delhi, 1984).

Arnold, David. *Police Power and Colonial Rule: Madras 1859–1947* (Delhi, 1986).

Athreya, V.B. *Vadamalaipuram: A Resurvey*, Working Paper No. 50, Madras Institute of Development Studies (Madras, 1984).

——. *Gangaikondan 1916–1984: Change and Stability*, Working Paper No. 56, Madras Institute of Development Studies (Madras, 1985).

Athreya, V.B., G. Djurfeldt, and S. Lindberg. *Barriers Broken: Production Relations and Agrarian Change in Tamil Nadu* (New Delhi, 1990).

Attwood, Donald W. 'Why Some of the Poor Get Richer: Economic Change and Mobility in Rural Western India', *Current Anthropology* 20, 3 (1979).

——. 'Capital and the Transformation of Agrarian Class Systems: Sugar Production in India', in M. Desai, S.H. Rudolph, and A. Rudra (eds.), *Agrarian Power and Agricultural Productivity in South Asia* (Berkeley, 1984).

——. *Rising Cane: The Political Economy of Sugar in Western India* (Boulder, San Francisco and Oxford, 1992).

Bagchi, Amiya Kumar. *Private Investment in India, 1900–1939* (Cambridge, 1972).

Baker, Christopher John. *The Politics of South India: 1920–1937* (Delhi, 1976).

——. 'Madras Headman', in K.N. Chaudhuri and Clive J. Dewey (eds.), *Economy and Society* (Delhi, 1979).

——. *An Indian Rural Economy 1880–1955: The Tamilnad Countryside* (Oxford, 1984).

Baker, C.J. and D.A. Washbrook. *South India: Political Institutions and Political Change, 1880–1940* (Delhi, 1975).

Baliga, B.S. *Studies in Madras Administration* (Madras, 1960), 2 vols.

Banaji, Jairus. 'Capitalist Domination and the Small Peasantry: Deccan Districts in the Late Nineteenth Century', *Economic and Political Weekly*, Special Number, August 1977.

Bandopadhyay, Arun. 'The Nature of Landownership in Tamilnadu from 1820 to 1855', *Calcutta Historical Journal* 3, 1 (1989).

——. *The Agrarian Economy of Tamilnadu, 1820–1855* (Calcutta, 1992).

Bayly, C.A. *Rulers, Townsmen and Bazaars: North Indian Society in the Age of British Expansion, 1770–1870* (Cambridge, 1983).

Bétteille, André. *Caste, Class, and Power: Changing Patterns of Stratification in a Tanjore Village* (Berkeley and Los Angels, 1965).

Bharadwaj, Krishna. *Production Conditions in Indian Agriculture: A Study Based on Farm Management Surveys* (Cambridge, 1974).

Bhatia, B.M. 'Growth and Composition of Middle Class in South India in

Nineteenth Century', *Indian Economic and Social History Review* 2, 4 (1965).

Bhattacharya, Neeladri. 'Agricultural Labour in Punjab', in K.N. Raj, Neeladri Bhattacharya, Sumit Guha, and Sakti Padhi (eds.), *Essays on the Commercialization of Indian Agriculture* (Delhi, 1985).

Bhattacharya, Sabyasachi, Sumit Guha, Raman Mahadevan, Sakti Padhi, D. Rajasekhar, and G.N. Rao (eds.). *The South Indian Economy: Agrarian Change, Industrial Structure, and State Policy, c. 1914–1947* (Delhi, 1991).

Blyn, George. *Agricultural Trends in India, 1891–1947: Output, Availability, and Productivity* (Philadelphia, 1966).

Bose, Sugata. *Agrarian Bengal: Economy, Social Structure and Politics, 1919–1947* (Cambridge, 1986).

——: *Peasant Labour and Colonial Bengal since 1770*, The New Cambridge History of India, III-2 (Cambridge, 1993).

Bouton, Marshall M. *Agrarian Radicalism in South India* (Princeton, 1985).

Bray, Francesca. *The Rice Economies: Technology and Development in Asian Societies* (Oxford, 1986).

——. 'Rice Economies: The Rise and Fall of China's Communes in East Asian Perspective', in Jan Breman and Sudipto Mundle (eds.), *Rural Transformation in Asia* (Delhi, 1991).

Breman, Jan. *Patronage and Exploitation: Changing Agrarian Relations in South Gujarat, India* (Berkeley, Los Angeles and London, 1974).

——. 'Mobilisation of Landless Labourers: Halpatis of South Gujarat', in Arvind N. Das and V. Nilakant (eds.), *Agrarian Relations in India* (New Delhi, 1979).

Breman, Jan, and Sudipto Mundle (eds.). *Rural Transformation in Asia* (Delhi, 1991).

Buchanan, Francis. *A Journey from Madras through the Countries of Mysore, Canara, and Malabar* (London, 1807), 3 vols.

Bugge, Henriette. *Mission and Tamil Society: Social and Religious Change in South India (1840–1900)* (London, 1994).

Cassels, Nancy Gardner. 'Social Legislation under the Company Raj: The Abolition of Slavery Act V 1843', *South Asia*, n.s., 11, 1 (July 1988).

Chandra, Bipan. *Nationalism and Colonialism in Modern India* (Delhi, 1979).

Charlesworth, Neil. 'Rich Peasants and Poor Peasants in Late Nineteenth-century Maharashtra', in Clive Dewey and A.G. Hopkins (eds.), *The Imperial Impact: Studies in the Economic History of Africa and India* (London, 1978).

——. 'Trends in the Agricultural Performance of an Indian Province', in K.N. Chaudhuri and Clive J. Dewey (eds.), *Economy and Society: Essays in Indian Economic and Social History* (Delhi, 1979).

——. 'The Russian Stratification Debate and India', *Modern Asian Studies* 13, 1 (1979).

——. 'The Origins of Fragmentation of Landholdings in British India: A Comparative Examination', in Peter Robb (ed.), *Rural India: Land, Power and Society under British Rule* (London, 1983).

——. *Peasants and Imperial Rule: Agriculture and Agrarian Society in the Bombay Presidency, 1850–1935* (Cambridge, 1985).

——. 'The Impact of the Interwar Depression on Agriculture in the Bombay Presidency: A Case of Further Arrested Development?' in Clive Dewey (ed.), *Arrested Development in India* (Delhi, 1988).

Chaudhuri, Binay Bhushan. 'The Process of Depeasantization in Bengal and Bihar, 1885–1947', *Indian Historical Review* 2, 1 (1975).

——. 'Eastern India', in Dharma Kumar (ed.). *Cambridge Economic History of India*, Vol. 2 (Cambridge, 1982).

Cohn, Bernard S. 'The Changing Status of a Depressed Caste', in McKim Marriott (ed.), *Village India: Studies in the Little Community* (Chicago, 1955).

Deloche, Jean. *Transport and Communications in India Prior to Steam Locomotion,* Vol. I, *Land Transport,* trans. James Walker (Delhi, 1993).

Desai, R.C. *Standard of Living in India and Pakistan: 1931–32 to 1940–41* (Bombay, 1953).

Dirks, Nicholas B. *The Hollow Crown: Ethnohistory of an Indian Kingdom* (Cambridge, 1987).

Djurfeldt, Göran, and Staffan Lindberg. *Behind Poverty: The Social Formation in a Tamil Village* (Lund, 1975).

Dubois, Abbe J.A. *Hindu Manners, Customs and Ceremonies,* trans. Henry K. Beauchamp, 3d ed., 3d Indian impression (Delhi, 1982).

Epstein, T. Scarlett. *South India: Yesterday, Today and Tomorrow* (London, 1973).

Evans, Barbara. 'From Agricultural Bondage to Plantation Contract: A Continuity of Experience in Southern India, 1860–1947', *South Asia*, n.s., 13, 2 (1990).

Farmer, B.H. (ed.). *Green Revolution? Technology and Change in Rice-growing Area of Tamil Nadu and Sri Lanka* (London, 1977).

Frykenberg, Robert Eric. 'The Silent Settlement in South India, 1793–1853: An Analysis of the Role of Inams in the Rise of the Indian Imperial System', in Robert Eric Frykenberg (ed.), *Land Tenure and Peasant in South Asia* (Delhi, 1977).

Fukazawa, Hiroshi. 'Agrarian Relations: Western India', in Dharma Kumar (ed.), *Cambridge Economic History of India* , Vol. 2 (Cambridge, 1982).

Ganesh, Kamala. 'Jajmani Relations in Tirunelveli District: A Case Study of the Kottai Pillaimar, 1839–1979', *Indian Economic and Social History Review* 22, 2 (1985).

Gough, E. Kathleen. 'The Social Structure of a Tanjore Village', in McKim Marriott (ed.), *Village India: Studies in the Little Community* (Chicago,

1955).

——. 'Caste in a Tanjore Village', in E.R. Leach (ed.), *Aspects of Caste in South India, Ceylon and North-West Pakistan* (Cambridge, 1971).

——. *Rural Society in Southeast India* (Cambridge, 1981).

——. *Rural Change in Southeast India, 1950s to 1980s* (Delhi, 1989).

Gough, Kathleen, and Hari P. Sharma (eds.). *Imperialism and Revolution in South Asia* (New York and London, 1973).

Guha, Sumit. 'Some Aspects of Rural Economy in the Deccan: 1820–1940', in K.N. Raj, Neeladri Bhattacharya, Sumit Guha, and Sakti Padhi (eds.), *Essays on the Commercialization of Indian Agriculture* (Delhi, 1985).

——. *The Agrarian Economy of the Bombay Deccan: 1818–1941* (Delhi, 1985).

——(ed.). *Growth, Stagnation or Decline? Agricultural Productivity in British India* (Delhi, 1992).

Guhan, S., and K. Bharathan. *Dusi: A Resurvey*, Working Paper No. 52, Madras Institute of Development Studies (Madras, 1984).

Guhan, S., and Joan Mencher. 'Iruvelpattu Revisited (I) (II)', *Economic and Political Weekly*, 4 & 11 June 1983.

Guilmoto, Christophe Z. 'Towards a New Demographic Equilibrium: The Inception of Demographic Transition in South India', *Indian Economic and Social History Review* 29, 3 (1992).

Hara, Tadahiko, Tsukasa Mizushima, and Hisashi Nakamura. *Socio-Cultural Change in Villages in Tiruchirapalli District, Tamilnadu, India*, Part 2, Modern Period, 1 (Tokyo: Institute for the Study of Languages and Cultures of Asia and Africa, 1983).

Hardgrave, Robert L. Jr. The *Nadars of Tamilnad: Political Culture of a Community in Change* (Bombay, 1969).

Harriss, John. *Capitalism and Peasant Farming: Agrarian Structure and Ideology in Northern Tamil Nadu* (Delhi, 1982).

——. 'Chapter 6: Knowing About Rural Economic Change: Problems Arising from a Comparison of the Results of "Macro" and "Micro" Research in Tamil Nadu', in Pranab Bardhan (ed.), *Conversations Between Economists and Anthropologists* (Delhi, 1989).

——. 'Agriculture/Non-agriculture Linkages and the Diversification of Rural Economic Activity: A South Indian Case Study', in Jan Breman and Sudipto Mundle (eds.). *Rural Transformation in Asia* (Delhi, 1991).

Haswell, M.R. *Economics of Development in Village India* (London, 1961).

Hayama, Teisaku. 'Shononoho no Seiritsu to Shono Gijutsu no Tenkai [The Development of Small Peasant Cultivation Methods and Techniques]', in Sasaki Junnosuke (ed.), *Zairai Gijutsu no Hatten to Kindaishakai* (Tokyo, 1983).

Hayami, Akira, and Matao Miyamoto (eds.). *Nihon Keizaishi* [Economic History of Japan], Vol. 1 (Tokyo, 1988).

Hazell, Peter B.R., and C. Ramasamy. *The Green Revolution Reconsidered: The Impact of High-Yielding Rice Varieties in South India* (Baltimore and

London, 1991).

Heston, Alan W. 'Official Yields per Acre in India, 1886–1947: Some Questions of Interpretation', *Indian Economic and Social History Review* 10, 4 (1973).

Heston, Alan, and Dharma Kumar. 'The Persistence of Land Fragmentation in Peasant Agriculture: An Analysis of South Asian Cases', *Explorations in Economic History* 20, 2 (April 1983).

Hjejle, Benedicte. 'Slavery and Agricultural Bondage in South India in the Nineteenth Century', *The Scandinavian Economic History Review* 15, 1 & 2 (1967).

Hurd, John II. 'Railways and the Expansion of Markets in India, 1861–1921', *Explorations in Economic History* 12, 3 (July 1975).

Imai, Rintaro, and Akihiro Yagi. *Hoken Shakai no Noson Kozo* [The Structure of Rural Villages in Feudal Society] (Tokyo, 1955).

Indian Council of Agricultural Research, *Sample Surveys for the Estimation of Yield of Food Crops* (Delhi, 1951).

Irschick, Eugene F. 'Peasant Survival Strategies and Rehearsals for Rebellion in Eighteenth-Century South India', *Peasant Studies* 9, 4 (Summer 1982).

——. *Dialogue and History: Constructing South India, 1795–1895* (Berkeley and Los Angeles, 1994).

Ishii, Kanji. *Nihon Keizaishi* [Economic History of Japan], 2d ed. (Tokyo, 1991).

Jayaraman, R. 'Indian Emigration to Ceylon: Some Aspects of the Historical and Social Background of the Emigrants', *Indian Economic and Social History Review* 4, 4 (1967).

Kapadia, Karin. 'The Profitability of Bonded Labour: The Gem-Cutting Industry in Rural South India', *The Journal of Peasant Studies* 22, 3 (April, 1995).

Karashima, Noboru. *South Indian History and Society: Studies from Inscriptions, A.D.850–1800* (Delhi, 1984).

——. *Towards a New Formation: South Indian Society under Vijayanagar Rule* (Delhi, 1992).

Kessinger, Tom G. 'The Peasant Farm in North India, 1848–1968', *Explorations in Economic History* 12, 3 (July 1975).

——. *Vilyatpur, 1848–1968: Social and Economic Change in a North Indian Village* (New Delhi, 1979).

Komoguchi, Yoshimi. *Agricultural Systems in Tamil Nadu: A Case Study of Peruvalanallur Village* (Chicago, 1986).

Kotowski, G.G. 'Pacht und Pachtverhältnisse in Tamilnad (Sudindien) von 1917–1939', in Walton Ruben (ed.), *Die ökonomische und soziale Entwicklung Indiens* (Berlin, 1959).

Krishnamurty, J. 'The Growth of Agricultural Labour in India—A Note', *Indian Economic and Social History Review* 9, 3 (1972).

Kumar, Dharma. *Land and Caste in South India: Agricultural Labour in the*

Madras Presidency during the Nineteenth Century (Cambridge, 1965; repr., Delhi, 1992).

——. 'Landownership and Inequality in Madras Presidency: 1853–54 to 1946–47', *Indian Economic and Social History Review* 12, 3 (1975).

——. 'A Note on the Term "Land Control"', in Peter Robb (ed.), *Rural India: Land, Power and Society under British Rule* (London and Dublin, 1983).

——(ed.). *Cambridge Economic History of India*, Vol. 2 (Cambridge, 1982).

Kumar, Ravinder. 'The Rise of the Rich Peasants in Western India', in D.A. Low (ed.), *Soundings in Modern Asian History* (Berkeley and Los Angels, 1968).

——. *Western India in the Nineteenth Century* (Oxford, 1968).

Kurien, C.T. 'Dynamics of Rural Transformation: A Case Study of Tamil Nadu', *Economic and Political Weekly*, Annual Number, February 1980.

——. *Dynamics of Rural Transformation: A Study of Tamil Nadu: 1950–1975* (New Delhi, 1981).

Ludden, David. 'Patronage and Irrigation in Tamil Nadu: A Long-term View', *Indian Economic and Social History Review* 16, 3 (1979).

——. *Peasant History in South India* (Princeton, 1985).

——. 'The Terms of Ryotwari Praxis: Changing Property Relations among Mirasidars in the Tinnevelly District, 1801 to 1885' in Robert E. Frykenberg and Pauline Kolenda (eds.), *Studies of South India: An Anthology of Recent Research and Scholarship* (Madras and New Delhi, 1985).

Macpherson, W.J. 'Economic Development in India', in A. Youngson (ed.), *Economic Development in the Long-run* (London, 1971).

Madras Institute of Development Studies, *Tamilnadu Economy: Performance and Issue* (New Delhi, Bombay and Calcutta, 1988).

Mayer, P.B. 'The Penetration of Capitalism in a South Indian District: The First 60 Years of Colonial Rule in Tiruchirapalli', *South Asia*, n.s., 3, 2 (1980).

——. 'South India, North India: The Capitalist Transformation of Two Provincial Districts', in Hamza Alavi, P.L. Burns, G.R. Knight, P.B. Mayer, and Doug McEachern, *Capitalism and Colonial Production* (London and Canberra, 1982).

——. 'Is There Urban Bias in the Green Revolution? Report on a Field Trip to North Thanjavur', *Peasant Studies* 2, 4 (1984).

——. 'Has India's Self-Sufficiency in Agriculture been Achieved at the Expense of Social Justice? Reflections on Recent Village Studies in Tamil Nadu', *South Asia Bulletin* 12, 2 (Fall 1992).

Mencher, Joan P. *Agriculture and Social Structure in Tamil Nadu* (New Delhi, 1978).

Menon, Saraswathi. 'Historical Development of Thanjavur Kisan Movement:

Interplay of Class and Caste Factors', *Economic and Political Weekly*, Annual Number, February 1979.

Miyakawa, Shuichi. 'Daitomai to Teishitsuchi Kaihatu [Great China Rice and Reclamation of Damp Lowlands]', in *Ine no Ajiashi* (Tokyo, 1987), Vol. 3.

Mizushima, Tsukasa. 'Minami Indo Noson no Ruikeika no Kokoromi [Some Types in Villages in South India]', *Shigaku Zasshi* 87, 7 (1978).

——. 'Village Records on Land Holding in South India and Ways for Processing Them', *Studies on Agrarian Societies in South Asia* 5 (Tokyo: Institute for the Study of Languages and Cultures of Asia and Africa, 1980).

——. 'Changes, Chances and Choices: The Perspective of Indian Villagers', *Socio-Cultural Change in Villages in Tiruchirapalli District, Tamilnadu, India,* Part 2, Modern Period, 1 (Tokyo: Institute for the Study of Languages and Cultures of Asia and Africa, 1983).

——. *Nattar and the Socio-economic Changes in South India in the 18th–19th Centuries* (Tokyo: Institute for the Study of Languages and Cultures of Asia and Africa, 1986).

——. *Minami Indo Zaichishakai no Kenkyu* [A Study of Local Society in South India] (Tokyo: Institute for the Study of Languages and Cultures of Asia and Africa, 1987).

——. 'Mirasi System and Local Society in Pre-Colonial South India', in Peter Robb, K. Sugihara, and H. Yanagisawa (eds.), *Local Agrarian Society in Colonial India: Japanese Perspectives* (London, 1996).

Moffat, Michael. *An Untouchable Community in South India* (Princeton, 1979).

Mukherjee, Nilmani. *The Ryotwari System in Madras* (Calcutta, 1962).

Mukherjee, Ramakrishna. *The Dynamics of a Rural Society: A Study of the Economic Structure in Bengal Village* (Berlin, 1957).

Mundle, Sudipto. 'Notes from a Palamau Village', in Arvind N. Das and V. Nilakant (eds.), *Agrarian Relations in India* (Delhi, 1979).

Murton, Brian J. 'Land and Class: Cultural, Social and Biophysical Integration in Interior Tamilnadu in the Late Eighteenth Century', in Robert Eric Frykenberg (ed.), *Land Tenure and Peasant in South Asia* (Delhi, 1977).

Naidu, B.V. Narayanaswamy and V. Venkataraman. *The Problem of Rural Indebtedness* (Annamalainagar: Annamalai University, 1935).

Nair, K.N., and A.C. Dhas. 'Agricultural Change in Tamil Nadu: 1918–55', in Sabyasachi Bhattacharya, Sumit Guha, Raman Mahadevan, Sakti Padhi, D. Rajasekhar, and G.N. Rao (eds.), *The South Indian Economy: Agrarian Change, Industrial Structure, and State Policy, c.1914–1947* (Delhi, 1991).

Nakamura, Hisashi. 'Disintegration and Re-integration of a Rural Society in the Process of Economic Development: The Second Survey of a Tank-based Village in Tamil Nadu', in *Studies in Socio-Cultural Change in Rural Villages in Tiruchirapalli District, Tamilnadu, India* 5 (Tokyo:

Institute for the Study of Languages and Cultures of Asia and Africa, 1982).

Nakamura, Satoru. 'Kindai Sekai niokeru Nogyo Keiei, Tochi Shoyu to Tochi Kaikaku [Agricultural Management, Landownership and Land Reform in the Modern World], no. 1,' *Keizai Ronso* 143, 1 (1989).

Nakane, Chie, and Shinzaburo Oishi (eds.). *Tokugawa Japan* (Tokyo, 1990).

Nakazato, Nariaki. *Agrarian System in Eastern Bengal, c.1870–1910* (Calcutta, 1994).

Nara, Tsuyoshi, and Tsukasa Mizushima. 'Neikuramu Mura Chosa Hokoku, 1 [Social Change in a Dry Village in South India: A Interim Report]', *Studies in Socio-Cultural Change in Rural Villages in Tiruchirapalli District, Tamilnadu, India* 4 (Tokyo: Institute for the Study of Languages and Cultures of Asia and Africa, 1981).

Pandian, M.S.S. *The Political Economy of Agrarian Change: Nanchilnadu, 1880–1939* (New Delhi, 1990).

Pandit, Dhairyabala. 'The Myths Around Subdivision and Fragmentation of Holdings,' *Indian Economic and Social History Review* 6, 2 (1969).

Panse, V.G. 'Recent Trends in the Yield of Rice and Wheat in India', *The Indian Journal of Agricultural Economics* 14, 1 (Jan.–March 1959).

Patel, Surendra J. *Agricultural Labourers in Modern India and Pakistan* (Bombay, 1952).

Patnaik, Utsa. 'Development of Capitalism in Agriculture', *Social Scientist* 1, 2 (Sept. 1972).

Prakash, Gyan. *Bonded Histories: Genealogies of Labour Servitude in Colonial India* (Cambridge, 1990).

——(ed.). *The World of the Rural Labourer in Colonial India* (Delhi, 1992).

Prakash, Shri. 'Models of Peasant Differentiation and Aspects of Agrarian Economy in Colonial India', *Modern Asian Studies* 19, 3 (1985).

Rajasekhar, D. 'Commercialization of Agriculture and Changes in Distribution of Land Ownership in Kurnool District of Andhra (c.1900–50)', in S. Bhattacharya, S. Guha, R. Mahadevan, S. Padhi, D. Rajasekhar, and G.N. Rao (eds.), *The South Indian Economy* (Delhi, 1991).

Raju, A. Sarada. *Economic Conditions in the Madras Presidency, 1800–1850* (Madras, 1941).

Ramachandran, V.K. *Wage Labour and Unfreedom in Agriculture: An Indian Case Study* (Oxford, 1990).

Ramiah, K. *Rice in Madras: A Popular Handbook* (Madras, 1937).

Ranga, N.G. *Economic Organisation of Indian Villages*, Vol. 1, Deltaic Villages (Bezwada, 1926), Vol. 2 (Bombay, 1929).

Rao, C.R. (ed.). *Data Base of Indian Economy* (New Delhi, 1972), Vol. 1.

Rao, G.N., and D. Rajasekhar. 'Commodity Production and the Changing Agrarian Scenario in Andhra: A Study in Interregional Variations, c.1910–c.1947', in S. Bhattacharya, S. Guha, R. Mahadevan, S. Padhi, D. Rajasekhar, and G.N. Rao (eds.), *The South Indian Economy* (Delhi,

1991).

Rao, K.V. *Tamil Nadu Land Reforms* (Madras, 1975).

Rao, V.K.R.V. *Taxation of Income in India* (Calcutta, 1931).

Ray, Rajat, and Ratna Ray. 'The Dynamics of Continuity in Rural Bengal under the British Imperium: A Study of Quasi-Stable Equilibrium in Underdeveloped Societies in a Changing World', *Indian Economic and Social History Review* 10, 2 (1973).

Ray, Ratnalekha. *Change in Bengal Agrarian Society* (New Delhi, 1979).

Reddy, M. Atchi. 'The Commercialization of Agriculture in Nellore District 1850–1916: Effects on Wages, Employment and Tenancy', in K.N. Raj, Neeladri Bhattacharya, Sumit Guha, and Sakti Padhi (eds.), *Essays on the Commercialization of Indian Agriculture* (Delhi, 1985).

——. 'Agrarian Structure of Nellore: Tenants and Tenancy 1800–1980', *Social Scientist* 166 (March 1987).

——. 'Work and Leisure: Daily Working Hours of Agricultural Labourers, Nellore District', *Indian Economic and Social History Review* 28, 1 (1991).

Robb, Peter (ed.), *Rural India: Land, Power and Society under British Rule* (London and Dublin, 1983).

Robb, Peter, Kaoru Sugihara, and Haruka Yanagisawa (eds.). *Local Agrarian Societies in Colonial India: Japanese Perspectives* (London, 1996).

Robert, Bruce. 'Economic Change and Agrarian Organization in "Dry" South India 1890–1940: A Reinterpretation', *Modern Asian Studies* 17, 1 (1983).

——. 'Structural Change in Indian Agriculture: Land and Labour in Bellary District, 1890–1980', *Indian Economic and Social History Review* 22, 3 (1985).

Roy, Tirthankar. *Artisans and Industrialization: Indian Weaving in the Twentieth Century* (Delhi, 1993).

Sarkar, Tanika. 'Bondage in the Colonial Context', in Utsa Patnaik and Manjari Dingwaney (eds.), *Chains of Servitude: Bondage and Slavery in India* (Madras, 1985).

Satyanarayana, A. *Andhra Peasants under British Rule: Agrarian Relations and the Rural Economy 1900–1940* (Delhi, 1990).

——. 'Commercialization, Money Capital and the Peasantry in Colonial Andhra, 1900–1940', in S. Bhattacharya, S. Guha, R. Mahadevan, S. Padhi, D. Rajasekhar, and G.N. Rao (eds.), *The South Indian Economy* (Delhi, 1991).

Saul, S.B. *Studies in British Overseas Trade, 1870–1914* (Liverpool, 1960).

Sayana, V.V. *The Agrarian Problems of Madras Province* (Madras, 1946).

Shah, Mihar. 'The Kaniatchi Form of Labour', *Economic and Political Weekly* 20, 30 (27 July 1985).

Shimizu, Yoji. 'Chuno Hyojunka Keiko to Nomin Keiei [A Trend towards Middle Peasants and Their Farm Management]', in Shigeaki Shina (ed.),

Famiri Famu no Hikakushiteki Kenkyu (Tokyo, 1987).

Shinbo, Hiroshi, and Osamu Saito (eds.). *Nihon Keizaishi* [Economic History of Japan], Vol. 2 (Tokyo, 1989).

Shivaraman, Mythily. 'Thanjavur: Rumbling of Class Struggle in Tamil Nadu', in Kathleen Gough and Hari P. Sharma (eds.), *Imperialism and Revolution in South Asia* (New York and London, 1973).

Sivakumar, Chitra, and S.S. Sivakumar. *Peasants and Nabobs: Agrarian Radicalism in Late Eighteenth Century Tamil Country* (Delhi, 1993).

Sivakumar, S.S. 'Transformation of the Agrarian Economy in Tondaimandalam: 1760–1900', *Social Scientist* 6, 10 (No.70) (1978).

——. 'Aspects of Agrarian Economy in Tamil Nadu: A Study of Two Villages', *Economic and Political Weekly,* 6, 13 & 20 May 1978.

Sivakumar, S.S., and Chitra Sivakumar. 'Class and Jati at Asthapuram and Kanthapuram: Some Comments Towards a Structure of Interests', *Economic and Political Weekly,* Annual Number, February 1979.

Sivaswamy, K.G. *Caste and Standard of Living versus Farms Rents and Wages* (Madras: Servants of India Society, 1947).

——. *The Madras Ryotwari Tenant* (Madras: South Indian Association of Agricultural Workers, 1948).

Sivertsen, Dagfinn. *When Caste Barriers Fall: A Study of Social and Economic Change in a South Indian Village* (Oslo, 1963).

Slater, Gilbert (ed.). *Some South Indian Villages* (Oxford, 1918).

Sonachalam, K.S. *Land Reforms in Tamil Nadu: Evaluation of Implementation* (New Delhi, Bombay and Calcutta, 1970).

Specker, Konrad. 'Madras Handlooms in the Nineteenth Century', *Indian Economic and Social History Review* 26, 2 (1989).

Srinivas, M.N. *Social Change in Modern India* (Berkeley and Los Angeles, 1966; repr., Bombay, 1977).

——. *The Remembered Village* (Berkeley, Los Angeles and London, 1979).

Stein, Burton. *Peasant State and Society in Medieval South India* (Delhi, 1980).

——. 'Idiom and Ideology in Early Nineteenth-century South India', in Peter Robb (ed.), *Rural India* (London and Dublin, 1983).

Stokes, Eric. *The Peasant and the Raj: Studies in Agrarian Society and Peasant Rebellion in Colonial India* (Cambridge, 1978).

Stone, Ian. *Canal Irrigation in British India: Perspectives on Technological Change in a Peasant Economy* (Cambridge, 1984).

Stuart, G.A.D. 'The Seasonal Factor in Crop Statistics: A Method of Correcting for the Inherent Pessimism of the Farmer', *Agricultural Journal of India* 14, 2 (1919).

Sugihara, Kaoru. 'Patterns of Intra-Asian Trade, 1898–1913', *Osaka City University Economic Review* 16 (1980).

Synthetic Gem Cutters Industrial Co-operative Society Ltd., Tiruchy. *History and Note on Gem Industry* (Tiruchirapalli, n.d.).

Tinker, Hugh. *A System of Slavery: The Export of Indian Labour Overseas,*

1830–1920 (London, New York and Bombay, 1974).

Thomas, P.J., and K.C. Ramakrishnan (eds.). *Some South Indian Villages: A Resurvey* (Madras, 1940).

Tomlinson, B.R. *The Economy of Modern India, 1860–1970*, The New Cambridge History of India, III, 3 (Cambridge, 1993).

Thurston, E. *Caste and Tribes in Southern India* (Madras, 1909), 7 vols.

Washbrook, David A. *The Emergence of Provincial Politics: The Madras Presidency 1870–1920* (Cambridge, 1976).

——. 'Economic Development and Social Stratification in Rural Madras: The "Dry Region" 1878–1929', in Clive Dewey and A.G. Hopkins (eds.), *The Imperial Impact* (London, 1978).

——. 'Progress and Problems: South Asian Economic and Social History c.1720–1860', *Modern Asian Studies* 22, 1 (1988).

——. 'Land and Labour in late Eighteenth-Century South India: The Golden Age of the Pariah?' in Peter Robb (ed.), *Dalit Movements and the Meanings of Labour in India* (Delhi, 1993).

Yagi, Hironori. *Suiden Nogyo no Hatten Ronri* [The Logic of the Development of Irrigated Rice Agriculture] (Tokyo, 1983).

Yamazaki, Ryuzo. 'Settsu niokeru Nogyo Koyo Rodo no Hatten [Development of Hired Agricultural Labourers in Settsu Area]', in Takamasa Ichikawa, Nobuo Watanabe, and Toshio Furushima (eds.), *Hoken Shakai Kaitaiki no Koyo Rodo* (Tokyo, 1969).

Yanagisawa, Haruka. *Socio-Economic Changes in a Village in the Paddy Cultivating Area in South India* (Tokyo: Institute for the Study of Languages and Cultures of Asia and Africa, 1983).

——. 'Mixed Trends in Landholding in Lalgudi Taluk: 1895–1925', *Indian Economic and Social History Review* 26, 4 (1989).

——. *Minamiindo Shakai Keizaishi Kenkyu* [Studies in the Socio-Economic History of South India] (Tokyo, 1991).

——. 'The Handloom Industry and Its Market Structure: The Case of the Madras Presidency in the First Half of the Twentieth Century', *Indian Economic and Social History Review* 30, 1 (1993).

——. 'A Comparison with Japanese Experience', P. Robb, K. Sugihara, and H. Yanagisawa (eds.), *Local Agrarian Societies in Colonial India* (London, 1996).

Yanagisawa, Haruka, and Tsukasa Mizushima. *Nijisseiki Hajime Minami Indo niokeru Kasuto to Tochihoyu Kozo no Hendo* [Caste and Landholdings in South India at the Beginning of the Twentieth Century] (Tokyo: Institute for the Study of Languages and Cultures of Asia and Africa, 1988).

Index